W9-CEZ-673

RESEARCH FOR DEVELOPMENT

RESEARCH FOR DEVELOPMENT

SECOND EDITION | A PRACTICAL GUIDE

SOPHIE LAWS, CAROLINE HARPER, NICOLA JONES & RACHEL MARCUS

Los Angeles | London | New Delhi
Singapore | Washington DC

Los Angeles | London | New Delhi
Singapore | Washington DC

SAGE Publications Ltd
1 Oliver's Yard
55 City Road
London EC1Y 1SP

SAGE Publications Inc.
2455 Teller Road
Thousand Oaks, California 91320

SAGE Publications India Pvt Ltd
B 1/I 1 Mohan Cooperative Industrial Area
Mathura Road
New Delhi 110 044

SAGE Publications Asia-Pacific Pte Ltd
3 Church Street
#10-04 Samsung Hub
Singapore 049483

Editor: Natalie Aguilera
Editorial assistant: James Piper
Production editor: Katie Forsythe
Copyeditor: Rosemary Morlin
Proofreader: Clare Weaver
Marketing manager: Sally Ransom
Cover design: Joni Strudwick
Typeset by: C&M Digitals (P) Ltd, Chennai, India

Library of Congress Control Number: 2012939392

British Library Cataloguing in Publication data

A catalogue record for this book is available from
the British Library

ISBN 978-1-4462-5236-9
ISBN 978-1-4462-5237-6 (pbk)

CONTENTS

ABOUT THE AUTHORS

Sophie Laws is head of policy and research for Coram, a UK charity that aims to develop and promote best practice in the care of vulnerable children and their families. With a PhD in sociology, she has long experience of managing practical research and evaluation in health and social care, mainly in services for children and young people, and is committed to clear communication and giving practitioners tools they can use. In addition to independent consultancy for UN organizations, UK government departments, UK and international charities, she has worked for save the Children, the College of Health, the Sickle Cell Society, and the NHS. Co-authored publications include: *So You Want to Involve Children in Research?* for Save the Children Sweden and the UN Study on Violence against Children; reports and articles on concurrent planning for young children, children's participation in Family Group Conferences, kinship care, and patients' experiences of medical treatment and research and *Reseach for Development, A Practical Guide* (Sage, 1st and 2nd editions, 2003 and 2013).

Caroline Harper has a PhD in social Anthropology and is currently Research Fellow and programme leader of social Development at the Overseas Development Institute. She has previously been Associate Director of the Chronic Poverty Research Centre, director of research programmes on childhood poverty, including the Young Lives longitudinal study, and research and poilcy manager at Save and Children. She has led multi-year, longitudinal and medium-sized programmes of research and polich analysis, including on childhood, gender, choronic poverty, exclusion and empowerment and she has undertaken work for multiple funders including multilateral and bi-lateral agencies and NGOs. Recent studies include: the impacts of the global economic crisis on chidren's and women's wellbeing; the nature of discriminatory social institutions and girls' exclusion; and the relationship between poverty and child protection. Her publications include *Children in Crisis: Seeking Child-sensitive Poilicy Responses*, (Palgrave Macmillan, 2012); *Research for Development, A Practical Guide* (Sage, 1st and 2nd editions, 2003 and 2013); Do the Facts Matter? NGO's Research and Policy Adcocacy, in Edwards, M. & Gaventa, J., *Global Citizen Action* (Lynne Reinner, 2001).

Nicola Jones has a PhD in Political Science and is a Research Fellow in the Social Development Programme at the Overseas Development Institute. She specialises in research, evaluation and policy advisory work on social inclusion, social protection, and the linkages between knowledge, policy and power. She has carried out work for a range of funders (African Child Policy Forum, AusAID, DFID, EU, IDRC, Oak Foundation, Oxfam International, Plan International, Save the Children, UNICEF, UNDP, UN Women). Her research is primarily qualitative and participatory, although she is also very interested in mixed methods approaches, and she prioritizes partnerships with local research organizations. She has published widely including the following co-authored book: *Gender and Social Protection in the*

Developing World: Beyond Mothers and Safety Nets (2013, Zed Books); *Knowledge, Policy and Power in International Development: A Practical Guide* (2012, Policy Press); *Children in Crisis: Seeking Child-sensitive Policy Responses* (2012, Palgrave Macmillan); *Child Poverty, Evidence and Policy: Mainstreaming Children in International Development* (2011, Policy Press).

Rachel Marcus is a freelance social development consultant with 20 years' experience of research, research management and practical development work, focusing particularly on social policy and children. She has worked as a research and policy advisor for Save the Children, a social development advisor for DFID and as a research and social development consultant for UNICEF and the World Bank. In the past few years her work has focused on the efforts of economic reforms on children and youth, on child protection and on social inclusion issues more broadly. She contributed to the first edition of this book, and has continued to work on practical research guidance for development workers, and in 2012 co-authored a web-based toolkit for analysing social development issues.

ACKNOWLEDGEMENTS

We would like to acknowledge first the tireless project coordination and writing support of Josiah Kaplan, which was greatly appreciated; the detailed and helpful research assistance inputs of Brenda Van-Coppenolle, Aminata Diop, Shreya Mitra, Johannes Rieken, Maria Stavropoulou and Arnaud Vaganay; excellent editorial support from Roo Griffiths; and expert inputs from Julia Pomares and Miguel Nino Zarazua on systematic literature reviews and quantitative methods, respectively. Additional case studies in the new edition were identified and provided by Cesar Bazan, Laurie Bell, Caroline O'Keefe, Shreya Mitra, Alan F. Newell, Bridget Pettitt, Pham Thi Lan, Save the Children, Eliana Villar and Matt Daw, who also provided photographs.

We would also like to thank the UK Department for International Development (DFID) for essential financial support to the first edition of this book, although the views and opinions expressed are those of the authors alone. DFID supports policies, programmes and projects to promote international development. Whilst now updated, much of the original content as produced by Laws, Harper and Marcus in 2002 remains true to the research endeavour today and much has been retained. The first edition was written by Sophie Laws with Caroline Harper and Rachel Marcus, who conceived the idea and use of such a book.

The writing of the first edition of *Research for Development* was possible only with the help and support of a large number of people. Thanks are owed to the members of the original advisory group: Rachel Baker (Edinburgh University), Sara Gibbs (International NGO Training and Research Centre), John Harriss (London School of Economics), Perpetua Kirby (independent researcher), Pat Kneen (Joseph Rowntree Foundation), Robert Lamb (Institute of Development Studies), Bridget Pettitt (independent researcher), Fiona Power (ID21) and Alan Thomas (Open University). We also took advice from development practitioners working in many countries, and are especially grateful to: Nicola Chapman, El Khidir Daloum, Clive Hedges, Tina Hyder, Lina Fajerman, Wendwessen Kittaw, Maddy Lewis, Peter Little, Robert McFarlane, Le Thi Minh Chau, Pham Thi Lan and Lu Yiyi.

Others who kindly read and commented on drafts were Roger Adams, Simon Mollison, N.K. Phuong, Joachim Theis, Chris Thornton and Roy Trivedy. Liz Kwast and John Wilkinson helped with advice on websites.

Many people kindly assisted in providing the original case studies. Some of these are referred to in the text and all informed our thinking. Thanks are owed to Mike Bailey, Ranka Bartula, Jo Boyden, Emma Cain, Olivera Damjanovic, Chris Eldridge, Irada Gautam, Yang Hai Yu, Guy Hatfield, Jutta Heering, Vanessa Herringshaw, Amanda Heslop, Andrea Hitzemann, Louise Illingworth, Edda Ivan-Smith, Victor Karunan, Sharfuddin Khan, Anne LaFond, Sheri Lecker, Pierre Lorillou, Maeve McAnallen, Isobel McConnan, Neil MacDonald, Chris McIvor, Ianthe Maclagan, Dumisani Mnisi, Anne Mulcahy Rahat Orozova, Sue Paganga, Jenita Rose Mary Perera, Peter Poore, Ranjan Poudyal, Jasmine Rajbhandary Vijay Rajkumar,

Helen Roberts, Judy Roberts, Shirley Robinson, Eddie Strong, Patti Strong, Sue Stubbs, Eddie Thomas, Chris Thornton, Kadiatou Touré, Mandai Urtnasan, Raya Ushurova and Andy West.

We are grateful for permission to reproduce the following material from other sources:

Cover image © Jenny Matthews /World Vision/PhotoVoice. From PhotoVoice's See it Our Way project, Pakistan. For more information visit www.photovoice.org

The children's drawings in Chapter 12 are reproduced from J. Boyden and J. Ennew (eds) (1997) *Children in Focus: A Manual for Participatory Research with Children*. Stockholm: Save the Children Sweden.

The diagram of sampling strategies in Chapter 10 is reproduced from L. Blaxter, C. Hughes and M. Tight (1996) *How to Research*, 3rd edn. Buckingham: Open University Press.

Figure 10.1 'Sampling strategies illustrated' on p.183 from Blaxter, L., Hughes, C. and Tight, M. (2010) *How to Research* © Open University Press. Reproduced with the kind permission of Open University Press. All rights reserved.

The material on pages 179 and 193 from Pratt, B. and Loizos, P. (1992) 'Choosing research methods: data collection for development workers'. *Development Guidelines 7*. Oxford: Oxfam, is reproduced with the permission of Oxfam GB, Oxfam House, John Smith Drive, Cowley, Oxford OX4 2JY, UK www.oxfam.org. uk. Oxfam GB does not necessarily endorse any text or activities that accompany the materials.

The material on page 186 from Nichols, P. (1991) 'Social survey methods: a field guide for development workers', *Development Guidelines 6*. Oxford: Oxfam, is reproduced with the permission of Oxfam GB, Oxfam House, John Smith Drive, Cowley, Oxford OX4 2JY, UK www.oxfam.org.uk. Oxfam GB does not necessarily endorse any text or activities that accompany the materials.

Table 12.1 'Example of preference ranking' on page 228 and Figure 12.2 'Example of a mobility map' on page 231 from Theis, J. and Grady, H.M. (1991) *Participatory Rapid Appraisal for Community Development*. London: International Institute for Environment and Development and Save the Children federation, are reproduced with permission from Joachim Theis and Heather Grady.

Tables 13.5A-C 'Simple tally sheets' on pages 272 and 273 from Hall, D. and Hall, I. *Practical Social Research: Project Work in the Community*, 1996, Macmillan, reproduced with permission of Palgrave Macmillan.

Permission has also been given for extensive use of material from the following sources:

Bell, J. (1987) *Doing Your Research Project: A Guide for First-time Researchers in Education, Health and Social Science*. Maidenhead: Open University Press (latest edition 2010).

Blaxter, L., Hughes, C. and Tight, M. (1996) *How to Research*. Buckingham: Open University Press (latest edition 2010).

Boyden, J. and Ennew, J. (eds) (1997) *Children in Focus – A Manual for Participatory Research with Children*. Stockholm: Save the Children Sweden.

Craig, G. (1998) *Women's Views Count: Building Responsive Maternity Services*. London: College of Health.

Denscombe, M. (1998) *The Good Research Guide for Small-scale Social Research Projects*. Buckingham and Philadelphia, PA: Open University Press (latest edition 2010).

Hall, D. and Hall, I. (1996) *Practical Social Research: Project Work in the Community*. Basingstoke: Macmillan.

Nichols, P. (1991) 'Social survey methods: a field guide for development workers', *Development Guidelines 6*. Oxford: Oxfam.

O'Laughlin, B. (1998) 'Interpreting institutional discourses', in A. Thomas, J. Chataway and M. Wuyts (eds), *Finding Out Fast*. Buckingham and London: Open University Press and Sage.

Pratt, B. and Loizos, P. (1992) 'Choosing research methods: data collection for development workers', *Development Guidelines 7*. Oxford: Oxfam.

Theis, J. and Grady, H.M. (1991) *Participatory Rapid Appraisal for Community Development*. London: International Institute for Environment and Development and Save the Children Federation.

HOW TO USE THIS BOOK

This book consists of three parts. The first concentrates on planning and managing research – giving practical advice on all the issues that arise in making research for development work happen. The second gives guidance on how to conduct the research itself. Finally, the third part gives guidance on how to analyse data, write reports, get your findings heard and assess your own research work.

Often, the same people manage research and carry it out, and there may be no clear line where one stops and the other starts. But experience tells us that much of what goes wrong in research for development work relates to planning and management. And most of the books about how to do research concentrate on the methods themselves, and neglect the many 'real life' issues that have to be decided in setting up research projects. Part 1 aims to put this right.

Throughout the book, there are checklists summarizing the main points. Some key tips are highlighted, as are common pitfalls. Activities are suggested for readers who would like to think actively for themselves about the issues – most of these could usefully be carried out with a group of colleagues. If you want to read further, a few recommended texts are listed at the end of each chapter and there is a guide to useful websites at the end of the book. A glossary aims to help you through the jargon of social research.

What are you looking for?

When we consulted development workers on how they might use a book like this, someone said something which rang very true. He said he would look at the manual when he had a problem, and would want to find the answer to his question in half an hour. For this reason, the book is full of checklists and tips, and has a good index.

Of course, we hope you will want to read the whole book, but just in case you don't have time, here are a few shortcuts:

- *New researcher starting work tomorrow?* Look at how to supervise them, Section 4.5, and skim the whole of Part 1.
- *Looking at a blank page, trying to write a research brief?* Chapter 14 tells you what should go in it.
- *A good idea of an area to look at, but a bit foggy about the details of the project?* Chapter 3 should help you to clarify your thinking, then read Chapter 7 and skim the rest of Part 2 when you are ready to choose methods.
- *Not sure if research is the right approach in this situation?* Chapter 1, especially 1.5.
- *Piles of data and a dead computer?* Chapter 13 to the rescue.
- Worried about whether your sample is good enough? Chapter 10 should help you.

- *A colleague has suggested you do some participatory research – but how?* Chapter 12, and parts of Chapter 4, on managing the process.
- *Heard there's some really good information on your subject on the internet?* Section 5.3 and Appendix 2 will get you started.
- *Wondering how to make sure your respondents are really happy to take part in your project?* Chapters 8 and 9 discuss consent.
- *Working in a language you don't speak?* Chapters 3 and 8 offer advice.
- *Want to know what a focus group is?* Section 11.3 will tell you.
- *Under pressure about your general approach?* Check on different philosophies of research in Chapter 2, and think about the quality of your work using Chapters 3 and 16.
- *About to consider hiring a researcher?* Read Chapter 4, but don't forget to check that the brief is clear (Chapter 3).
- *Draft report on your desk, but it's not quite right?* Chapter 14 will give a framework for making it better, and Chapter 15 will help you to plan a strategy to promote your findings.
- *Want to build your organization's capacity to use research in its work?* Chapter 6 suggests some approaches.

Part 1: Introduction and planning your research

Part 1 starts with a discussion of why development workers can benefit from using research, and gives ideas on how to tell when research is the best approach to a problem. Chapter 2 looks at the main research approaches, and at the two main types of purpose for which research is used in development work – to inform programme planning and to influence policy. Quality is a key issue in determining how much influence your research can have, and Chapter 3 discusses what is meant by quality in research work, across the broad spectrum of different types of research. Chapter 3 also contains guidance on the critical tasks of clarifying your research focus and questions and writing a research brief. Chapter 4 offers further help on how to supervise research work, and how to estimate costs and timescales. It also discusses some other important aspects of managing research work – negotiating access, managing participatory research and relating to funders.

Chapter 5 discusses the first step for most research projects – finding out what is already known about your subject. It looks at how to go about conducting a review of existing evidence, using libraries and the internet and seeking out information informally. Chapter 6 gives guidance on how to help people to learn more about research, suggesting a range of ways in which you can build up skills and knowledge. Training workshops are discussed, but learning by doing, with advice from more experienced researchers, is recommended.

Part 2: Collecting data

Part 2 is a basic guide to how to gather and manage data for research. In Chapter 7, we arrive at the point where people often try to start – the choice of research methods and a description of the techniques themselves. This chapter suggests that it is useful to distinguish between broad approaches to research and the specific techniques you will use to gather the data. It is recommended generally to abandon the search for a single perfect method to use, but to use the approach known as 'triangulation' – looking at things from a number of angles, using a variety of different techniques. Having looked at how to choose which methods to use, and before moving on to consider specific techniques like interviews or observation, Chapter 8 suggests ways to make sure any kind of data collected are of good quality.

Chapter 9 addresses a crucial matter in the quality of the work you do: the ethical challenges of research for development work, including detailed discussion of responsibilities to respondents as well as wider accountability.

How to choose a sample is discussed in Chapter 10 – talking to the right people. Different kinds of sampling are discussed, including both quantitative and qualitative approaches. A special section offers advice on how to include 'hard-to-reach' people in your study.

Chapter 11 describes five tried and tested research techniques, giving information on their strengths and limitations, and when it is appropriate to use them. A first section offers advice relevant to many techniques on how to ask questions – what kinds of questions to avoid and how to evaluate the questions you want to ask. Then the chapter deals with interviews, focus groups, questionnaires, documentary sources and observation.

Methods that facilitate participation, such as ranking and scoring techniques; visual methods like drawing, mapping and video; and drama and role play are described in Chapter 12, which also discusses participatory approaches more broadly, including some critiques of these.

Part 3: Analysis and research communication

This last part concentrates on two important areas for managers of research projects to consider – promotion and assessment. Both need to be considered throughout the life of a research project, not just at the end. Practical tips are offered on a range of ways of both promoting and assessing your work.

Chapter 13 helps you to analyse your data in a convenient way and to an adequate standard. We begin by discussing how to get organized, as well as the core principles underlying analysis. We then discuss approaches to analysis for qualitative and quantitative data, emphasizing straightforward techniques that inexperienced researchers can use with confidence. Data analysis software is introduced. Finally, you are encouraged to step back and consider how to bring together your findings and clarify what they really mean overall.

Chapter 14 guides you through the process of writing up the findings of your research – looking at both what to write and how to write it. It contains sections on what needs to go into your report and how to present quantitative data clearly, with illustrative graphs. This chapter should be read alongside Chapter 15, which encourages you to look at how to get your message across, both in writing a report and in communicating your research findings in a variety of other ways.

Chapter 15 also shows you how to formulate an effective communications strategy so your work is distributed to, and read by, those you wish to influence. This chapter focuses particularly on how to get your findings heard in relation to policy issues, and offers tips as to how to deal with the media.

Finally, Chapter 16 looks at some common approaches to evaluating research projects and also at ways you can assess the uptake of your research by key audiences, as well as how to measure the impact you have achieved at the programme and policy levels.

The book concludes with two appendixes. Appendix 1 gives a short summary of key ideas in monitoring and evaluation, since this is such a common use of research methods in development work. This book is not designed to give comprehensive guidance on monitoring and evaluation, as there are many excellent sources already available, but this appendix draws out the links between the research guidance contained in *Research for Development* and evaluation work. Appendix 2 contains a guide to useful websites, both for research methods and for some development issues.

PART 1

INTRODUCTION AND PLANNING YOUR RESEARCH

1

INTRODUCTION: WHY DEVELOPMENT RESEARCH MATTERS

What is research? What is the best approach to research for development work? What are the different ways in which research is used in development work? This chapter aims to lay the foundations for the rest of the manual by attempting to answer these questions.

The book is written for development workers, and is intended to give you the tools to use research as effectively as possible in your work. We draw on examples from international development work and from work in the UK to improve the wellbeing of disadvantaged communities. We take a definition of human development compatible with the following, that 'human development aims to expand people's freedoms – the worthwhile capabilities people value – and to empower people to engage actively in development processes, on a shared planet. And it seeks to do so in ways that appropriately advance equity, efficiency, sustainability and other key principles' (Alkire, 2010). For development workers, research is one approach to improving social wellbeing. Ideas are proposed to assist in deciding when a research approach is the best one to take.

Research is used in development work for a variety of purposes. It may set out to explore an issue in order to plan a programme; it may, more broadly, ask people in an area about their own needs; or it may aim to collect in-depth information about a specific issue, to make a case for change. Research methods are also used in programme monitoring, evaluation and review. What we call research can range from very small local pieces of work (perhaps just reviewing existing information) to major international projects.

Research involves collecting new information in a systematic way, and effective research often challenges received wisdom and ideas that are taken for granted. So, what can be achieved through using research in development work? We begin with some real-life examples focused on various aspects of child wellbeing.

In the first example, research into the situation of children working stitching footballs in Pakistan gave information which could be used both to plan Save the Children's own programme of work and to influence policy on child labour internationally.

FOR EXAMPLE

Child Labour Project, Sialkot, Pakistan

Save the Children's research in Sialkot was the foundation for its involvement in a coalition working to phase out child labour in football production. The research provided detailed information about why children stitch footballs, their working conditions, the problems they and their families face and how to help them exit the workforce. It challenged some of the myths that were floating around, for example that the work prevented child stitchers from attending school, and revealed for the first time the large numbers of women football stitchers. On the basis of this new and important information, Save the Children was able to plan its own contributions to a programme to assist children's transition out of the workforce.

The research was also very timely. The initial findings were available at the same time as the International Labour Organization was planning its own programme, and the completed research was ready by the time most of the partners in the Sialkot programme were starting to plan their activities. It was thus possible to use them to influence other partners' activities to promote family welfare, for example by finding ways women could continue working after their children stopped. The research provided the basis for broader advocacy on child labour issues with industry, international organizations and consumers, among others.

In Pakistan and internationally, the research played an important role in establishing Save the Children as a credible actor on child labour issues. The fact that it was rigorous – based on a carefully thought-out methodology – and was widely seen to be impartial was important in Save the Children's ability to exert an influence on the programme and to speak with authority on the issue.

Source: Save the Children UK (1997a)

Research is also important to ensure that development programmes are appropriate to the needs they aim to address. In addition to carrying out research themselves, development organizations should encourage the greater use of existing research. Especially in emergency situations, there is often a failure to seek out relevant research – for example work produced by anthropologists on a group suffering a crisis – and this can compromise effective intervention.

FOR EXAMPLE

Appropriate aid for nomads in Somaliland

A failure to read ethnography on Somaliland, led agencies in the immediate post-conflict phase to build schools in pastoral nomadic communities which would normally move continuously with their herds to water sources. Schools created a focal point for settlement but also provided a target for grenades: by bringing people together they rendered them more vulnerable to attack.

Making use of existing research to identify mechanisms to address school violence

Cruel and humiliating forms of psychological punishment, gender-based violence and bullying remain a daily reality for millions of schoolchildren. Aiming to stop this growing global problem, Plan launched the Learn Without Fear campaign (http://plan-international. org/learnwithoutfear) in October 2008.

In order to inform the campaign with the most updated, relevant and actionable evidence, Plan commissioned a review of existing research from the Overseas Development Institute to identify policies, programmes and legal instruments that address school violence in the developing world, and to draw implications for policy, practice and research.

The paper (http://plan-international.org/learnwithoutfear/files/painful-lessons-english) focused on bullying and sexual violence in school contexts only. This choice of focus was influenced by an international consultation process undertaken by Plan in 2007.

The report shows that:

- Girls as young as ten are being forced to have sex by their teachers to pass exams and threatened with poor grades and failure if they refuse.
- In a multi-country World Health Organization study, between 20 and 65 per cent of school-aged children reported having been verbally or physically bullied over the past 30 days.
- Gender-based violence in schools is reinforced by sexist and discriminatory content of educational materials. In Nicaragua, for instance, educational authorities approved a conservative religious-inspired module on sexual education, popularly known as the 'catechism of sexuality', to be used in schools.
- Girls' likelihood of molestation increases with the distance to school.
- Bullying is also seen to be linked to experiences of domestic violence, as children learn that violence is a primary mechanism for negotiating relationships. Children who suffer from family violence are more likely to be bullies and/or to be bullied.

Violence in schools ruins the one real chance of a better and more prosperous life for many children, and denies to communities and countries a vital national asset. Since violence against schoolchildren is preventable, Plan will continue to use research to guide campaign and programme work to ensure children's right to a safe school environment.

Development agencies are increasingly using participatory research methods. These enable community members to have a say on both the issue itself and how the research is carried out. Participatory work can contribute both to programme development and to influencing policy at national or international level.

Participatory needs assessment in Vietnam

A participatory needs assessment in four communes in Thanh Chuong district, Nghe An province, Vietnam, looked at livelihood strategies and credit and savings. The purpose was to improve the quality of Save the Children's assistance and enhance its impact on partner agencies and beneficiaries. The assessment had the goal of obtaining a better understanding of local conditions and needs; constraints and problems; and opportunities and potential. The participatory process was to lead into communities participating in project design and implementation and management in the longer term.

(Continued)

FOR EXAMPLE

FOR EXAMPLE

(Continued)

Multidisciplinary teams, including a credit specialist, an agriculturalist, a district representative and two representatives from each commune, carried out the research using a mix of techniques and a variety of sources of information. Observation, semi-structured interviewing, diagrams, livelihood analysis and ranking enabled analysis of elders, children, leaders, women, men, the poor, the better-off, etc. The teams could thus gain a more informed understanding of the locality and the issues facing the population. The use of records and observation verified information gathered. The process yielded a set of priorities for interventions based on community members' experience and views.

Source: Save the Children UK (1993)

FOR EXAMPLE

The contribution of older people to development: Ghana and South Africa

Older people are often invisible in development issues, although they make up an increasing proportion of the population of developing countries. HelpAge International carried out a major study of the contribution of older people to development, including Ghana and South Africa case studies. The purpose was to help policies and services respond better to the needs and capabilities of poor and disadvantaged older people in African and other countries.

Fieldwork took place in a number of locations in each country. Approaches included interviews, focus group discussions and methods drawn from Participatory Learning and Action, a development from the tradition of Participatory Rapid Appraisal. These emphasize visual work – mapping, diagramming, ranking and scoring exercises – which enables participants to share information and to debate its meaning as a group.

Findings drew attention to the different kinds of contributions older women and older men make: in addition to being income generators, older people are health- care providers, asset managers, educators, mentors and carers. The research then began to feed older people's views into policy discussion on ageing in Ghana and South Africa. It again involved older people directly at the point when the findings were presented to national-level government officials, as HelpAge saw it as a catalyst to develop processes to include older people in mainstream decision making about issues that affect their lives.

Source: HelpAge International (1999)

Another style of participatory research – peer research, led by young people themselves – influenced UK politicians on the issue of support to care leavers. The research helped the young people to get their experience and views listened to.

FOR EXAMPLE

Peer research by young care leavers in the UK

Every year in the UK, thousands of young people leave local authority care, some of them having spent all their lives in residential or foster homes. Many are only 16 years old when they face the challenge of living independently. Previous research has produced worrying statistics on the numbers becoming homeless and experiencing other problems.

Save the Children asked a group of young people who had left care not long before to investigate the issues. The group planned and carried out their own research, supported by youth workers and a research advisor. They presented the research to a well-attended meeting at the Houses of Parliament, and MPs from several parties agreed to take up the issue. The research contributed to an increase in concern for this group of young people, and subsequent legislation increased local authorities' duties to assist young people after the age of 16, although there remains much room for improvement.

Source: West (1995)

1.1   So what *is* research?

A major challenge in writing this manual is that what we mean by research covers a large and diverse group of processes. And everything about research is argued over. There is fierce debate between researchers and those who use research about the validity of different approaches. It would be so much easier to explain something like plumbing, where it is so much less a matter of opinion whether things work or not.

When we consulted practitioners on what they would like to see in this manual, they asked for clear answers to the questions: What is research? What are the 'rules of the game' if you are doing research? These are reasonable questions, but huge numbers of books exist discussing the answers – and not just academic ones: the debate emerges regularly in daily life for those doing research for development work.

Evaluating community health development projects: the debate

FOR EXAMPLE

Save the Children in the UK and internationally sets up community development projects to improve the health of different groups of people. Usually, these work in partnership with government health services. At a certain point, Save the Children staff meet with government research staff, often practitioners of public-health medicine, to discuss how to conduct the necessary evaluation.

Typically, public health practitioners insist that the only valid evaluation compares objectively measurable 'health gains' – children growing taller, people living longer – in the area where the intervention occurs and in a 'control' area where no such development work is going on. The model is the randomized controlled trial. Many issues arise, though: What are appropriate measures of success? How could the effect of the intervention be isolated from other changes in the area? How can the cost of such a major study be met?

An alternative approach may then be suggested, which concentrates attention on community members' views on the development work and the issues they raise as important. Development is about the empowerment of community members, not about fulfilling aims set by outsiders. And the process of carrying out an intervention, as much as the direct outcomes, may be valuable in the long term. Importance is placed on learning throughout the project rather than just making a judgement at the end.

A complex discussion then takes place, which community development workers usually find enraging. Questions of values, practicalities, costs, validity, philosophies of knowledge (What counts as a real effect? Whose opinion counts?) and possible research methods all fly around the room in a chaotic muddle.

The medical model of research is particularly well defined. Also, doctors hold great authority in most societies, and may have an influence on the survival of health-related projects. This makes negotiations of this sort particularly fraught. It is crucial to any partnership process to agree an approach to evaluation that will be acceptable to the key partners, but sometimes there seems to be no way through the conflicts. Focusing on evaluation and research does not soften any differences of approach; rather, it usually sharpens the outlines of the matters at issue.

Similar patterns can crop up in dealings with economists, agronomists and psychologists, among others.

This book has been prepared by professional researchers who have frequently supported development workers in situations like this. But there is no simple solution. Arguing about whose truth matters is important – it is an important part of the process of development to try to ensure the voices of less powerful people are heard.[1] Equally, it is essential to argue about how we can measure the success of our work in a way that is convincing to those who need to be convinced (see, for example, Davies et al., 2005 and DFID, 2006). What this manual hopes to achieve is increased confidence for development workers when they take part in this kind of discussion.

1.2 'But I'm not a researcher': the contribution of the development worker

This handbook is designed to be accessible and useful to a wide range of readers, including students and first-time researchers who are looking for an introduction to designing and conducting research projects related to international development. That being said, it is written primarily with development practitioners in mind – professional people who do not intend to become full-time researchers – to give them a greater sense of control in using research in their work. Looking at things from a more research-oriented point of view can help in avoiding mistakes in programme design resulting from ill-informed assumptions about a situation, as the following examples illustrate.

FOR EXAMPLE

Why were children missing school in northern Iraq?

Save the Children was concerned about low school attendance within a Kurdish community in northern Iraq. The organization had assumed that the cause was parents' lack of money. However, when researchers talked to children, they found teachers were beating them so severely that they were afraid to go to school. There were also allegations of sexual abuse. The agency was then able to discuss with the local authorities a programme of teacher training to address how children should be treated as well as how to convey information.

FOR EXAMPLE

Identifying an effective intervention: Child Labour Project, Sialkot, Pakistan

The research into children stitching footballs aimed partly to identify how Save the Children could intervene most usefully. Some campaign groups were pressing for the building of more schools, but the research established that it was not a lack of schools that was preventing children from attending. Rather, the key factors were the high cost and low quality of schooling, as well as families' need for income. In this case, it would have been ineffective to set up more schools.

How do you feel about research?

Without thinking too much about it, jot down the feelings, ideas and images that emerge when you think about 'research'.

- What about the words 'enquiry' and 'investigation'?
- What do these feelings mean for you in thinking about how you will use this manual?
- Where do they come from? Experience at work? Your schooling?
- Doing this as a group could be useful.

ACTIVITY 1.1

Ordinarily, development practitioners do some similar work to researchers. They are very likely to undertake needs assessments. They investigate people's opinions and probe their explanations of problems in their lives. They work with people to help them to analyse their situation – to make sense of things beyond the individual.

They also use some of the same methods as researchers. Both may conduct interviews, undertake observation, hold discussions and ask groups what is most important to them. However, development workers generally specialize in being with people in an informal way, to build trust. This makes it possible for people without the confidence bred by formal education to discuss issues of importance to them.

It is not the intention of this manual simply to re-label development workers' methods as research. All of the many schools of thought about research have a set of rules defining 'good data'. Development work has its own, different, standards and priorities.

Take the example of a development worker discussing unemployment with a young person. Like a researcher, they are likely to be listening for themes they have heard from other young people they have talked to, so as to understand what is important to the whole group. But the development worker will also be observing the conversation for ways to enable the young person to feel more in control. They might let contradictory statements pass, if they are at the stage of building trust with the person.

A researcher would be much more concerned to record things exactly as the young person puts them. If they are engaged in work of any depth, and they hear apparently conflicting points of view, they will gently ask questions to tease out the way the person is thinking. The researcher is not trying to effect change in the young person, but to understand the situation.

If the young person says something which offends the development worker's principles, for instance taking the blame for events the latter regards as caused by wider social forces, the development worker is likely to challenge that interpretation. Depending on their school of thought regarding different approaches (see Section 2.2), a researcher may simply record such a comment, or they may put forward a different view, usually in a neutral way, such as 'some people might say …', and then record the response.

In encouraging development workers to learn more about research, the hope is they will take from the disciplines of research the things that could be most useful to them. Doing research does change your point of view.

Meanwhile, development workers' skills and knowledge have a great deal to contribute to research processes. One key role is that of identifying issues for research. With their knowledge of the situation and the needs of a group of people, combined with an understanding of broader social processes, they can frame issues which are 'live' and meaningful to those concerned. Second, development workers' skill in building relationships with people, including those who face discrimination, is invaluable in facilitating research that actively involves community members.

A different way of seeing – through researchers' eyes

- A questioning approach to everything, including everyone's pet theories;
- Concern to understand what people say very accurately, to hear them without bias;
- Appreciating that how we ask questions can determine the answers we get;
- An analytical approach – that is, looking for patterns in things, probing behind surface appearances;
- Trying to get inside how people make sense of things – especially when the sense is not immediately obvious;
- Becoming ever more conscious of the researcher's own impact on people and their responses.

Research methods can be seen as a set of tools you can use in various ways – but they are complex tools and there are risks attached to their use. It is important to learn to use them properly in order to avoid accidents.

Accordingly, some types of research are best left to experienced research professionals. Large-scale surveys, complex statistics and subtle qualitative research on sensitive issues are best done by researchers with specialist training. Development workers may wish to commission this type of work; Chapters 3 and 4 aim to help them to do so. But many kinds of research approach are straightforward to use and can enable development workers to understand the issues they are working with in more depth and represent people's views more accurately.

1.3   Who should do research for development work? The broader issues

This section discusses wider questions arising from choices made about who does what research. Development workers are in the business of creating social change, and need to take a pragmatic approach to the use of research. At times, it may well be that an expert view from a famous university is exactly what is needed. However, some broader issues need to be considered, beyond the immediate piece of work.

The traditional model of development research has, until relatively recently, concentrated internationally recognized expertise in a few elite centres. Historically, much of the research into Southern issues has been carried out by people based in or coming from the North. In recent years, though, there has been a welcome trend of growth in development research centres, think-tanks and academic departments throughout the South, which now produce a large volume of cutting-edge research on both local and international themes. Deep inequalities persist, however – as Girvan (2007) notes, 'knowledge hierarchies' favouring Northern over Southern knowledge remain deeply entrenched in the development community.

With this in mind, it is important to remember some issues which may well arise in the production of development knowledge within elite Northern research centres:

- These centres are typically not situated in the countries or among the people in question. Meanwhile, knowledge in any country is more likely to be concentrated in elite, urban centres – heightening the geographical as well as conceptual divide between the researchers and the 'researched' (see, for example, Utting, 2006). Centres also tend to be closer to funding institutions, which can raise issues of impartiality and independence.
- Research is often done by highly paid academics or consultants who make brief visits to poverty-stricken areas and then return to their base with their data, which may never return to the place they relate to. This can encourage the dangerous perception that answers lie with outsiders and not with those directly involved.
- Without sufficient awareness of competing Southern perspectives, the traditional predominance of Northern approaches and ideologies in development thinking, which have come to be seen as universally applicable, can all too easily be replicated in research. Indeed, these approaches are often unthinkingly favoured over 'local' knowledge which is equally, if not far more, relevant to the context.
- Overreliance on Northern research centres can lead to fewer opportunities for Southern people or non-academics to learn from research processes.

Of course, many excellent Northern knowledge centres take great pains to address such concerns, and the continuing growth of Southern knowledge production (including North–South and South–South research cooperation) continues to improve the situation. Nonetheless, these challenges remain embedded in the fabric of development knowledge production, and should be considered carefully in any research project.

Cartoon by Peter Maddocks, reproduced with kind permission of id21/Insights.

There are, of course, more and less sensitive ways in which researchers/consultants can operate, but a power imbalance seems an inevitable part of this pattern. (See Chapter 9 on undertaking ethical research for more on issues of power in research.) One purpose of this manual is to encourage development workers to play a role in supporting researchers in the South and in disadvantaged communities in the North. In this way, it will be possible to do more research closer to communities whose lives are its focus.

Checklist: developing research skills in disadvantaged communities

☑ Where possible, hire researchers from Southern countries/disadvantaged groups.
☑ Build some training and development work for local workers into any research brief, so they can learn from a variety of research processes (see Chapter 6 on learning development research skills).
☑ Seek to develop research ideas which are locally generated and owned, so there will be demand to keep the data locally, even if research is conducted by outsiders.
☑ Ensure that if data are removed from the context, they are copied or returned to those who can use them for development purposes (unless issues of confidentiality prevent this).
☑ Give appropriate feedback on findings to local agencies and community members[2] themselves as well as to decision makers.
☑ Ensure research processes are carried out in an open way and demystified for all participants.
☑ Organize participatory training workshops in research skills as part of your ongoing staff development work.
☑ Ensure that, where researchers are relatively inexperienced, they have a clear brief and sufficient support – coaching and supervision from those with relevant experience (see Chapter 3).

1.4   Research and social change

Development work usually aims to create social change of some sort. It might aim to assist a minority community in moving out of poverty, or be directed towards increasing educational opportunities for children and adults across a whole region. There are many theories as to how social change takes place, and on top of these many more as to how development workers can and should intervene in these processes. One way of thinking about the use of research-type activities within development is to focus on how they can contribute towards processes of change.

There are a number of different ways of looking at this. Perhaps the dominant model is what you might call the rationalist, or engineering, approach. This suggests we have a social problem (and its definition is straightforward). Information is needed to understand it better in order to solve it. Research collects such information, and policy will change in light of such findings. Researchers are seen as engineers, providing technical data to solve technical problems.

There are many problems with this model. In reality, things are much more complicated. There may not even be agreement about the nature of the problem. Policy change does not automatically follow on from research – the process is much more contradictory (see Chapters 3 and 15). The assumptions behind this model see governments and the powerful in general as benignly and openly seeking to improve things: the complexities of political reality are left out.

Much participatory research works with a quite different model of the links between research and social change (see Chapter 12). Ordinary people are seen as important, and research aims to empower them to better understand their situation and hence take action to change it. Information is not neutral, but reflects different standpoints. The key is to give voice to the experience and knowledge of oppressed people.

For non-governmental organizations, campaigning can be a route to social change – in this case, research is seen as providing 'ammunition'. This is really a kind of engineering approach, but it sees public opinion as important, whereas the traditional model aims to influence decision makers through nothing more than the strength of the evidence.

Finally, development organizations routinely seek to effect social change by directly engaging policymakers through research. Under this model, research knowledge can be a decisive factor in shaping the development of evidence-informed policy. As a result, it is conducted with an eye towards policy relevance, and is promoted strategically so as to maximize its chances of uptake by policymakers (see Chapter 15 for more).

Which approaches are chosen depends on many things. It may be a tactical choice, depending on the issue in question and the kind of change desired – for example legal, economic or a change of ordinary people's attitudes. But it may also spring from professionals' own beliefs about how change takes place. Some place their faith in parliamentary processes, others in grassroots education and action.

Suppose, for example, the aim is to influence some aspect of professional practice, perhaps in social welfare. Some see the best hope of achieving this as being through scientific-style research which aims to 'prove' the success of a particular method. Others want to engage directly with the professionals in cooperative enquiry. Still others want to give information to service users or the general public to encourage them to pressure the professionals to change their practices.

It is worth reflecting on these issues in reading this manual, so you can be conscious of the framework you are working within. It is not surprising that the research we do in development is so diverse, when it is performing a number of very different functions in each organization's work for change.

What model of change do you use?

In the table below, list projects you are familiar with which you think fit into each approach. How many fit squarely in one category?

Ask two other people to fill in the table separately, then discuss any issues that arise.

If the fit is bad, can you think of a better way of describing the model of social change behind your work?

Model of research for social change	Projects fitting this model
1. Rationalist/engineering	
2. Empowerment	
3. Campaigning	
4. Policy influence	

ACTIVITY 1.2

1.5 How to tell when research is the best approach to a problem

Development workers have other tools at their disposal: this manual does not intend to suggest that research is appropriate to all situations. Indeed, it has certain built-in disadvantages in many instances. Where people do not read or write, or have been taught not to criticize, research approaches are difficult for them to get to grips with. Although many methods can enable non-literate people to contribute to data collection and, to some extent, analysis, a research approach will still tend to introduce barriers to their full participation. This does not mean research is illegitimate in these situations – agencies need information for their own reasons. But research is unlikely to be the best method when the key aim is to directly empower people.

If you are planning a participatory project, remember there are many different ways of working alongside community members to investigate their issues and to help them to express their needs and views.

FOR EXAMPLE

Making videos about dynamite fishing in Tanzania

Dynamite fishing is a major problem on the coast of Tanzania. In 1994, a group of fishermen and women learnt at a conference that authorities typically blamed the environmental destruction on local fishers' ignorance. During the next six days, they made a video in which they explained their perceptions of the true situation to fellow villagers and to 'an establishment of anonymous decision makers'. Participants were able to exert control over production by watching and approving the results of the day's shooting every evening. 'People [...] want to speak loud and clear. Many of those who have never had access to modern, public fora seem to love the concept of being seen saying something for the records.' The participants revealed the dynamiting of fish and the destruction of the local marine environment, even giving the names of corrupt police and dynamite dealers.

When the facilitator of this project returned to Tanzania in 1996, he discovered that the video had had an extraordinary impact. It had engendered community mobilization on a massive scale, bridging regional and ethnic divisions between villagers, instilling confidence and inspiring action – only for villagers to be let down time and time again by corrupt local police and fisheries officers. 'The video really did make policymakers listen to villagers, even when they seemed unable to act. [...] We have an amazing video statement of an almost shocked MP who makes analogies with burning a forest or bombing a village.'

Source: Johansson (1994), in Holland and Blackburn (1998)

A range of creative approaches can be effective, as can more traditional community development methods.

Some poor and disadvantaged communities, both in the global North and in parts of the South, complain of too much research being done 'on' them. Different researchers keep appearing in people's homes, asking similar sets of questions, but nothing seems to be done as a result. It is essential to make sure the information you need is not already available before undertaking new research, especially with people who are as hard-pressed for time as are those living in poverty.

In some situations, it may also be that, when you want to start a project, doing research to investigate needs can create a focus on the negative that is counterproductive. Mollison (2000) contrasts the 'appreciative inquiry' approach of a highly successful Bombay-based community organization, Pratham, with the conventional approach. Rather than asking what people's needs are, appreciative inquiry (Elliott, 1999) looks at community resources, and asks 'What have been our most inspiring experiences?' and 'How can we have more of them?'

> The 'normal way' to start an education project is to study why poor children do not go to school. [...] Typical findings are that the poor do not expect to do well in school, that poor families need their children to work because of poverty and that poor children feel that they are treated badly in schools. Sometimes the physical infrastructure is also found wanting. Once these problems have been identified a project is designed to tackle them. Thus, for example, a project plan might aim to reform the existing education system [...], to mount a major school repair or building programme and to establish income generating projects [...].

> Had Pratham taken this approach they would have needed a huge budget from the beginning and might still be struggling to succeed on a small scale. They might also be finding that many of the originally intended 'beneficiaries' had somehow been excluded from the programme. The potential enthusiasm for education that Pratham have in fact unleashed would not have been uncovered. Instead, the project would have demonstrated to the poor (assuming it reached the poor at all) that it is we who want their children to go to school and that we are willing – for a while – to pay for it. (Mollison, 2000)

Table 1.1 Conditions for research

When research may be an effective approach	When research is not likely to be helpful
✓ When no one has much information on a situation;	✗ When it is clear what needs to be done, but no one is getting on with it;
✓ When there is only 'anecdotal' evidence of a 'hidden' problem;	✗ When your programme is trying to decide where to start, in a known environment;
✓ When the group you are working with feels their point of view has not been heard;	✗ When political conflict or state repression are particularly intense;
✓ When policymakers are considering a policy change and want to investigate its possible impact;	✗ When communities have already been the subject of many research projects;
✓ When it is important to show you have represented people's views accurately;	✗ When the main purpose is to increase people's participation and build their personal development;
✓ When you know past attempts to address this issue through programmes have made mistakes.	✗ Where there are no resources to follow up research with any action;
	✗ To avoid making a decision.

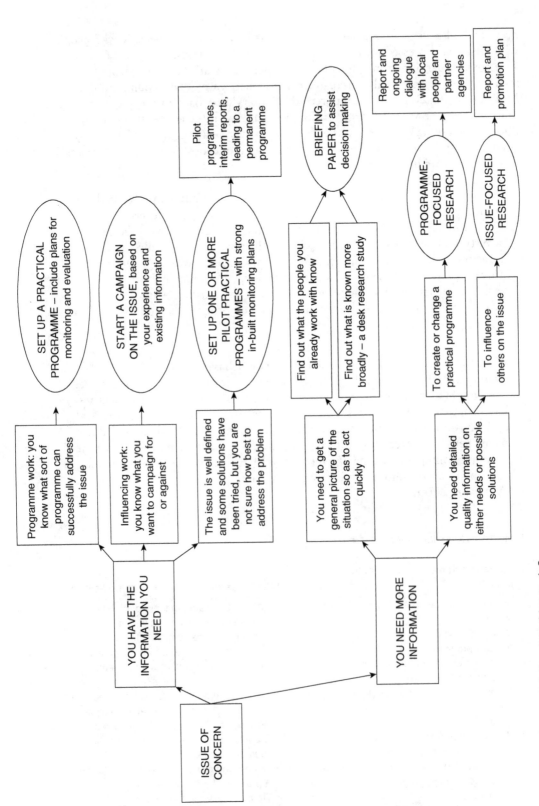

Figure 1.1 Is research the right thing to do?

1.5.1 What role will your research play?

Research can fulfil different roles in a process of working for change. It will be helpful to be clear where you are in the process and what you hope to achieve through the research.

Table 1.2 Different roles for research in development processes

Policy-focused research	Programme-focused research
• Raising a new issue in the public domain; • Putting forward a new perspective on a 'live' issue or reframing an existing issue in a new way; • Producing strong evidence of the benefit or harm of a particular policy; • Drawing together learning from different studies to support a policy position.	• Investigating the needs of a community or specific group of people; • Investigating the need for a particular programme; • Demonstrating convincingly the effectiveness of a particular programme (evaluation).

Each of these situations has its own key requirements for how the work is carried out. You need to think of the research work as linked closely into either advocacy processes – perhaps an organized campaign to influence policy – or programme planning and development. To be an effective part of development work, research needs to be planned and carried out in cooperation with others with related responsibilities.

15.1.2 If in doubt ...

Perhaps you are not sure that research is the right approach to the problem you hope to address. Research is not the only way of investigating a question, and it may not be the most useful one. At times, a much simpler investigation is all that is required, more like what a journalist might do to gain a greater understanding of an issue or to dramatize it for their readers. Calling it 'research' may overcomplicate your task.

If in doubt: things you could do before starting a full-scale research project

Small-scale internal fact finding

Find out what people inside your organization and those working closely with you already know about the issue – and what they think should be done. This can be done more or less formally (a meeting, a short questionnaire), as appropriate.

A mini-literature search and review

Spend some time collecting existing research on the issue you are interested in, and write a summary of what you have found. Make an effort to contact people

(Continued)

(Continued)

who have grappled with the same type of problems in different geographical areas.

Carry out a small pilot study

After clarifying your research questions, carry out a small study to get some general impressions of the information you could collect. For example, carry out five interviews with local people on your issue, or raise it at a group meeting that is already scheduled and facilitate a short discussion. Make sure you record your data properly, as you may need them later if you proceed to do more extensive research.

Test the idea for the research project

If you are concerned about committing your organization to a research project, it may be helpful to carry out a Strengths, Weaknesses, Opportunities, Threats (SWOT) analysis on the project, making guesses about future outcomes. (This tool is introduced in Section 3.4.) And do the same for any alternative strategy you can think of.

The amount of energy you put into research-type exercises should depend on the use you intend to make of the material you collect. There is no one recipe – what you do needs to be appropriate to its purpose (see Chapter 3 on planning for effective research).

 # Key points from this chapter

This chapter has aimed to show the positive contribution research can make to development work. It suggests that development workers have an important role in identifying issues that require investigation, and in planning and carrying out research. The contested nature of ideas on research is discussed, and readers are encouraged to try to understand these issues sufficiently so as not to be intimidated in defending their methods. It is important to be conscious of the various issues of power inequality involved in research work. Different approaches to research in development work are considered in relation to what they say about how change comes about. There is also a discussion on how to tell when research is the best approach to take to a problem, and what other courses of action might be considered.

Checklist: using research in development work

☑ Research can be a powerful tool in working for social change, and can be used in a variety of different ways.
☑ Development workers need a good understanding of research because it is important in their jobs whenever they need to produce, or assess, evidence for any claim about what is really going on.
☑ There is debate about most research issues!

☑ Development workers do many similar tasks to researchers, but their training leads them to approach these in different ways.

☑ A research perspective can contribute a questioning attitude, a concern to hear people's views accurately, an analytical approach and reflection on how our own actions determine the responses we get.

☑ It is very important to build research capacity in the South and in disadvantaged communities in the North.

☑ Research is a useful approach in only some situations – there are others where it would be useless, wasteful and possibly harmful.

☑ If in doubt as to whether research is needed, there are a number of things you can do, short of a full-blown research project, which will give you a better sense of the issues in question.

Further reading

Bulmer, M. (1982) *The Uses of Social Research: Social Investigation in Public Policy-making*. London: George Allen and Unwin.

Offers models for thinking about the relationship between research and decision making in public policy.

Desai, V. and Potter, R. (eds) (2006) *Doing Development Research*. New Delhi, Thousand Oaks, CA, London: Sage.

A comprehensive introduction for anyone carrying out research in developing countries, this brings together experts with extensive experience of overseas research and presents an overview of the core methodologies used.

Mikkelsen, B. (2005) *Methods for Development Work and Research: A Guide for Practitioners*. New Delhi, Thousand Oaks, CA, London: Sage.

This book provides an introduction to a variety of methods and methodological considerations to help the development practitioner to match issues and approaches in their research. Based on long experience, it offers practical guidance and critical reflection on methods for development work and research.

Notes

1 See, for example, Holland and Blackburn (1998) and Robb (2002). Some of the fundamental difficulties in 'hearing' the voices of the less powerful are explored in Spivak's seminal article 'Can the Subaltern Speak?' (1988).

2 'Community member' is used as a very broad term to refer to those the development worker/researcher relates to. They might be villagers, young women or disabled people, for example. Community links and support may be strong or weak.

2

USING RESEARCH IN DEVELOPMENT WORK

This chapter gives some of the background the reader will need to feel confident working with researchers, briefly describing some of the important schools of thought about research. It suggests that, rather than searching for the 'right' methods of research, we should accept that a wide range of approaches can be useful for different purposes.

In development work, research is undertaken for two main types of reason – to inform a programme (either as a needs assessment before starting or as monitoring and evaluation as the programme develops) or to learn more about issues with a view to influencing policy. This distinction will crop up throughout the manual, as the primary purpose of the research has important consequences for the way it is carried out. Here, we look at some of the issues involved in carrying out each type of research.

2.1 So what is the right approach to research for development work?

This manual would have been a lot simpler to write if it was setting out to sell a particular set of research methods. Participatory methods, for example, are clearly of great value for development work, and it is quite straightforward to advocate these and explain how to use them.[1] But actually there is value for development workers in a number of approaches to research.

At times, for example, an agency needs to argue an unpopular case at the political level. Then it is helpful to use evidence that a variety of powerful players will accept as valid: it is not a good idea to set up a situation in which you have to defend both the case itself and the validity of the evidence. Here, it can be worth using more conventional methods to make an important point convincingly.

A musical interlude

We might think of research as a bit like music. There is no point in arguing the virtues of one type of music against another – they are not in competition; each obeys its own rules and each may fit different needs at different times. There are, of course, people who appreciate only Mozart or Bob Marley. And we may find traditions very remote from those we grew up with difficult to tune into. But if we don't try, we miss a lot that is going on in the world.

Research and music are both about communication and coherence. If there is no emotional link to anything the user knows about, they won't listen to it. Equally, if it doesn't hold together and make sense in itself, it is unattractive, and the user turns away. Music, and research, can also be done well or badly, and even those of us without any great training can tell the difference.

Our point is that, first, we need to appreciate a wide range of styles of research and, second, researchers of all sorts need to make efforts to make their work accessible to a wide audience. The most traditional methods – for example a census, asking very simple questions – may be totally appropriate for some purposes, such as to establish the number of females and males in a population. But explaining any imbalance in these numbers would require the investigation of many factors in a variety of ways. Are any biological factors involved? What social structures surround the survival of girls and boys? Is sex pre-selection or female infanticide occurring? Finding answers to these questions obviously involves a more subtle approach.

Objections can be made to any given approach. For example, records of deaths are not necessarily the 'simple facts' we might expect them to be. A suicide or indeed an infanticide will often not be recorded as such, for understandable social reasons. That such statistics are unreliable does not mean they are meaningless and should not be collected: research is always imperfect. It is a very valuable part of the scientific tradition that we treat any 'truths' we arrive at as provisional and open to question. Quality is defined by the internal logic of a piece of research, and by how well it is defended. There is no absolute standard of right and wrong out there.

2.2 Two major research approaches

Research is all about the power to define reality. Saying you are doing research suggests you are undertaking systematic investigation with a view to making some claim about the world. But different research traditions see this issue differently.

Traditional scientific research tends to deny the power dynamics around research, claiming that *the scientist is a disinterested, unbiased observer who can produce objective truths about a straightforward reality*. Social science that follows this tradition, such as mainstream psychology, aims to get as close as possible to the natural sciences, such as physics or chemistry. This is often called 'positivist' research,[2] and there has recently been a trend to apply it to qualitative as well as quantitative studies. Proponents claim that the same logic of inference underlies good design in both cases, and that the social scientific approach applies equally to both (for example King et al., 1994).

There are others in the social sciences who challenge the view that a truly objective science is possible, showing how the observer's standpoint affects what is seen at every level. We tend to see what we are looking for; hence reality is to some extent constructed by our views of it. These schools of thought go by many names, which can unfortunately come across as rather daunting. Widely used ones include 'social constructionism', 'phenomenology', 'critical theory', 'grounded theory' and 'postmodernism'.

What these latter traditions have in common is that they are interested in *the ideas people themselves generate*, rather than looking at social reality through categories determined by the researcher. They often challenge definitions and aim to reduce bias through what is called 'reflexivity' – open reflection on researchers' own point of view and how it influences their perceptions (see, for example, Alvesson and Skoldberg, 2009). Background assumptions about people and situations – the 'taken-for-granted' aspects – can be examined, and 'hidden' issues can be brought into the public sphere in a relatively safe way.

There are many elements to the inequalities of power that create, and are created by, poverty and disadvantage. Economics, social structures and access to natural resources are important. But part of the problem for less powerful groups is that their reality is not visible to others. Oppressed people often say that one of the worst things is other people's view of them. For example, disabled people often find others' attitudes just as oppressive and personally damaging as inaccessible buildings and transport systems.

Naming something can in itself have an important impact. For example, when feminists began to look at women as an oppressed group, this enabled women to reconsider issues they had thought of as individual personal problems, to see them as part of a wider social system. This released a huge amount of energy and creativity.

To give a simple example of how these different approaches affect research processes, let us take the case of a development worker who wants to commission a study of the situation of children in a longstanding refugee camp. A traditional, positivist approach might weigh and measure children, using well-tested questionnaires or checklists and comparing results with standard measures of child development. They might interview parents or those who work with the children, looking for evidence of maladjustment. They might want to know how many children go to school, how many suffer from physical or mental illness, how many commit offences and how many teenage pregnancies occur, for example.

A social constructionist researcher might instead spend time in the camp getting to know the people and observing the situation. They might seek broad information about health and welfare indicators, but would concentrate more on what the children themselves and their parents think about their situation. They would ask open questions about what children and adults consider to be the benefits and drawbacks of life in the refugee camp for children. They would not take it as given that life in the camp is worse for the children than the place they came from, but would ask questions about this. Aware of power dynamics, they would try various ways to enable children (and mothers) to voice their point of view, away from community leaders and camp authorities.

Both approaches have their strengths. Since expert views and international standards of child welfare are valued within donor agencies, a positivist report might be effective in attracting funds to a particular programme. The second approach is more likely to generate action by refugees themselves, and could identify issues that an approach which makes assumptions about people's problems might miss.

Which kind of research?

If you would like to think further about these different traditions of research, it may be helpful to see whether you can identify the sorts of research philosophy behind research projects you are familiar with.

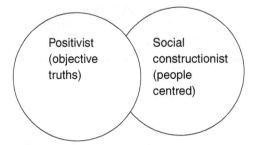

Positivist (objective truths)

Social constructionist (people centred)

Think of as many research projects in your area of work as you can, and put a cross to locate them on this diagram. We represent them as two interlocking circles because there is an overlap between the two types – some projects draw on both traditions.

Quantitative and qualitative research

The major divide in research approaches is sometimes presented as that between quantitative and qualitative research, the first being seen as concerned with numbers and the second more with meanings. A quantitative approach asks how many people share a particular characteristic or hold a particular view. A qualitative one looks more at what people think and feel and why.

However, it is not usually particularly meaningful to debate the virtues of one approach against the other. Most social research for practical purposes contains some element of both, and a 'mixed methods' approach is increasingly common: researchers seek to use both types of evidence to strengthen their arguments and 'triangulate', or test, their findings (see, for example, Brannen, 2005 and Creswell, 2009). It is more useful to understand the philosophical basis for each general approach – positivism and social constructionism – as discussed above. These issues are explored further in Chapter 7 on choosing methods.

2.3 Types of research in development work

Many kinds of activity that could be called research are present in development work. People use a variety of terminologies to refer to these, and there is a tendency to invent new jargon every few years to describe different methods or packages of methods. However, with a grasp of the most common methods and the key issues surrounding them, it is easy enough to understand any new 'magic formula' that comes along.

We suggest there are fundamentally two types of research commonly carried out in development work: that which relates primarily to the programme and that which addresses issues beyond the programme. Issue-focused research is usually undertaken with the intention of having an influence on policy.

Within each of the circles in Figure 2.1 is a great variety of kinds of research, but they all share some key characteristics related to the final purpose of the exercise. Is it fundamentally to inform the programme? Or does it seek to influence policy more broadly by gathering information on issues? Participatory research may fit into either of the two circles, and there can be a greater or lesser degree of participation within research for the programme or research for policy influence. In this, as in all other research, it is still important to keep a focus on the final purpose of the exercise.

However, Figure 2.1's two circles overlap because there are important areas of overlap between programme-focused and issue-focused research.

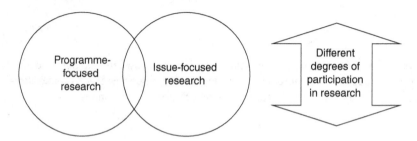

Figure 2.1   Purposes of research and levels of participation

---

FOR EXAMPLE

Research for programming and for policy advocacy: a poverty assessment in Ho Chi Minh City, Vietnam, 2000

Save the Children UK carried out a poverty assessment in three districts in Ho Chi Minh City, with a special focus on children and on disability, as part of a larger effort by the World Bank to analyse poverty in Vietnam. This was the first participatory poverty assessment (PPA) to be carried out in Ho Chi Minh City and it had a significant impact on donors and the government.

As a result of it, the World Bank realized that living standards survey data underreported poverty in Ho Chi Minh City. The PPA also put urban poverty and the situation of unregistered migrants firmly on the agenda of donors in Vietnam, in a remarkable experience of collaboration. PPAs at the community level were accompanied by regular meetings in Hanoi to discuss poverty and poverty alleviation, with the attendance of donor representatives and officials from a number of key Vietnamese ministries and departments.

The results of the PPA were also used to inform Save the Children UK's programme in Ho Chi Minh City, where the process generated an unprecedented level of cooperation and collaboration between non-governmental organizations (NGOs), mass organizations and government departments. To complement advocacy on policy issues, practical follow-up at city level is crucial to respond to the expressed needs of communities and the expectations of city authorities.

So you cannot always put a piece of work in one category or the other. One common area of overlap is when a needs assessment or community profiling is undertaken with a view to broader influence as well as to plan a specific programme of work. NGOs often hope to demonstrate the impact of national or international policy on people through study of a particular community. Another case in point is when evaluation is designed not only to enable the organization to learn the lessons of a project, but also to demonstrate the value or problems of a particular way of working to a wider audience. This manual therefore includes further guidance on these areas.

The reason it is helpful to look at the two types of research separately is that the main purpose of the project should shape how the work is undertaken in many ways. Sitting on the fence, you may find that neither purpose is served adequately.

This manual focuses mainly on research for policy influence, because many other resources offer guidance on programme-related research.[3] This chapter focuses on the purposes of research rather than how it is carried out, so we divide approaches according to the purpose, not their technical features. For example, in the category 'research for advocacy', you might find anything from a public opinion poll, to an ecologist's study of environmental damage in an area, to peer research by young people. Equally, community needs assessment can be undertaken in a wide variety of ways, from large-scale surveys to focus group meetings.

The distinction here is different to the one discussed in Section 2.2, between positivist and social constructionist approaches. Those are whole intellectual traditions, whereas this section focuses more pragmatically on the uses you wish to put your research to. Research for both programme and policy purposes can work within either tradition. Equally, both types may use qualitative and/or quantitative methods; either may involve surveys, interviews, focus groups or observation.

2.4   Programme-focused and issue-focused research

Many different terms are used to describe different types of research work used for practical purposes. The box identifies just a few of the terms you may have come across – you will be able to think of many more.

2.4.1   Programme-focused research

Some types of programme-focused research

- Needs assessment;
- Community profiling;
- Stakeholder analysis;
- Action research;
- Monitoring and evaluation;
- Participatory research – people defining their own issues, for example PPA;
- Participatory Learning and Action (was Participatory Rapid Appraisal).

(Continued)

(Continued)

Key features of programme-focused research

- An appropriate focus is dictated by practical aspects of the programme, not by theory.
- It should lead to action for change in the immediate area.
- Joint working with partner agencies is likely to be most productive.
- Participation by 'the researched' will lead to greater ownership of findings and hence greater likelihood of action being taken.
- The research process needs to be managed close to the programme.
- Researchers need an understanding/experience of the issues facing practitioners.

FOR EXAMPLE

Programme-focused research: assessing the needs of young people and of disabled children in Serb Sarajevo

The aim of this project was to demonstrate a model of community-based social welfare that includes partnership between agencies and the communities they serve. The project was conducted in Serb Sarajevo, Republika Srpska, where close to one-third of the population was at that time internally displaced. It was initiated by Save the Children UK in the context of an agreement for action with the Ministry of Health and Social Welfare Public Fund for Child Protection and the Centre for Social Welfare.

Using a community profile approach, the first step was to carry out research within the community to assess needs and to present solutions to the problems of youth and of disabled children, as seen by them and by others in the community. The priority was not to produce some academic research, but to facilitate a process whereby local people gained self-confidence, learnt about their community, were involved in assessing local needs and could use the results to progress action.

The research recruited a cross-section of representatives from the youth community and parents as advocates for children with disabilities. The youth group consisted of ten young people aged between 16 and 21, five female and five male. They were from varied backgrounds in terms of academic achievements, but all shared the problems of being displaced. Advocates for the children with disabilities consisted of six parents – five mothers and one father. None of them had any experience in any kind of research.

Training involved a basic grounding in research methods, including questionnaire formulation, interview methods, ethics, quantitative and qualitative approaches and concepts of community. It was based largely around group discussions, with people able to put forward their own views and reflect consciously on important local issues.

Each of the groups chose a method they felt was appropriate to the task. The youth group decided on a semi-structured interview approach based on a questionnaire and, with some assistance, agreed a set of open-ended questions. They carried out their interviews in cafés, on the street, in public buildings and in people's homes. Their sample included people of a similar age or younger than themselves, selected by convenience and by 'snowballing', whereby contacts are made by word of mouth. A total of 175 semi-structured interviews were conducted.

The group of parents decided in-depth interviews would be more appropriate for their work with parents of children with disabilities. After some discussion and assistance, they selected relevant questions as prompts. They carried out interviews in respondents' homes.

The sample was taken from a list provided by the Centre for Social Welfare: in total, 24 families with disabled children were visited and interviewed.

When the interviews were complete, the field researchers analysed their data, first grouping the responses, then quantifying the data and selecting illustrative quotes for inclusion in the report. The report, 'Community Appraisal of Life in Serb Sarajevo for Young People and Children with Disabilities', gave a vivid, often painful, description of life in the community seen through the eyes of its members. It highlighted precisely and subtly the problems for disabled children and youth; at the same time, it offered realistic and practical solutions. Issues related to employment, accommodation, criminality, education and transportation were the most important.

The report was presented to representatives of the local community and potential donors. For Save the Children UK, it was the guiding light for projects that followed.

2.4.2 Issue-focused research

Some uses of issue-focused research

- Research for policy engagement – to engage with policymakers on a semi-regular basis on areas of interest;
- Research for campaigning – to argue a point;
- Comparative thematic research looking at experiences in a number of countries;
- Reviewing what is known on an issue;
- Helping the voices of less powerful people be heard by decision makers;
- Reframing an issue – incorporating new data and events or applying new theories to existing case studies.

Key features of issue-focused research

- It should lead to action for change beyond the local area.
- It may involve direct participation by 'the researched', or may be carried out to support a participatory advocacy process.
- It involves researchers being knowledgeable about the broader context of the issue and able to contextualize findings within this.
- It is crucial to be clear about the audience and what is required to influence them.
- To ensure the greatest likelihood of influencing policy, it is critical to think strategically at the planning stage (see the discussion of tools for planning policy impact in Chapters 3 and 15).

Issue-focused research: 'the missing link'

Millions of poor rural children are taught in a language they do not use in daily life, meaning that they drop out or fail at school.

Save the Children UK's education team had for many years been working to promote bilingual education based on children's first language. Although there were successful pilot projects,

(Continued)

FOR EXAMPLE

(Continued)

there was little government support in many developing countries for large-scale change in the languages used for teaching. There was no clear consensus among the donor community that language was a major problem, so governments were not receiving clear messages from development partners that change was needed. Language seemed to be the 'missing link' in understanding how to get the poorest children into school and learning well.

There was plenty of evidence about the damage caused by teaching a child in an unfamiliar language, but much of it remained at the level of academic papers and had not been articulated clearly to education decision makers. There was no material that explained why high-level decision makers should prioritize language over all the other pressing issues involved in expanding educational access and quality. In 2009, Save the Children secured funding from the Centre for British Teachers Education Trust to support the production of a policy report on the language used in teaching children in low- and middle-income countries.

The resulting study, *Language and Education: The Missing Link* (Pinnock, 2009), had a large impact on global child education policy. It received supportive media coverage worldwide, and has been referenced in education policy literature. Save the Children UK's research also served as an impetus for a British Council initiative aimed at improving awareness of language and child education among key policymakers in Pakistan.

The Sialkot research on child labour in football stitching in Pakistan gives an example of issue-focused research that was also important to programme planning. This study is also referred to later in the book in further case study examples.

Issue-focused research: influencing policy and practice – the Child Labour Project, Sialkot, Pakistan

FOR EXAMPLE

In 1996, following media campaigns by US-based and European pressure groups against child labour in Pakistan's football stitching industry, Save the Children was invited to join a coalition of organizations working to solve the problem. Initial visits to the area – Sialkot district in the east of Pakistan – and discussions with children, families, local NGOs and industrialists called into question some of the claims on which campaign work had been based. For example, early discussions showed no evidence that children were working as bonded labourers.

Although several other organizations had commissioned studies of child labour in football manufacture, it was clear that none had discussed the issue in any depth with child football stitchers, or with women, who make up a high proportion of stitchers. However, there was strong pressure to act fast and there was concern that action might well be taken on the basis of incorrect information and thus lead to an ineffective programme or, worse, one that actually undermined children's and families' wellbeing. It was important to undertake an in-depth, rigorous situation analysis to check the accuracy of early impressions and of the different claims being made about the situation of child football stitchers.

Furthermore, child labour is a politically and emotionally charged issue at the best of times, even more so in this case, given the constant Western media spotlight. This meant being sure the research was rigorous – carefully designed so it provided an adequate basis for drawing conclusions, carried out accurately and analysed carefully to be sure the findings were based on the data that had been collected. One of the main audiences, international and local football manufacturers, was particularly interested in the numbers of children involved. It was therefore important that the research be carried out on a large enough scale to provide a basis for estimating the numbers involved. Because football stitching takes place throughout a district of 2,600 km^2, Save the Children wanted to interview people from a sample of towns and villages across the district, to illuminate differences in working conditions, rather than concentrating on those closest to Sialkot city, as other investigations had done. Finally, the researchers were aware that numbers carry weight. Overall, 428 households were surveyed in 30 villages and two towns, and 745 children and 1,004 adults were interviewed. Villages were selected on a stratified random basis to give coverage of the entire district.

The survey had two parts: one collected detailed information about family size and income, numbers of children stitching, their ages, how long they had worked, how much they earned and their school attendance. The second asked respondents more open-ended questions, such as 'What is your view on children stitching footballs?' and 'What would be the effects of phasing out child labour?' In Pakistan, as in many other cultures, it is common for male heads of household to answer questionnaires on behalf of their family members. It could be difficult to find out women's and children's views of their situation through the survey. Save the Children also wanted to provide opportunities for people – men, women and children – to discuss more freely issues related to child labour, education and the football industry. Forty-six different focus group discussions were therefore organized. The groups were based on gender and involvement in football stitching and, in the case of children, also age and school attendance. For example, some of the discussions included girl stitchers aged under ten who attended school or boy stitchers aged ten to 13 who did not; mothers and fathers of child football stitchers; and community leaders.

Source: Save the Children (1997a)

One important way in which issue-focused research can be influential is through re-framing the way in which issues are understood. The following example is a piece of work which is controversial, but which has had an important impact as a result of its re-framing, that of Fairhead and Leach (1996) on environmental change in West Africa.

Deforestation in West Africa: is it a problem?

Parts of Guinea in West Africa feature patches of dense, semi-deciduous forest, which orthodox thinking has tended to view as relics of previously more extensive forest cover. The belief that this situation has resulted from farmers destroying vegetation has been dominant since the 1890s, and has been used to justify repressive measures against the inhabitants' land-use practices.

Fairhead and Leach (1996) looked at the historical evidence in relation to Kissidougou prefecture, particularly air photographs and more recently satellite pictures, from 1952 up to 1992. They found that, 'in many zones, the areas of forest and savanna vegetation have remained remarkably stable during the 40 year period which today's policy-makers consider to have been the most degrading. Where changes are discernible these predominately involve increases in forest area.' Landscape descriptions and maps from earlier periods 'clearly falsify assertions of more generalized forest cover.'

The researchers further collected oral information from local inhabitants, who described how village forest islands are usually formed through human settlement and management. Observation of more recent settlements confirmed this. People value the forest islands around their villages for a variety of reasons, and habitually do a number of things to positively

(Continued)

FOR EXAMPLE

(Continued)

encourage their development. Fairhead and Leach suggest that, rather than being half-empty, the landscape should be seen as half-full. This challenges the notion, which they trace to colonial times, of African farmers as ignorant and careless of their environment. It also challenges current policy towards farmers.

A Northern example where a new perspective is brought to an issue focuses on children's safety and freedom.

FOR EXAMPLE

Are children safer, or just less free?

Hillman et al. (1990) noted that road accident rates for children had actually fallen in the 20 years to 1990 in England and Germany, despite huge increase in car ownership. The explanation proposed lies in the great restrictions parents came to place on children's independent mobility. Children of about nine and a half in these countries in 1990 had the freedom (for example to go to school on their own) that children of seven had had 20 years before. A total of 91 per cent of UK seven to 11 year olds owned a bicycle, but only 35 per cent were allowed to come home from school alone. Hillman et al. also drew attention to the cost to children's health and sense of self caused by the restrictions traffic imposes on them.

The following case study illustrates research that made use of existing data rather

than undertaking new data collection, where a participative process enabled the gathering of more accurate information and wide ownership of the learning process, leading to action to address the issues identified.

Issue-focused research: sub-national situation analyses in Vietnam help local authorities address children's issues

FOR EXAMPLE

The development of a situation analysis (SitAn) of children and women is a key piece of research supported by the United Nations Children's Fund (UNICEF) as part of its international mandate to strengthen evidence-based policy planning and decision making to promote human development and fulfil children's rights. This is a comprehensive assessment and analysis of child-relevant issues in a country which provides recommendations and suggests solutions to tackle child-related priorities.

A SitAn is typically conducted at the national level in countries where UNICEF works. In Vietnam, however, in a context of strong fiscal and administrative decentralization, stark regional divergence in key challenges for children and significant data gaps and dispersion, particularly at the sub-national level, UNICEF has gone one step further, commissioning provincial-level SitAns in selected provinces. Three SitAns have been undertaken, namely, in the mountainous North-Western province of Dien Bien, in An Giang in the Mekong Delta and in Ninh Thuan in the Central Coast region. In these provinces, UNICEF is supporting the promotion of evidence-based and participatory socioeconomic development planning.

Provincial SitAns have three key objectives: 1) to consolidate information and analyse the situation of children in the context of a province's socioeconomic development with a focus on intra-provincial disparity; 2) to identify challenges affecting knowledge on child rights and the advancement of these rights; and 3) to provide recommendations to improve children's situation for incorporation into planning and budgeting decisions.

Importantly, SitAns do not collect new data, but capitalize on existing data and research, mainly from official sources already being used by different levels of government. As such, the novelty comes from their comprehensiveness, as they compile all available national and provincial data on different sectors such as health, education and child protection, to draw up a holistic picture of children's situation in each province. Second, they advocate for a human rights-based approach by focusing on the roles, responsibilities and capacities of duty bearers and rights holders in addressing children's issues through the lens of the UN Convention on the Rights of the Child.

The SitAns are produced in close partnership with the provinces and through an intense participatory process. This process consists of extensive consultation during various research stages, including agreement on the research plan, provision of data and joint analysis and dissemination. This improves the accuracy of the data and ensures the research outcomes and recommendations are both relevant for provincial policy decisions and fully owned by sub-national authorities.

Political ownership was demonstrated by the statements of the leadership of Dien Bien province. Proud of their new flagship report, in particular its comprehensiveness, the provincial People's Committee wanted the SitAn to be 'the reference document to undertake socioeconomic development planning by provincial line departments and agencies'. Extensive local and national media coverage and wide dissemination of the SitAn further strengthened the province's resolve to use its findings in planning and monitoring across sectors, and in leveraging the support of other development partners to address children's priorities in the province.

For more information, visit www.unicef.org/vietnam/

One key message to be drawn from dividing up research for development work into these two types is that the overall purpose of the exercise needs to be the central factor in deciding on the methods used and how the research is undertaken. Throughout this manual, there will be reference back to the distinction between programme-focused and issue-focused research. Because of the different audiences involved, and the different level of scrutiny that can be expected, the two types have different needs at many stages of the research process. Table 2.1 describes some of the key differences.

Common pitfall

Expecting policymakers to be interested in research you do for your own programme planning purposes

Common pitfall

Expecting a study of an issue automatically to tell you what the programme should be doing about it

We next discuss consultation with communities, and some other activities which are a bit like but may not exactly be research. The two following sections look in more depth at the two main types of research for development work – for programme development and for policy influence.

Consultation is an important activity for development workers. Involving local people in decision making of various kinds is a core element of their work. However, consultation is not the same as a research process. A dictionary definition of 'to consult' is 'to have regard to; to ask the advice or opinion of; to refer to; to deliberate together; to serve as a consultant' (www.merriam-webster.com/dictionary/consult). It is about taking advice from people, asking their opinions, and not just about recording their experiences or collecting information.

Table 2.1   Key characteristics of the different types of research

	Programme-focused research	Issue-focused research
Audience	Primarily local or regional, includes community members	Diverse – could include high-level decision makers
Timescale	Dictated by programme requirements	May be dictated by key decision points of others within the policy cycle; may be in your control
Quality standards	Good enough for planning purposes; timeliness may be more important than depth	May need to stand considerable external scrutiny
Level of community participation	Variable	Variable
Who should do it	Depends on nature of project	Consider audience; credibility
Promotion of results	Likely to take place throughout the life of the research; local audiences key	Needs planning alongside the main project; promotion crucial to usefulness

In UK policymaking, community consultation has become increasingly common, for example on health service priorities. Service users are actively engaged in giving feedback on decisions relating to a service, in a way which often uses research-type methods but is not the same thing as research. This is a directly political process, and its constraints are about political realities – whereas research has different priorities. One important distinction to keep in mind here is that, in some cases, the intention is to consult people because they have had a particular experience, and in others simply as members of the public. However, there is some overlap between the two kinds of process.

Consultation and research: shared concerns?

- To be fair about who is involved;
- To ask questions in a way that is seen to be unbiased;
- To ensure people are consulted in a way that enables them to participate properly – clear communication;
- To report findings accurately and honestly.

Thus, research traditions may have many useful things to teach those involved in consultation, but consultation exercises can be undermined if they are turned into research projects. Research ideas can impose unnecessary constraints on consultation processes, whose 'life' comes from the real engagement of people with the issues. For example, a consultation process may need to meet people who are easier to contact than others, whereas a research project that aims for findings that can be generalized to other populations would need to be more rigorous in its sampling processes. Organizations also need to do the consultation they can afford and will be able to listen to – there is no point elaborating the process so it becomes overwhelmingly difficult and expensive.

Many of the methods described in this manual could be useful for consultation processes, which can be done for both programme development and policy influence. The key question in assessing both consultation and research is this: How confident do you feel about taking action on the basis of this evidence?

2.5 Using research for programme development

The most common reason for development workers to use research in their work is to inform the planning of their programme. They may want to look in more depth at what issues local people perceive as important, or to understand more about why things are as they are. Sometimes, this will mean a broad look at a wide range of issues seen to be affecting a community; sometimes, research will be targeted at a particular issue, for example health care for young children. Increasingly, development workers like to engage the community directly in the process of deciding priorities for their work, rather than regarding it as primarily a technical exercise.

Included here are processes like stakeholder analysis, whereby a development worker systematically investigates the views and plans of agencies, individuals and groups which have a 'stake', an interest, in a particular issue. This stands on the borderline between research and planning and can be done in a more or less formal way. There are texts giving specific guidance on many approaches within this category of work, for example on community profiling[4] and on Participatory Learning and Action (see Chapter 12).

At times, programme-oriented research is required to investigate the impact of interventions. It cannot be taken for granted that development initiatives are effective, and there can also be unintended consequences.

FOR EXAMPLE

Help or hindrance? Infant feeding in Kosovo

During the crisis in Kosovo in 1999, large amounts of infant formula and other infant feeding products were sent as unsolicited donations through the UN and the North Atlantic Treaty Organization, or directly by road convoys. This added to the huge stocks of breast milk substitute in the refugee camps. A study was undertaken by the Institute of Child Health with Save the Children to investigate whether breastfeeding practices were being undermined.

2.6 Using research to influence policy

The use of research to influence policy is increasing in development work. When and how does this occur? This is not an easy thing to find out, as it is difficult to identify what degree of influence particular research evidence has on particular decisions.

ACTIVITY 2.2

Which research projects have influenced you?

Let us start by drawing on your experience of research within your own work.

Either alone or with a group, brainstorm a list of research projects that have had an influence on you. What has really affected your thinking? It may be helpful to include areas outside your immediate professional concerns – think also about research that has influenced choices you make in your own life. Then think about why this research has been able to influence you.

Brainstorm:

- What research has influenced you?
- Why did it have this influence?

ACTIVITY 2.3

Assessing the influence of research projects

Identify three issue-focused research projects you are familiar with that aim to influence policy. They need not be ones undertaken in your own organization, but they need to be complete. They can be at local, national or international level. Consider what evidence you can use to assess what influence these projects have had on policy. For example, they may have led to a change in the law, or to changes in the allocation of resources. Think about what features of these research projects, in your view, helped them to have an influence.

	Evidence of influence on policy	Features that enabled this research to have influence
Project 1		
Project 2		
Project 3		

Was it difficult to assess influence? Or perhaps you had difficulty identifying projects you were confident had an influence. You may like to make a note of ways *not* to have an influence!

Features that prevent research from having an influence

How could influence be increased?

If you can involve some colleagues in this activity, ask them to make their own assessments of the same projects. Discuss the ways in which you have judged influence. Consider what this means for planning for influence.

Some researchers have studied the issue of the influence research has on policy. Academic research often has less impact than researchers might hope. Nutley et al. (2007) confirm that the influence is often inconsistent, sometimes succeeding in achieving an impact and other times failing to gain notice. Nevertheless, the increasingly well-established paradigm of evidence-informed policymaking means social research today plays a more important role in informing policy decisions than ever before.

This is a role that is played out at the so-called 'research–policy interface' – the point at which policymakers receive, process and, ideally, make use of research to improve and adapt a particular policy or change the broader policy environment. (Chapter 15 explores in greater depth tools and strategies for bridging the interface.)

Furthermore, it may be that those directly engaged in development work are in a better position to set up research that is relevant to important issues, and to feed findings into policy processes in a way which increases their influence.

The Research and Policy in Development (RAPID) programme at the Overseas Development Institute in particular has been looking at the links between research and development policy for several years. The box summarizes areas highlighted by the RAPID programme as factors making for influential research (derived from Start and Hovland, 2007) – context, evidence and links.

Factors determining the influence of research

- The political *context*: the broader political events and influences that drive what policymakers are interested in and how they are thinking about an issue.
- The *evidence*: the quality of the research, the credibility of the source and *how and when* the research is communicated, that is, its relevance, timeliness and actionable recommendations.
- The *links*: the pre-existing and working relationships between all actors involved in the research, which may facilitate, for instance, the communication of findings when they challenge the status quo or do not conform to user expectations.

2.6.1 The political context

The political context, the interests and assumptions of policymakers, new events and appetite for new ideas inevitably have a big impact on the influence that research is likely to have. For these reasons, RAPID advises development researchers to get to know policymakers, their agendas and their constraints, to identify potential supporters and opponents and to keep an eye out for new opportunities or 'windows' for influence.

Policymakers are likely to be on the lookout for new ideas, but like any professionals will also have a set of deep-seated assumptions and worldviews. The challenge for researchers is knowing when and how far to challenge these, and when an idea is too new or different to be acceptable. The available literature highlights a contradiction between seeking to influence policy through 'challenging the status quo' and 'conformity to user expectations'. 'Conformity' is defined by Weiss and Bucuvalas (1977) as research which supports the individual policymaker's values and construction of reality and their own experience and knowledge . The challenge factor relates to research which challenges existing assumptions and institutional arrangements, implies the need for a major change in philosophy, organization or services, raises new issues or offers a new perspective. Researchers will have to make informed decisions about the best strategy given the particular political context for a piece of work.

2.6.2 The evidence

Quality is a key issue in terms of research utilization. Whether research is 'good enough' is not only a formal issue of adherence to rules, but much more fundamentally a question of whether the research can be believed. In relation to research for development, it may be more useful to talk about credibility or 'trustworthiness' (Oakley and Roberts, 1996) than about the standard technical terms 'validity' and 'reliability'. Chapters 3 and 8 look in more detail at the importance of quality in research for development.

Also crucial to the impact research has is *how* and *when* it is communicated. Research may come too late to be relevant, or be overtaken by events. And the attention paid to it is determined by how ideas are presented to their target audience, the language used and the format and media chosen.

2.6.3 The links

The RAPID programme has found that policy impact can be enhanced by getting to know other stakeholders and actors with an interest in the research and building strong working relationships before, during and after it. This could involve establishing a presence in existing networks, building coalitions with likeminded stakeholders or building new policy networks and working groups.

Effective policy-oriented research, then, can usefully learn from the development tradition, in that it requires relationships to be built at all levels. People learn best from processes they are actively engaged with, and this goes for high-level policymakers too. An interactive approach at the planning stage and throughout the research process, drawing in those you hope to influence, as well as those you hope will benefit from any changes you bring about, will set a strong base on which to build your project.

Letting powerful people see the 'inner workings' of a project may make us anxious, but a transparent process is much more convincing than one that obscures key processes. A strategic approach is required: analyse at what level the decisions you hope to influence are made, then work out what sort of evidence could have influence and whom you need to consult. It simply does not work to carry out research, however excellent, in isolation from those who need to learn from it and then expect them to be interested in it.

Street children in China: the importance of working in partnership with government

The phenomenon of increasing numbers of children living or working on the street, often separated from their family, became an issue for the government of China in the late 1990s. The Ministry of Civil Affairs and its departments at provincial and other levels were responsible for developing a response. In 1999, Save the Children UK began to work with these agencies on the issue.

One site for the partnership was the province of Xinjiang, in northwest China. This is an autonomous region, with a high percentage of ethnic minority people, especially Muslim Uighurs. It is also a poor area, and many people migrate eastwards – children are part of such migration, both within the province and outwards; many are trafficked.

In order to understand the situation better, it was decided to carry out research in addition to testing out different methods of work. For research to be recognized and used in the future, and for methods of work to be sustainable and maintained, it was crucial to involve the government in both design and implementation. Save the Children facilitated a multi-sectoral meeting of interested government departments, mass organizations and academies, at which participants agreed an approach.

The research was commissioned by Save the Children, with the Street Children Centre, and conducted by the Academy of Social Sciences. The initial results were fed directly back to civil affairs and other officials and influenced the next stage of work. The involvement of a range of government departments ensured wider awareness on the issue, and the research results further heightened this. The partnership approach meant the results were keenly awaited and taken up in policy and practice. Without government involvement, the research would have had first to be completed, then to be presented to officials; then government would have had to be persuaded to pay attention and take it up. The involvement of local agencies in the research gave them a stake in seeking out responses to the issues raised.

FOR EXAMPLE

On the other hand, the following example, taken from an impact assessment report by the UK Department for International Development (DFID) on a project which looked at DDT use in Zimbabwe, shows how scientifically excellent research can miss its time in terms of having an influence (DFID, 1998).

Too late: DDT use in Zimbabwe

DDT was widely and successfully used to control tsetse fly in Zimbabwe in the 1960s and 1970s. By the 1980s, its use there had become controversial, partly because of the effects of its residues on non-target wildlife and partly because of its persistence in temperate climates where it was already banned.

(Continued)

FOR EXAMPLE

(Continued)

The objective of this research was to produce a better understanding of the environmental costs of using DDT vis-à-vis alternative insecticides in ground spraying against tsetse. It was implemented between 1987 and 1992 at a cost of £866,000. However, an evaluation found that, although the research was successful in terms of its immediate scientific objectives, it did not achieve benefits commensurate with its costs, that is, it is unlikely to have a significant impact on tsetse control policy and practice. Higher-level policymakers were insufficiently involved, and the research design was too narrow to be as useful as it might have been. Even if these shortcomings had been recognized and addressed, the research project was set up too late to influence decisions on DDT use within Zimbabwe, and might never have been able to do so because of the public prejudice against DDT. The policy debate was too far advanced to allow the research findings to have any impact.

 ## Key points from this chapter

A key distinction is made in this chapter between research for the programme and research on issues, for policy influence: these two broad types have different requirements in a number of respects. Research for policy influence is discussed further, including what factors lead to effective influencing work, drawing on the RAPID framework. Some findings from research into this question are presented, and readers are asked to consider it in relation to their own experience. (The concepts of research for policy influence are introduced here; practical guidance on how to promote research to policymakers is discussed in greater depth in Chapter 15 on promoting research uptake.)

> ### Checklist: understanding research for development work
>
> ☑ In order to achieve policy influence, research needs to consider and adapt to the wider political context and be credible, well communicated and timely.
> ☑ Researchers need to build strong relationships and partnerships with all relevant actors and institutions before, during and after the research.

 ## Further reading

Carden, F. (2009) *Knowledge to Policy: Making the Most of Development Research.* New Delhi, Thousand Oaks, CA, London: Sage.

Using case studies from around the world, this book investigates the impact of research in the field of international development. It shows how research can influence public policy and decision making in at least three ways: by encouraging open inquiry and debate; by empowering people with the knowledge to hold governments accountable; and by enlarging the array of policy options and solutions available to the policy process.

Department for International Development (2006) *Maximising the Impact of Development Research: How Can Funders Encourage More Effective Research Communication?* London: DFID.

This summary highlights the importance of seeing communication as a two-way process, with researchers engaging with stakeholders and being much more imaginative and proactive in how they communicate their findings. It includes a guide to drawing up communication strategies and working with the media and other knowledge intermediaries.

Start, D. and Hovland, I. (2007) *Tools for Policy Impact: A Handbook for Researchers.* London: Overseas Development Institute.

This handbook addresses various factors that need to be considered to enable research to have an impact on policy, and provides a comprehensive selection of practical tools that can be used when attempting to turn research into policy influence.

Notes

1 This has already been done: see recommended reading for Chapter 3.
2 See Glossary for definitions of unfamiliar terms.
3 See, for instance, Gosling (2003) and Mikkelsen (2005).
4 See, for example, Hawtin and Percy-Smith (2007).

3

PLANNING FOR EFFECTIVE RESEARCH

So you've decided to do some research. A certain mystique tends to surround the process, but do not be deceived. The first step is to realize that research projects need to be planned and managed, just like any other activity within your work. There are a number of processes involved in this, which may need to be done in a different order in different projects.

Research planning and management: key tasks

- Conceive the idea, agree research focus and questions.
- Consider who you want your research to influence and how.
- Draft a research brief.
- Agree the brief with other stakeholders, including community members.
- Consider whether and how the project can enable more people to learn research skills.
- Decide who will undertake the research.
- Work out the timescale.
- Negotiate access to information/respondents.
- Estimate costs.
- Arrange appropriate support and supervision for researchers.
- Set up an advisory group.
- Apply for funding.

In most research exercises, the most difficult parts of the process are at the beginning and the end. This chapter concentrates on ways to assure the quality of your research at the very start of a project – in choosing a topic, writing the brief and agreeing it with all those with a stake in it. The next chapter looks at how to estimate costs and timescales, who should do the research and ongoing management issues.

3.1 Quality in research

How can development workers ensure the research they undertake is of good quality? For that matter, what is meant by quality in research work if, as Chapter 2 showed, there are many approaches that follow different rules? This section argues it is crucial that development organizations recognize the importance of quality in research work, in relation to the process as well as the products. It proposes some quality standards which summarize the key issues. Finally, it offers some guidance as to the practical steps to take to ensure your research meets these standards. (Chapter 8 continues this discussion in detail by offering practical direction on ensuring quality in data collection.)

3.1.1 Getting the balance right between quality, cost and time

Perhaps it is obvious that the quality of the research affects how seriously it is taken. But, as there is never enough time or money to do the perfect piece of work, aspirations have to be scaled down to what is possible.

Project managers think in terms of a 'project triangle' (see Figure 3.1) when deciding how to balance resources in a given project. Of the priorities 'fast', 'good' and 'cheap', you can pick only two; the third will necessarily suffer. Research projects are no different: research managers need to make a decision based on the specific context of their work as to what level of quality is achievable within the available time and budget (Lewis, 2010).

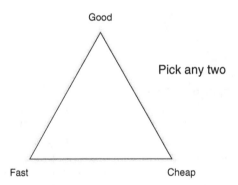

Figure 3.1   The project triangle

It is crucial to find an appropriate balance between rigour and relevance (Harper, 1997). More in-depth work takes longer and costs more but may have much greater influence. Equally, there is no point in doing elaborate academic work on fast-changing situations where information is needed very quickly. However, it is not wise to try to hurry too much with research, since below a certain level of quality it is simply of no use.

Research can be expensive, and it is important that resourcing be kept in balance with that for other types of development activity. However, it is also important that research is good enough for its purpose: there are real limits to what can be achieved on a very small budget. It is worth taking some advice about what exactly can be done at different levels of resourcing. A rule of thumb might be to think about the research effort in proportion to the resources involved in the programme or policy decisions that will depend on its findings.

This is really the key: the quality of the research needs to be sufficient for the decisions that will rest on the results. It may be better to do one excellent piece of research in a year than three 'quick and dirty' ones that may not be taken seriously. In a different situation, the reverse may be true. Overall, it is helpful to stand back a little from the immediate situation when planning research. Some of the driving urgency surrounding development work is constructed by the culture of the organization carrying it out (Barnett and Finnemore, 2004; Edwards and Hulme, 1995). It should not be assumed that longer-term, better-quality research is not possible.

Audience is an important issue when making decisions about what priority to give to quality. Different audiences care about different aspects of quality, and the measures you need to take to assure it depend very much on whom you hope to influence.

If development organizations aim to influence policy, research needs to stand up to potentially hostile scrutiny in public settings. Journalists may ask awkward questions and often enjoy finding faults in claims made in research work. If journalists, and indeed politicians and other policymakers, are to take an argument seriously, they need to be convinced the claims made are credible. Meanwhile, partner agencies may value the genuine participation of community members in the process of the research.

3.1.2   Indicators of quality

As Chapter 2 showed, different research traditions have important differences. However, some standards are very widely accepted. The essential integrity of a piece of research is readily identifiable, whether or not it is undertaken within a tradition you are sympathetic to. Here, we summarize some key indicators of quality in research for development work. These are not the same as those for academic research – development work has different priorities. Research of different types has different key imperatives – this is merely a simple checklist for the non-specialist.

You might want to use this list of standards when:

- discussing practice issues with a newly appointed researcher;
- forming a research team for a particular project;
- assessing a completed piece of work before publication;
- assessing a whole body of research work, with a view to developing better practice.

Some quality standards for research in development

Research planning should

- be about an important issue;
- be needed, that is:
  - not duplicate other research;
  - not be a substitute for action;
  - be relevant to the organization's mission – an issue on which it could follow through with further work if appropriate;
- be aware of where the idea for the research came from, and prioritize ideas which come from 'the researched';
- have a clear brief, including aims and objectives and suitable research question/s;
- be planned in cooperation with relevant agencies and representatives of community members affected by the issue;
- have transparent organizational structures which make researchers answerable to all those with a legitimate interest in the research, including respondents;
- be planned with a view to increasing local or national research skills;
- include a strategy to promote learning from the findings.

Research processes should

- question taken-for-granted ideas and explanations;
- involve interaction with respondents based on respect and a concern for clear and open communication;
- aim to enable participants to have a say in the original design and in identifying key issues from their point of view, as well as in data collection and analysis (for participatory research);
- entail a sample adequate to the purpose of the research;
- involve the piloting and revision of research tools before use;
- entail systematic data collection, with care taken to preserve the integrity of the data, that is:
  - questions should never be 'leading';
  - recording should be as exact as possible;
  - quotations should not be taken out of context so that meaning is distorted;
  - the process of information gathering should be systematically observed and recorded;
- be planned with an awareness of the impact of power inequalities, both between different groups in the population and between researchers and respondents. Power relationships in the 'private sphere', within the family (gender and age hierarchies), are especially important;
- actively consider ethical issues as problems arise, in particular ensuring that:
  - respondents' consent is properly sought, and they understand what they are agreeing to when they give it;
  - no pressure is applied to respondents to participate in research;

(Continued)

(Continued)

- ○ where undertakings to protect confidentiality of data are given, they are fully complied with;
- ○ where respondents wish to be anonymous, their identities are protected throughout the life of the project, from initial contact to publication and subsequent promotional activity;

- establish good communication with respondents; where different languages are involved, interpreters who understand the process and are able to give accurate and full translations must be used;
- lead to explanation in reports of exact procedures involved in drawing the sample, with reflection on the strengths and weaknesses of the sample used;
- involve reflexivity and openness about researchers' own perspectives and the influence these have on the research process;
- ensure statistical procedures are explained briefly for a lay readership, with the meaning of findings expressed clearly;
- make checks on the validity and reliability of research tools (quantitative research), that is:

- ○ that they measure what they claim to measure;
- ○ that responses are consistent if, for example, a questionnaire is repeated with the same people at a different time.

Interpretation and analysis should

- take great care to avoid laying researchers' own interpretations on respondents' comments, with uncertainty of meaning acknowledged where this occurs;
- include consideration of alternative interpretations of the data and reasons why these do not hold;
- have regard to the policy context, including research information beyond the current project, and comment on its relevance to the issue at hand;
- not make claims which go beyond what can be supported by the evidence.

Promotion of research findings should

- involve concise reports which include all the information necessary to assess the quality of the research;
- include making a summary of the final report, which is essential to having an influence;
- create recommendations which are based on the findings;
- feed findings back to the respondents of the research and to all agencies and individuals who contributed towards it, in formats which are accessible to them;
- identify and fully reference other research which is quoted from or referred to, to enable readers to locate the item;
- disseminate findings in a targeted way, with special attention to ensuring those with related policy responsibilities are informed of relevant results.

Chapter 16 on assessing development research revisits these standards.

3.1.3 Simple ways to improve the quality of your research

Consult experienced researchers

On some of the issues listed above, there is no substitute for getting advice from an experienced researcher. For example, if you wish to make generalizations from your sample, it is essential to talk to a statistician *before* the fieldwork to ensure you have sufficient numbers and the structure of the sample is suitable. Equally, you may wish to seek advice on ethical practice in research if you are not familiar with the ways in which researchers practically go about protecting respondents.

This manual advises you to consult an experienced researcher at a number of points in the process of carrying out or commissioning your research, as a way of improving the quality of the work. It is a good idea to show someone with more experience a draft of any research brief, and to consult on your choice of methods or on sampling issues. You may well want them to read drafts of a final report.

Expert researchers' criticisms may not always be comfortable. You may want to get more than one opinion. And you do not have to take the advice you are offered. But the principle of defending your work against likely criticisms is a useful one, and experienced researchers can help you to do this.

Checklist: consulting an expert researcher

- ☑ Ask for a response to the work as a whole before starting to look at the details.
- ☑ Expect to hear criticism.
- ☑ Explain clearly the purpose of your research and the needs of its audience – researchers may be more oriented to an academic audience.
- ☑ Find out what school of thought (see Chapter 2) the researcher belongs to early on. If they use obscure terms, get them to explain in straightforward language.
- ☑ Ask questions to establish what level of decision any criticism relates to. For example, is the problem in the research focus and questions themselves, the methods proposed or the sampling scheme?
- ☑ Don't despair!

Learn lessons from previous research exercises

We should not always be in the position of working out as we go along how to run research projects: organizations should aim to ensure a wide group of people learn from the experience of each project they undertake. For this to take place, a record must be made of how things were done, difficulties encountered and how these were dealt with. A group discussion at the end of the project will assist people in learning the lessons for next time.

FOR EXAMPLE

Learning from consultants' visits: Ethiopia

One strategy aid agencies can implement is to shadow international experts. A member of staff can be assigned to shadow the expert and write up an account of the work done. The staff member learns from observing the way the consultant works (even if the methods are not successful) and is able to share this learning with colleagues long after the consultant has left.

Focus on the quality of the process as much as the product

When we think about quality in research, we tend to focus first on the product. That is, does the final report succeed in persuading readers of its argument? Does the methodology (the whole approach to the problem, including methods) hold water? Is the material well presented and credible? Are the recommendations based firmly on the evidence presented?

But it is also important to think about the quality of the *process* of the research work. In a development context, this is likely to include issues such as the quality of the involvement of community members at each stage of the research – conception, development, data collection and analysis. Some issues to consider are:

- Who defines the research objectives? Have 'the researched' had a say?
- Are relevant partner agencies fully on board?
- If you are a Northern or international agency, are you building research capacity among Southern partners as well as investigating the issue?

And, of course, for all research projects, a key question is about ethical standards of conduct in relation to respondents – that the research does no harm and takes proper care in relation to consent and confidentiality.

ACTIVITY 3.1

Assessing quality of process and product

Consider the overall quality of a piece of research you are familiar with, looking in broadbrush terms at its strengths and weaknesses in relation to the quality of the product and the process. Make notes on the following table of issues which arise.

	Strengths	Weaknesses
Quality of product		
Quality of process		

A strong process should produce a strong outcome. However, in development work, concern for process may overtake concern for the final product. Equally, traditional research may sacrifice ongoing relationships with stakeholders in pursuit of the perfect final report. You need to consider the priorities for your piece of work to decide what is most important – although ideally process and product should not be in conflict.

The next two sections look briefly at some sticky issues in relation to the quality of research work – the ideas of objectivity and of generalizability.

Objectivity and reflexivity

The idea of objectivity in research is very important to the mainstream tradition of scientific research. Researchers have traditionally been seen as 'disinterested' and able to rise above human conflicts of interest. This idea remains powerful, and it is important to take this into account where an organization is aiming to have influence on policy in a highly contested area.

However, as Chapter 2 discussed, an alternative strand within research challenges the notion of a value-free social science. This tradition draws attention to the inevitable biases human beings introduce into research simply through the way their expectations influence perception. The social constructionist tradition (see Section 2.2) argues there will always be an influence on research from the researcher's own values, beliefs and interests. One method of dealing with this is for researchers to be open about where they are coming from, to allow the reader to evaluate their work on this basis. This is known as 'reflexivity'.

In international development, this idea has had important implications in recent years. For example, some have questioned the conventional use of large-scale surveys, once seen as accurate and objective. Where no account is taken of local knowledge, questions may be entirely irrelevant to real life, and survey results can be meaningless or simply wrong. Importantly, such mistakes reflect less on the limitations of the tool itself and more on how researchers apply it. Nonetheless, some see more interactive approaches, where the people under study are engaged with as equals, as better suited to avoiding such mistakes. Participatory Learning and Action (PLA) approaches have become common practice among development agencies.[1] Newer techniques involve those being researched in agreeing policy recommendations and include citizens' juries and techniques to build grassroots consensus, such as the Charette and Delphi methods.[2]

In all these methods, the emphasis is placed on hearing the views of those involved and of negotiation between different perspectives, rather than identifying an overarching truth about a situation (Alvesson and Skoldberg, 2009). However, participatory methods are best used to strengthen – rather than replace – large-scale surveys. For instance, it can be helpful to use such methods to explore an issue and then use the results to design a large-scale survey questionnaire.

These approaches have been an important corrective to traditional research thinking which elevated the idea of objectivity in such a way as to suppress new ideas, in particular those coming from relatively powerless groups. However, there is a danger, following this line of thinking, of arriving at a position where there can be no knowledge beyond the opinion of an individual. Everything is relative; no 'truth' is possible. In practice, most of us actually operate with a pragmatic sense of reality which allows us to see that differently located people will have different perspectives on an issue. At the same time, we accept there can be evidence for or against claims made about an issue which go beyond the individual. We evaluate evidence on the basis of how it has been produced as well as who has produced it. A conscious decision therefore needs to be taken in each project on how the issue of objectivity versus reflexivity is addressed, and this must be made clear in the final report.

What is reflexivity?

You are being reflexive when

- you think about what is influencing the way you interpret what people tell you;
- It is helpful to discuss with colleagues your different ways of seeing the same piece of data; and to ask respondents for their reflections on their experience of the research process – 'How did you feel about this interview?'
- as a researcher, are open about your viewpoint on or involvement in an issue – this might include your personal

   o beliefs;
   o interests;
   o experience of the topic;
   o expertise.

To give an account of how these might have a bearing on findings, the researcher is likely to need to draw on personal details, for example their

- social background (class, family, environment);
- age;
- sex;
- ethnicity;
- religion;
- sexuality;
- education and qualifications;
- work experience and skills;[3]

FOR EXAMPLE

Working with interpreters

Undertaking research with a translator requires reflexive thought not only on the researcher's presence and interpretation but also on the influence of the translator. Undertaking multiple research programmes across China with translators, social researchers with the UN had to take note of the translator's gender, ethnicity and attitude when interviewing minority peoples. Translators would be changed as necessary according to the group or individuals being interviewed; for social issues, interpretation of the data had to take into account the influence of the translator in enabling or inhibiting certain types of responses. Reflexive thought allows one to qualify certain findings and to be clear on the circumstances which influence the information being revealed – in this case deep suspicion of other ethnicities and gender restrictions.

Source: Caroline Harper, personal communication

Generalizability

Research quality standards often include 'generalizability of findings' as a key standard. Indeed, the UK National Health Service's research and development funding system will fund only research which allows generalization. The intention is that research should always enable statements to be made about a broader population than the one directly studied. This is an important principle of sampling for quantitative research.

However, it is not appropriate to apply the principle to all research. Qualitative research which explores meanings and aims to generate ideas about a social phenomenon can be valuable without being generalizable. Case study research will also not usually allow generalization. Any research on minority groups or socially hidden phenomena will have problems if it is required to be generalizable. Minorities are often under- or misrepresented in official statistics, for a variety of reasons, and this makes generalizations problematic. Any group which fears officialdom can best be researched by working through friendship networks and trusted organizations, a process which cannot yield a strictly representative random sample. Of course, those minority people who are in touch with such organizations may not be entirely representative of those who are more isolated – but there may be no choice. It is better to learn something about hard-to-reach groups than to let a purist approach block such learning.

Ensuring your research is of good quality: a summary

So what do you need to do to ensure your research is of good quality? Very briefly, some key points are as follows.

> ### Checklist: practical steps to assuring quality in research work
>
> ☑ Good early planning;
> ☑ Clear brief/terms of reference (ToR) shared with all those involved;
> ☑ Clear researchable questions that match the methods selected;
> ☑ Staff with sufficient relevant experience;
> ☑ Project allocated sufficient resources to undertake research of adequate quality;
> ☑ Supervision by experienced researcher;
> ☑ Advisory group established, involving policymakers from relevant agencies, research advisors, representatives of the researched group;
> ☑ In participatory research, participation planned for throughout the project;
> ☑ Promotion planned for throughout the project;
> ☑ Final reports read and commented on by a range of people;
> ☑ Evaluation and feedback on the research process built in;
> ☑ Chapters 4, 12, 13 and 15 give more detail on all of these points.

One of the best ways to assure the quality of your research is to think about it carefully upfront and spend time agreeing the exact focus, methodology, 'deliverables' (end products) and an achievable work plan before you begin. The following three sections discuss how to choose a focus for your research, define clear research questions and write a research brief.

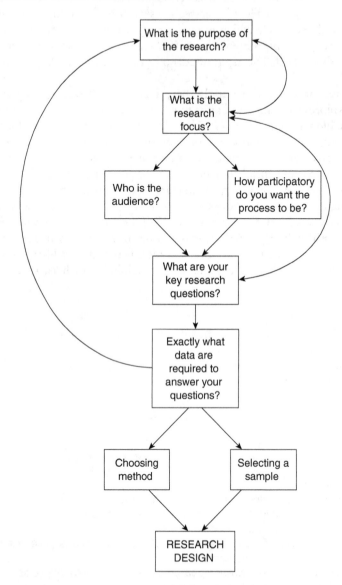

Figure 3.2   Research planning – the key questions

3.2   Choosing a research focus

Getting the research focus right is crucial to planning a good piece of research. Chapter 2 explored how research in development work is most frequently used either to inform a programme or to influence policy. Because good research is costly and time consuming, it should never be undertaken for its own sake, but should

have a clear purpose that fits within your organization's wider strategy and objectives. Think about what you want to achieve and why research is necessary to do this. What is the 'problem' you are trying to fix? If the purpose is to convince others or influence policy, who is your target audience and what evidence do they need?

Try to remain open-minded for as long as possible about exactly how you will focus the research. A decision will have to be made, of course, but discussing the issues with others will throw up new possibilities, and you may find your original ideas need to be reconsidered to get to a project which is both feasible and appropriate.

As Chapter 5 discusses, reviewing existing evidence can be a key step. It can also be very helpful to work with a group of colleagues or stakeholders to clarify the focus for a piece of research. Experienced researchers can also give helpful advice, as they will have a greater awareness of existing research, current projects happening elsewhere and what will be feasible within your timeframe and budget.

! ————————— CONSULT A RESEARCHER NOW ———————— !

You may also want to consult policymakers directly and look at how your ideas fit into wider policy frameworks, the current political climate and the interests of the people and institutions you are hoping to influence.

Expert informed reviews

It has become more common for a serious investment to be made in reviewing existing data through a process of systematic reviews. Systematic reviews are common in evidence-based medicine and randomized controlled trials, and these methods are now being applied to the social sciences. A systematic review aims to provide an exhaustive summary of literature relevant to a research question. These reviews systematically select from a literature search to derive an understanding on a particular issue.

They have been adapted into expert-informed reviews and purposively selective reviews for areas where data are limited and fragmented. Expert-informed reviews consult with experts, including practitioners, along the way to ensure expert views are incorporated and the research questions are fit for purpose and ultimately new and productive, not repeating existing research but building on it.

For more information, see Bergh et al. (2012); Hagen-Zanker et al. (2012); EPPI Centre (2009).

What follows are some activities and thinking points to assist you in finding the right focus for your research project.

A brainstorming workshop to help define the research focus

Invite some colleagues to a workshop, telling them it is not a decision-making meeting but a way to generate and explore new ideas. Schedule it for one hour at the most. Make sure you invite people who do not know much about the problem but are good at asking critical questions.

Give people a very brief introduction to the broad area you want to research and your objectives. Then ask each participant to write down separately three proposals for a research focus. These should be areas where they think more knowledge will help to achieve your objectives. Pin their ideas on the wall and have everyone look at them and respond. Use the group to assess whether these are things where information already exists, or whether further research is needed.

A similar process could be carried out at a distance by post or email, although people are less likely to engage so readily with your question at a distance.

Source: Adapted from Robson (2002)

3.3 Defining the research questions

Once you are clear on the general focus, the next task is to identify the specific big questions the research as a whole will aim to answer. These are not the same as the questions to be asked to respondents as part of the research.

These need to be *researchable questions*, both in principle and through methods that it is feasible for you to use. The broad issue the research is concerned with (the research focus) needs to be broken down into sub-problems (the research questions) which can be addressed using the available evidence, and which, when answered, will achieve the objectives of the research. Do not expect your research to answer too many questions – ensure the scope you set for it is achievable within the resources at your disposal.

Tip

Locate your project within a broader strategy or programme

In talking about research, we tend to think in terms of individual projects. But this may make us think too big or indeed too small to cope with the problem we are grappling with. It may be more appropriate to think in terms of developing a *research strategy* or *programme* which involves a series of different projects that contribute towards elucidating a shared set of questions.

Common pitfall

Setting too many research questions, or questions that are too broad to answer within your resources

It is a good idea to have detailed discussions within the research team to clarify the research questions. It may be worth making a long list of all the questions you would ideally like answered, before narrowing it down to the questions you will be able to address in this project.

Clarifying the research questions: the impact of water metering on low-income families in England

Researchers from Save the Children UK undertaking a study of the impact of water metering on low-income families produced a whole series of sub-questions. These are just some of them:

- What measures do people take to save water?
- Is water saving linked to income?
- Do charging systems influence people's behaviour?
- Have individual families' behaviours changed with the change in charging system?
- Are people aware of the system being used to determine their water costs?

(Continued)

FOR EXAMPLE

(Continued)

- Are families using measurably less water as a result of the economies they report?
- Is there harm to children's health resulting from sharing baths or flushing the toilet less often?
- Are epidemics of diarrhoeal diseases occurring more frequently in areas where water is metered?
- What do people/parents think about water metering?
- Are some families more affected than others? Those with more children? Those with medical conditions requiring extra washing? Those with young babies?

Investigating different questions on this list would require very different procedures. For example, an objective detailed measure of people's water use would involve the researchers putting measuring devices on each appliance, which seemed excessively invasive and expensive, although some such studies have been done. Other questions could be investigated only through medical records, which would rely on these being very complete and up-to-date. The best sort of study for the purposes would have been a comparison between metered and unmetered families. As this was not possible, the study focused on people's own accounts of their behaviour and views and their actual water use. The total volume of water used per household could also be established using people's water bills.

Source: Cuninghame et al. (1996)

Activity 3.3 should help you clarify your research questions.

ACTIVITY 3.3

Draw an issue tree

Write down your research question, then create branches off it which break down the main questions you will need to answer in order to be able to answer the high-level question. Then create further branches off these sub-questions, and so on.

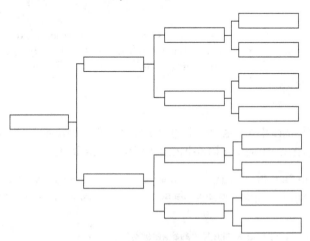

For example, if the starting question is, 'How can we most effectively increase employment rates through improving access to child care?', the next layer in the tree might comprise two further questions:

- What are the most effective forms of child care to help parents into work?
- How can government best support parents in accessing these forms of child care?

The answers to these two questions should provide the answer to the original, higher-level question. These two questions will then be further broken down, and so on, until a level of questions is reached that address the fundamental root causes of the original issue. Specific analysis can then be designed to address each one.

Having taken the question apart, you will need to put it together again. The intention is not to push the project towards more and more abstract questions. Non-governmental organizations (NGOs) are not in the business of fundamental theoretical research, but this procedure will help you to be conscious of the assumptions you are making, which helps to define good research work.

It is also important to be as clear and specific as possible in wording a question. One project may begin with the aim

To understand civil society's attitudes to education

After breaking the issue down, this could be changed to the much more focused

Why do so few girls go to school?

The first aim is huge and is unlikely to address the key concerns of the investigators. In addition, 'civil society' is difficult to define for research purposes. However, the main issue is that the aim does not identify any problem or question – it simply seeks to understand more. The second formulation is much more specific and reveals the problem of concern very directly.

Checklist: setting research question

☑ Are you looking at a question, or is it really a statement you wish to make?
☑ Are the different factors involved defined in a clear and unambiguous way?
☑ Can items of evidence (such as data collected) be identified to answer the question?
☑ Are there value judgements embedded in the question which make some factors problematic to measure (for example 'a good education'; 'a healthy lifestyle')?
☑ Is a comparison implied? If so, this needs to be made explicit. Is information available to enable comparisons actually to be made?
☑ List some possible answers to the question you have set. Will this type of answer meet your needs?

! ——————— CONSULT A RESEARCHER NOW ——————— !

3.3.1 A positivist approach to research questions: hypothesis testing

Many texts on research will tell you all research needs a hypothesis. Much traditional scientific positivist research (see Chapter 2) sees its central aim as attempting to disprove a hypothesis. A hypothesis is 'a logical supposition, a reasonable guess. [...]

It may direct your thinking to the possible source of information that will aid in resolving the problem' (Leedy, 1997).

We make simple hypotheses all the time. For example, 'Since I can see the sun is shining, I hypothesize that I may be able to get my washing dry outside today.' We also make much more complex hypotheses. One broad hypothesis might be that it is possible for famine to occur in countries where sufficient food is present but where social divisions prevent its distribution to those in need. In principle, these are both testable hypotheses.

Hypothesis testing essentially deals with 'why' questions – explanations – and is highly relevant to much academic scientific research, which aims to develop generalizable theories about the world. It looks at cause and effect in a focused way.

Researchers working in non-positivist traditions reject the idea that all research needs a specific hypothesis, and the sort of research development workers most often carry out may not require a formal hypothesis. Research can bring to bear a new perspective, perhaps describing a situation from the point of view of the people concerned rather than setting out to 'prove a point'. The investigation may be at too early a stage for it to be appropriate to test hypotheses – it may be more a matter of generating some relevant hypotheses that could be tested later.

However, it is a good discipline, when you are working to clarify your research plan, to try to turn your research focus into a set of hypotheses. If you do this, you will make explicit the theories that lie behind your way of seeing the problem, clarifying the assumptions you are making.

For example, let us look at some ways of writing a research question, structured as a hypothesis and then in a more open way.

Hypothesis

That significant physical violence and abuse towards children is more common in families where there is physical violence towards adult women (usually the mother)

Non-hypothesis question

What are the effects on the incidence and type of violence or abuse of children of the presence or absence of violence towards adult women in the family?

These are both difficult issues to investigate, given social norms of 'family privacy'. Both formulations beg many questions about definitions. Using a specific hypothesis encourages researchers to define terms as tightly as possible before investigation. This has its pros and cons: for example, might sexual abuse or neglect be missed in our example if questions are directed very tightly towards physical violence?

3.4 Writing a research brief

The next step in planning involves writing a research brief. Any researcher who has worked in NGOs will tell you that a large proportion of the problems people encounter in research work could be avoided by them writing better briefs at the start of research processes. For this reason, a lot of space is given to the process here.

Many different terms are used to describe research plans. Research proposals, terms of reference, scoping notes, concept notes and briefs all refer to the same type of document. We use the term 'brief' because it expresses the idea that the document communicates a job to be done. Briefs are different from research protocols and contracts, which fulfil other functions, as Table 3.1 shows.

Table 3.1 Research planning documents

Type of document	Also called	Definition	When written
Brief	Proposal, ToR, scoping note, concept note	Describes and justifies the research plan	During planning, often before applying for funding
Research protocol		Detailed procedures for carrying out research, used in addition to a brief	Start of implementation. Useful when many people are involved, the methodology is complex or consistency is important
Contract		Formal agreement of roles and responsibilities when employing staff – may refer to the brief or include individual ToR	If employing staff specifically for the research project

3.4.1 When should you write the brief?

It is best to start writing the brief as early as possible, and to expect to revise it many times. You could start out with just some notes about the purpose of the exercise. Do not put off committing your thoughts to paper – it is the best way of enabling other people to become involved. You can always add the more technical details later.

Common pitfall

Starting out on a research project without a written brief

Strengths, weaknesses, opportunities, threats analysis

One straightforward, but versatile and effective, planning tool that can help start efforts at thinking through a research brief is SWOT analysis.[4] This exercise asks you and your team to think carefully about your research plans by focusing on assessing the internal strengths and weaknesses of your current research strategy, and asks you to consider the external opportunities and threats which surround it.

Using a simple two-by-two matrix like the one below, identify these strengths, weaknesses, opportunities and threats in a group setting. It is important to be clear from the start what your research objectives are. Also, consider as many real examples as possible to provide grounding and clarity.

ACTIVITY 3.4

(Continued)

(Continued)

Strengths	Weaknesses
Opportunities	Threats

You should also rank the responses you come up with. Which threats are most pressing or serious? Which opportunities are most exciting or attractive? This will help you to prioritize the next steps.

Finally, pay close attention to any suggested solutions and recommendations that emerge from this activity, as they will be of immediate relevance in the midst of your planning process.

3.4.2 Who should write the brief?

The main drafting of the brief should be undertaken by the person with the clearest view of the research being planned. This may be a manager, but also may be a development practitioner or an in-house researcher. External consultants should not be asked to write briefs for their own projects. Whoever does the main writing, responsibility for ensuring the brief is adequate to its job remains with the manager of the project. If the brief does not make sense in terms of its contribution towards the overall goals of the development work the agency is undertaking, there will be a problem.

Where a proposal is being submitted to an academic research funder, it may be planned jointly with academic or independent researchers. In this case, the researchers may take lead responsibility for writing the brief and approach a development organization to be a partner in the bid. The development agency needs to concentrate on clarifying what will be expected of it as a result of its involvement. For example, will the agency be used as a link to community members? If so, do frontline staff members agree this will be feasible and acceptable? Have ethical issues been addressed properly? Are the researchers expecting the agency to provide administrative help, and can this be delivered? Will the agency be expected to do any of the analytical work?

3.4.3 Who should be consulted?

To write a good brief, you will need to consult a wide range of people – partner agencies with an interest in the topic; staff (and/or external researchers) who may be involved in carrying out the research; and perhaps funders. The very process of writing the brief will lead to fruitful discussions.

Key stakeholders need to be involved from the start. No one likes to hear about research in their 'field', especially if their help is required, after all the main decisions have been made. Support at a later stage is much more likely to be forthcoming if people have some ownership of the project from the start.

It is important for staff within the commissioning agency to be happy with the brief, and to see that it makes sense in relation to the other work they are doing. Partner agencies should also be consulted, as it is likely they will be involved, either in contacting informants or in implementing recommendations. This also applies to members of the local community: where possible, community organizations should be shown a draft brief for comment. You might want to call an open meeting for community members to discuss your plans.

> **Tip**
> Working out a research brief is a major piece of work, and time needs to be allowed for it.

Particularly if you hope to attract research-oriented funders, considerable work will be required to satisfy them that you both know about existing research and are competent to undertake the work you propose. Most research proposals go through several drafts, with major changes made before they are agreed – it is important not to be put off by critical comments from colleagues on early drafts of the proposal. Time spent at an early stage will certainly pay off in the long run. Proposals for major projects can take anything from two weeks to several months to prepare.

3.4.4 Stakeholder analysis

One important tool in identifying key stakeholders at this stage of planning is stakeholder analysis. Here, key actors are identified and visualized using a simple matrix in order to plan a strategy of engagement.

To begin, you should have a clear idea of the research objective you are pursuing – tools like an *issue tree* can help prepare you. Your next step is to carefully think through all the potential stakeholders and interest groups associated with the issue or topic you are researching. Here, the bigger and more varied your brainstorming group, the more comprehensive a list can be developed – a good number is between six and eight. Stakeholders themselves can be a range of different actor types. Table 3.2, adapted from Start and Hovland (2007) offers a good starting point:

Table 3.2 List of potential stakeholders in research projects

Private sector	Public sector	Civil society
• Corporations, businesses	• Ministers, advisors (executive)	• Media
• Business associations	• Civil servants and departments (bureaucracy)	• Religious bodies
• Professional bodies	• Elected representatives (legislature)	• Schools and universities
• Individual business leaders	• Courts (judiciary)	• Social movements and advocacy groups
• Financial institutions	• Political parties	• Trade unions
	• Local government	• National NGOs
	• Military	• International NGOs
	• Quangos, commissions	
	• International bodies	

3.4.5 What should be included in the brief?

Table 3.3 gives a typical structure for a research brief, which can be adapted to different needs. It also gives references corresponding to each element of the brief to sections in the wider text of this volume. It is followed by some thoughts about different areas to emphasize in different types of research project.

Table 3.3 Outline of a research brief

Select section headings from the below list as appropriate to your project.

Outline of research brief	Discussed in detail
Setting the scene: introduction and background, existing information, gaps and rationale	Below; Chapter 5; Appendix 2 Useful websites.
Aims and objectives	Chapters 1, 2 and 3
Research focus and questions	Chapter 3
Audience	Chapters 2, 3 and 15
Learning and participation plan	Chapters 6 and 12
Methods	Chapters 7, 11 and 12
Sample	Chapter 10
Analysis	Chapter 13
Outputs: reports, presentations, interim reports, training sessions, etc.	Chapters 14 and 15
Plan for dissemination/influence/implementation	Chapters 3 and 15
Quality assurance for the research	Chapters 8 and 16
Accountability: support and supervision	Chapters 4 and 9
Advisory group	Chapters 4 and 13
Ethical considerations	Chapter 9
Timescale	Chapter 4.4
Budget	Chapter 4.4

Obviously, a brief needs to reflect the scale of the research being proposed in terms of how elaborate it is, and the contents and style will need to reflect its purpose. Different types of research need different emphases:

- Research that is essentially part of a programme of development work needs a brief which emphasizes the practical *outcomes* desired and which encourages regular, appropriate *feedback* to partners.
- Research to influence policy requires consideration of exactly *who the work is addressed to* and *how it fits* into an influencing strategy. The methodology needs to be convincing to the audience. The participation of key stakeholders in planning and implementation should be defined, and the role of the researcher/s in writing up and *dissemination* should be specified.
- If *capacity sharing* through developing staff or partners' research-related skills is part of the purpose, this should be made explicit and time allowed for it.
- If the research is very participatory, with end users defining the research questions, this needs to be specified, identifying empowerment explicitly as an important outcome.

If you plan to seek external funding, you must obtain the guidelines for research proposals used by the funder/s you have in mind.

Setting the scene

It is easy to feel that the introduction to a research brief is unimportant, as you are probably very familiar with the material that goes into it. But to the reader it is crucial.

The introduction needs to answer a number of questions:

- Why is this research important to the development work your organization is involved in?
- What is the wider background to the subject? Is there national or international legislation or guidance relating to this issue? Looking to the future, are key decision points coming up?
- What do we already know that is relevant to the questions you are raising?
- Why this research now?

Aims and objectives

Research for development needs research questions for intellectual clarity. But this type of research is done for practical purposes, and so also needs aims and objectives, similar to those you would set for any other sort of project. This is a matter of making explicit the outcomes you hope to achieve by carrying out this piece of work.

An aim is a broad statement of what the research hopes to achieve. An aims statement answers the question: Why are we doing this piece of work?
For example, 'to find out how maternal mortality is affected by distance from health centres and whether this is a primary factor'.

An objective is a specific, realistic and measurable statement of the change you want a particular piece of work to achieve. *A statement of objectives answers the question: What do we hope to achieve?*
For example, 'using the information obtained make recommendations to the Ministry of Health and donors on the location and efficacy of health centres in relation to reducing maternal mortality'.

Objectives should relate to the ultimate purpose or desired outcome of the research. Why are you undertaking the research and what do you hope to achieve? For example, you may wish to influence national or local policy in a specific area, persuade others about an issue or inform a programme.

Objectives can also include desired outcomes from the *process* of conducting the research as well as from its final products. For example, it is important to assess whether objectives that relate to capacity sharing – process outcomes – are possible. A project working with young people with experience of using mental health services as peer researchers could have as a specific objective increasing the confidence of at least four young people in speaking up on mental health issues.

It is particularly important that objectives be concrete and capable of assessment. It should be possible to tell whether or not the objective has been achieved at the end of the project.

FOR EXAMPLE

Including rural people's perspectives: studying drought in Malawi, Zambia and Zimbabwe

The primary objective of a PLA study on the 1992 drought in Malawi, Zambia and Zimbabwe was to investigate its effects on rural livelihoods and responses to it from the perspective of rural people. Most previous evaluations had focused on programmes organized by UN agencies, government ministries and NGOs. They consequently overlooked, or at least underestimated, the major role villagers had played in mitigating the effects of the drought. A secondary objective was to provide training and field experience to Ministry of Agriculture staff (in Zambia and Zimbabwe) and NGO staff (in Malawi).

Source: Eldridge (1993)

A common confusion is to mix up methods or activities with objectives. Thus you get an objective reading 'to carry out a survey' or 'to run five focus groups with xyz'. This is unhelpful, as it does not tell us what purpose is being pursued by carrying out the survey or running the groups. Methods or activities are the ways you pursue your objectives; they are not ends in themselves. This distinction is very important: if we fail to make it, we can get hooked into doggedly continuing to carry out particular activities as if they were an end in themselves, even when they are not working well. It would be better to step back and look more broadly for other ways the aims we have in mind could be reached.

Audience

Who is the research for? Research is all about communication, and most research undertaken as part of development work has quite specific audiences. These are, however, diverse. They range from community members to politicians at national and indeed international levels. What is needed to convince these different groups of a case may be very different. Some audiences are much more wedded to traditional research methods than others. You need to think about your audience in relation to the design of the research itself, and also in planning the promotion of the findings. A different writing style will be needed for different audiences.

The standard and style of your research needs to be fit for its purpose, and part of that purpose is defined through a consideration of audience. List all the possible audiences for a particular piece of work – but do not stop there. You need to decide which audiences have top priority in relation to this piece of work. It may be that the same data will be of interest to a very wide group of people but, even if this is so, it is likely you will need to use different methods to communicate your message to different groups. For example, politicians will require less detail than professionals, who may also want information on the methodology used.

Busy senior managers and politicians do not read long and complex research reports. It is essential that findings be summarized if they are to be read by people with decision-making power. It is also crucial to realize that people bring their own agenda to your research. Take account of the terms in which powerful people are

Table 3.4   Some audiences for research

Research into child labour in the sports goods industry in Pakistan	• The sports goods industry • International donor agencies • Pakistani government and NGOs • International Labour Organization • Campaigning NGOs • Private sector working in developing countries
Needs of young people and disabled children in Serb Sarajevo	• Local people: parents and other adults, children and young people • Potential donors • NGOs • Ministry of Health and Social Welfare
Sustainability in health sector	• UN Children's Fund, World Bank, World Health Organization (WHO) • UK Department for International Development • Other international donor agencies, especially in health • Governments of countries studied • Other Southern governments • Academics in development studies
Studies of child sexual abuse in Pakistan, South Africa	• Adults in community • Children themselves • Local NGOs
'Leaving care' research	• UK government • Young care leavers • Politicians with an interest in young people leaving care • Local authorities • Social workers

thinking – what they think the problem is. You need not agree, but to get their attention you must relate the problem as you define it to their specific understanding.

Bilingual education: 'the missing link'

As mentioned in Chapter 2's example, Save the Children UK conducted research in order to have an impact on policy on bilingual child education. To this end, the Save the Children UK education team decided to produce an international policy report that would do three things:

1 Summarize the evidence around language in children's education for international donor agencies and national education decision makers in low- and middle-income countries;
2 Make it clear why, and in which circumstances, improving language in education should be a top priority for national education policymakers and donors;
3 Explain the implications of not taking action on language in these 'top priority' circumstances, and offer clear and practicable recommendations for donors and national policymakers.

The team identified the top priorities of target audiences as cost effectiveness, national stability and competitiveness in the global knowledge economy. They conducted desk research

(Continued)

FOR EXAMPLE

(Continued)

to identify links between these priority areas and evidence on how learning in an unfamiliar language affects children's educational achievement and prospects.

The research framework developed for Save the Children's research on financing of education in conflict-affected fragile states was useful. The team found evidence that the way education and other public services are managed can affect conflict and fragility, by either increasing or reducing the divisions between ethnic and linguistic groups. When some groups fail in education because they don't understand the language used to teach, this is likely to worsen such divisions. Based on this analysis, they matched countries with high conflict or fragility against data on countries where children are least likely to have education in their mother tongue. This allowed for the production of a list of the countries most at risk of worsening stability if they did not take action to improve how language is used in teaching.

The focus on conflict and fragility was distinctive, and readers found the report clear and relevant. *Language and Education: The Missing Link* (Pinnock, 2009) has been referenced frequently in education studies and policy publications worldwide. It received positive media coverage in *The Guardian* in the UK, and in online newspapers in Canada, Bangladesh, Indonesia and Thailand. The link made between school language policy and conflict was used as the basis for the core arguments in a key British Council report on language and education in Pakistan, which presented language in education as a crisis which will fuel further conflict and instability. The British Council report received strong coverage and has helped to put language higher up the agenda among stakeholders in education in Pakistan.

It is equally important to think about audience in relation to research which primarily addresses a local community or a particular group of people. At times, the key purpose of a research project is to raise the issue publicly in a community. Some HIV-related research has been of this nature. Another example would be research that shows how people are not taking up pensions and disability benefits to which they are entitled. In this case, the accessibility of the methods used is absolutely central, and thought must be given to how this group can best contribute to and learn from research.

Respondents themselves are always one of the audiences of a research project. Studies of child domestic servants which ask questions of their employers are an example of how research can have an impact on respondents simply by raising new questions. People employing children as domestics may find the process of answering these questions draws their attention to children's welfare in a new way.

Getting clear about the audience may also enable you to think about whom to involve in advising you about the research. It is helpful to directly involve people like those you hope to influence – or indeed those people themselves. This enables ongoing dialogue about what evidence is seen as important and relevant and what is not.

Methods

The research brief should give a general idea of the kind of methods the research will use. But do not feel you have to specify every last detail. If the brief is to be used to employ an experienced researcher, it is a good idea to leave them some room to advise you on the methods they think would be most appropriate to your research questions.

In participatory research, too, it will be best to leave choices of exact methods to those who will be carrying it out. Often, several possible approaches could be taken, and there is no need to specify too early the methods to be used.

You may want to state roughly the scale of the research, for example how many people will be interviewed. But until you are clear about the difficulties you may encounter, it is worth leaving some leeway. In proposals for quantitative research, you will need to give some specific figures, but consult an experienced researcher on sampling first.

Ensure that you remember to pilot any research tools (for example questionnaires, focus group topic guides) before they are used. Time needs to be allowed for organizing a small pilot study and for reflecting on the results and making the necessary changes.

See Part 2 for more on research methods.

Analysis

Although you may not want to think about analysis yet, it is at the point when data collection is complete, and analysis and writing should start, that many research projects threaten to collapse. This can be a huge waste of resources. If you hope to get funding for the project, research-oriented funders will want to see a clear and detailed statement of the procedures to be followed in interpreting and analysing the data.

Analysis is the process of organizing the information you have collected to relate your data to the research questions. It requires you to interpret what people have said and to decide on the categories you will use to organize your material. It is not a good idea to plunge into the process of collecting data before you are clear about how you are going to analyse it. While you may be able to hire somebody to make sense of the data once they are in, it is far preferable to involve them in the early planning stages. If you do not, it may not be possible to get from the data the information you require. Questions asked in slightly the wrong way can be impossible to analyse.

This applies to both quantitative and qualitative research. Analysis is part of the design of research work, and any research materials, like questionnaires, should be designed with a view to the final methods of analysis. There is nothing like knowing that you yourself will be responsible for writing up the research to make you focus on getting the right data in the first place.

Many research projects include an element of both quantitative and qualitative data collection. It is usually best to think about the analysis of these two elements separately, although you will need to bring them together again in the end. Where a large amount of data is to be collected, careful thought needs to be given to the technicalities of analysis. If you plan to analyse your data using specialist statistical software, you should identify the right software and its requirements before starting collection. Computer software exists for both quantitative and qualitative data analysis – but don't jump into using it just because it looks good on your proposal. As software packages are often expensive, look into the practicalities of buying them, or using others' facilities, in advance.

Chapter 13 discusses the advantages and disadvantages of computer analysis for the different types of data. Remember that qualitative analysis always takes considerable time and skill, whatever technology you use to help you. Quantitative analysis can be very straightforward or extremely subtle, depending on the type of project.

It is quite difficult to anticipate how you will need to analyse your data, and therefore how you should collect it. This is something one learns from (sometimes bitter) experience. Ask someone who has been involved with two or three completed research projects to have a look at your plans and comment on how best to make the data collection process suitable for the analysis you intend to undertake.

! ————————— CONSULT A RESEARCHER NOW ————————— !

See Chapter 13 for more on analysis.

Outputs and dissemination plan

Although you may need one, few people are filled with joy at the thought of reading a conventional research report, even if it is about something they are extremely interested in. Think creatively: How have you yourself learnt about research findings? What communication methods reached you?

Some projects need to produce two or more reports: one, perhaps, for those most directly involved with the community group in question and one for a wider audience of policymakers. The wider audience will want less detail about, for example, the history of a particular programme, but may need more background information to put the findings in context. Respondents should have access to its findings – and be able to respond to them. You may want to write a shorter, more direct report for them.

It may be that the research is intended as an internal piece of work to be read by small groups of colleagues, stakeholders and partners, or that the intellectual property belongs to the funders of the work. But if research is intended to influence policymakers, win support and change the way people think about an issue, you will want to think about your research communication strategy, including the use of in-person feedback approaches, videos, blogs, etc. (discussed in more depth in Chapter 15).[5]

It can be a good idea to write your research communication strategy into the brief from the start. If employing someone, you can specify that you wish them to write articles and present seminars as well as to write a report. Too many research projects employ researchers only up to the point when the 'long and boring' final report is complete, leaving no one to present the findings in more accessible ways. It is important to employ a researcher with the writing skills you need (see Section 4.2 on who should do the research and Chapter 14 on writing effectively to aid your decision here). An alternative is to split these roles, asking someone with journalistic skills to carry out the promotional element of the work.

Reports often go through several drafts and, if they are published, there will be further work involved in getting the design right. Incorporating changes required by readers of a first draft can be a substantial piece of work, and this should be acknowledged in the brief. For reports aiming to influence policy, it is important that recommendations be written in an appropriate way (see Chapter 15 for more detail).

Accountability, support and supervision

Research does not look after itself. The brief should state to whom the researcher is accountable, and where they will get support. Some of a researcher's accountability may be through an advisory group, but this can lead to confusion if it is the only or main line of accountability. Generally, it is best to have a clear line of accountability through an individual who is responsible for overseeing the research as a whole and for linking the project with other related activities. The line manager should be a member (or perhaps chair) of any advisory group established, and share responsibility with the researcher for ensuring discussions in this group produce clear decisions to enable the research to proceed.

Researchers should receive regular supervision in relation to their progress towards meeting their aims and objectives, just like any other staff. In addition to management supervision, they may also need support and supervision from another researcher with experience of the type of work in question.

Advisory or steering groups

Beyond the smallest piece of investigation, all research projects benefit from setting up an advisory group to assist staff through the various stages. As well as offering support and a sounding board for researchers, an advisory group ensures partner agencies that may be affected by the research process or findings have an opportunity to be represented. Those the project hopes to influence can be invited to take part, so they can learn from the project as it goes along and ask questions if they have doubts about any aspect. The research should also be accountable to those whose lives it concerns – community members, including perhaps children and young people. Finally, funders may wish to be represented and have a say in how the research proceeds.

These groups are sometimes called steering groups, but this implies they are responsible for managing the project. It is difficult to be accountable to a group: what happens if members disagree? Perhaps this term sends the wrong message to members. To call the group 'advisory' makes it clear that members' views will be taken into account, but that it may not be possible to do everything they suggest.

Members might include:

- representatives of funding organizations;
- researchers/policy experts in the substantive field of study (for example early years education);
- researchers with experience of a range of relevant methodologies;
- representatives of partner agencies – government departments, NGOs, local authority or health authority managers;
- representatives of community members/those being studied;
- senior management of the 'host' organization;
- people who are, or are similar to, the people you hope to influence (for example someone from the Ministry of Health).

All members of the research team may attend meetings, or one or two people may represent the others. It is important that information flows freely between the advisory group and members of the research team: researchers should feel confident to bring any problems they encounter to the group. Groups do not need to meet frequently – three or four times in the life of a project may be enough. Staff should not feel they have to refer every small decision to the group: this can seriously impede progress. People can be consulted by post, email or telephone if they are unable to attend meetings.

FOR EXAMPLE

A multi-agency research management committee: pre-school education in Mongolia

In Mongolia, Save the Children assisted in developing a study of the pre-school sector, using a management committee to ensure ownership of the project by those with a stake in the work. This consisted of all those involved in pre-school work, from the Ministry of Health and Education, to the National Children's Centre (a quango), to pre-school specialists. The committee was empowered with money and the role of writing the ToR. Save the Children provided only advice on the ToR, procedures and research methods.

The resulting research was owned by the committee and expertise was retained in country. The committee itself brought together a group of people who had previously been locked in competition over retaining resources for the pre-school sector. They worked together to raise funds and committed themselves to common objectives and to taking the whole process forward.

Chapter 4 on managing research gives more details on managing research projects, including advisory groups.

Timescale and budget

See Section 4.4 on managing costs and time for a full discussion on how to establish a realistic timescale and budget for your project.

Ethical considerations

In writing a research brief, it is important to discuss any ethical issues you see arising in the project. You should describe any procedures you intend to use to overcome these. Ethical issues can arise at any point in the life of a research project. Chapter 9 discusses these in more detail.

A key ethical issue is how you ensure people who choose to take part in the research do so on a genuinely voluntary basis. This is called 'informed consent': drawing attention to the need to ensure respondents understand what the research is and what their participation means. There may be concern about how informed consent will be obtained if respondents have limited experience and understanding of research, as may be the case with children or people without formal education. The brief should explain how you hope to ensure respondents understand what they are being asked to do.

The central ethical issue to consider at the outset is whether any risks or costs to participants involved in the research process are justified in relation to the benefits to be gained from the project as a whole. See Chapter 9 for more.

Key points from this chapter

This chapter has concentrated on the practical aspects of planning research for development. It has looked in detail at the different elements that need to be included in a research brief. The next chapter moves on to look at the ongoing management of research, such as ways of estimating costs and timescales as well as issues related to negotiating access, sharing research capacity, managing participatory research and relating to funders.

Checklist: effective research planning

- ☑ Expect to actively manage the process of initiating and overseeing a research project as you would any other project – and allow time for this.
- ☑ Carefully consider key stakeholders you want to involve in your research, and identify potential issues and opportunities before they arise. Use tools like issue trees and stakeholder and SWOT analysis.
- ☑ For research aimed at influencing policy, use the planning tools provided in Section 15.3 at an early stage to improve impacts among policymakers.
- ☑ Concentrate on the brief: writing a good brief is the key to planning effective research, and includes a standard set of headings.
- ☑ Discuss briefs thoroughly with all concerned before they are finalized.
- ☑ In drafting the brief, defining the purpose, focus and key questions for the research is the central task, and should be given time.
- ☑ If you want your project to have influence, consider carefully the audience for the research and how the results will be disseminated. Plan for influence throughout the life of the research.
- ☑ Work out a project timetable and budget which allows realistic resources for each of the tasks involved.
- ☑ Ensure recognition and support from your organization's management.
- ☑ Consider community involvement in relation to every aspect of the project, from identifying the research focus to promoting its findings.

 Further reading

Bell, J. (2010) *Doing Your Research Project: A Guide for First-time Researchers in Education, Health and Social Science*, 5th edn. Maidenhead: Open University Press.

Provides step-by-step help and useful suggestions for first-time researchers, including on how to choose and plan a research project. Written in a very clear and informative way and has an easy-to-use index.

Blaxter, L., Hughes, C. and Tight, M. (2010) *How to Research*, 3rd edn. Buckingham: Open University Press.

Aimed at people involved in small-scale research projects at college or work, this helpful book includes good advice on how to focus a research project.

Denscombe, M. (2010) *The Good Research Guide for Small-scale Social Research Projects*, 4th edn. Buckingham and Philadelphia, PA: Open University Press.

Gives pragmatic advice on how to do 'good enough' research with limited resources. Very useful general guidance on how to use a number of research methods and approaches, including mixed methods.

May, T. (2003) *Social Research: Issues, Methods and Processes*, 3rd edn. Buckingham: Open University Press.

The book is divided into two parts, with Part I examining issues and perspectives in social research and Part II exploring different methods and processes.

Robson, C. (2002) *Real World Research: A Resource for Social Scientists and Practitioner-Researchers*, 2nd edn. Oxford: Blackwell.

Provides an overview of various strategies, methods and research designs for use in social research, combining quantitative and qualitative research in a critical realist paradigm. Contains a useful discussion on how to establish trustworthiness.

Notes

1 The Participatory Planning, Monitoring and Evaluation Online Resource Portal brings together useful information on these methods: http://portals.wi.wur.nl/ppme/index.php; also see Holland and Blackburn (1998).
2 Slocum (2003); also www.excludedvoices.org/democratising-agricultural-research-food-sovereignty-west-africa; gives an account of how citizens' juries were established in Mali to deliver verdicts on governance of food and agricultural research.
3 Denscombe (2010) contains a useful discussion on reflexivity in ethnographic research.
4 SWOT analysis is explained in Start and Hovland (2007).
5 See, for example, DFID (2006) and the chapter on communications in Start and Hovland (2007).

4

MANAGING RESEARCH

This chapter aims to assist managers in the most important aspects of implementing and overseeing a research project, in five sections. The first looks at relating to funders when managing a research project. The second looks at the issues involved in deciding whether a piece of research should be undertaken in-house or commissioned from others. The third describes the process of employing professional researchers, whether as employees or as freelance workers. The fourth and fifth parts look at managing costs and timings and ongoing supervision of researchers, respectively.

4.1 Attracting and engaging with funders

Research is not cheap, and thus funding issues are critical for any research manager to consider. Some research that development workers undertake or commission is paid for by their own organization as part of their work programme. However, quite often, funding is obtained from another organization, which may be oriented specifically towards funding research or may fund research as part of a development programme. The two main ways in which such research is undertaken is on the basis of grant funding and through contracts. With grant funding, researchers may be left to make their own decisions on methods, sampling, etc.; with a contract, the funder is actively involved in these decisions (Hakim, 2000).

Engagement of funders throughout the life of a project is a much-overlooked part of managing research. When we think about funders, we may think in terms of 'us and them'. They give us money and we give them reports. However, any funding arrangement is a type of interagency deal (Mordaunt and O'Sullivan, 2010). It is essential to consider what the funding body wants out of its grant giving and to cooperate with them in that endeavour. It may also be possible to influence their ideas about appropriate directions for their future funding based on the agency's experience. But the first step is to accept that funders have a legitimate stake in the outcomes of their funding operations.

4.1.1 Applying for funding

Top of most funders' list of criteria will be whether the issue in question is important enough to merit attention. Making this case persuasively is key if funds are to be attracted. Too often, by the time an application is written, the issues we want to work on are so familiar to us, we take it for granted they are important, rather than arguing this in a convincing manner. A study of grant applications refused by the US National Institutes of Health found that 33 per cent were rejected because 'the problem is of insufficient importance or is unlikely to produce any new or useful information' (Leedy, 1997).

Different funders take very different approaches to their work, and it is important to get information from the ones you are interested in and adapt your ideas to their frameworks. Much development research is funded as part of a package which also includes practical development work 'on the ground'. Where this is true, it is essential to make it clear how the work will be relevant to the donor's aims.

Some of the largest social research funders take a very proactive approach. The Joseph Rowntree Foundation and the Nuffield Foundation, for instance, publish quite detailed research strategies in their areas of concern and invite bids on research that pursues particular sets of questions. These funders encourage people who wish to submit proposals outside such programmes to discuss them with funders' staff first. It is a waste of time all round to submit proposals that have no hope of success.

Non-governmental organizations (NGOs), as 'users' of academic research, can be consulted on the research strategies of funding bodies. Funding bodies like the UK's Economic and Social Research Council (ESRC) place emphasis on involving users in discussions about research directions. In the ESRC's guidance on writing a good proposal, key questions asked include 'Have I identified potential users of this research outside the academic community?' 'Have I involved/consulted them in my planning?' 'Have I arranged for their continuing involvement in the research process in an appropriate way?' (www.esrc.ac.uk/funding-and-guidance/guidance/applicants/application2.aspx).

This trend has encouraged academics to involve voluntary organizations in their research proposals, with a view to ensuring their relevance to practice. Some fruitful partnerships have emerged. As NGOs become increasingly oriented towards influencing policymaking, many have gained extensive experience in working with academics during the research proposal process. Nonetheless, tensions can still arise around practical and cultural miscommunication. For example, busy organizations can find themselves receiving a flurry of phone calls from academics the day before a deadline for application asking to put the name of the organization on their bid. This sort of involvement may be completely token, but also may drain an organization's resources as it tries to engage with a project into which it has had no creative input.

New trends, such as the increasing prevalence of practitioners taking part in Masters-level development studies programmes at academic institutions and the growth of 'bridge-building' institutions such as the International NGO Training and Resource Centre (INTRAC) in Oxford and the Hauser Centre for Non-profit Management at Harvard, are helping to decrease the likelihood of such situations. Nonetheless, as Roper notes, you should remain ready to confront potential issues of miscommunication from the academic–practitioner divide as they arise (2002). Here, the best approach relies on self-awareness and concerted efforts at mutual understanding between both groups.

NGOs need to think carefully about their role when seeking research funding. The perception of many funders is that only universities are capable of undertaking rigorous research. For some types of funding, for example from the ESRC (UK Economic and Social Research Council), it may be necessary to form a partnership with a university. The potential benefits of such partnerships extend far beyond funding strategies, however. Their real value ultimately lies in bringing together the perspectives, resources and expertise of the two groups for the purposes of producing more fruitful insights into development issues.

Development workers are best advised to seek funding which draws on their strengths in terms of active engagement with stakeholders and their ability to link needs assessment with participatory processes and service provision as well as influencing policy. Getting academic research funding is difficult for academics and almost unheard-of for those outside academia. However, there are other types of funders who want to see research undertaken with communities. Some, for example Comic Relief, emphasize community participation in their principles for grant giving: 'we would expect to see people who will benefit from projects – as well as those who could influence the success or failure of the work – being consulted at the outset and their views incorporated in project design' (www.comicrelief.com/apply-for-a-grant/vision-principles-uk-grant-making).

Others, such as the UK Department for International Development (DFID), are increasingly interested in research impact and thus increasingly fund partnerships among think-tanks, universities and NGOs (through what are called development research consortia). NGOs may be in a good position to ensure that policy engagement and research communication aspects are followed through, compared with, for example, academic researchers, who operate within institutions where these types of achievements are only weakly incentivized.

4.1.2 Engaging with funders throughout the project

It is important to agree with a funding body on the form and frequency of ongoing engagement at the outset of a project. Different funders take very different approaches to their work, and it is important to adapt your working style accordingly. Some expect to give input into the research process and decision making, or require regular progress reports. When the Joseph Rowntree Foundation funds a project, for example, it takes a close interest in it throughout its life, and requires it to convene an advisory group usually chaired by a member of its staff. It also publishes and distributes a short summary of the findings in a standard format.

However, even if you are dealing with a funder that has minimal requirements for feedback, it is wise to keep them informed of developments. The better a relationship you can build with them, the more hope you have of further funding in the future. On the whole, funders understand that changes may need to be made to the details of the proposal they agreed to, but will want to be told about any major changes of plan and the reasons for it.

4.2 Deciding who should do the research

This section assists managers in making decisions about how to undertake a particular piece of research. The key decision is often whether to undertake the research in-house, using existing staff, or whether to hire researchers specifically to carry out the work, as employed staff or as freelance consultants.

Certain questions need to be answered in making this decision. Who you need to do it depends on what type of research it is. Is it primarily programme-focused research, like needs assessment, or is it aiming to have a wider influence on policy? How much community participation will be involved? Table 4.1 shows some typical roles in a research project and can be used to plan who will do what.

Table 4.1 Who can do the research?

	Lead researcher	Supervision	Fieldwork	Writing and dissemination	Enabling participation	Admin support
Development staff						
In-house research staff						
New research staff						
Community member						
Freelance researcher						
University academic						
Research agency – commercial or voluntary sector						

You can divide research tasks up in a number of different ways, depending on the scale and complexity of the project. Some projects are essentially carried out by one person, for example desk studies or small-scale qualitative studies. A participatory project is likely to involve community members, a researcher/advisor (who may be one of your staff or an external consultant) and at least one other worker to support the community members. Sometimes, a development worker will run the whole project herself. A large-scale survey might involve many people – a lead researcher, a supervisor/manager, interviewers, administrative staff doing coding and data entry, perhaps a specialist transcriber, a statistician to advise on data analysis ... a cast of hundreds!

As with all projects, the more complex the division of labour, the greater the need for coordination. This complexity makes it advisable to contract out any very large survey work to an organization that is geared towards delivering this sort of project.

4.2.1   Doing research in-house or commissioning it out: factors to consider

Whether to do research in-house or to commission external researchers depends on the nature of the research itself, so it will be easier if you have a clearly defined, agreed-on brief for the project, as described in Chapter 3. The following checklist sets out some criteria to consider, which are discussed in more detail below.

Checklist: should research be done in-house or not?

- ☑ Capacity – research skills: do you have the right skills in-house?
- ☑ Capacity – workload: do in-house staff have the time?
- ☑ Credibility: will the research be more credible if an independent, specialist or academic researcher conducts it?
- ☑ Audience and level of scrutiny: will in-house authors persuade your target audience?
- ☑ Methods to be used: are specialized skills required?
- ☑ Benefits to the wider programme: does doing research in-house make sense in terms of the broader programme?
- ☑ Role confusion: what makes sense in terms of ongoing community relations?
- ☑ Capacity building: is capacity building an aim for this project?

4.2.2   Capacity – research skills

Many staff will have some knowledge of research methods from their training. However, knowing how to evaluate and criticize research and how to actually carry it out are two very different things!

If you are hoping to undertake a piece of research within your current staffing set-up, the first step is to match the skills profile of existing staff with the requirements of the task. The box sets out the core skills involved in undertaking research. Not everyone who is involved in research must have this whole range of skills developed to a high degree. This model is offered as it may help you to anticipate the range of skills a project will need and arrange for support or training as necessary.

Skills for research

Library/internet/information searching

- identifying and locating relevant information sources;
- making effective use of sources;
- compiling annotated bibliographies;
- contacting outside organizations/informants.

Summarizing/précising skills

- structuring overall content
- organizing and condensing information into a coherent form;
- summarizing the essence and content of a body of writing/research.

Work planning and organization

- planning a work schedule;
- keeping a research diary;
- time management;
- working under pressure;
- management of research files;
- organizing meetings.

Teamwork

- working constructively and critically within a group;
- learning to give and take criticism;
- working towards collective goals.

Research design skills

- defining appropriate and relevant data for a study;
- designing a questionnaire;
- planning a research project or research strategy;
- devising/implementing appropriate sampling strategies (quantitative/qualitative);
- designing a programme of fieldwork.

Interviewing skills

- locating and recruiting informants;
- conducting a series of interviews (structured/semi-structured/unstructured);
- organizing/conducting group discussions;
- developing appropriate recording skills.

Observation skills

- negotiating access to field of observation;
- preparing theoretical grounds for watching;
- selecting an appropriate observational role;
- carrying out observations (participant/non-participant);
- developing field recording skills (field notes).

Analysis skills

- processing and organizing a body of data;
- developing an analysis strategy (quantitative/qualitative);
- analysing and interpreting data;
- describing and summarizing a dataset.

Report writing

- planning a dissemination strategy;
- planning report contents;
- writing a research report/article/document to a deadline.

Research presentation and communication

- organizing and conducting a briefing session;
- effective verbal communication (to colleagues, outside agencies, respondents);
- clear and concise writing skills;
- presenting research findings at seminars/conferences.

Information technology skills

- use and application of, for example, word-processing, databases, internet research and visual presentation packages;
- skills in the use of specialist statistical software packages, for example Stata and SPSS.

Numerical skills

- processing and analysing numerical information;
- applying statistical techniques;
- presenting data in graphical form;
- skills in specialist statistical techniques.

4.2.3 Capacity – workload

Don't underestimate the work involved in your project. Development organizations frequently report being surprised by how much work is involved in a piece of research – for managers as well as practitioners. If in-house staff are to take a leading role, this will have a major impact on their existing workload. The project must be seen as a key objective for them for the next period of time.

A number of elements of the research process can be difficult to fit in with other major commitments. The fieldwork stage is often best undertaken intensively, and analysis and writing are extremely difficult to complete if one can work on them only in fits and starts. Concentrated quiet time is essential.

4.2.4 Credibility

Will your research have credibility if it is carried out by staff of your organization? Whatever you believe about objectivity in research, the people you need to influence may wish to see someone they regard as independent taking a key role. University academics tend to be seen as independent.

On the other hand, an element of the credibility of evidence from the point of view of decision makers depends on the general reputation of the organization or individuals producing it. Where an agency is held in high regard, and known to be expert in a particular area of work, its research may be seen as having credibility.

4.2.5 Audience and level of scrutiny

It is important to consider what will be convincing to your target audience. Will the intended audience accept as valid findings that come from those you plan to carry out the research? Development workers may be better at communicating with community members or partner agencies (often important targets for research); more experienced researchers may be needed if high-level policymakers are the key target.

Politics is also a key factor. How much pressure will be placed on the integrity of the research findings? Where an issue is highly controversial, the agency needs to be very confident its findings can be defended. Even research on issues not immediately perceived as risky can draw attention. It is important that your researchers can assure the level of quality you need, given the scrutiny the piece of work will be under.

4.2.6 Methods to be used

Another issue to consider is that some research methods are more difficult to use than others and may require greater experience or expertise. Nevertheless, it is important to use the methods best suited to your research question and not to let the methodology be determined by the competencies of those concerned.

Practitioners may be familiar with interviews and group work for development purposes, but research interviewing and focus group research require a somewhat different approach and some different skills (see Chapter 11 for more on each).

In some cases, it simply does not make economic sense to expect development workers to undertake certain types of research. For example, very large-scale surveys can be carried out much more efficiently by organizations that do them frequently, which employ professional recruiters and interviewers and have systems for questionnaire design and analysis ready and waiting.

4.2.7   Benefits to the wider programme

There may be clear benefits for development organizations in undertaking research themselves. For example, if a needs assessment is undertaken as a way of consulting local people on what they hope for from a development project, it makes sense for the workers to do the work themselves. It can also have benefits further down the line, when it comes to reviewing programme impact: development workers will have a much more vivid image of the changes they hope to see. Assessments in emergency situations are a particular example of studies of this type.

4.2.8   Role confusion

However, problems might arise when people perform different roles with the same community. Where the research involves an element of evaluation of a project's work, it may be inappropriate for those responsible for delivering services to enquire about people's views of them. Service users may not feel free to make critical comment and may be afraid of jeopardizing their access to services. More subtly, if an organization is involved in providing personal support to an individual, it may be very difficult for the person to refuse to assist with any research. Ethics require that people have a free choice in whether or not to participate in research.

A broader issue about roles arises when a development worker has been engaged with a particular group of people for a while. If the worker then decides to undertake some research, she is taking up a different role in relation to these individuals, with potential long-term consequences, for example if she is trusted with sensitive information as part of her research role.

4.2.9   Capacity building

The decision to undertake research in-house or to hire in external skills also depends on whether an aim of the project is to build the capacities of staff, including local staff. Developing the skills needed to undertake research in-house can be costly, and may necessitate formal training, additional supervision and coaching. But the benefits are considerable. Where an agency wants to influence policy on the basis of its practical experience, research-type approaches provide very useful tools for capturing this experience. Many of the skills involved are also transferable from and to other areas of development work. In general, research teaches a questioning, analytical approach which is also very useful in programme management activities.

The downside of hiring in a researcher for a particular project, especially on a short-term basis, is that they leave when their contract finishes, taking with them important skills and learning which the organization needs.

Supporting national researchers in the South is a very important development aim in itself, with potentially long-term spin-offs beyond the life of any project. If you are bringing in expert researchers, it is good to ensure local staff shadow them, or that they formally train local researchers. Beware of throwing people in at the deep end, however. Plan to offer adequate support if new researchers are relatively inexperienced at research. Ensure research supervision is provided, and in particular get advice on the brief at an early stage. It may be helpful to encourage staff to register for further qualifications that include formal research training, so they have built-in support while they undertake research, if they see their careers taking this direction in the longer term.

In this decision-making process there is often a chicken-and-egg problem. The decision about who should do a project depends on the brief. However, clarifying the brief is often the first task to be undertaken. Negotiating better research briefs is a skill learnt over years of research practice. It may be worthwhile asking advice on defining the brief from an experienced researcher, while reserving judgement on who will carry out the work itself. You could pay a small fee for such advice on a consultancy basis, or seek advice from in-house research staff.

! ——————— CONSULT A RESEARCHER NOW ——————— !

4.3　Selecting and appointing external researchers

The key benefit of employing a professional researcher is obviously that they are already in possession of most of the skills you need. They have had lengthy professional training and work experience. Some may have weaker skills in terms of participation with community members, but many are learning to work in this way. Some universities now teach participatory research alongside traditional methods.

Researchers usually have strong analytical and writing skills, which others can find difficult to develop. They also have the practical skills and understand the discipline needed to record data properly and to be careful in interpreting it. You may also be able to recruit researchers who have a strong knowledge base in a particular policy area, which can take years to develop and may be crucial to positioning your research.

If you are clear that you need to bring in new people, it is important to think through the issues involved in going about doing this. Researchers are a variable breed, and whom you hire will have a major impact on the piece of work you end up with. This section looks at the process of commissioning research and describes the different ways in which you can employ researchers.

4.3.1　Employed or freelance?

One way to bring in the specialist skills or capacity you lack in order to undertake research is to hire professional researchers as regular staff members. Increasingly, as the need for research work grows, agencies find it economical to employ researchers as permanent staff. One of the virtues of this is that other staff in effect receive coaching on research methods as an ongoing part of the researcher's presence in the work team.

There are a number of issues to be considered in choosing between hiring research staff and using freelance workers or consultants, contracted to undertake specific projects.

Deciding between employed or freelance research staff: some issues to consider

- Will you still need research capacity when this project is over?
- How long will the piece of work take? Really?
- How specialized is the knowledge you need them to have?
- Over what period of time will you need to call on the researcher? This may extend into the dissemination phase.

You need to consider the market locally in terms of the supply of suitable researchers. There can be difficulty in finding researchers skilled in using qualitative or participatory methods, especially in the South, where investment in this type of skills training has been minimal. Consultants with strong skills of this sort need to be booked up early.

If you need a high level of experience, and cannot afford a high-level, full-time post in the long term, you may need to have the work done on a freelance basis. When employing freelance consultants, it is important to look into the tax situation in the country in question, and establish what your responsibilities are as a contractor. Fees (often quoted as a daily rate) asked by freelance workers tend to look high compared with salaries. This is often because self-employed people receive no contribution from employers towards any national insurance payments or pension, and must make their own arrangements to cover sickness and holidays. They also carry the expenses of their own office base. Freelancers may be good value when you need someone who can work intensively on a particular task and who has strong specific experience, skills and/or knowledge which will enable them to undertake the task efficiently.

Increasing numbers of researchers now work on a freelance/consultancy basis. However, recruitment processes can be costly and, if a sequence of research work is planned, it may be best to avoid a whole series of short appointments.

In addition to employing individual researchers, there are several other options to consider:

- academic institutions;
- think-tanks;
- commercial research agencies;
- voluntary sector research agencies;
- small research organizations – a group of consultants who work together.

It may be appropriate to set up a contract with a particular agency rather than an individual. Many, though not all, independent research agencies, including commercial ones, do high-quality work. If you decide to commission work from another organization, make sure you know who exactly will undertake the work. Sometimes, work is delegated to someone more junior than those who negotiate for the contract.

4.3.2　Working with researchers

NGOs relate to professional researchers in a number of different ways. They can simply commission work from them on a fee-for-service basis. In addition, they may suggest ideas for research to a research institute, then seek funds from research funders to carry out the work.

Most research carried out at universities is funded by funding bodies specifically oriented towards academic research. These may be governmental bodies like the ESRC or independent charities like the Wellcome Trust (on health issues). These funders rarely give grants directly to voluntary organizations to undertake research, but they encourage academics to work closely with voluntary organizations as 'research users'.

From the point of view of the voluntary organization, the important thing to remember about researchers is that they have an agenda and priorities of their own. They will be pursuing a sequence of research work in a particular area and are likely to have a distinctive perspective on the issues involved. If you do a deal with them, make sure you are happy for their agenda as well as yours to be a feature of the finished work.

Research careers are advanced primarily by publishing in academic journals and books and by giving papers at academic conferences. Many researchers are also committed to social change, and hence to disseminating their findings to practitioner and lay audiences, but they are always under pressure to give priority to academic audiences.

4.3.3　Selection processes

Appointing research staff is just like appointing staff to any job. Whether you are appointing people as staff or on a freelance basis, some sort of selection process will usually be needed.

Look for *evidence* that the researcher can produce work to the standard you require.

There are several ways of going about this – you can treat the process more like other jobs, or focus very much on the piece of work. It may be helpful to produce a person specification, in addition to the job description, to help you to focus on the particular skills and knowledge you require for the job.

Selecting the right person

- Ask candidates to show you some written materials they have produced, preferably published, which are not jointly authored with others. Younger people will have less to show, but anything written can give an indication of what the person will produce. Look for independent thinking, clarity of expression, sound, well-grounded conclusions and honesty.

- If the job includes giving presentations and persuading people of your case, ask candidates to make a short presentation as part of the interview process. Exercises like this should be as realistic as possible, without creating an unreasonable amount of work for candidates.
- If working closely with community members or other stakeholders is involved, it can be helpful to involve these people in the selection process, either in setting criteria or in taking part in the panel. They can be asked to assess in particular the candidate's attitudes and ability to communicate with people like them.
- Ask for references and take them up. Where interpersonal skills, and the skills of promoting participation, are as important as writing skills, this can be the best way of judging them. You can ask if referees can be telephoned rather than written to, and specific questions about the referee's experience of the person.
- Writing a person specification at the start of the process can help you to focus on the key skills you require. This can help you to avoid being distracted by fine qualities and impressive qualifications candidates have which may not actually be relevant to the task in hand.
- Don't be afraid to ask directly about researchers' opinions on the issues in question, or about their perspectives on research methodologies.
- Ask them to talk about an example of a piece of work they have done which involved a particular method you are interested in.
- Although attitudes and values are important to a person's suitability for a job, don't concentrate too much on this area as it can distract attention from a focus on the skills necessary to carry it out.

Experience shows that many more people are good at talking about the issues around research in an interview than are able to deliver finished work to tight deadlines. If you require the researcher to write, and they cannot show you anything which approximates the qualities you require, you should not employ them. Looking at material they have written should also help you to understand their perspective, which will be very important in how they carry out the tasks, as well as enabling you to see what quantity and quality of work they have actually produced.

4.3.4 Writing a person specification

The following items might be useful to adapt to your needs in setting a person specification for a research task.

Some possible items for a person specification for a research post/contract

- Experience of using a range of research methods/a particular method;
- Knowledge of a particular field;
- Analytical skills;

(Continued)

(Continued)

- Ability to write to a high standard/for particular audiences;
- Experience or knowledge of your type of organization;
- Excellent communication skills (verbal and written)/specify particular purpose;
- Ability to encourage participation of community members;
- Ability to work to deadlines and within budget;
- Commitment to relevant values (participatory research, equality of opportunity, children's rights, community development approaches, etc.).

As with all person specifications, if you ask for *experience* in a particular area of work, you are setting a higher, and more assessable, standard than if you ask for just *knowledge*. You need to decide whether, for example, having taken a course which covered a particular issue can be regarded as evidence of sufficient knowledge. You may want to require that people have direct experience of using a particular type of research method. However, beware of setting unrealistic person specifications.

It will be helpful to formulate points to specify the reason skills are needed. For example, 'excellent communication skills' could be broken down to specify groups of people the person should be able to interview; types of group work; negotiation skills; and the type of writing needed.

You should, of course, pursue the same types of equal opportunities employment practices as in other types of work. Only essential characteristics should appear on the person specification, as any extra ones will disqualify people who could in fact do the job. Setting exercises such as making a presentation and asking to see examples of written work should reflect the requirements of the post and focus the selection process on its specific needs.

Note that if the researcher you are employing will have significant unsupervised access to children through their job with you, you should consider child protection issues within your selection process (see Section 9.2 for more).

4.3.5 Invitations to tender

Where you are appointing someone to do a defined task, rather than to fill a post, it may be appropriate to invite a number of individuals or organizations to make proposals, saying how they would do it. You need to set a clear brief and then ask candidates to say what methods they would use to carry it out. It is worth following this procedure only for fairly large projects, as it creates quite a lot of work all around.

Some organizations do not specify the amount of money available, and ask those tendering to say how much they reckon will be needed. Others do give a figure, but ask those tendering to say what they would be able to do for that figure. From the point of view of those writing tenders, it is hard to respond if the amount of money available is not specified, as research can generally expand or contract to fit a budget.

Tendering for research work is quite an onerous task, and standard practice is to approach three or four agencies or individuals for tender. Do not make the volume of work promised in relation to the fee the main criterion – it is important to establish whether those tendering have the experience to be realistic about what can be achieved.

4.3.6 Contracts

When you employ either an organization or an individual to carry out a particular task, you need to set a contract with them to cover a number of issues, in addition to the brief for the project. The box describes the matters which need to be covered.

Research contract outline

- Tasks and responsibilities;
- Basis and timing of payment;
- Who is contracted to undertake the work;
- Fee;
- Expenses;
- Status and liability (tax issues);
- Insurance;
- Consultant's obligations;
- Employer's obligations;
- Confidentiality;
- Whose property the data are;
- Termination of contract;
- Copyright.

Some issues from this list which require particular thought include the following.

Tasks and responsibilities

This specifies exactly who is responsible for which tasks. This is a matter of putting on paper your assumptions, to ensure these are clear from the start. In addition to the core research tasks, include other important aspects. For example, do you require the final report from the researcher in electronic copy? Will any administrative support be available to the research staff?

Ownership of outputs and data

Organizations often expect to own reports and data generated in research they pay for, in which case the researcher/author must seek permission to use information elsewhere. Researchers like to own knowledge and ideas they feel they have created. Respondents, too, have a right to the information they have given. Conflicts can arise, with often no clear-cut answer.

Where published material is in the public domain, whoever has paid to have it written, or to publish it, may reasonably expect to have copyright. Sometimes, authors and commissioners share copyright. Researchers should negotiate in advance with the organization if they wish to be able to publish elsewhere.

Meanwhile, in terms of raw data, organizations often want ownership, so they can use it in later exercises. But do not assume your organization owns the data generated for a study. From the point of view of respondents' confidentiality, it may be appropriate for the researcher to own the data, although the employing organization is likely to want access. There can also be issues of confidentiality and integrity: researchers may be best placed to ensure that data are not taken out of context. Thus, it might be useful to build in some requirement that, if data are used for other purposes, some check be made with the researchers.

Where confidentiality is not a concern, for example where the data are in effect already in the public domain, as in a participatory research exercise, it may be appropriate to take steps to ensure a community group retains control. Communities have protested at researchers taking away information they have participated in gathering and need for their own purposes, for example to make a case for funding on a specific element of an investigation such as access to clean water.

4.4 Managing costs and time

Common pitfall

'Perhaps the most common practical mistake in research proposals is to grossly underestimate the budget in time and money required for a project. [...] Research budgets that allow no room for manoeuvre, or for any mistakes, can create significant problems' (Hakim, 2000)

A crucial part of planning is to sort out the timescale for the research and the costs it will incur. It is a safe bet that, when you think it through, you'll realize a piece of research will cost more than you had hoped. Time and money are tied up together – more of one can be used to balance less of the other, and vice versa.

So let us start with time, returning to other aspects of costing research later in this section. A research project involves a series of tasks which are quite different from each other but may overlap in time and interrelate in a complex way. It is worth working out a detailed 'work plan' at the start. The first draft of this should form part of the brief; it should be updated when you know more about your team and any constraints.

A work plan is like a timetable, but breaks down the activities involved to show the timing and duration of each. You may not be able to stick to it exactly, but at least it gives you a way of looking ahead at the consequences if things start to slip. It also gets everyone on the same page at the start of a project, so each team member knows their own schedule and objectives, as well as those of others (Lewis, 2010).

A number of software packages can be used to prepare and monitor work plan implementation. Microsoft Project Manager, Excel and Lotus are among the most commonly used. One of the most common types of work plan is a Gantt chart. This planning tool shows the order in which various tasks must be completed and the duration of each. More complex ones will tell you the resources (including people hours) needed for each activity, so you can plan team inputs and cash flow, and also what 'dependencies' exist between different tasks (which activities must be done before you can begin others).

Table 4.2 shows a Gantt chart for one kind of research process, to give an idea of how to plan research work. It gives possible timescales for a typical (fictional) medium-sized qualitative study using focus groups to clarify the key issues and then in-depth interviews for the main data collection. It is not intended to be prescriptive either of the activities involved or of the time taken for them.

Table 4.2   Research planning timetable

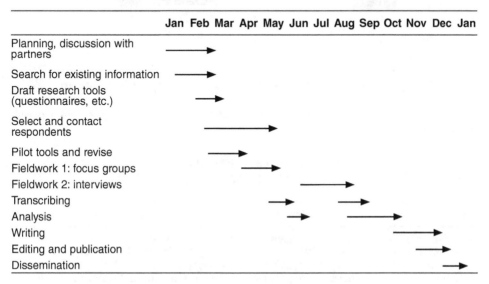

	Jan Feb Mar Apr May Jun Jul Aug Sep Oct Nov Dec Jan
Planning, discussion with partners	
Search for existing information	
Draft research tools (questionnaires, etc.)	
Select and contact respondents	
Pilot tools and revise	
Fieldwork 1: focus groups	
Fieldwork 2: interviews	
Transcribing	
Analysis	
Writing	
Editing and publication	
Dissemination	

Gantt charts are useful for planning research in real time – that is, they estimate how long the different stages of the process will actually take to carry out. Another way of planning work is to draw up a 'work schedule' to estimate how many days' work each stage will take. This is particularly useful for working out costs.

Table 4.3 gives an example work schedule. The different elements can take very variable lengths of time, so boxes are left empty for you to fill in.

Table 4.3   Work schedule

Task	Time required	People required	Costs
Clarifying the focus, setting questions			
Literature survey			
Drafting research tools			
Pilot study			
Selecting and contacting respondents			
Fieldwork			
Transcribing (if needed)			
Analysis			
Report writing			
Commenting and editing			
Design and printing			
Presentations			
Total			

Planning for a participatory poverty analysis in Vietnam

Below is a real example of a planning grid for a participatory poverty analysis (PPA) exercise in Vietnam.

Tentative work schedule for PPA in Ho Chi Minh City
(deadline for final report: 30 June 1999)

Dates	Duration	Activity/event
1–12 February	2 weeks	Preparations for initial PPA workshop
22–4 February	3 days	Meetings to introduce and discuss PPA with city and district officials and to researchers
1–19 March	3 weeks	Preparations for PPAs in three (or two) poor districts (two wards per district): permits, logistics, teams, team leaders ...
22–4 March	3 days	Training of three PPA teams
29 March–9 April	**2 weeks**	**PPA in Ward A (three districts simultaneously)**
12–23 April	**2 weeks**	**PPA in Ward B (three districts simultaneously)**
26 April–8 May	2 weeks	Writing up
10–23 May	2 weeks	Translation of reports: as reports get out, start translation as early as possible
24–31 May	1 week	Review of reports and recommendations for synthesis report
1–30 June	4 weeks	Synthesis report
		Poverty workshop (after the summer)

The time taken for many of these tasks depends in part on who undertakes them. Experienced researchers will be more adept at avoiding problems and will certainly find tasks like analysis and writing much easier than people without such experience. However, it may be important to encourage a wider group of staff and indeed community members to learn research-related skills. In this case, it will be necessary to allow time for them to make their mistakes and put them right again. Where training is part of the objectives of a research project, it will be necessary to schedule time for this, even if it is not to be undertaken in any formal way.

There is more detailed guidance on planning time and resources for research projects in Chapter 3. This section concentrates on person-time over the life of the project.

4.4.1 The search for existing information

Some of the most valuable information may be available only with some effort. You may need to visit donor agencies or research institutes, or contact other researchers, both of which take time. Sometimes, people will need to be talked into assisting you. It is also important to set deadlines for literature search work.

4.4.2 Planning and drafting research tools

This takes time, as all questionnaires and other tools need to be thought about very carefully and to go through many drafts before they are complete. Piloting is also nearly always a good idea. Designing a questionnaire can take anything from eight to 24 hours.

4.4.3 Contacting respondents

'Negotiating access' is a piece of researchers' jargon which refers to the process of getting permission to approach people, or indeed to use archive material or unpublished official statistics, as part of the research process. Discussions of sampling tend to sound as if you as the researcher were swooping down from on high to pluck those you select out of a pool of willing participants … – if only!

> **Tip**
>
> Making contact with respondents is one of the most variable elements in the time research takes – it can both involve a lot of work and be slow to sort itself out.

When we set out on a research project, our own enthusiasm often makes it difficult to remember that others, whether local community members or staff of partner agencies, will not always readily wish to be involved. People meet your research project with expectations of their own, which you cannot guess. There is often some suspicion of your motives, and there is always competition for people's time. Do not underestimate the work involved in gaining people's trust and cooperation.

Referring to international NGO research, Pratt and Loizos (1992) argue:

The right of an agency to operate in another country depends upon the will of the host country. Permission to do research should normally 'have' been part of a Country Agreement which set out the conditions under which the development agency operates. If for some reason research has been omitted from the agreement, or had conditions attached to it, then negotiations might have to be undertaken with an appropriate Ministry to get permission to do research. If political conditions in the country generally, or in the area you are working in, are good, and your agency has a positive image with the relevant Ministry, research permission should be readily forthcoming. But if the country is riven by bitter internal conflicts, or your agency is operating in a climate of mistrust or suspicion, then a relatively simple research project may present itself to official minds as a major diplomatic issue, and you will need all your patience, tact and persuasiveness to get the project accepted. Under such difficult conditions, research sometimes simply 'isn't on'.

Alternatively, you make take the view that anything which is not explicitly forbidden by your Country Agreement, and which is covered by your general statement of agency aims, is clearly defensible, and go ahead with your research without seeking official clearance. This strategy might initially save you time and trouble. But be prepared for misunderstandings, and be ready to explain your research in a calm, and diplomatic way if an anxious and ill-informed official – from the police, for example – decides that you are engaged in some form of spying activity, or something else harmful to the interests of the government. Social researchers are used to having their inquiries misunderstood.

It is a better tactic, if you want to make a rapid start and cut through the red tape, to notify your most friendly senior contacts in an appropriate Ministry informally that you wish to do some research on a specific topic – agricultural productivity, or mother-child health issues – in a particular locality. Then, in the event of misunderstandings, you can say to inquirers 'Mr X and Mrs Y at the Ministry know what we are doing here, and can tell you about our work'.

What goes for governments also goes for all kinds of other organizations whose permission you may need to carry out your research. In some cases, there may be formal procedures for the granting of permission to carry out research. Universities also have ethics committees to scrutinize their own research. In addition, a decision will need to be made by the senior managers of the organization in question – yet another reason to involve partner agencies at an early stage. Informal authorities within the community can also of course throw up barriers to research.

At the community level, there can be hurdles to be overcome, usually in terms of persuading 'gatekeepers' (who may be village leaders or official organizations), who control access to other people, of the value of the research. Gatekeepers hold power in different ways – they may be a government minister, the local doctor, the village chief or a respected older woman. The (reasonable) cynicism of ordinary people in impoverished areas towards those claiming to help them can be reflected in barriers thrown up by their leaders. This can entirely block a piece of research if they are unsympathetic to it. It is better to take the time needed to win over any authorities whose permission you require to undertake your work.

Sometimes, it is best to establish an intermediary – a local person with useful contacts and a range of expertise concerning power relations and key players in the local community. Indeed, it is typical practice for both aid workers and field researchers to employ such contacts – often called 'fixers' – who can offer project support in everything from basic logistics to the valuable local introductions, cultural advice and guidance outside researchers routinely need to navigate through such gatekeepers.

On the other hand, development projects may have no problem at all contacting respondents if they plan to do their research with a community they already know through their existing service provision. However, if the research concerns a sensitive subject (for example mental health, money, domestic violence), people may still be reluctant to take part, even if they have some trust in those initiating the project. Time will need to be taken to put people's minds at rest.

The preparatory work involved in organizing any sort of research should not be underestimated.

4.4.4 Participatory research

It is extremely common for reports on participatory research projects to emphasize the need for time to be allowed to win the trust of those taking part and for participants to gain the confidence to act assertively within the research. Where a strong practice base already exists, this may be less of an issue, but where new relationships need to be forged, it will take time for communities' (reasonable) cynicism to be overcome.

Participating in research can be stressful for people, for a variety of reasons. In particular, if the issues to be researched are close to home for those involved, and perhaps still painful for them, time needs to be allowed to assist them in coping in a positive way with the feelings that arise.

4.4.5 Fieldwork

A half-hour interview takes about half an hour to arrange plus the time to get there – remember to allow enough travelling time. If you are not filling in a questionnaire at the time, allow another hour to write up your interview notes. Many interviews take longer, and interviewers also need to spend time with respondents before and after to ensure they understand the research and are comfortable with it. It is a good idea to allow time between early interviews or focus groups to reflect on the process and make adjustments.

Arranging a focus group with ten participants can take about an hour and a half where telephones can be used, and much longer where they are not. The time taken for interviews depends on the type of interview – whether you want simple quantitative information or more in-depth responses. About four to six straightforward interviews of up to 45 minutes, three longer qualitative interviews or two one to one-and-a-half hour focus groups can be completed in a day.

Do not schedule too much fieldwork for each day – it becomes impossible to listen properly after a certain point, and the quality of the information collected will suffer. Group work is more tiring than individual interviews.

It is important to fit in with people's schedules, so you may be able to conduct interviews only in the evenings or afternoons or on days off. There may also be a seasonal cycle which means people are extremely busy at some times of year and much freer at others. For any research where trust is needed, it is good to call on people at home or in their workplace to ask whether they will take part – this also takes time.

The business of actually contacting respondents can be particularly fraught with difficulty when working with disadvantaged groups. People who have many demands on their time may break or forget appointments. Your research is not their priority. Allow some time for the likelihood that some planned arrangements will fail and you may need to go back to complete an interview.

4.4.6 Recording data

Time must be allowed for this, whatever method of recording you are using. Data that are not recorded during or very soon after an interview or focus group are lost.

The only way to get a verbatim version of what people actually said in an interview or focus group is to record it and transcribe it. An hour of recorded speech can take anything from four to eight hours to transcribe. If the researcher present at the interview is a good typist, it is helpful if they do the transcribing – it is more difficult to hear accurately what people said if you were not present at the time. It is also possible to get transcribing done by freelance typists who specialize in this. It can be a false economy to ask in-house administrative staff to transcribe tapes unless you brief them very well on exactly how you want it done. Voice recognition software may be another option in the near future, but is currently unsuitable for interviews or group work, being able to only transcribe one voice at a time (Matheson, 2007). Whoever does the transcription, expect to check the transcript carefully and make corrections.

Transcribing is a lot of work. An alternative method is to listen to the recordings and take notes, and then to transcribe the most interesting passages. If you do not record your data, you need to allow time throughout the fieldwork for notes to be written up.

4.4.7 Data entry

In large surveys, it takes substantial time to 'clean' (sort out inconsistencies in) and organize the data for analysis, whether by hand or by computer.

4.4.8 Analysis/interpretation

Allow time for this! People often forget about it when planning research, and it is a crucial part of the process. It is a separate process from writing, and qualitative analysis especially can be very time consuming; with quantitative research, it is the data coding and entry and sorting out of any problems that emerge which takes the time – the actual analysis can be very quick. Qualitative analysis requires continual reflection on the categories used and the management of large amounts of text. It is not a process which can be rushed without seriously compromising quality.

4.4.9 Writing

Again, this needs to be given time. Someone will almost certainly need to take a solid stretch of time with few other responsibilities to write up a research project of any scale. One consultant allows about half the time allocated to fieldwork to write up the report. Thus, if data collection takes four weeks, at least two will be needed to write the report. Others think that analysis and writing together can be reckoned to take about the same length of time as data collection. This obviously varies with the volume and complexity of the data and how much analysis and writing are done during the fieldwork. It also depends on the level of stakeholder engagement and how many people provide comments on drafts, which take time to incorporate.

4.4.10 Estimating research costs

Working out the costs of a research project is never easy. With experience, researchers get better at it, but advice should always be sought from someone who has undertaken a similar project. Very often, the situation is more that you have to work out what can be done for the money you have available or you think you can obtain.

! ————————— CONSULT A RESEARCHER NOW! ————————— !

Salaries or fees are the largest part of the cost for any such project. The guidance above on working out a work plan for a piece of research will give help in calculating these. However, some important other costs may need to be taken into account.

Possible costs of research projects

- Research wages or fees;
- Interpreters, translators for research materials or data;
- Travel and subsistence expenses of researchers, including visas for international travel;
- Premises; venue hire;
- Payments to community researchers and respondents;
- Computer hardware and/or software;
- Training for staff and/or community participants;
- Purchasing books, journals and other reference material, fees for use of libraries;
- Digital voice recorders, batteries, microphones, headsets, etc.;
- Transcribing costs;
- Administrative assistance;
- Administrative costs, for example phone calls, postage;
- Costs of advertising to contact potential respondents;
- Flipcharts and other visual aids for group work;
- Data analysis – it can be sensible to pay someone to analyse statistical data, but they need to be involved earlier as well;
- Advisory group travel and other costs;
- Printing and publication;
- Making findings accessible, for example translation, short simple versions, child-friendly versions, multimedia products (audiovisual and online), Braille, etc;
- Advertising and distributing the results, for example printing flyers, holding workshops, launch events, webpages;
- Other dissemination costs, for example travel to events, conference fees.

What you need to spend also depends on what you already have in the way of equipment and what you can do without. Staff costs are generally the largest item: if spending on other items can save staff time, it may well be worthwhile. For example, if paying incentives to respondents means an adequate sample can be contacted in a shorter time, savings may be made on salaries wasted during time otherwise spent being unable to proceed with fieldwork.

A note on overheads

The term 'overheads' refers to all the costs you incur simply by being there, whatever it is that you are doing – rent, heat and light, phone rental and someone to answer the phone, someone to pay wages and keep track of finances, management costs, etc.

Financing overhead costs is often a huge headache for voluntary organizations. Funders like to see concrete results for their money, and prefer to fund only specific projects, not the general costs of running an organization.

In a large organization, the overhead costs of research projects, which can be relatively low, may be able to be absorbed into general running costs met from central funds. Small agencies are likely to need to specifically allow for a contribution towards overhead costs. You can work out overheads in two ways; it is worth considering which will be most attractive to anyone you are applying to for funding. One approach is to specify in detail what you will be spending the money on. The other is to add a percentage to the overall cost of the specific project. Some UK universities add 40 per cent or more to grant applications, others 15 or 25 per cent. Some funders refuse to pay any overhead costs on research grants; others set a ceiling on the percentage they are willing to pay. It is generally worth finding out a funder's attitude towards overhead costs before submitting a proposal to them.

Table 4.4 shows a hypothetical budget template for a short-term research project in a Southern context.

Table 4.4 Sample budget template

Reimbursables and communications	Rate	Units/persons per site	Person days per site	Sites	Amount
Venue		1	n/a	3	
Project coordinator		1	8	3	
Junior researcher		2	8	3	
Staff per diems		3	8	3	
Digital recorders (3 sets of 2)		2	n/a	3	
Local/village guide		1	8	3	
Respondent reimbursements		27	n/a	3	
Translation transcripts (5 pages)		18	n/a	3	
Subtotal					

4.5 Supervising researchers

As discussed above, research projects need two types of supervision:

- management supervision – overall monitoring of progress towards the aims and objectives of the research;
- research supervision by an experienced researcher, advising on methodology and ensuring quality standards for research are met.

These may, or may not, be given by the same person. It may be appropriate to make special arrangements for research supervision with an external agency, or another part of a large agency, where the line manager is not able to provide this. It is possible to build into a research project the provision of research supervision on a consultancy basis, or it may be that an appropriate person at a local university will be able to offer supervision as part of their post. Even if this is done, however, the line manager should not relax! *Management* supervision is still key to ensuring the agency's aims are met by the research.

Research is a specialized area, and if researchers are to learn from their work and do it effectively, they need contact with others in their profession, as well as those they work with on a day-to-day basis. A research supervisor can also assist the researcher in keeping the project in touch with related work elsewhere.

One role of a research supervisor is to encourage self-reflection about the researcher's own role in the research, for example the impact their gender, background or manner may have on the research process. It should be possible to talk about the emotional impact research can have, and to unpack what this may mean for the work. (See Section 3.1 for more on objectivity and reflexivity.)

Table 4.5 suggests a possible division of labour between management and research supervisors, if these jobs are not performed by the same person.

Table 4.5   Management and research supervision

Management supervision	Research/professional supervision
In cooperation with the researcher to ...	
• Clarify aims and objectives • Ensure proper links are made with senior managers within the organization, facilitating wider use of the research • Ensure steady progress towards aims and objectives • Set timescales and targets • Deal with resources issues • Manage research advisory groups • Facilitate links with partner agencies • Support participatory processes • Support the process of working out recommendations from findings • Ensure feedback to policymakers and/or community members is in an appropriate format	• Ensure professional standards are met in research practice • Assist with identifying relevant literature • Assist in making links beyond the immediate area with relevant researchers and others • Draw on experience to assist in planning timescales • Advise on research methods • Ensure people with appropriate knowledge are invited onto advisory groups • Consider emotional responses to the research process and their consequences • Advise on methods of analysis • Assist in dealing with ethical dilemmas • Assist with any writing for academic audiences

Where different people provide managerial and research supervision, it will be useful for them to meet from time to time, to consolidate plans and ensure everyone is working towards the same ends.

Researchers are often independent spirits and may expect to work rather separately from others. But in research for development, it is important that projects keep in touch with the broader work of the organization and that learning occurs in both directions. Further, it may be important to involve partner agencies – managers who are also involved with the practice side may find this easier to facilitate. If partners are involved at an early stage, it is more likely they will be influenced by the findings.

Supervision should not be strongly directive in terms of how objectives are fulfilled, but should keep an eye on the larger picture. The supervisor needs to support the researcher in sorting out a sound methodology for the project.

Where a development practitioner is managing a researcher, the former can be confident they have a legitimate, and indeed crucial, role in relation to a research project. However skilled and experienced researchers are, they come to any project from a different perspective to that of development workers, who are permanently committed to their particular area of work. Development workers need to ensure a piece of work meets *their* needs.

Managing research for development work effectively

First, check the brief is appropriate, especially the aims and objectives, output and outcome indicators and research questions,
Matters for ongoing monitoring:

- Progress towards aims and objectives is going well.
- A set of 'milestones' along the way – interim reports, etc. – is planned and achieved.
- Written materials (make sure the final report is not the first thing you see) are clearly expressed and appropriate to their audience.
- Appropriate partner agencies have been informed or involved, and all stakeholders are kept informed of progress.
- An advisory group is convened as appropriate.
- Formalities have been observed, such as informing local authorities of the work.
- Reports include an appropriate balance between description and analysis.
- Draft recommendations meet the agency's needs. How are recommendations to be arrived at? Is consultation on these planned – and appropriate?
- Ethical standards are being upheld. Are procedures for obtaining consent and ensuring confidentiality working well?

Finally, remember to give positive feedback to the researcher whenever possible – research can be a lonely business. Researchers generally welcome the interest and involvement of development workers and managers.

4.5.1　Managing freelance consultants

Freelance consultants are employed in relation to the task, not to time spent on work. The relationship with them is different in some respects, but it is best to think of them as employees in terms of providing support and supervision.[1]

Checklist: getting the best from freelance consultants

☑ Give them space to advise you on matters of method and style – let them draw on their experience – while you keep an eye on your objectives.
☑ Expect to work closely with them – meet them regularly.

> ☑ Work out a series of deadlines for the completion of elements of the task, in discussion with the consultant, and take the schedule seriously.
> ☑ Include deadlines for interim reports and require a draft final report well before the absolute final deadline.
> ☑ Tie payments to tasks rather than time, where reasonable.
> ☑ Set out clearly to whom they are accountable, and expect to offer supervision.
> ☑ And, once again, make sure the brief is clear and achievable.

Employers of freelancers dread paying them a lot of money and then not getting the product they hoped for. The guidelines above should protect them from this. If a trusting relationship is developed, the freelancer will inform the employer of any problems arising in meeting the brief, just as an employee would.

The employing organization is best protected by a contract which ties payment of fees to the performance of particular tasks rather than to time spent on the job. For example, an element of the fee might be paid only on delivery of a satisfactory final draft of a report. However, freelancers have to eat too: it is reasonable to pay some of the fee upfront. With large tasks over long periods, a regular payment is a reasonable arrangement, although clear deadlines should be set for the delivery of particular tasks.

Development agencies report consultants producing a draft, comments being collected and then huge delays occurring in getting the changes incorporated into the report. This can be anticipated by writing the process of incorporating agreed changes resulting from readers' comments explicitly into the brief. The consultant allows time for it, is paid to do it and sees it as part of the brief, not as an extra. If this process is expected to be particularly time consuming, it may be appropriate to tie an element of the fee to completing it to the agency's satisfaction.

4.5.2 Managing unsatisfactory performance

What do you do when a researcher, either employed or freelance, is producing unsatisfactory work? As in all things, prevention is better than cure. At the risk of repeating points made elsewhere, this checklist gives guidelines.

> ### Checklist: avoiding problems with research staff[2]
>
> ☑ Write a clear brief.
> ☑ Make a good match between the skills needed and the person appointed.
> ☑ Get evidence of the candidate's skills before making an appointment.
> ☑ Ensure a clear line of accountability and decision making for the project.
> ☑ Give both management and research supervision regularly. Agree objectives with all staff members at the start of a project and conduct regular performance appraisals.
> ☑ Break down the tasks necessary – in large projects ask for interim progress reports.
>
> *(Continued)*

(Continued)

☑ Give encouragement and support as well as critical comment.
☑ If it appears a task is being avoided, discuss it in detail. Research involves many different processes and people may lack confidence in some areas.
☑ Make sure material is written up as the process goes along – do not allow researchers to leave all the writing to the end.
☑ If hiring on a freelance basis, tie some element of the payments to tangible products.
☑ Ensure contracts made with consultants enable you to cease their employment if their work does not reach adequate standards.

Dealing with problems once they are evident involves the same managerial process as for any other staff. It is essential to pick up on problems early, and to communicate to the person very clearly exactly what it is you want to change. Give the person a chance to explain what the problem looks like from their point of view. Aim for an agreed, timetabled plan to set things right.

One scenario involves a researcher writing a report that is very different from what those who commissioned the work hoped for. The first step needs to lie in giving comments to the researcher and asking her to make changes. However, where the problem is great, experience shows that a long period of stagnation can follow. Make sure you set clear deadlines and follow up if nothing has happened. Researchers usually do the best they can on their first attempt, and it is likely they will have difficulty producing something very different from their first draft. Assess the scale of the problem and, if necessary, pay whatever is due for the work done to date, take the work back and give it to someone else.

 ## Key points from this chapter

Checklist: research management

☑ Make sure you understand what a funder wants from its grant giving, and exactly what its remit is, before you write an application.
☑ Keep funders involved and informed. Agree at the start the format and frequency of ongoing contact.
☑ Establish clear lines of accountability, preferably to individuals rather than groups.
☑ Set up appropriate research and managerial supervision arrangements.
☑ If necessary, buy in professional research supervision.
☑ Establish regular liaison to ensure confusion does not arise between the advisory group, any external supervisor and the line manager.
☑ In deciding who should undertake the work, balance the needs of the particular project with the need to build research skills in your organization.
☑ If appointing external researchers, look for *evidence* of a candidate's abilities.

☑ Write a person specification as well as a brief, to help you focus on the post's needs.
☑ Write a work plan and return regularly to it to check on progress.
☑ Provide management *and* research supervision to researchers.
☑ Freelance consultants also require supervision: set out a series of deadlines, including for interim reports if appropriate.
☑ Establish a carefully considered and realistic budget plan.

This chapter has considered the issues involved in deciding how to undertake a piece of research, including *who* should undertake it. Costs and benefits of using in-house development workers and of hiring new researchers are considered. A skills framework for research work is presented to help in making these decisions. We have also discussed how to go about appointing new staff or consultants, how to plan their work, including the costs and timings involved, and how to provide supervision. Time spent upfront in careful planning, plus regular oversight, should help you avoid problems.

 # Further reading

Gosling, L. with Edwards, M. (2003) *Toolkits: A Practical Guide to Planning, Monitoring, Evaluation and Impact Assessment*. London: Save the Children UK.

See especially Tool 8 (page 262), which gives guidance on using consultants.

Lewis, J. (2010) *Project Planning, Scheduling and Control,* 5th edn. New York: McGraw Hill.

A beginners' guide to project management, describing best practice in taking a team through each project stage, including the design phase, planning, implementation and monitoring and evaluation.

Moore, N. (2006) *How to Do Research: The Practical Guide to Designing and Managing Research Projects*, 3rd edn. London: Facet.

Provides clear, helpful guidance on designing and managing a research project, including day-to-day project requirements, and comprehensive discussions on funding proposals, budgeting and the use of in-house research, subcontractors and team management. Aimed at professionals undertaking research and evaluation and undergraduate and postgraduate students.

ReStore 'The Managing Research Projects Toolkit'. Available online at www.restore. ac.uk/mrp/services/ldc/mrp/resources/resproskills.

Online toolkit developed by the ESRC's Research Development Initiative. Designed around interactive web modules for researchers at all levels of experience to build their own knowledge of collaborative research team building and development.

Roper, L. (2002) 'Achieving successful academic–practitioner research collaborations', *Development in Practice*, 12 (3–4): 338–45.

Identifies several common impediments to academic–NGO collaborations and proposes several different collaborative models and practical recommendations to eliminate such tensions and ensure longer-lasting relationships.

Tarling, R. (2006) *Managing Social Research: A Practical Guide.* London: Routledge.

A guide to the practical aspects of managing a research project, including managing stakeholders, applying for funding, negotiating contracts, managing research staff and project planning.

Notes

1 Tool 8 in Gosling and Edwards (2003).
2 For a good introduction to best practice processes for managing staff performance, see Pettinger et al. (2007).

5

REVIEWING EXISTING EVIDENCE

5.1 How to look

Please read this chapter! Development workers may feel their own local community's experience is the most important thing, and the prospect of searching out existing information on an issue may not make them happy. But research is greatly strengthened by placing your new information in the context of what is already known.

Researchers call this process a literature search, survey, review or study. 'The literature' refers to all the available research on a subject. A search locates the material and a survey simply describes the existing literature. A review or study critically assesses the information collected and makes sense of it in relation to your own research questions.

A good literature review is a key feature in a good-quality piece of research. It guards against duplication of work already done and justifies the choice of focus. It should also enrich the arguments to be made from the new material and add authority to the whole exercise. Sometimes, a whole project is essentially a literature review – mobilizing existing information to answer new questions.

Development organizations often find it difficult to take the time to carry out a literature review on an issue. Going to a library and searching the internet do not look like 'proper work' in the way other activities might. But it really is worth it! The time, and any money, you may spend, for example on key texts in the area, will certainly be repaid by the weight added to your final report. Meanwhile, if you fail to identify key information on your issue, it will be obvious to others that you are not on top of the existing research material. This can be highly discrediting when you come to use your own findings to argue your case.

Common pitfalls

Ignoring important existing research which could support (or undermine) your case – publishing your new research findings in isolation

Of course, the difficulty of identifying and locating relevant information will vary greatly depending on where you are based and how organized and accessible information sources are. Some countries have desperately inadequate libraries and research resources, and it is a real struggle to get information. But do not assume no information exists because the local area you work in is very poor or because libraries are not readily available. Ask for help from someone located closer to good information sources. The growth in internet availability in the developing world, as well as the increasing accessibility of journals and books online, is opening up new possibilities for research in poorer areas (see Section 5.3 on using the internet for research and Appendix 2 for a list of useful websites).[1]

5.1.1 Taking a critical approach

Think carefully about where to look for relevant information. Only some sorts of knowledge make it onto databases and into libraries. If you want to locate research that validates the knowledge of people like those you are working with, you will have to search hard. In this, informal networks sometimes work better than libraries; however, sometimes the traditional methods work really well – it is always worth a try.

Stubbs (1999) proposes the following criteria for reading 'the literature' for her research:

1 Are the 'facts' reliable, can they be trusted? How do you know?
2 Are the facts really facts – what definitions (for example of disability) are used?
3 Are key concepts examined critically?
4 Are concepts considered from a cross-cultural perspective?
5 Have key concepts been exported from the North and transplanted uncritically into other cultures?
6 Are the perspectives of key stakeholders represented?
7 If the writers are 'outsiders', do they write with a self-critical awareness?
8 Is the issue of ownership, participation in and control of research addressed?
9 Is local knowledge and practice acknowledged and drawn on?
10 Is there a discussion of power and resource issues in relation to global development, including the role and status of multilateral and bilateral agencies?

Stubbs was seeking information on the education of disabled children in the South and found that much of the material her literature search threw up was problematic. She warns against 'building towers on quicksand': often, the same few academic writers are quoted over and over again and their work takes on what may be undue authority.

It is important to locate a writer's approach within the field by considering their theoretical assumptions, the sources they cite and the policy prescriptions they favour (Blaxter et al., 2010).[2] This will enable you to see patterns in the material and decide how much weight to give their work.

Be attentive to what is *not* there too. Do not be swept along into the traditional way of seeing an issue just because that is what the literature concentrates on – if you want to develop a new perspective, you may have to do it without much support.

5.1.2   Putting your work on the map

It is important to deposit your own reports, and those of Southern partner agencies, in national 'copyright libraries' such as the British Library and the US Library of Congress, which are supposed to hold everything that is in print, as well as in relevant specialist and university libraries. Getting an International Standard Book Number (ISBN) for publications, and generally making sure they 'exist' for the wider world, is really worthwhile. Otherwise, existing research may continue to be inaccessible to researchers. ISBN numbers are issued by different national agencies worldwide, such as the ISBN Agency for the UK and the Republic of Ireland and R.R. Bowker LLC for the USA. Contact information for agencies in other countries can be found on the International ISBN Agency website (www.isbn-international.org/agency). The fee varies by country – it is \$125 for a number in the USA, for instance.

You should also consider whether and how to use the internet to publish your work. Think carefully about who you want to read your work, and which websites, online journals and blogs will have the most credibility among your target audience. If you are undertaking the work on behalf of an organization, check they are happy to make the work accessible on the web (see http://cloud2.gdnet.org/cms.php?id=disseminating_research_online). Also, be aware that subscription fees and copyright laws can prevent many, particularly those in poorer countries, from accessing work published in professional and academic journals.

5.1.3   Challenges in conducting a good literature review

The challenges of conducting a good review of development research must be understood in the context of how contemporary social science research is carried out and disseminated.

1   **Going beyond internet search engines:** the internet has revolutionized how research is conducted. You only need a couple of keywords and you are a click away from thousands of pieces of information. However, the quality of this information needs to be scrutinized carefully. A blind search may turn up large amounts of poor-quality or distracting information. Specialized search functions, such as Google's dedicated search engine for academic publications – Google Scholar – can help, but you should remain aware of this limitation (see also Section 5.3). Also, especially when dealing with theoretical contributions, don't forget the classics and seminal works on your research interests, which may not be online!

2   **Beyond English:** English is the working language of much academic research. However, knowledge generation has become ever more unequally distributed, with knowledge produced and disseminated in languages other than English seldom incorporated into mainstream academic circles. If the issue focuses on a specific country or region, reading in the local language is a valuable asset in mapping research produced locally.

3   **Taking the diversity of knowledge production into account:** development research is now produced and disseminated through several types of organizations, not only academic ones. Think-tanks, multilateral banks and private foundations are

among those commissioning and producing development research. Their products may not reach a library, so you need to diversify your search to find them.

4 **Going beyond methodological divisions in current social science research:** over the past two decades, a division of labour has become clear between quantitative and qualitative scholars, resulting in a shortage of exchange between the two. Recent calls for triangulation and mixed methods have created room for dialogue, but you might need to look hard to obtain research on an issue using different types of methods, especially because some journals or conferences welcome only studies based on a specific method or technique.

5 **Development research crosses disciplines:** development research combines contributions from a range of disciplines, including economics, sociology, political science and anthropology. Therefore, looking only at development-specific journals may mean you miss interesting contributions from other fields. The same can be said for region-specific journals.

5.1.4 How to conduct a literature review

Four steps are discussed below: getting organized, focusing your literature review, systematizing the results and writing up the literature review.

Step 1: Getting organized

Perhaps it is obvious that you need to create a record-keeping system for the information you gather. You need to be able to share what you find with colleagues and to find it again yourself easily. Also, your readers should be able to trace each item you cite from the reference you give. Proper referencing is part of your accountability – it enables others to check your claims for themselves. The references in this book follow the conventions you should use.

It may be tedious to write down or electronically record all these details but don't think you can avoid it or get anyone else to do it, and don't put it off! As soon as you start reading, start taking notes, and above all keep exact information on all the sources you use. There is nothing as time wasting as having to trace your references all over again when you come to write up your work because you did not keep good enough records.

Most people nowadays store records of their references on the computer, using spreadsheets, databases or specialized software. Those without access to a computer or who prefer to do without it can use the traditional file card system. In each case, the principles are the same: you need to keep the standard set of information required to give a proper bibliographic reference. It is also helpful to give each item some key words so you can search or sort by subject later. And you may want to write some notes to remind yourself what was interesting to you about it, or who suggested looking at it. Again, these things are remarkably difficult to remember later on.

For a project of any scale, it is really worth having easy, regular access to a computer to regularly enter and check information as you accumulate references. The computer makes it easy to search for relevant material, sort references alphabetically or by date or simply look up an individual record. You have also got the typing over with and can draw directly on your computerized records when you come to write up your report. If you don't have or don't want to use a specially designed software package, you can create a suitable database in any database package. You could also use a word processing program or spreadsheet, although a database is more flexible.

What information must be kept? Table 5.1 shows the key material needed.

Table 5.1 Sample layout for a reference spreadsheet

Last name	First name	Year of publication	Title	Publisher	Edition	ISBN	Location or link	Notes
Tarling	Roger J.	2006	Managing Social Research: A Practical Guide	London: Routledge	1st	978-0415355162	Class mark in library or online link	

For journal articles, it is important to include the volume and issue number as well as the exact date and page numbers for the article itself. Articles in edited collections need to be referenced alongside full details of the books in which they are found. The format of your references must be consistent throughout, using any one of a range of referencing 'traditions' in social research scholarship, as outlined by several influential 'style guides' – but always check first with your organization to see if a particular style is recommended, and look at recent publications by your organization. Most referencing traditions derive from or combine one of two distinct styles proposed by the Chicago Manual of Style or Harvard referencing. The specifics of formatting may differ, but in general you should decide between one of these two broad traditions. Table 5.2 outlines the basic differences between two of the most common referencing styles used in social science research.

Table 5.2 Referencing styles

Style	Notes	Example
Harvard	'Parenthetical referencing'. The author, publication date and page number (where appropriate) are included, within parenthesis, in the text itself. Full references are provided at the end of the article, in alphabetical order.	In-text: *Research for Development* provides guidance for undertaking research in development settings (Laws, 2003, p.1). **End of article bibliography:** Laws, S. with Harper, C. and Marcus, R. (2003). *Research for Development: A Practical Guide*. London: Sage.
Chicago	Footnotes provide full bibliographic details at the bottom of each page. The first time a source is referenced, all details are included. Subsequent references provide abbreviated information. Full references are provided at the end of the article, in alphabetical order.	**First reference:** *Research for Development* provides guidance for undertaking research in development settings.[1] 1. Laws, S. et al. (2003). *Research for Development: A Practical Guide*. London: Sage. **End of article bibliography:** Laws, S. with Harper, C. and Marcus, R. (2003). *Research for Development: A Practical Guide*. London: Sage.

Step 2: Focusing your literature review

One worry about undertaking a literature review is that you might get lost for weeks, wandering among a lot of not-very-relevant material. First, you need to define a set of research questions for which you are seeking answers. These need to be precise: avoid too open questions such as 'What works in anti-poverty programmes?' A better one would be 'What is the impact of conditional cash transfer (CCT) programmes on gender equality in Latin America?'

It is important to scan possibly useful books and articles rather than settling down to read every word. Keep a clear focus on the information you need to find. Break your 'big questions' down into sub-questions, and refer back to the research focus, the research questions and the broad aims and objectives of your study at regular intervals to help you to find your way through the material.

Identify six or eight key words derived from your research questions to use in searching for relevant material – although be careful when using terms that have recently become fashionable (such as 'governance'). Select combinations of your keywords and timeframe. (Are you interested in what has been published over the past decade only, or over a longer period?) Then conduct a bibliographical search on academic databases, which gather a large number of journals so you don't need to browse each one. Accessing these databases as well as the content of journals requires a paid subscription, so you need to find a library where you can do this. You might need to refine your keywords (for example, if you retrieve 10,000 results or just 3!) A good start for the aforementioned example on CCTs in Latin America would be: gender, impact, assessment, "Latin America", "social protection", conditional (using double quotes for terms with more than one word to keep the term intact in the search). Finding the right keywords might be a dynamic enterprise at the beginning of the search. In addition, as you find useful references, looking at their keywords might help you to refine the keywords for the problem at hand.

It may be helpful to make a visual image of the field you are looking at and to note issues related to your focus. You could draw a spider diagram like the one in Figure 5.1.

This process identifies related fields, where material you read will not directly address your core problem but may contain information of relevance. It is worth looking fairly broadly around the topic you are interested in, so as to be aware of the debates that have been taking place to date. This will help you to be confident as to when there is an existing controversy you will need to relate your work to and when you are genuinely opening up new areas for discussion.

Step 3: Systemizing the results

You have now collected loads of material and don't know what to do with it! Make a first scan of a reasonable amount of sources and try to spot the most influential contributions (for example those quoted more often). Use these as a starting point to get into the topic. If possible, talk with a scholar specializing in the topic to identify the key trends and to help you to organize the material. Write an extended abstract of the most important contributions to systematize the different perspectives on the topic derived from your research questions before writing up the report.

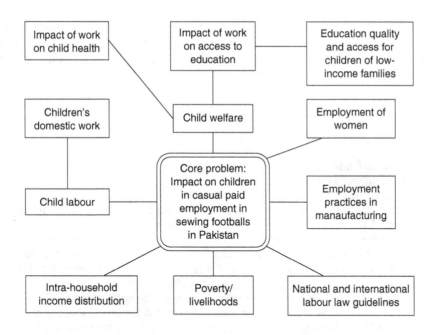

Figure 5.1 Child labour in Pakistan's football industry – breaking down the issues

Step 4: Writing up the literature review

You may well want to include a discussion of the existing research as part of your final report. Such a discussion needs to contribute to the argument you are making and be strongly focused on your own research questions. It should help you to make your case.

This can be a difficult task. It is best to start by writing an early draft to enable you to gather your thoughts and to see what conclusions can be drawn from the existing material. This is the best way to identify what is most important and to spot gaps for further investigation. You need to start focusing very tightly on the questions you set out to answer; do not be tempted simply to recount what each source says – this is very boring for the reader! When you get to the end of your own research, you can rewrite this draft into a tighter literature review with greater confidence.

Don't panic at this point! A good start is to define the structure of your report (different sections and subsections based on your research questions) and to identify the core areas of consensus and dissent on the topic. Is dissent borne out of different methods, theoretical frameworks or empirical evidence? What ideal research project would tackle the weaknesses of the current research? You might feel everything has been said on the topic, but learning is a dynamic and collective enterprise and you can always look at an issue from a different angle or add new empirical evidence.

Leedy (1997) suggests that, to get the proper psychological orientation, you should 'consider the review of related literature section in your document to be a discussion with a friend about what others have written in relation to what you plan to do' .

As with all writing, keep it as brief as possible. It may be best to interweave information from existing research with your own material rather than writing it as a separate section.

If you locate material which appears to provide evidence that does not suit your argument, do not be tempted to try to sweep it under the carpet. It will greatly strengthen your hand if you discuss what any different findings mean – do they undermine your case? If not, why not?

Checklist: writing up your literature review

- ☑ Write a draft early and revise it after doing your own original research.
- ☑ Be clear about where you are going in your thinking.
- ☑ Have a plan.
- ☑ Specify clearly the boundaries of your literature review: what you cover and what you don't. A good set of research questions is key to get this right.
- ☑ Identify schools of thought within the literature and present your findings critically. A literature review is not a summary or description of research done by others but a critical assessment of the state of the art, identifying gaps and directions for future research on a specific subject.
- ☑ Organize the material into sections that group together related research.
- ☑ Use visual tools (diagrams, figures, tables) to support the text. These can show linkages between concepts or different perspectives on the research question.
- ☑ For each piece of research you introduce, explain how it relates to your own research problem.
- ☑ Don't just describe others' work – assess it in relation to your own questions.
- ☑ Summarize what you have said – what does it all mean?
- ☑ Annex to your literature review an annotated bibliography of the 25–30 most important sources on the issue.

5.2 Where to look

This section will make frustrating reading for people working in areas where access to information is a big problem. Lack of resources of this type is a huge barrier to both scholarship and development in some countries. But many development workers do or could have access to reasonable library resources, and most have access to the internet. In this regard, this section should help you to find what you need more efficiently.

5.2.1 Using a library

The large development agencies have resource centres. These hold some useful material, and information staff will have good ideas about finding it. However, you are likely to need direct access to a library if you are doing research in any depth, although the internet is becoming increasingly valuable.

University libraries have many resources, which you may only need occasionally but which will then be extremely helpful. If you are setting out on a piece of research, you may already have links to an academic. Ask them whether some arrangement can be made to enable you to use the library of their institution. Anyone who is registered for a course will automatically have access to the library. Otherwise, it may be a good idea for your organization to make some formal link to a department of a university interested in the kind of work you do. Many universities welcome links to development organizations.

It is usually a good idea to consult a librarian on the best way to search for the information you need. University libraries have subject-specialist librarians who will have good ideas about how to find information. New technology means that the databases of many libraries are now available online, allowing you to search for and even request books prior to your visit.

As well as books and journals, libraries have a number of other useful facilities.

Indexes and abstracts

Every subject has its own huge indexes, which list references for articles on a wide variety of subjects. Many include an abstract, or summary, of the article as part of the entry, so it is easy to assess how relevant the article is to your research problem. Examples include the PubMed and the Social Sciences Citation Index. These used to be held as very large books, but nowadays are available online or in electronic format.

It is particularly useful to know about Ulrich's International Periodical Directory (www.ulrichsweb.com). The easiest way to access this is online. Ulrich's website contains information on more than 300,000 periodicals of all types, including academic and scholarly journals, open access publications, peer-reviewed titles, popular magazines, newspapers and newsletters from around the world and in 200 languages.

Photocopy requests and inter-library loans

If the book you are after is not available in your immediate area, it is often possible for librarians to request a loan from other libraries. Within the UK, it is possible to borrow books via any participating library, through the British Library's website (www.bl.uk). For a fee, you can also request journal articles to be photocopied and posted, or scanned and emailed, to you anywhere in the world. This is particularly useful if you don't have access to the internet or the journal article you are after is not available online.

Efforts are increasingly being made throughout the development research community to promote the practice of 'open access' publication. This means encouraging publishers to make articles freely available for use over the internet for the benefit of researchers who may not have access to copyright-enabled research libraries, particularly those based in poorer settings. One of the most useful resources for such publications is the Institute of Development Studies (IDS), located at the University of Sussex. IDS runs a 'family of knowledge services', including Eldis, a web-based gateway for sharing emerging open access research in development, policy, practice and research (www.eldis.org). Eldis hosts a continually expanding collection of full-text, online reports, articles, scholarly materials and publications selected by an editorial team from thousands of separate development organizations, all freely available for download. See Section 5.3 for more.

Translations of articles

When an item you pick up in a literature search is published only in a language you cannot read, it is worth checking whether it has been translated into English. The British Library Document Supply Centre holds a very large number of translations of documents of all kinds, particularly journal articles, mainly from Japanese, Russian, French and German. You can request a particular item through the British Library website and a search will be made to see if such a translation has been made.

5.2.2 Out of the library

TIP

> Contact a few knowledgeable people directly: most won't mind answering a few questions.

The most efficient way of finding out what is known on development issues is asking for help from a number of people.

Individuals

To get hold of the most relevant and up-to-date material, there is no substitute for asking advice from someone who knows the field in general and can consider your particular question. Try to locate people who could help you like this – someone you have some link to – and ask their advice about other people you can ask. You could ask for the top five things they think you should read.

Organizations

Many organizations aim to help development workers to access information on key issues – through information centres, research units, policy study institutes and so on. These may publish briefing papers which will quickly give you references for the most important published research on an issue. Ask for this assistance – they can only say no! You can look up their website, make a phone call or write a letter.

For international development issues – some places to start are IDS, including Eldis, the International Institute for Environment and Development, and the Overseas Development Institute. (See useful websites list in the Appendix for further information.) Also online materials from major deveolpment agencies and NGOs.

Campaigning organizations and non-governmental organizations (NGOs) often produce useful publicly available information and materials, usually referred to as 'grey literature'. Schöpfel and Farace (2010) define grey literature as 'information produced on all levels of government, academics, business and industry in electronic and print formats not controlled by commercial publishing'.

In using this kind of material, it is essential to locate its choice of questions and conclusions within its particular institutional discourse. O'Laughlin (1998) suggests the following steps for best making use of this type of material:

- Step 1: register the complete reference.
- Step 2: study the title page. Note down the title, date of publication, institutions, etc.
- Step 3: read the executive summary. This is good for reconstructing policy discourses and debates on the issues, but may not reflect the body of the report.
- Step 4: skim the substance.
- Step 5: survey the quantitative data. Copy any useful primary data – this may be your only chance to do so.
- Step 6: review the bibliography.
- Step 7: take notes.

O'Laughlin's advice is to leave reading this type of material until you are fairly clear about your field of study and what you are looking for. This puts you in a better position to treat these reports as 'data' and to assess them with a critical mind.

Most development partners' websites offer the option to sign up for mail alerts on specific topics or publications. Take some time to surf and sign up for those related to your research interests. You can also browse the tables of contents of academic journals: you do not need to subscribe to a journal to use this service. Store these emails in labelled folders so you can access them easily when you need them. You might want to create a folder for each topic of interest. For the more tech savvy, another time-saving option is to subscribe to the RSS feeds of development partners' websites through platforms such as Google Reader.

Official publications

These are obviously an important source in carrying out policy-related research work. Governments publish a surprising amount of useful research material, in addition to legislation and guidelines, which you need to know about and take account of. Such documents often contain useful reviews of the literature around a particular policy issue.

In the South, you can usually get copies of government documents that are available to the public from the relevant ministry or a central information office. Documents are also increasingly available online. Development cooperation offices, for example the Food and Agriculture Organization, the UN Development Programme (UNDP), the UN Children's Fund (UNICEF) or the World Bank, will usually have paper copies of their publications freely available from their office or on their website. European Union publications are available online (http://europa. eu/documentation/index_en.htm and http://epp.eurostat.ec.europa.eu/portal/page/ portal/eurostat/home).

Publications by international bodies can be located in a number of ways. UN agencies usually publish a directory (see the Appendix). There is also the listing in Ulrich's International Periodical Directory, as mentioned above, which should give useful prompts for organizations you might not have thought of.

In the UK, many government publications can be obtained from the Stationery Office (www.tso.co.uk), but do not make the mistake of thinking they all can. Each department or agency can and does publish material itself as well. So first search with the Stationery Office, but then check for other material on departmental websites or using the National Archives Government Web Archive.

5.2.3 Finding useful statistics

Development workers often use secondary data in the search for statistical information on the group of people a programme is interested in. This section looks briefly at the types of information which may be available to you – but first some words of warning. The quantity and quality of information available on a population are extremely variable. In some countries, nothing is published, and requests for information to the government will yield, at best, no more than a few poorly referenced spreadsheets. Meanwhile, in the North, and in some Southern countries, there is a long tradition of collecting information on the population, and a potentially overwhelming quantity of local- and national-level information exists. The quality of this material is variable – it is essential to treat all official statistics with deep suspicion!

Checklist: questions to ask when faced with a statistic

☑ Who says so? Or who has undertaken and who has written about the research?
☑ How do they know? Or what method has been used and what is the sample?
☑ What's missing? Or what information is not there? What statistics are not given?
☑ Does the result answer what the question asks?
☑ Does it make sense? Or has the assumption the statistic is based on been proved?

Source: Huff (1973)

However, even if it is likely that the figure you are looking at may be inaccurate by 10 per cent each way, for example, it is worth knowing about. You can also check the likely accuracy of statistics by triangulating them – seeking alternative sources of the same type of information. If more than one source or study says it is true, it is more likely to be. Or you could ask yourself what else you would expect to see if you were to believe a set of statistics. Does it gel with other facts you know about a subject area? For example, if one set of statistics tells you 3 per cent of a country's children are double orphans, and elsewhere you have seen that 2 per cent of children are maternal orphans, you know one of the statistics is wrong.

It is well worth spending some time searching for relevant statistics, as they are so helpful in giving context to your own research work. You have to make a judgement on how much time to give this, in light of your knowledge of how likely it is you will be successful in finding anything useful. Good websites for development statistics include those of the World Bank (data.worldbank.org/) and the Organization for Economic Co-operation and Development (OECD) (www.oecd.org). Table 5.3 suggests ideas for what statistics may exist and some ways of finding them, both in the UK and worldwide.

As we have seen, UN agencies are an important place to start – many countries have UN information centres. Get their most recent report and follow leads you find there. In the South and the North, it is worth asking for information from local universities and colleges. Specialist NGOs may also be able to help.

Table 5.3 Some sources of quantitative information

Type of information	Worldwide	UK
Demographic – age, sex, ethnic origin, household/ family type, etc.	Census of population; population surveys; UN reports; local births and deaths registration; national statistics offices; county statistics offices	Census, carried out every 10 years by the Office of National Statistics – local details from local authority research departments; health authorities' annual reports; British Household Panel Survey; Families and Children Study; Youth Cohort Study; *Social Trends*
Poverty, income, welfare	Household living standards surveys; demographic and health surveys; World Bank living standards measurement surveys (for some countries only); World Bank and UNDP Human Development Indicators	Census; Households Below Average Income statistics; living standards surveys; Family Resources Survey
Health	Health surveys; maternal and infant mortality data; World Health Organization country reports; health ministry studies; UN Administrative Committee on Coordination Sub-committee on Nutrition – reports on world nutrition situation	Department of Health; health authorities; Public Health Observatories such as ChiMat, the Child and Maternal Health Observatory

(Continued)

Table 5.3　(Continued)

Type of information	Worldwide	UK
Child welfare	Ministries of social welfare studies; UNICEF studies, for example State of the World's Children (annual report)	Local authority education and social services departments; National Child Development Study (longitudinal survey); Families and Children Study; Youth Cohort Study
Economy and labour market	Labour force surveys; World Bank; agricultural reports (may include useful information on other aspects and are sometimes more up-to-date than census-type data); International Labour Organization; OECD Employment Outlook	Training and enterprise councils; local authority planning and economic development departments; employers' organizations; trades unions; UK Labour Force Survey
Housing/shelter	Census; UN Human Settlements Programme reports; living standards surveys	Census; House Condition Survey; local authority housing and planning departments; housing advice agencies
Environment	Agricultural reports; UN Environment Programme reports	Environment agency; local authority environmental health departments

Some other sources of information

Newspapers

It is worth keeping newspaper cuttings that relate to your area of work. These can provide data on how events are perceived, as well as on what is happening.

Anthropologists' reports

These often contain extremely useful information and interpretation on an area, even if the focus is quite remote from yours. They may also give you new ideas and lead you to other helpful sources.

5.3　How to use the internet for research

As we have seen, the internet offers relatively easy, quick and free access to an extensive amount and range of development resources. It also offers increasing opportunities to share knowledge and participate in forums and professional networks of people with mutual research interests. Finally, it provides several ways of keeping up-to-date with the latest news and developments on topics or areas of interest. However, given that quality control continues to be an issue, we need to know how and where we can find what we want; that is, we need to use precise keywords and reliable websites and check the sources of information we decide to use. This section gives further assistance in this regard.

5.3.1 Searching the internet

The most common way to find information online is to use a *search engine* such as Google; you enter some words, a list of results containing any or all of them appears and then you scan and choose the most relevant ones. If you end up with a list of irrelevant and inappropriate research material, you have to refine your query and select precise keywords or a combination of keywords; you can also use the Boolean operators (the words AND, NOT and OR) and the wildcard symbols (including *, # and ?) as far as they are recognized by the search engine you use.

It may be better to use more *specialist search engines* such as Google Scholar, which offers access to academic literature, or development portals. Using portals with well-structured resources on key development topics, such as the Eldis Resource Guides, is a good way to get an overview of what is available and where it can be accessed. Zunia is another well-updated knowledge-sharing portal. It has thematically and country-organized resources published by various development agencies. SciDev.Net has a focus on science, technology and environment issues, and the One-World Group has thematic development guides (see Appendix).

Development guides: Eldis

An integral part of IDS Knowledge Services, Eldis is a knowledge-sharing portal with a wealth of resources on major development issues. Aiming to bridge research, policy and practice, and to facilitate professional communication, it offers free access to thousands of documents selected from over 7,500 publishers, from reports and research papers to articles and manuals, organized by theme and country; links to key development organizations and their resources; subject guides; regional and country profiles; several thematic and country e-bulletins available on subscription; RSS feeds for the latest news and research updates; announcements of events, training and employment opportunities; and online communities of professionals to share and discuss issues of interest.

Undoubtedly one of the most useful services Eldis can offer and a good starting point for a thematic search is the resource guides included in its topics section. These cover key development topics and put forward related research and policy documents, key subthemes and relevant resources, country information, links to organizations working on the topic, the related Eldis community and newsfeeds. In addition, several dossiers intend to provide an introduction to emerging development issues and some resources.

For those more interested in a specific region or country, Eldis also offers regional and country profiles, with publications organized by development topic, reference access to related resources kept in the British Library for Development Studies and links to international agencies such as UN bodies and NGOs working on this particular area.

Another option is to go directly to the *website of a research institute or development organization* you think would have the information you need, search its publication/research/resource databases and download relevant resources (the Appendix presents a basic thematic guide to such websites). Many websites offer links to related sites or resources, and you can always search within your results and downloaded documents to find other publications of potential interest. If you are unable to open a link, check it is correct and try again at a different time of day when the internet traffic is less heavy. Meanwhile, despite the online dominance of English language, many UN documents are available in the six official languages; regional organizations also use Spanish, French and Arabic and many government policy documents are available online in the national language. These can be translated easily by an online translation service such as the one Google offers.

Apart from research papers, policy documents and methodology manuals, the internet also offers access to various economic and social development *data and statistics*. The websites of international organizations such as the OECD, UNDP and UNICEF have specific sections, with users able to select indicators of interest to generate their own tables, charts or even moving graphs, using interactive visualizing applications such as StatPlanet and Gapminder. Such tools not only support your work but also make it more appealing to your audience. However, again, be very careful with the data and statistics you select, and always check and cite their sources. In fact, using several reliable websites, critically assessing the material you come across, selecting resources that represent different approaches to your topic and citing fully are all essential to good results.

Another helpful aspect of the internet is that it enables you to access *online library catalogues*, identify resources of interest and, in some cases, purchase a copy. However, most library catalogues offer only reference services, and you will have to visit the library to consult the books and periodicals you are interested in. In addition, you can access online journal catalogues, find articles and read their abstract or the full text. Where you can identify the title, author and publisher of a book, you can also check if you can access its online version or a free preview. For example, many publishers offer free previews of their books, and such services are also available on Google Books, which even provides access to almost all of the text of some books.

5.3.2 Storing and sharing information

The internet also provides you with the necessary tools to *save the links to websites with useful material, organize them and even share them* with other users working on the same or similar topics. Connotea is a free online reference management application which enables academic researchers to save links to webpages just by assigning keywords (tags) to their references and, if they want, to share these references with their colleagues (www.connotea.org). Social bookmarking systems such as the popular Delicious also allow users to save links to their favourite pages, discover relevant links saved by others and share their own (www.delicious.com). And wikis – a form of website which permits the collaborative creation and editing of multiple hyperlinked pages – can be a very productive way of allowing a research team to collectively add to a shared pool of knowledge. You have probably heard of Wikipedia (www.wikipedia.org), which uses this same platform on a massive scale to produce a collaborative encyclopaedia (whose content must be treated with caution).

Moreover, the internet offers you the option to join *development social networks and online forums* in order to connect with other people working on the same issues, exchange views, ask for assistance and share resources from references to documents. An example of such online groups of people with mutual development interests are the Eldis communities. And think about whether you might want to contribute to a shared data archive – see Chapter 8 for more.

5.3.3 Keeping up to date

Keeping abreast of new developments and research in your subject area should be viewed as an essential part of your work, and again the internet can be a helpful tool in this. After having identified useful websites (whether for libraries, research institutes, development organizations or journals), you can usually subscribe to receive *email updates* of new additions, regular email *newsletters* or bulletins or frequent *news feeds* (such as the popular RSS feeds) alerting you on website updates.

Another option for getting informed about the latest news, publications and issues is to read *development blogs*: there are several good ones written by researchers, practitioners and journalists on various topics. You can also listen to *podcasts* or watch online *videos* of conferences and lectures on current development challenges. Last but not least, if you are interested in a particular country, you can check online versions of *newspapers* from all over the world. Also check the few excellent *specialist news sites* on development and humanitarian issues which provide access to various resources from breaking stories to analysis reports (see Appendix).

5.3.4 A word of caution

Always remember, the great thing about the internet is the world of information at your fingertips – but the danger is there is no quality control! Any information you access online needs to be checked carefully and potential biases considered. For politically or culturally sensitive issues, be aware of what webpage you are accessing data from, and what its affiliations are. With statistics in particular, find out the source given for any statements made, and check that too. And while websites can themselves be valid references, try whenever possible to give preference to published, peer-reviewed or official material.

Key points from this chapter

Checklist: reviewing existing evidence

Locating key literature:

☑ Find and study carefully any recent reviews of the 'state of the art' in the field you are working in. These may be found in official documents or academic publications.
☑ Look 'sideways' from your central subjects.
☑ Don't confine yourself to one discipline (for example anthropology, nursing, psychology). There may be relevant data in a number of fields, and you may need to seek them out specifically, as cross-referencing can be weak.
☑ Ask people!
☑ Use the internet when you have ideas about where to look for information – specific sites or specialist databases.

Reviewing the literature:

☑ Do a good search, including library and internet searches and contacting knowledgeable organizations and individuals.
☑ Review the literature by critically assessing the material you have collected and analysing the different approaches it represents.
☑ Note what is not there as well as what is.
☑ Be aware of the political forces which operate in determining whose knowledge becomes part of 'the literature' and whose does not.
☑ Keep the aims and research questions of your own study in your mind.
☑ Write a first draft of your study of related literature as soon as you can – this will help you greatly in your thinking.

Conducting research on the internet:

☑ Conduct a well-defined keyword search of reliable portals and databases.
☑ Refer to library catalogues and check for quality sources.
☑ Create and foster research networks.
☑ Keep up-to-date with the latest information on your areas of interest.
☑ Check and cite your sources carefully, especially the data and the statistics you use.
☑ Be aware of the 'politics of writing' and try to combine and use your resources critically.

 ## Further reading

Babbie, E. (2009) *The Practice of Social Research,* 12th edn. Belmont, CA: Wadsworth.

Blaxter, L., Hughes, C. and Tight, M. (2010) *How to Research*, 3rd edn. Buckingham: Open University.

Both texts provide good overviews of several themes covered by this chapter. Babbie provides a useful introduction to using the internet for research, and a guide to library research in the appendix. Blaxter et al. discuss issues involved in planning, conducting and writing up a literature review, as well as internet and library-based research techniques.

European Commission (2008) *Open Access – Opportunities and Challenges: A Handbook*. Brussels: European Commission.

A comprehensive introduction to the concept and practice of open access research, aimed at stakeholders, researchers and practitioners interested in promoting the practice in their own work. Provides practical guidance on implementing open access models in publishing.

Ridley, D. (2008) *The Literature Review: A Step-by-step Guide for Students*. New Delhi, Thousand Oaks, CA, London: Sage.

An in-depth guide to conducting a systematic review of existing research, showing how to conduct searches quickly, parse and synthesize information and write a literature review. Useful best and worst practice examples from real life are offered throughout.

Rumsey, S. (2008) *How to Find Information: A Guide for Researchers,* 2nd ed. Maidenhead: Open University.

An excellent general resource for researchers who wish to learn more about locating, accessing and evaluating information. Very accessible introductions to search strategy design, web-based and database searches, using libraries and keeping up-to-date with new developments in emerging research.

University of California Berkeley *Finding Information on the Internet: A Tutorial*. Available online at www.lib.berkeley.edu/TeachingLib/Guides/Internet/FindInfo.html.

This web-based workshop guides the user through a comprehensive introduction to using search engines, finding and referencing research material online and evaluating the credibility of sites. Also has a very helpful dictionary designed for first-time users to decipher internet jargon.

Notes

1 See Chapter 20 of Flick (2009).
2 See Chapter 4, and in particular Box 55.

6

LEARNING DEVELOPMENT RESEARCH SKILLS

This chapter is for those who want to build research skills for themselves, their colleagues and those they work with. Making effective arguments for wider change is increasingly seen as part of practical development work with communities. Research has an important role to play, as it is one way of making the case for change. There are a number of ways research skills can be shared and development workers can be assisted to undertake the work they need to do.

The chapter starts by considering the different aspects of the research process for which you may want to increase skills. Exercises throughout this manual aim to help in building skills in the different areas, but the area of general analytical skills is often identified as problematic. A short section suggests some exercises to develop critical thinking. The next part of the chapter looks at some approaches to skills development: courses, training workshops, joint working, coaching and on-the-job learning as part of a practical project. Finally, we step back and look more broadly at how development organizations can support Southern researchers.

A skills gap: studying the impact of HIV in Ethiopia

A study aimed at minimizing the impact of HIV in a region of Ethiopia identified two sets of skills limitations:

- **Research and data collection skills:** qualitative research demands a high level of skill and precision in data collection. Because of language and cultural barriers, it was not possible for the (expatriate) consultant to collect data directly, nor even to supervise the data collection. Save the Children research team members supervising the work were also new to the particular research skills involved. The time available for training team members did not allow for sophisticated skills development. As a result, focus group discussion facilitation was more formal than was ideal. This limited the quality and extent of the data collected.

- **Details lost through translation:** the raw data from the focus groups were summarized and translated from Amharic and Oromo into English for the consultant to analyse. This inevitably resulted in a loss of fine detail, which was reflected in the broad-brush nature of the results.

6.1   Where to start?

If you are a manager considering the needs of an organization, you will want first to consider at what level you need to improve research skills, and in what ways this should be done. Are you looking at:

- The whole organization?
- Some individual staff members?
- Whole teams of staff members?
- Managers or practitioners?

You may want to hire new people who have the skills you need or perhaps set up a whole new department. Or you might want to make an arrangement with an organization which has the skills you need. If you decide that in-house or external skills training is required, you will need to carry out a training needs assessment exercise with the staff concerned. This means looking at job descriptions and tasks required, and comparing what is needed with the existing skills profile of the staff concerned. It is also extremely helpful to consult staff about their own perception of the skills they need to learn, and their learning and development goals for the future. People rarely get much out of training they perceive as imposed from 'on high'.

Common pitfall

Setting up a one-day workshop on research methods in the hope that this will make the whole team capable of planning and carrying out a major research project

As this manual shows, 'research' is a big subject, and the skills and knowledge involved are quite broad and complex. You need to consider exactly what skills you require for your work, what the priorities are at this point in time and what is feasible in terms of the available resources. Skills development is often costly, time consuming for staff involved and disruptive to everyday work. Is this an investment you can justify in terms of the overall project, budget and organization?

Some of the typical areas for skills development you may wish to consider are:

- the role of research in development work, and different approaches to research;
- planning and managing research;
- how to choose methods for research projects;
- data collection techniques: interviewing, focus groups, observation, visual techniques, etc.;
- data analysis;
- writing and promotion of ideas.

Within any of these areas, you may want to take a participatory approach, and this involves some special skills as well. There is also the general area of developing better analytical skills, a critical approach, which may need attention. And you may also need to learn about the specific issues involved in research with particular social groups: disabled people, refugees or children, for example.

It is important to realize that, while learning practical techniques is useful, the whole area of attitudes and behaviour, within fieldwork and within the planning and management of research, is also crucial. Learning to listen carefully while thinking about the next question, to approach people confidently but respectfully, can be difficult. Carrying out new tasks is stressful, and researchers need help to convey a positive attitude and not to share their anxieties with the respondent.

Some tasks are more difficult than others. Collecting responses to a standard survey is much easier than carrying out a less structured in-depth interview. Focus group facilitation is particularly demanding. Research planning and management sometimes runs really smoothly, with clear aims and skilled researchers. Sometimes it is a nightmare. See Chapters 3 and 4 for ideas about breaking down a research project and involving different people in different tasks. Different training or other educational work may also be needed by different parts of a research team. As with all learning processes, inexperienced people should undertake some tasks where success is reasonably easy to achieve before tackling more challenging ones.

The other chapters of this manual suggest some activities to help people to learn about research. Most of these can be done on your own or with a group. An underlying skill essential to many aspects of research work is that of taking an analytical approach. The next section suggests some ways of working on this.

6.1.2 Developing stronger analytical skills

A critical, analytical approach is crucial to research. You need to question your own research questions; why people are giving the responses they are; and then how you interpret these. Small children ask a lot of questions, but this is knocked out of many of us by authoritarian schooling, which in effect teaches a fear of questioning authority. Confidence is needed to ask sharp questions, as you are exposing your thinking to others' scrutiny. Working in a foreign language adds to the barriers.

Organizations can help to increase staff confidence by building a culture where it is acceptable to make mistakes, to say the wrong thing occasionally, but perhaps less acceptable to be passive and say nothing. Timid people should not be slapped down when they make a suggestion. Praise is important.

Innovative work involves an element of risk: mistakes will inevitably be made. When trying out new things, it will not be possible to get everything right first time. Any mistakes should been seen as opportunities to learn rather than to blame.

Any exercise which encourages people to think for themselves and then to argue their point of view is useful. One effective traditional method is to set up formal debates, with people speaking for and against a motion, to push people to question and defend their ideas. Another is simply to regularly make a practice of reading one another's pieces of work and commenting on them.

Methods commonly used include brainstorming, 'red teaming' (whereby one part of the group takes on the role of stakeholders likely to oppose an idea) and 'critical friending' (where colleagues go over your work in detail and ask probing, difficult questions). Finally, 'pinpoint sessions', where a facilitator helps participants build on each other's ideas by drawing out themes and issues they identify, can encourage the development of strategic thinking.[1]

These methods can help participants to learn to accept critical comments without feeling they have done something wrong. This is essential – to expect and welcome critical comment on your work. If no reader has anything to say about what you have written, you need to ask why! It may not mean it is good – but that it is boring.

Some fearful words – a game of eight squares

ACTIVITY 6.1

Many words are used loosely in everyday speech, and then have specific meanings in social science. This can be especially difficult to grasp where people are working in a second language.

Early on in the research process, use the examples given here. Later, during analysis and writing, the game can be adapted using examples from participants' data or writing.

Concept	Fact
Theory	Assumption
Explanation	Analysis
Understanding	Description

Facilitators need to prepare three or four large game boards (on stiff card, about the same size as a flipchart sheet), and mark each one up clearly with the words given below.

You should also prepare two sets of cards, labelled 'definitions' and 'examples' (using those given on the answer sheet below), for each group, placing each set in a marked envelope. An answers sheet should be prepared for each facilitator, making sure the participants do not see this.

So, each player or group of players has a game board, a set of definitions and a set of examples. The object of the game is to match each word on the game board with the correct definition and example.

It is helpful to discuss why people have put things in different places and explore any disagreements. Try to think of other examples from your work for each of the words.

Word on game board	Definition	Example
Concept	An abstract or general idea which is important to how we think about a subject.	Sexual exploitation is based on situations of power between men and women, adults and children.
Fact	A justified, true belief (based on information that has been properly collected and analysed).	Medical tests and records show children treated with oral rehydration therapy (ORT) tend to recover better from diarrhoea than children who are not given ORT.
Theory	Ideas or principles which explain, or seek to explain, something.	If children's rights were respected, their welfare would improve.

(Continued)

(Continued)

Word on game board	Definition	Example
Assumption	A belief that is taken for granted and (perhaps mistakenly) used as the basis of a statement or research question.	People on low incomes lack knowledge about a healthy diet.
Explanation	Statements which make sense of something about why things are the way they are.	The increase in skin cancer in some areas is caused by thinning of the ozone layer.
Analysis	The logical process of examining data to see what they mean.	In a study of 450 15-year-old Indian boys, 25 per cent were found to work full time. Of these, 85 per cent were found to have been unwell in the past 14 days, compared with 32 per cent of those who did not work. This suggests full-time work in childhood may be harmful to health.
Understanding	Our perception of the meaning of something.	Ali's view is that he cannot get a job because employers think he is too old to be worth training.
Description	A verbal account of places, events, people or situations.	In the market on Saturdays, there are usually five stalls selling fabrics, all run by women.

Source: Boyden and Ennew (1997)

6.2 Some ways of learning research skills

People learn in different ways, but for all of us, the more actively we are involved in learning research skills, the more likely we are to remember what we have learnt. Approaches vary in terms of their cost, length and frequency, and whether they are self-led, co-led or taught, whether they take place in groups or alone and whether they take place in the workplace or outside. Approaches include:

- training workshops;
- reading and learning on your own;
- formal courses, qualifications and degrees, including by distance learning;
- learning on-the-job through coaching and as part of a real research project;
- joint working, coaching and consultancy.

We look at these areas in more depth below. However, there are many kinds of initiative you could take to encourage people to learn more about research work; some are suggested in the following checklist. Don't assume a workshop is the right approach: experience shows that other approaches may be more effective.

Checklist: learning about research through special initiatives

☑ Set up small low-risk projects, part of whose aim is to develop staff and/or community members' research skills – and ensure time is released to carry these out.

☑ Arrange in-house training – offering training in interviewing skills is a good way of introducing broader research issues.

☑ Involve people from partner agencies in training workshops, where appropriate – this is especially useful when working with innovative methodologies which need to be 'sold' to partners.

☑ Sponsor staff to undertake external research training.

☑ Facilitate networking among people doing similar work to promote mutual learning.

☑ Work through activities from this manual individually or with colleagues.

6.2.1 Training workshops

First of all, as ever, be clear about the purpose of any training session you set up. Check which areas of research and skills (see Section 6.1) you need to cover. Find out directly from potential participants what they feel their needs are. If a real need exists, consider alternative ways to address it. Is a training session the best solution?

If you are planning a specific project, it should be possible to tailor the training to address the particular issues raised, for example by adapting the exercises and case studies used or using real-life examples from the project. It may be best to wait until you are close to the time when the work will be done, so people can link abstract ideas to practical tasks. The most effective training allows trainees to practise newly acquired skills through a practical piece of work.

One benefit of training workshops is that they can be a way both to build a team of people and to support them. It represents a safe place to work out any controversial issues raised by a project.

Checklist: guidelines for training in research methods

☑ Acknowledge and build on participants' existing knowledge and skills, and consider their personal development goals.

☑ Model the approach to people that you want to see in practice.

☑ Try to find trainers who are familiar with the local situation and fluent in the local language – if this is not possible, trainers should team up with a co-trainer who knows the area and speaks the language.

☑ Involve someone with experience in adult non-formal training techniques.

☑ Use active methods like role play, practical tasks and open debate.

☑ Use examples to practise on that are relevant to participants' own work.

☑ Don't try to pack too much into a short time.

☑ Include an element of practical research, however small.

☑ Evaluate and reflect on the training, as you hope participants will evaluate and reflect on their research practice.

6.2.2   Reading and learning on your own

Many books can give guidance on different aspects of research. Reading on the different areas of the research process is recommended at the end of each chapter of this manual. The best approach for many people is to have books with you to refer to when you have questions, rather than expecting to work through them from start to finish.

Formal courses, qualifications and degrees

Many professional training courses, especially undergraduate and Masters degrees, contain an element of teaching on research skills. Pursuing a degree by distance learning can be extremely rewarding, but it is important to research the course thoroughly before committing to it. Look for courses that require you to carry out a small project yourself.

Increasingly, a number of universities worldwide offer distance learning opportunities, including training, diplomas, certificates and first-degree and postgraduate degrees in development studies, and management courses intended for those working in the voluntary sector. These courses require access to the internet, although in some cases they may also send printed materials by post. The UK-based Open University's Development Policy and Practice Centre, for instance, offers a distance-based taught Masters programme, diplomas and certificates in social research methods in general.[2]

The Open University is, of course, just one of many such institutions. In exploring the wide range of programmes now available, a good place to start is the Development Studies Association, which offers a thorough listing of first-degree and postgraduate courses offered by 50 UK- and Ireland-based universities. Many of these offer distance learning arrangements (www.devstud.org.uk/directories/course). A similar online directory can be found at Studying Development (www.studying-development.org) and the training section of the UN Office for the Coordination of Humanitarian Affairs' Reliefweb (http://reliefweb.int/trainings/), both of which list international programmes. Many other organizations run distance learning courses: the list of useful websites in the Appendix should give you some places to start. In using these resources, however, don't overlook the important step of consulting with colleagues and academic contacts for advice on which courses have the best reputation in your particular field of interest.

6.2.3   Learning on the job

This manual aims to make the planning process as straightforward as possible. Start with a small and relatively simple project, to build skills and confidence. You could invent a small piece of work to practise on, one which would benefit your agency's work. But just get started! The most useful learning is gained by being involved in a project from the beginning to the end, having some responsibility for the results. Then you learn about the successes and problems of the methods you try in a very direct way.

6.2.4 Joint working, coaching and consultancy

One of the best ways of learning about research is to work alongside an experienced researcher. This is why there are points throughout this manual where it is recommended you consult such a person. You could make a stable arrangement with someone that they will advise throughout a project, or indeed throughout the year, as research issues arise.

If you normally lack access to an experienced researcher, but hire them in for a specific project, consider building it into their brief that they will work closely with staff who would like to learn from them. You could ask them to run a specific training or feedback event, so relevant people gain some direct learning from a project as it happens. Ask them to discuss openly the methodological choices and problems a particular project raised, and this will assist you when you next have to plan research.

> ### Checklist: some ways of sharing research skills as part of an ongoing project
>
> ☑ Involve people who want to learn as observers, for example note taking at focus groups or at interviews.
> ☑ Have in-house staff lead a project, and arrange research supervision for them from someone more experienced.
> ☑ Enable staff to be involved in projects from start to finish, so they learn about how their decisions and actions early on affect the final results.
> ☑ Invite relevant development workers onto research advisory groups – for their contribution as well as for them to learn.
> ☑ Make the task of facilitating the learning of others part of the brief when you involve more experienced researchers.

6.3 Supporting Southern researchers

Researchers, and development workers learning research skills, in the South can face a very difficult environment. Development agencies can invest in skills development in a number of ways: networks to link up researchers and identify common or complementary research agendas and to allow strong North–South partnerships to be forged; dissemination of research papers; enrolment of staff in local postgraduate programmes; and research capacity strengthening (including in research administration and management) (Jones et al., 2007).

A number of important challenges are as follows:

- insufficient time horizons and long-term commitment;
- limited impact of research on policy;
- limited demand-led research;
- lack of research quality assurance;
- exclusively local projects tending to be less fruitful than North–South partnerships;
- a lack of gender analysis and gender balance within research capacity initiatives;
- a need for more industry–university cooperation to enhance the utility of efforts;

- inadequate monitoring and evaluation mechanisms;
- limited inroads into general institutional strengthening.

However, the same review identified a number of good practices which could be built on to strengthen research capacity for development. Table 6.1 summarizes these.

Table 6.1   Summary of good practices in research capacity building in Africa

Dimensions	Examples of good practice
Coordination among donors	• The Partnership for Higher Education in Africa coordinates seven independent foundations' funding for higher education development in Africa. During 2000–5, the founding partners contributed more than $150 million to fund research, institutional research units, research-focused graduate training and infrastructure in six African countries. • A joint Hewlett Foundation and International Development Research Centre (IDRC) initiative supports West and East African social policy think-tanks through core funding and research capacity strengthening, with planned funding of $150 million over 10 years. • Consultative Group on International Agricultural Research (CGIAR) research centres are funded through a central mechanism.
Long-term commitment and funding	• The Rockefeller Foundation has funded research capacity-building for about 50 years. • The Norwegian Agency for Development Cooperation has been supporting research capacity strengthening for over 40 years. The current Programme for Development, Research and Education provides funding for five years. • The International Science Programme, the Swedish International Development Cooperation Agency (Sida) and the World Health Organization (WHO) have trained researchers and provided core support to universities and research institutes in Africa for at least 30 years. Their end vision is the capacity of countries to produce doctoral candidate graduates so local researchers can tackle development issues.
Understanding of political context	• IDRC's functions have been decentralized to three regional offices in Africa, which allows for closer collaboration with recipients and better local knowledge. • International Relief and Development has an extensive network in Africa: 36 per cent of its staff work overseas, 600 of its technical staff are from the South and foreign researchers are directly involved in research. • A number of donors are increasingly funding projects through their embassies.
Supporting existing capacity, expertise and institutions	• Strengthening Capacity for Agricultural Research in Africa, funded by the UK Department for International Development, and University Science, Humanities and Engineering Partnerships in Africa – a consortium of independent foundations – were both begun and led by an African institution and then funded by Northern donors.
Southern demand-driven partnerships	• IDRC's proposals are led by Southern institutions. • The Carnegie Corporation's funding mechanisms provide Southern partners with greater voice over resource allocation. • WHO responds effectively to Southern demand in its research capacity development. Southern partners set the focus and have decision-making power over many issues. Northern involvement is increasingly informal and Southern partners are actively sought.

Dimensions	Examples of good practice
Research management and knowledge management	• International research institutes and networks based in Africa are intermediaries between local research institutions and donors, and support local partners in project management and donor reporting as well as research capacity building. Examples include CGIAR centres and networks such as the African Economic Research Consortium. • Sida grants universities funds to use for faculty research and fellowships to improve fund management capacities.
Building partnerships with national governments to ensure harmonization with broader national policies/plans	• In Mozambique, Sida was invited by the Science and Technology Minister to help develop a research strategy which incorporated training of ministerial staff in relation to research and policy. • The World Bank and International Fund for Agricultural Development (IFAD) support the Agricultural Research Centre in Ethiopia, which links national and regional governmental, researcher and practitioner stakeholders in coordinating research agendas, priority-setting and implementing and communicating research.
Capacity-building throughout the knowledge generation and translation process	• A joint initiative by the Wellcome Trust and IDRC to support social policy think-tanks is an example of support to policy research and bridging research and policy. • The Danish International Development Agency (Danida) supports partnerships involving Southern and Northern researchers in planning research relevant to the host country's development and the dissemination of research results. • DFID's Research into Use programme is key.
M&E of research capacity	• IDRC evaluated the policy impacts of its development research over 20 years, many of which include strong research capacity components. The evaluation sought to tease out crosscutting lessons from development research in diverse sectors and implemented in diverse country contexts.

Source: Jones et al. (2007)

When working in developing countries, three kinds of capacity building should be considered: capacity within the agency itself, that of the people you work with and that of partner agencies.

Three key types of capacity building

Earlier work on research capacity building focused on technical and resource transfers (Kharas, 2005, in Jones et al., 2007), but more recent analyses have increasingly adopted a broader definition, emphasizing the importance of differentiating between various levels of capacity building.[3] These are commonly divided into individual, institutional and system approaches.

At the **individual** level, capacity-building initiatives focus on building up a critical mass of researchers competent in a particular thematic, disciplinary or methodological

(Continued)

(Continued)

area, typically through the provision of postgraduate training or small research grants. Individual-level approaches have expanded to include a broader range of stakeholders in knowledge generation, translation and uptake processes (Costello and Zumla, 2000).

At the **institutional** level, the concern is with improving organizational structures, processes, resources, management and governance issues (including institutional reward systems that encourage partnership modes of working), so local institutions are able to attract, train and retain capable researchers.

Although a comparatively newer area of focus, the **system** approach is designed to improve national and regional innovation environments. The emphasis here is on the development of coherent policies and strategies and effective coordination across sectors and among governmental, non-governmental and international actors. It includes attention to funding transparency, remuneration, continuing education and access to information, as well as strategic planning, priority setting, knowledge management and demand creation (Nuyens, 2005).

Partners may include local or national government, national research bodies and universities. Past reflections on World Bank-led participatory poverty assessments in a number of countries considered it an important outcome that there are now people with experience of the benefits of participatory approaches within the governments and donor agencies concerned (Norton, 1998). However, this often entails tackling complex power relations.

Any initiative to support research capacities needs to tackle power relations between Northern donors and providers of research capacity-strengthening services and Southern 'beneficiary' organizations. Marouani and Ayuk (2007) argue that there are two problems in the field of research capacity development: 'money aid', often with conditions; and 'ideas aid', whereby key concepts, discourses and policy analysis are produced disproportionately by donors' research policy units and/or commissioned by experts or think-tanks in the North with the aim of influencing other donors and policy research institutions in the North and South. They emphasize that think-tanks in Africa are often very dependent on donors for both money and ideas, 'and are thus a good channel for donors to strengthen their influence on policymaking and research agendas'.

Accordingly, in order to ensure sustainability, it is critical to promote both capacity-strengthening efforts which are informed by a nuanced understanding of the local socio-cultural and political context (Harris, 2004) and local ownership over research priorities and agendas (Velho, 2004). Costello and Zumla (2000), for example, call for a phasing-out of the 'annexed site' approach, whereby foreign-led and foreign-funded research in developing countries remains semi-colonial in nature and dominated by Northern research priorities and research management.

Capacity building needs to be re-envisioned as a two-way collaborative process whereby Northern partners stand to learn as much as Southern partners (Marouani and Ayuk, 2007) and greater investment is possible in South–South, public–private and and/or in-country partnerships (Oyelaran-Oyeyinka, 2005). Oyelaran-Oyeyinka (2005) argues that getting the institutional context right for partnerships is demanding. Building a culture of innovation among all actors is a long, multifaceted and context-specific process, which requires soft skills such as team building, competing while cooperating, resolving competing priorities and mobilizing resources.

Voices from the South

Northern partners can be an asset if they are motivated to work with African researchers and help them to get research published. Often, Northern researchers simply take the data and publish them themselves. Only if they are willing to support and help local young researchers to get published is the partnership worth anything (Kathryn Touré, Educational Research Network for West and Central Africa, 2007).

'The main problem with donor approaches is that it is often assumed that there is no existing capacity at all. There is always previous experience and expertise somewhere, and it is this pool of people that capacity strengthening should aim to expand' (Ebrima Sall, Council for the Development of Social Science Research in Africa, 2007).

Most African universities are very fragile, they are largely dependent on donor funding and government goodwill. In this kind of situation, there is no stability over time and little opportunity to accumulate intellectual capital. Long-term institutional stability should be the government's – rather than the donors' – responsibility. Instead, donors should work with those institutions that are stable and have the most capacity and potential. (Johann Mouton, Centre for Research on Science and Technology, 2007)

Source: Jones et al. (2007)

Key points from this chapter

Checklist: learning about research for development work

☑ Be clear about which part of the research process you need to learn about.
☑ Build in learning as part of a real research project.

☑ Arrange for joint working and coaching from an experienced researcher to gain the most learning from practical work.
☑ Involve partner agencies and community members, as appropriate, in training workshops.
☑ When planning training, ensure that the principles you want to see followed in the research work are reflected in the training methods.
☑ Plan to make a contribution to the broad task of supporting the development of appropriate research skills within disadvantaged communities worldwide.

 ## Further reading

Chambers, R. (2002) *Participatory Workshops: A Sourcebook of 21 Sets of Ideas and Activities*. Oxford: Earthscan.

This sourcebook provides 21 sets of ideas and options for facilitators, trainers, teachers and presenters, and anyone who organizes and manages workshops, courses, classes and other events for participatory learning and change.

Hare, K. and Reynolds, L. (2005) *The Trainer's Toolkit: Bringing Brain-friendly Learning to Life*. Bancyfelin: Crown House Publishing.

The book contains tools, techniques, example sessions and activities for in-house training. It focuses on how to help people learn productively.

Highmore Sims, N. (2006) *How to Run a Great Workshop: The Complete Guide to Designing and Running Brilliant Workshops and Meetings*. Harlow: Prentice Hall.

This guide is designed for managers – people whose main role is not training – and takes readers through a simple step-by-step process to create stimulating, fun and effective workshops and presentations.

Slocum, N. (2003) *Participatory Methods Toolkit: A Practitioner's Manual*. Bruges: UN University Institute on Comparative Integration.

This toolkit consists of ten in-depth participatory methods and a brief overview of almost 40 other participatory techniques. The introductory chapter provides a comparative chart for choosing between the various options and general guidelines for running participatory sessions.

Notes

1 See 'Encouraging Creativity' chapter in Prime Minister's Strategy Unit (2004).
2 A particularly useful course for people wishing to apply many of the skills described in this manual to a real-life project is the Development Management Project. This is the final module in the Development Studies MSc but can be taken as a standalone course. It takes students right through planning, conducting and writing up a project. See www3.open.ac.uk/study/postgraduate/course/TU874.htm/.
3 It is important to point out from the outset that there is a regional and disciplinary bias in the literature on research capacity-building initiatives. Empirical analyses largely concern capacity-building initiatives outside Africa, and experiences in the health and science, technology and innovation sectors, with few sources documenting research capacity-building initiatives in the non-economic social sciences and humanities.

PART 2

COLLECTING DATA

7

CHOOSING METHODS

This chapter assists you in deciding on methods for collecting and analysing data for your project. Research methods should always be embedded into a study's broader design, as part of which you need to make two kinds of decisions. First, which overall research approach do you intend to take to your research? Second, which specific techniques for collecting and analysing data will you use (such as interviews, observation, questionnaires, ethnography, grounded theory or regression analysis, etc.)? The choices you make about the overall research approach should guide your choice of techniques. As it is often best to use more than one technique – to triangulate the evidence you collect – you are not engaged here in a search for one perfect technique.

7.1 Choosing a research approach

Choosing the overall research approach involves getting the purpose of the research as clear as possible in your mind:

- the research focus;
- the aims and objectives;
- the research questions;
- the audience/s.

Look back at Chapter 3, and if need be have another go at clarifying the brief. Writing out some precise research questions and identifying a set of hypotheses are likely to help you in establishing the methods to use. Are you asking 'how many?' or 'yes/no' type questions? Or do your questions tend to concern how or why people do things? Do your questions concern individuals or groups? Try to imagine what kinds of answers you might find to these questions– then consider what methods might lead to this sort of information. The purpose of the research will ultimately guide the choice of the overall research approach and specific techniques, so it is important to take a step back and consider the research's aims.

The following are some of the key issues to consider.

- Purpose/audience?
- Positivist or social constructionist?
- Quantitative and/or qualitative?
- Primary or secondary data?
- Individual or collective methods?
- Level of participation of community members and other stakeholders?
- Short- or long-term research?

Each of these issues is discussed here. Look back at Part 1, especially Chapters 2 and 3, and recall which approach you are intending to take within these broad frameworks. It may be helpful also to look at Chapters 11 and 12, which discusses various packages of methods commonly used in development work. It would also be worth looking at Chapter 16, on assessing research for development work.

7.1.1   Purpose/audience?

The distinction made in Chapter 1 between programme- and policy-focused research is important here. You need to decide what evidence will be good enough for you to rely on, given your purpose. Think about not only the quality but also the nature of the information you need, and the kinds of processes that will be helpful to your project.

Who needs to have confidence in the findings of your research? What are their values and ideas about what is valid evidence? Are they interested in community members' views? Or do they principally value traditional 'scientific' approaches? In answering these questions, the Research and Policy in Development (RAPID) Context Evidence Links (CEL) framework can be a helpful tool. It offers a range of conceptual questions to help to identify the purpose and audience of policy research (see Chapter 16).

Having said this, most decision makers will say they favour 'hard facts', usually meaning large surveys, for more or less any purpose. But it is important to remember that this type of research it not always relevant and, even when feasible, its messages are not necessarily heard. Participatory and qualitative styles of research can influence decision makers where they see the work as having credibility. A strong case study which explores relevant themes in a convincing way can also be influential. So don't necessarily take at face value what people say about the kind of research they trust. Consider the politics of the situation: if you need to make a highly controversial point, it is generally not wise to try to make it through research that uses highly controversial methods.

7.1.2   Positivist or social constructionist?

The first decision to make when deciding your research approach is whether you are aiming to work within a positivist or a social constructionist framework. Section 2.2

discussed this distinction. Positivist approaches see research as an unbiased investigation of reality, which is 'out there' to be observed. Social research should in this view be as like the natural sciences as possible.

Social constructionist approaches maintain there is no one 'right answer' out there waiting to be identified. Research should accept that 'the researched' are actively engaged in constructing their world, as is the researcher. There will always be different ways of seeing things and a range of interpretations.

The key is to make conscious decisions in light of your research purpose. What really makes for bad research is failing to decide which sets of rules you are playing to, and therefore producing work which meets the criteria for neither approach.

7.1.3 Primary versus secondary data?

You might want to consider using existing data, at least to answer some of the questions you are interested in. This leads us to an important distinction between primary data, generated directly for the purpose of a study, and secondary data, generated for other purposes and/or pre-existing the study. Secondary data sources might include census statistics or administrative records. These can be extremely valuable, as you can use information you would not be able to collect on your own (for example census data) that is seen as 'neutral', having been collected independently of your study. However, considerable effort needs to go into working with such data, and researchers need to know how they were put together. What samples were used? What is the timescale covered and what is the unit of analysis? It is only by asking these questions that a judgement can be made about whether these data can be used in a particular study.

7.1.4 Quantitative and/or qualitative?

The choice between research that gives you numbers and research that produces mainly words has long been seen as a key issue in social science. However, it is not helpful to feel you need to pick sides on this. Very often, you do need qualitative information, but you also need some sense of the scale of things, some element of quantification. It is best to view quantitative and qualitative data as a continuum from the most quantitative to the most qualitative.

Many of us are prejudiced in one way or another by our past experience in relation to quantitative or qualitative methods. Leedy (1997) advises that 'hating maths is not a good reason for choosing a qualitative study'. Equally, fearing the complexity of the answers you may get is not a good reason to avoid qualitative work. Your own skills come into the decision as to whether you undertake the research yourself, and what types of help you may need to buy in, but they should not restrict the kinds of information you are able to consider collecting.

Some common techniques, for example semi-structured interviews, typically collect both qualitative and quantitative information. However, it is not OK to start quantifying, for example, how many people make a particular point in a focus group. Within a group discussion, you cannot place too much importance on whether or not individuals mention particular issues – they could simply have nodded when one person said something. If you want to collect some information on an individual basis alongside your group work, you could, say, ask participants to fill in a questionnaire before or after the focus group.

7.1.5 Individual opinions or a collective view?

Some research methods are focused on individuals, others on groups of people – village communities, interest groups or households. It is important to be clear what type of information, and what kind of process, you need. Traditional positivist research has tended to focus on the individual, aiming to collect information in as private and confidential a way as possible. Participatory approaches, and action research in particular, tend to be more interested in the collective level (see Chapter 12). There are advantages and disadvantages to both – as ever, it depends on the purpose of the research as to which one is best.

People respond differently depending on the context in which they are asked questions. The impulse to give 'socially acceptable' answers may be an issue in any research, but is stronger when working with groups. However, in close-knit societies, people may be more likely to be able to misrepresent their situation, for example in relation to their economic resources, when interviewed individually.

One specific issue to consider is that, in assessing the wellbeing of members of a household, it cannot be assumed that men, women, children and older people share their resources in an equitable way. Or that they do not. However, it may be socially challenging to ask to talk to people separately – it may be assumed that the head of the household should answer for the others. This has been a big concern for researchers (Pratt and Loizos, 1992). One approach is to assign someone in your team to talk to the men of a household while another goes around to the kitchen and talks to the women, or out into the yard to see the children. The question for your piece of research is what do you really need to know? What information can you actually use?

A combination of methods will make it possible to get information of both kinds, from individuals and from groups. Whole-village meetings will inevitably be dominated by whatever local groups hold the most power – men, the better-off, those with most education. However, it is possible to specifically convene

---

Common pitfalls

- **Avoid false certainty about people's class:** people who belong to a certain type of class may be difficult to define (such as the 'popular classes' in Latin America), and people do not necessarily feel part of the class they are supposedly members of.
- **Do not assume solidarity:** to share a characteristic is no guarantee of a sense of having 'something in common'.
- **Do not assume community:** living near to each other does not automatically lead to something called 'community spirit'.
- **Do not read rural patterns into urban contexts (or vice versa):** don't assume people in rural and urban areas have similar ideas of, for example, community or family.
- **Avoid overreliance on particular informants:** 'most key informants will have their own biases and their own perspectives [...] and any information from them needs to be cross-checked or validated against the views of other people'. Consider, for instance, that your interpreter may give you a 'cleaned-up' version of the interviewee's account or may not be well integrated (culturally) with the interviewee(s).

Source: Pratt and Loizos (1992)

group discussions with people whose view you are interested in but who might not otherwise speak up – younger women, landless labourers, minority ethnic groups. To counteract group bias, it may be best to ensure some information is also collected from individuals.

The key point is again to be conscious of the choices you make. When you get to analysing the data, it will be important to be clear as to whether you have information relating to individuals or groups. Data from group and individual discussions are quite different types of material, and need to be analysed differently.

7.1.6 Level of participation of community members and stakeholders?

There are many issues to consider here, discussed at length in Chapter 3. If community members are to be involved in deciding on which methods to use, it is important that they can practise a range of methods, so they have a real choice. Otherwise, they are likely to pick whatever is most familiar to them – in the South perhaps participative methods (Chapter 12), in the North perhaps questionnaires or interviews (Chapter 11).

7.1.7 Short- or long-term research?

Some research methods involve data collection and/or analysis that inherently take a long time. Major surveys are usually in this category, as are complex case studies. Other methods may look quick and simple but turn out differently. For example, it can be quick to run a focus group discussion with a group that meets together anyway for some other purpose, but if you are bringing people together expressly for the focus group, the process of organizing it can be time consuming. Analysis and writing are also rarely as quick as anyone hopes.

Much research in development work is done to extremely tight timescales. In some cases, so little time is taken it is hard to see how there could be much reflection on the data collected. There is a risk that, rather than investigating what is going on in an open and transparent manner, a pre-existing framework is being taken and tried out on a new situation. While such an approach may have its place, it is very important to be transparent about its limitations.

At times, of course, there are very good reasons for undertaking research in a hurry. With policy-oriented research in particular, it is important not to 'miss the boat' by failing to produce your evidence in time for the relevant decision-making process. However, sometimes it seems to be assumed that only very rushed research can be attempted, perhaps because of the urgency of the issue under consideration. But working fast has real costs in terms of the quality of the output. In particular, building trust with both community members and other organizations is slow, but if it is not done, sources and quality of data available to you will be severely limited.

Many of the issues which require investigation in development are actually deep rooted and long term in nature. Where this is the case, it is unlikely that research conducted at a breathless pace will get to the bottom of the matter. It might be better to invest in a solid piece of research that can produce more reliable results than to expect several short-term projects to add up to substantial evidence.

Some of the most powerful research designs involve comparisons over time. In evaluation research, collecting information before and after an intervention, or at stages throughout its life, greatly strengthens the ability to draw conclusions. The same applies to studies of the impact of a particular policy change. To follow the fortunes of a group of people in the context of the AIDS epidemic or after economic liberalization, for example, a series of 'snapshot' studies at intervals over a number of years could be much more convincing than a study carried out at one point in time only.

The use of multiple methods can sometimes allow for an early report on the findings of elements of a piece of research, enabling action to proceed in light of these, while the more in-depth research proceeds more slowly. Remember also to check whether it is really necessary to collect new data. Existing data can be easy to obtain and can be a good option for research tied to strict schedules.

7.2   Choosing research techniques

Once you are clear about the broad research approach you want to take, you need to move on to choosing specific techniques. These can be selected from the key techniques described in Chapters 11 and 12, or you may use other less common ones or invent new ones. However, you need first to take some further issues into account: good communication; recording and analysis; issues in working on sensitive subjects; and whether you are looking at experience or opinion.

7.2.1   Good communication

Your research will only be as good as your communication with the people you are working with. Consider carefully what types of communication they find most comfortable, and those with which they may have only negative experiences.

Some people cannot read or write, and some will also be unfamiliar with drawing. Although people can learn some new techniques, they may be most at home just talking to you. However, this should not be assumed. Where people are used to it, for example some groups of school children, asking respondents to fill in a questionnaire is a very confidential and straightforward way to collect data. Other people will associate forms with threatening dealings with officialdom.

Group work is familiar to some people, but they may be used to using it for different purposes. For example, for a research-oriented focus group you would need to brief participants that they do not need to agree with each other, or to come to any consensus. Some will not be accustomed to speaking up in group settings and will not find it easy to participate.

Any group may contain people with some communication impairment – those who are deaf or hard of hearing, those who do not see well, those with speech difficulties. Some may have had more limited education than their neighbours. You need to think carefully about including and communicating with all these people. More guidance on this is given in Chapters 8 and 11. Another problem can be how to get people's attention; sometimes, choosing an unusual, attractive research method can make a real difference. One solution is to use valued technology. Consider the favourite communication routes of the group whose attention you seek.

7.2.2 Recording and analysis

When you are deciding on which techniques to use, consider the whole process you will follow in collecting and analysing the material, not just the face-to-face situation. In recording data, for example, if you choose to ask people to fill in questionnaires themselves, check they are actually giving you the type of responses you need (see Chapter 8 on recording methods). Piloting your data collection method generally identifies problems of this kind. Make sure to pilot test your methods of analysis too: it is only when you try to analyse the material you collect that you are forced to connect what you get from people with the questions you set out with. The other reason to worry about analysis early is that you need to establish whether you can do it yourself or whether you will need help (see Chapter 8 for more information about pilot testing).

7.2.3 Sensitive subjects

Sometimes, research for development work concerns issues everyone is happy to talk publicly about, but often we are trying to open up issues that are traditionally kept hidden. These may relate to sexuality, domestic violence, HIV and AIDS or trafficking, although income is a sensitive subject too in many cultures. If you work closely with community members, they can guide you as to what people may have difficulties speaking about.

People's fears are likely to be based on a rational calculation of the risks involved. For example, a violent man may be provoked by his wife taking part in research he disapproves of. Researchers need to be careful that their project is worthwhile in terms of any risks to which it potentially exposes respondents, as well as making all possible arrangements to avoid harm to respondents, of course.

Using appropriate methods can help a great deal in approaching difficult subjects in an acceptable way. Other factors, like ensuring you have proper consent from respondents (see Chapters 8 and 9), are also important, whatever methods you use. But do not jump to conclusions about which methods people will find most suitable. What seems private and safe to one group may seem threatening to another.

Focus groups have been used successfully for a wide range of issues that might be assumed to be too private to discuss in a group. If people know others in the group are in the same position they are in, they will often greatly enjoy sharing experiences that attract stigma in the broader society. For example, groups have discussed HIV prevention and treatment for incontinence without difficulty, and groups of terminally ill cancer patients valued discussing their own care. What makes the difference is the sense of equality and sharing among the group. Where there is hierarchy between participants, the dynamic is very different.

Getting people to be hypothetical can also encourage people to talk about sensitive issues. Here, you ask participants to think about people in general and imagine their response. To illustrate this, rather than asking a nurse or a group of nurses working with elders 'Have you ever used force against an elderly patient?', you could ask 'What in your view could be done to prevent elder abuse or neglect in workplaces like yours?'

The use of some sort of stimulus material, or warm-up exercise, can also encourage people to talk openly about subjects they find difficult. But don't beat about the bush! If you are embarrassed, you will convey your embarrassment to your respondents.

7.2.4 Experience or opinion?

It may be helpful to consider whether the material you need to tap is essentially a matter of gathering information about people's experiences, or whether you want to encourage them to give their opinions. When collecting views and opinions, it is important to realize that people may not have fully formed views on the issues you are investigating. This is why yes/no questionnaires can be so frustrating. What weight can you give to the box people tick if it is likely they have not really thought through the issues?

There are two points to make here. First of all, in gathering opinions, there can be a problem of people having limited experience, and hence only limited ideas about what might improve their lives. Group work can give strength in numbers and enable more creative thought, whereby one person builds on another's ideas. In both group and individual situations, if you want imaginative answers you need to give people time to think: don't just tack on questions about what might be better at the end of an interview.

Second, if you want to gather both types of material, make sure you allow time for people to tell their story properly, so you do not shortcut the process of understanding people's experiences in your haste to get on to asking their opinions. Experience is the more stable thing – opinions may change as people think further about the issues.

7.2.5 Get advice

It is essential in choosing your methods to ask advice from one or more experienced researchers. When you have worked on several research projects, you will have a much better 'feel' for the data generated by different research methods. Many researchers will be happy to give you their view on this.

7.3 Triangulation: using more than one technique

Triangulation is a term borrowed from navigation, where it is used to measure where something is located by getting a fix on it from two or more places. A calculation is then made, using the known properties of triangles to work out distances. The idea is to look at the same thing from different points of view and in different ways. Triangulation in social research means using multiple methods, different investigators/ analysts and different sources (for example informants) to increase confidence in the results.

Another tradition expresses this idea through 'mixed methods research' – the application and combination of more than one research perspective in the study of the same phenomenon. This yields completeness because quantitative methods can further develop findings derived from qualitative research, and vice versa. The methods *complement* each other, providing richness or detail that would be unavailable from one method alone.

As the example below shows, triangulation can also be used within the participatory learning and action tradition. Here, it refers to the use of different techniques, asking questions of different groups of people and the involvement of a range of investigators, perhaps with different kinds of training or different sensitivities.

Triangulation in practice: studying drought in Malawi, Zambia and Zimbabwe

A Participatory Learning and Action study of the 1992 drought in Malawi, Zambia and Zimbabwe used a range of methods in 24 villages in each country. Mapping, calendar tables, interviews and scoring techniques were used with men, women and children from three different wealth categories. Several cross-checks were used to validate the results: internal consistency within one household; internal consistency between several households; checks between answers given by individual households and those given in group discussions; secondary data; and direct observation. In addition, six of the villages were visited in a follow-up study. The objectives of this were to discuss and check the results and policy conclusions with smallholders. In all six cases, they endorsed and in some cases enlarged on the findings and recommendations.

Source: Eldridge (1993)

FOR EXAMPLE

Why is it thought important to collect information in different ways? Essentially, it is because the means through which data are collected has an effect on the findings. If we want to build confidence in the trustworthiness of our research, it is helpful to collect information in different ways. This links development workers to the familiar process of taking account of the views of all stakeholders. For example, if you were investigating water use, you might want to do some observation, as well as detailed interviews with different types of people, to supplement people's account of the community's needs as given in a group session.

As noted above, you will likely want to include some element of quantitative data collection alongside qualitative methods. But the key to triangulation is to see the same thing from different perspectives, and thus to be able to confirm or challenge the findings of one method with those of another. The sequence in which methods are used is important, and there should be opportunities to reflect on the meaning of any apparent contradictions.

The image of triangulation can be questioned, however. A social constructionist approach would suggest no one social 'thing' can be seen from different angles – and that the accounts collected from different perspectives may not match tidily at all. There may be mismatch and even conflict between them. A mismatch does not necessarily mean the data collection process is flawed – it could be that people just have very different accounts of similar phenomena. You need to critically examine the meaning of any mismatches to make sense of them.

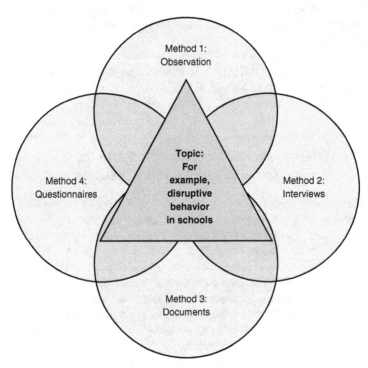

Figure 7.1 Methodological triangulation

 ## Key points from this chapter

It is often tempting for an applied researcher to rush through the design phase of a study to data collection and analysis, which are more tangible and give you the comforting sense that 'the work is being done'. However, as you will see in Chapter 8, experience shows this could well be a mistaken view, considering the very negative consequences a poor research design can have on the validity of your conclusions.

Checklist: designing a study

☑ Methods must be chosen in the light of the research focus, aims and objectives, research questions and hypothesis (if there is one).
☑ It is usually best to use more than one research technique in any project, to 'triangulate' the information you collect.

☑ The audience you want to influence is a factor to consider in your choice of methods.
☑ Think ahead about how you will record and analyse your data when you choose a method.
☑ Take account of what you know about communication with this group of people in choosing techniques.
☑ When you have chosen a technique and are pilot testing it, if you find major problems, consider adapting your technique or changing to a wholly different one.

 Further reading

Alasuutari, P., Bickman, L. and Brannen, J. (2008) *The Sage Handbook of Social Research Methods*. London: Sage.

A must for every social science researcher, this charts the new and evolving terrain of social research methodology, covering qualitative, quantitative and mixed methods in one volume.

Creswell, J.W. (2009) *Research Design: Qualitative, Quantitative and Mixed Method Approaches*, 3rd edn. New Delhi, Thousand Oaks, CA, London: Sage.

The third edition of this bestselling text enables readers to compare three approaches to research – qualitative, quantitative and mixed methods – in a single research methods text.

Della Porta, D. and Keating, M. (2008) *Approaches and Methodologies in the Social Sciences: A Pluralist Perspective*. Cambridge: Cambridge University Press.

This volume makes a persuasive case for a pluralistic approach to social science. A broad range of approaches is presented by their leading exponents so the reader can judge in what ways they might be enlisted in the study of markets, politics and societies.

Gilbert, N. (2008) *Researching Social Life*, 3rd edn. New Delhi, Thousand Oaks, CA, London: Sage.

A number of useful features, such as worked examples, case studies, discussion questions, project ideas and checklists, are included throughout the book to help those new to research to engage with the material.

Trochim, W. and Donnelly, J. (2008) *The Research Methods Knowledge Base*, 3rd edn. Mason, OH: Cengage Learning.

Covers everything from the development of a research question to the writing of a final report, describing both practical and technical issues of sampling, measurement, design and analysis.

8

COLLECTING AND MANAGING QUALITY DATA

8.1 Introduction

Having looked at how to choose which methods to use, and before we move to consider specific techniques like interviews or observation, it is important to think about what you can do to make sure that any kind of data collection is of good quality. The issues discussed in this section are at the heart of the matter of doing research properly. They are greatly emphasized to researchers in their training. Making sure your audio recorder is working, making sure your respondent realizes you are not able to give them practical help, making sure the questions you are asking make sense to people – not very exciting, but crucial.

The chapter starts with a summary of three key characteristics of quality data: that they are well scoped; based on commonly agreed concepts; and credible. The next section looks at ways to improve quality: piloting materials; being reflective about your own role; using plain language; and attending to how you present yourself. More specific issues are then considered relating to working in non-literate contexts; in languages other than your own; with children; and with disabled people. The next section looks at some practical matters at the core of the process of collecting, recording and managing data – in particular securing consent, assuring confidentiality and ways of recording, transcribing and archiving. Finally, we look at how ensure 'trustworthiness' by making sure to leave an audit trail recording key decisions.

8.2 Three characteristics of good-quality data

The purpose of research is not to collect simply any kind of data, but data that will most accurately describe the phenomena you're interested in: your data will deserve a 'quality label' only if you could not find a better measure of the issue at hand in the big collective toolbox that is empirical research. If that sounds a bit worrying, this chapter is for you. Here, we identify three of the most important issues, referring you to Chapter 3 for more general reflections on the issues of quality in research.

The first section shows how important it is to collect the right data – those which will allow you to respond to your 'big' research question. We then present the connection between concepts and data, which can be particularly tricky when doing research in a foreign country. Finally, the main issues behind measurement are addressed.

8.2.1 Quality data are well scoped

Missing, redundant or inconsistent data are a rather unpleasant surprise to a researcher writing her final report. Alas, as this situation is almost inevitable, your objective should be to make the gap between your data 'needs' and your data 'stock' as small as possible.

First, your study needs to be comprehensive, in that it needs to capture all the variables that might partially explain the phenomenon you're observing. Failing to do so will invariably result in a spurious analysis of the situation – for example, if you try to correlate shoe size and reading test scores in a survey of pupils, you are very likely to find a positive and statistically significant association between these two measures, but the claim that shoe size explains reading ability is somewhat far-fetched. If you control for age, the association will disappear, shedding light on a much more probable outcome: it is age that explains both shoe size (up to a certain limit) and reading ability.

Second, your study needs to be parsimonious (the word means 'mean' in the sense of highly economical), that is, it should exclude any irrelevant information. It can be very tempting to explore the frontiers of a research question, but the further away you venture from your initial research question, the more likely you are to generate data that are related to it only weakly, and thus to make inconclusive arguments. As such, make sure you understand which factors are essential in the question you're observing and spend more time on these. In addition, keep all interesting questions that do not strictly belong to your project for later: they might be new perspectives for further research, for inclusion in the conclusions chapter, for instance.

There are two complementary ways of checking the scope of your data collection. First, a thorough review of the literature will highlight the factors most likely to be instrumental in the situation you're analysing (see Chapter 5). It might also save you a lot of time and energy. For instance, if previous studies converge to indicate no systematic difference in the health status of women and men living in rural areas in the region you're studying, do not reinvent the wheel unless you think you have a very good reason to doubt that evidence.

8.2.2 Quality data are based on commonly agreed concepts

At this stage, your data collection plan should be reasonably well scoped. However, this does not mean the information you will gather will accurately reflect the concepts that underpin your study.

So, just as you should make sure your data stock matches your data need, you should give extra thought to the way you intend to bridge the gap between your measures and what you claim to measure. This is seldom an issue when measuring certain physical attributes (for example weight in pounds or kilograms), but is a real challenge in studies using socially defined concepts or constructs.

There are several steps to take to ensure your study makes sense in this way. The first is to conduct a thorough review of the literature. Again, the key idea is to build on previous results rather than replicating existing work.

It is always good practice to ask the same question using different methods (triangulation). For instance, if you can come to the same conclusion using administrative data and in-depth interviews, you can have confidence in your findings (Trochim and Donelly, 2008).

8.2.3 Quality data are credible

It is of course key that research is trustworthy and can be believed. In the positivist tradition, this aspect is expressed by reference to the idea of *reliability*, that is, that findings will be consistent or repeatable. Another investigator who repeated the study should find the same results. Data are said to be reliable when there is virtually no difference between the *real* or *true value* of a measure and the value you collected. As we have seen, this is a bit tricky: no one knows the true value of a measure since the value we collect is the best approximation of this supposedly true value – provided you took all the advice given in this book! You should always assume that every measurement in your study contains a certain amount of error (Shadish et al., 2002).

Essentially, there are two reasons for failing to capture the real score of, say, an individual on a given variable. The first might be the environment, the circumstances or anything else beyond your control, which might lead to *random error*. People's mood is a typical example of random error: there is not much you can do about it and, overall, it does not really matter, since some people can be in a good mood just as others are in a bad mood and the sum of all these moods is very likely to be zero.

Second, any factor systematically affecting the measurement of a variable across your sample is called systematic error: bias that is embedded in your research process. For instance, if you come dressed in a suit and a tie to a series of interviews taking place in a remote rural area, you might involuntarily introduce a bias in the data you collect, as your interviewees can be positively or negatively impressed by your outfit and modify their answer accordingly. This kind of measurement error gives either positive or negative results consistently, and it should be corrected.

It is not possible to calculate precisely the reliability of research – the best you can do is to limit measurement error to the best of your ability before, during and after the data collection phase (see also Chapter 13 on analysis).

8.3 Ways to improve quality in data collection

Whatever methods you use, some practical measure will greatly improve the quality of your work: piloting research instruments; being reflective about your own role; using plain language; and attending to how you present yourself. The following section looks at ways to work better with specific kinds of respondents.

8.3.1   Piloting

In research, we are always inventing new questionnaires, topic guides, interview schedules, observation schedules. It is vital to pilot these first: it is a terrible waste to collect data from large numbers of people in such a way that you do not get the information you need. Even if you are carrying out only one focus group discussion, you still need to test your topic guide carefully, to make sure people can follow your questions.

The best way to do this is to try it out on a small group of people who are potentially or actually part of your sample. Before that, try it out on some friends or colleagues. Reading over a questionnaire is not the same as actually trying to fill it in. Ask people to use the materials as they are intended, not just to glance through the text.

At times, even with good piloting, problems with a questionnaire become clear only after you have completed the first batch of proper interviews. It is still usually worth making changes, to ensure you get the most useful information from the majority of your respondents. You may then have questions for which there are missing answers (from the first batch), but you can acknowledge this.

When quantitative data are collected, running a pilot means applying the selected statistical model to data already collected, usually halfway through the process, to see how the model 'fits' the data. Subsequent changes might be needed.

8.3.2   Reflecting on the role of the researcher

An important way of maintaining quality is to pay attention to your own feelings and actions, and how others respond to you, and to reflect on their impact on the research process. Do you think people are giving you answers they think you want to hear? Are you hearing more from some people than others because you are a man or a woman, because of your age, your background, your perceived status? Are you frustrated with your work, and is this coming through in how you deal with respondents?

As you carry out fieldwork, it is a good idea to write notes about how things went after each interaction. What went well? What might you do differently another time? And you might want to write some notes about what you expected to find and what actually happened.

If the research is a large part of your work over a period of time, it is really useful to keep a regular research diary, to record your thoughts about the research – the content and the process – as you go along. This develops the habit of reflection, and can also be therapeutic. It also creates a record of your expectations and struggles, which can be referred to later on. An ethnographic project would include this diary writing as part of a more intensive process of recording observations of all relevant aspects of daily life.

Finally, when you are part of a research team, reflection should be built into your work process (see Chapter 16). Each phase of the process should be discussed, and suggestions for improvements made. However, don't rush to criticize when people are finding their feet. In giving feedback, for example, first ask the person who conducted the interview to give their own reflections on how it went and what might have been better. Only then allow others to give their opinions, and temper negative comment with praise of anything that was done well.

8.4 Improving communication with respondents

This section looks at a number of issues relating to communication – language, style and working in non-literate contexts. There is brief consideration of some issues relating to work with disabled people and children. We then look in a little detail at how to proceed when you do not share a language with your respondents.

8.4.1 Language

We discuss below the complex issues involved in research with people whose language you do not speak. But it is also important to think about the kind of words you use in your own language. Jargon and technical terms can be very confusing and intimidating to respondents: use language you know is familiar to your respondents and put things as simply as possible.

It is very helpful to check if people have grasped key points by politely asking them to explain them back to you. Pay attention to non-verbal signals that your respondent has lost the thread (looking confused, gazing around the room, etc.). If you are giving important information, repeat what you have said at least once and ask if it is clear.

You need also to check you have understood the other person correctly. It is very tempting to pretend you are following someone when really you are not. Be assertive and honest – if you don't, you are lost! Rephrase back to the person what you think they just said, and check on areas you are not sure of.

8.4.2 Style

How you present yourself in terms of dress, posture and so on is part of your communication with others. What is informal and relaxed in one setting can be positively rude in another. Equally, dressing in an overformal way can make you and your different background more conspicuous than it needs to be. Aim to be as informal as possible, while dressing formally enough to show respect. Think about the particular group you are working with and what their norms are. But be yourself! You won't blend in by adopting dress or behaviour you are unfamiliar with.

Remember that appropriate body language is quite culturally specific. In Western cultures, direct eye contact is used to establish a person's honesty and openness. But in some cultures, direct eye contact between strangers is seen as aggressive. All cultures have complex rules around gender relations which need to be negotiated carefully.

If you are interviewing people in their own home, it is important to balance the role of a visitor (for example accepting hospitality) with the professional role you have as a researcher – and indeed avoiding people expending scarce resources unnecessarily.

You can demonstrate listening and respect by:

- sitting at the same level as your respondents;
- using appropriate eye contact (varies by culture);
- making small encouraging movements (nodding, etc. – also varies by culture) and noises;
- adopting an open, relaxed posture (avoid folding arms, turning away);
- not interrupting.

8.4.3   Working in non-literate contexts

It is important to adapt research methods to the abilities of the people you are working with. Interviews and focus groups build on the basic skills of conversation. It can be helpful, whether or not people have literacy skills, to use visual materials as a focus. Action research has developed many methods intended to facilitate the active involvement of non-literate people – mapping, diagrams (such as seasonal calendars) and various ranking and scoring techniques (see Chapter 12, Section 12.4.). These use local materials to create a visual representation of the issues under discussion or, for example, to describe the area. However, they are generally not ends in themselves, but ways of encouraging discussion about the issues in question. For example, building a map of the area with local people using materials that come to hand is a means to implement a discussion about local problems, while at the same time affirming local knowledge and skills.

Don't use these techniques rigidly, but adapt them to the local context. People can find diagrams just as puzzling as words on paper, and may not readily see the purpose of, for example, ranking exercises. Methods should be used only when they are meaningful to participants and when they can produce information relevant to the exercise in hand. Where there is a strong oral tradition, people may actually be very comfortable with discussions, regardless of level of literacy.

8.4.4   Working with people whose first language you do not share

Carrying out successful research where you cannot speak directly with people requires considerable care and preparation. You will have to invest some time in making sure you have good arrangements for interpreting and in explaining the purpose of your research to the interpreter.

When you involve someone else in communicating with people, it is important to be clear about the capacity in which you wish them to act, be it research assistant (who can ask their own questions), advocate (to encourage respondents to put forward their views) or interpreter (simply to translate the exact content of the conversation).

If interpreting is what you need, it is best to use professional interpreters, not colleagues or professionals with other roles.

You should discuss with your interpreters exactly what the issues are that you are investigating. In addition, concepts (including common terms like 'household', 'work', 'child') may not translate directly. Your interpreters will be able to help you to ask questions in an appropriate way, given their knowledge of the language and culture. However, you also need to make it clear you want to know exactly what respondents are saying: you don't want your interpreter to censor or edit what is being said, whatever their own views on it.

In some areas, many communities from a number of different language groups co-exist. This can be problematic, particularly if communities have very different backgrounds and ambivalent attitudes towards each other. A London focus group on screening for breast cancer, conducted in Turkish, included women from Cyprus, Kurdistan and Turkey. Some hostile comments were made, arising from political tensions between the communities.

Sometimes, where a number of different languages are spoken, you will not be able to find an interpreter who can talk directly to all your respondents. Is it worth proceeding in a situation where you need two stages of translation to communicate – someone who can translate into the national language, for example, and then someone else who can translate into English? This depends on the skills of the interpreters, and what type of information is required. It is a problem to exclude groups of respondents on the basis of their language group, as they may have particular experiences you should hear about. But you cannot gather subtle and sensitive information with a room full of interpreters!

It is important to spend time with the interpreter immediately after each interview, going through your own notes and checking anything you were not sure about. Matters may have been taken for granted between the two people sharing a culture which could usefully be made explicit for you at this point. Equally, you may simply not have understood exactly what was meant from a short translation of a complex statement.

8.4.5　Research with children

In the 1990s, a body of work emerged which proposed a new approach to research with children.[1] Rejecting then-traditional approaches to children, which essentially saw them as defective adults, the new philosophy suggested seeing them as 'social actors' in themselves. We should be interested in children's points of view for their own sake, not just to measure them against adults' perceptions. Children were placed at the centre of the process of investigation, with research to take a lead from children's own agenda.

What does this mean for how we actually carry out research with children? Do not assume it is automatically necessary to use special techniques. The whole range of research approaches and techniques discussed in this manual can be used with children – where appropriate. But the way any research is carried out is critical – children are excellent observers of adults, and researchers' behaviour and attitudes will come through very clearly. It is crucial to show them respect and, as part of this, to take enough time to develop trust and a rapport with them.

It is best to think of children as like other disempowered people, and to direct your efforts to finding ways of equalizing the power imbalance between you and them. Meanwhile, advice throughout this manual about handling different stages of the research process is equally important if working with children. For example, we should be just as concerned not to waste children's time with un-thought-out research that will result in no change, as we would adults'.

You may need to be flexible about your research techniques in working with children, and take more time with children to get the right approach sorted out. In some situations, formal research methods can be suitable, but there is a danger that structured interview techniques will feel to children like a sort of test. It is helpful to spell out that there are no right or wrong answers to your questions.

- **Asking open questions:** let children tell you their story in their own way. Even if they begin somewhere way off your subject, let them continue, if necessary guiding them back to what you are interested in.
- **More structured approaches:** with children who are reasonably comfortable with reading and writing, it actually grants very good confidentiality to ask children to fill in a questionnaire or write a short essay on a subject. These methods have been used in relation to teenagers' experiences of sexual abuse (Kelly et al., 1995) and ideas about families (Morrow, 1999). 'Draw and write' is a helpful technique with younger children (see Chapter 12).
- **Group work:** children may gain confidence from the presence of their friends (chosen pairs or larger groups), as opposed to one-to-one time with an unfamiliar adult, which may feel threatening. All the same drawbacks apply to group work with adults (see Chapter 11, for example), but so do the advantages.
- **Stimulus materials:** children may find ideas easier to grasp if they are made concrete in some way. For example, using drawings or photographs, or offering 'vignettes/scenarios' (very short stories which illustrate or dramatize the issue), can be helpful, as can references to either fictional or factual elements of popular culture (soap operas, news reports). Young people often enjoy working on practical problems, and you can then probe for the reasons behind their judgements. But don't let your materials take over – they should generally only introduce discussion which moves on to a deeper level in relation to children's own experiences.

Where children have a trusting relationship with professionals, it may be a good idea to ask them to work alongside you. For example, a youth worker can sometimes 'lend' you the trust they have built with young people by introducing you and working with you. However, it may be best to avoid working closely with those with direct authority over children, such as teachers or social workers, even if they have a good relationship. It depends on the subject you are looking at.

Finally, it is generally best to spend time with children in places where others can see you. There is no need to be completely alone with individual children. You need to strike a balance: give your respondents some privacy while avoiding making them feel isolated and vulnerable and guarding against any possible accusation of abuse.

Researchers are often concerned about what to do if a child discloses to them that they or others are at risk of significant harm. See Chapter 9 on ethics for discussion of these issues.

8.4.6 Communicating with disabled people

Some disabled people have conditions which mean their communication is impaired, through deafness, blindness and/or a learning disability. But most disabled people have difficulty getting anyone to listen to them, because of negative social attitudes. Erroneous assumptions are often made about their abilities. There are no different rules for communicating with disabled people – having respect, taking time, observing how they communicate with others are key. You do not need to be an 'expert' to talk to disabled people.

Most people with impaired hearing can communicate successfully through a mixture of lip reading and signs, which usually build on signs people in their culture use routinely. A minority use a formal sign language and can conduct complex discussions through an interpreter.

Remember that many elderly people and quite a few young people have a hearing impairment. This can become particularly stressful in group situations. Raising your voice is unhelpful. Make sure people speak in turn and indicate when they are speaking. Speakers need to turn towards the person with impaired hearing and avoid covering their mouths. Before you start, think about the layout of the room, to check everyone can see each other. These measures will be helpful for other people in the group as well.

In order to make written materials accessible to those with a visual impairment, reading them out loud or audio recording are the most helpful (see Section 8.5.2). Large print (preferably at least 14pt) will help many. Braille is extremely helpful for the minority who have learnt to read it, but many blind or partially sighted people never get the chance to learn.

8.5 Collecting, recording and managing data

This section deals with data management. The guidelines given below should allow you to collect and manage data legally, safely and in a way that facilitates future reanalysis. This section looks at practical issues in gaining consent and ensuring confidentiality – there is more discussion of the ethical considerations behind this in Chapter 9. Analysis is discussed in Chapter 13.

8.5.1 Securing consent

Securing consent may be a particular issue for development workers: potential respondents may associate them with development programmes and think participating will affect their likelihood of benefiting. The issue of how to explain research to respondents so they really understand is a practical one which needs to be addressed in every research project.

It is important to remember that people may have no experience of the kind of research you are doing, and may jump to unexpected conclusions. For example, a respondent approached by one of the authors of this book in the course of her field research thought she was making a TV documentary, even though this respondent had already had two conversations and received a detailed letter about the nature of the research.

Rehearse what you will say to people and eliminate all jargon from your account. It is also crucial to be clear that people will not benefit personally from taking part, nor suffer any ill consequence from not taking part. Be specific about this – for example, if the research is collecting views on an aspect of health care, it will be helpful to say something like 'whether or not you participate in this research will not in any way affect your medical treatment'.

You need to ask specific permission to record what people are saying, whether you are taking notes or using an audio recorder. If you want to record the interview or focus group, people will sometimes refuse consent, and you need to be prepared to cope (that is, be ready to take notes instead). In asking permission, emphasize that only you and perhaps one or two other people (who can be named) will hear the recording. People sometimes imagine themselves on national radio when they see an audio recorder!

There are two easy ways respondents can give consent: first, by signing a consent form, which should be written in plain language, and second, by giving oral consent, if the interview is audio recorded. Alternatively, any written communication in which the respondent agrees to answer your questions can be considered evidence of consent, provided it is properly identifiable (with the respondent's name and yours), referenced (by, say, the title of your project) and dated.

8.5.2 Assuring confidentiality

Like consent procedures, this is discussed in general terms in Chapter 14, but the practicalities are of the essence. First, you need to decide what sort of undertakings about confidentiality to make. For some sorts of research, where community involvement is central, confidentiality is irrelevant, and no undertakings should be made to protect people's identities. In these situations, the whole process needs to be in effect a matter of public record, and people are not able to contribute unless they can stand by their evidence publicly. However, in many situations, it is appropriate to enable respondents to tell their story with the reassurance that identities will be protected and their names will not appear in any final report.

Disempowered people generally have realistic concerns about what is known about them, whether by their landlords, social security or social services officials. A study of the help given to ex-child soldiers in Liberia had to abandon audio recording because respondents were too fearful to allow this after prolonged conflict and repression (Peters et al., 2003). There may be real risks for them in trusting you with sensitive information. You need to be prepared for people to be sceptical of your ability to keep information confidential, and willing to explain why you think you can do so.

Be as specific as possible in explaining to people exactly how you will protect their identities. It is best to avoid ever writing names and identifying details on questionnaires, and you can, for example, show respondents that their names are kept on a separate card and a code number assigned to them; explain that filing cabinets are kept locked. Tell people exactly who will see or hear the material they give you.

With qualitative research, it can be worth saying that you will disguise stories you are told, if you think they are so unusual that they might identify the respondent to others. You may want to offer respondents the chance to look over the information they have given you and check they are happy for you to use it. It is easy for people to get carried away in telling their tale and forget the purpose of an interview. Consent is a process, not a one-off event – people need to be able to withdraw it at any time. You could either read back the notes you have made at the end of an interview or show the respondent a draft of your report, and then ask them to confirm that they are happy for you to use the material you are quoting from them.

Having assured respondents of the confidentiality of data, you must then follow this through by being scrupulous about office procedures which will actually make it so. It is also important, of course, to be rigorous about not verbally breaking confidentiality. Professionals who are used to sharing personal information about people they are involved with may expect researchers to similarly tell them what people have said – you need to tactfully remind them of the different rules that apply to research information. As noted above, there will be times when you cannot guarantee confidentiality, and it is important then to make that clear too.

8.5.3 Recording

It is crucial to the success of your fieldwork that you choose an appropriate method of recording the information you set out to collect. Even methods which are to some extent self-recording, like participative mapping, require you to record the discussion taking place while the work is going on. Recording for research should be as complete as possible – you should summarize and analyse later, not as you note what people are saying. Details whose importance you do not see at the time may come to the fore later on in your research process. This is where not jumping to conclusions comes in – keep an open mind, and simply record as much as you can. It is worth writing on only one side of the page: it stops you getting in a muddle when analysing the material.

Making notes during the interaction

This is sometimes the only option. It is important to learn to make notes as unobtrusively as possible. It can be difficult to maintain sufficient eye contact with a respondent sufficiently to make them feel at ease while furiously scribbling notes. You get better at this with practice.

One of the problems of semi-structured and in-depth interviewing is that you need to be thinking about the next question at the same time as writing notes from the last one – you inevitably miss some material.

Making notes after the interaction

This is obviously the least intrusive method of recording fieldwork events. However, it relies on the memory to store a large amount of information and reproduce it accurately. You will inevitably lose some. If working in this way, it is essential to do your note taking as soon as possible after the event. We forget a lot very quickly; by the next day, a lot of information will have gone forever. In this situation, you could return to the respondent after you have written up your notes to check any matters you found you were uncertain about.

While it can be a good thing if respondents are not made aware at the time of your recording their words, it is important in terms of ethics to ensure they understand that they are taking part in research.

Using an observer to make notes

This is common practice with focus groups, whereby an observer can free the facilitator to concentrate on the group process. This means introducing a non-participating person into the group, which may put some people off, but if they are unobtrusive they are soon forgotten. The observer can also note non-verbal communication as it happens.

It is also possible to use an observer in an interview situation. One person leads the interview and the other writes notes – this frees up the interviewer. This practice, for interviews or focus groups, also has the benefit of giving a second person a role in the fieldwork setting without throwing them in at the deep end. Make sure they are briefed to make complete notes, not summarize. They can observe how a more experienced person carries out an interview, and can discuss how it went afterwards. Similarly, novice interviewers can be supported by someone more experienced.

Flipchart notes

Writing flipchart notes produces a summary of what has been said – it is not the same as a detailed record. However, it is helpful in enabling participants to see the picture being built up from what they are saying. This can reinforce their sense of being heard, and can reduce repetition of key points. It can enable a group to agree a summary at the end of the session, which can avoid the researcher's distortion of the group's intentions – although it can implicitly give the message to the group that they are expected to agree with each other, which may suppress minority views. You may like to say 'one point of view was this, another was that'.

Recording

Voice recording creates a complete record of what has been said. This avoids the problem of the interviewer getting distracted from the interview by the process of recording it. It also captures people's own way of saying things, which can bring a report to life. However, it also has several drawbacks. Audio recording can make people self-conscious, although if you present a recorder in a clear and low-key way, people will usually soon forget it is there. Transcribing a recording is a lot of work, and generates very detailed information which can be difficult to analyse. Its use depends on whether you need the details of people's points of view or only the gist.

As mentioned above, you need to be prepared to cope if people refuse to let you record the interaction. You also need to be mentally prepared for recorders failing – in which case you may need to write notes quickly after the event. Always check the recording has worked.

It is best to use a digital recorder, which allows you to upload the interview onto your computer (with, in principle, the guarantee of a back-up). A small microphone which lies flat on the ground is useful for recording group sessions, and one with a suction pad is good for recording telephone interviews.

8.5.4 Transcribing

Before deciding to rely on voice recording, think ahead about transcribing. Transcribing is a skilled task for which you need to be able to type well and quickly. Transcribing an hour of audio recording takes anything up to five hours for an experienced transcriber. Focus groups are more difficult to transcribe than interviews. Freelance professional transcribers can be of good value if you need a large amount of transcribing done.

Do not assume an administrator can carry out transcribing easily – experience shows this is not necessarily the case. You need to give detailed instructions about how you want the work done (for example you want every word as it is said), and it is always important to check transcripts against the recording.

You could both audio record and take notes or, rather than fully transcribing recordings, listen to them and take detailed notes only at key points. You can then use the recording to get important quotes or to check on that point when the dog barked and you got distracted. Audio recorders have counters which enable you to make a note of where you were on the recording at any given point in the interview, so you can go back to it later.

Whatever method you use to record fieldwork interactions, you should also write notes as you go along, recording your observations of the context you are working in, any interactions which occur 'behind the scenes' that may be relevant and your own thoughts about what you find.

Working with interpreters adds another dimension to the recording process. Ideally, you would record the whole interaction. In one case, a researcher working in London found that the interpreter (actually a community worker without specialist training in interpreting) was not translating what her elderly Chinese respondents were saying, but putting forward her own point of view, by getting another Chinese speaker to transcribe the recording. It is to be hoped that you have worked out an excellent relationship with your interpreter, and this sort of thing could not happen! (See Section 8.4.4.)

8.5.5   Archiving

The issue of archiving data is often neglected by busy researchers rushing through their final report. Anybody involved in the collection of personal data has the legal and moral obligation to keep these data in an appropriate way. Governments from a number of countries have recently strengthened their legislation (and enforcement procedures) in response to new technological developments and growing social concerns.

Where you collect substantial data, including qualitative data, consider contributing this to a shared data archive. The UK's data archive (http://www.data-archive.ac.uk/home) holds much valuable material both about UK issues and for some international studies, such as the Young Lives study of childhood poverty. Of course, you need to get consent to this from respondents at the start.

Data archives should meet two requirements: facilitating *legal* access to the data (by respondents requesting to check their personal data, legal authorities and other research teams wishing to reanalyze it) and preventing *illegal* access (by individuals and organizations trying to harm) as well as *unlawful* access (by individuals and organizations unaware of their obligations).

Meeting these requirements implies a mix of technical solutions and organizational procedures. Technology is needed to save the data in the appropriate format, store it in a password-protected area, prevent intrusions and possible viruses, find appropriate backup solutions, etc. Established procedures will help your organization to enforce its data protection policy even as staff change: an ethical charter published on your website will give your organization credibility and brief new staff about the research ethos; standard consent forms will be produced; procedures to grant access to the data by other research teams will be put in place; metadata and documentation will be made available to facilitate reanalysis, etc. You might find that some training is necessary to make sure the data protection policy is enforced across the organization.

When you conduct field research in a foreign country, a minimum requirement should be to abide by the data protection legislation of the country in which you operate. However, a simpler and safer solution is to systematically follow the rules of 'strict' countries such as the UK, where extensive legislation has been in place since 1998 (see www.data-archive.ac.uk/home).

Finally, the best way to make sure your data are handled correctly without creating too much extra work is to embed these procedures in the research process and enshrine them in the brief. In this area also, anticipation is the key to high-quality research.

8.6 Ensuring 'trustworthiness'

One big challenge to qualitative research in particular is the charge that we find what we set out to find – in effect that we select only those parts of respondents' testimony which suit our argument. And indeed, the same is sometimes said about quantitative work – for example, it is true that pharmaceutical companies generally only publish the results of drug trials when the results are positive. A key way of keeping traditional scientific research 'honest' is the principle that it should be possible to replicate (copy) exactly what was done in the research and come up with the same findings. This is the reason why the exact methods used are always given in research reports. Although for some sorts of research replication is impossible or irrelevant, the principle that it should be possible to trace exactly what was done is an important one.

You should leave a 'paper trail' which could be followed by someone else, documenting important processes and decisions. This is important in relation to sampling, data collection and particularly analysis. It should be possible to see why you have arrived at the categories you use – or at least at which point these decisions were made. This discipline can also be useful if someone else needs to pick up your work from you.

Key points from this chapter

Checklist: for quality in data management

Quality data:

- ☑ are well scoped;
- ☑ are based on commonly agreed concepts;
- ☑ are credible/reliable.

Improving quality in data collection:

- ☑ Pilot to allow you to fix possible mistakes before it is too late.
- ☑ Reflect on the influence you may have had on the situation of interest when collecting data.

Improving communication with respondents:

- ☑ Make sure your non-verbal signals demonstrate listening and respect.
- ☑ Take time to build rapport and observe how people usually communicate before asking questions.
- ☑ Use simple language and avoid jargon.
- ☑ Adapt your ways of communicating to the group of people in question, and don't make assumptions about their abilities.
- ☑ Never pretend to have understood when you have not.
- ☑ Check that your respondents are understanding you by asking for feedback.

Take care in collecting, recording and storing data:

- ☑ Ensure your procedures to secure respondents' consent and protect confidentiality are carried out consistently.
- ☑ Be very careful to ensure you are getting genuine informed consent to participating in your research.
- ☑ Find an appropriate method of recording your data and use it systematically and consistently.
- ☑ Archiving of data should be done according to the highest standards.
- ☑ Keep notes of all research decisions you make and the reasons for them.

Further reading

Boyden, J. and Ennew, J. (eds) (1997) *Children in Focus: A Manual for Participatory Research with Children.* Stockholm: Rädda Barnen.

Denscombe, M. (2010) *The Good Research Guide for Small-scale Social Research Projects,* 4th edn. Buckingham and Philadelphia, PA: Open University Press.

Includes useful practical guidance on how to use a number of research methods and approaches.

McCrum, S. and Hughes, L. (1998) *Interviewing Children: A Guide for Journalists and Others.* London: Save the Children.

Ward, L. (1997) *Seen and Heard: Involving Disabled Children and Young People in Research and Development Projects.* York: Joseph Rowntree Foundation.

Note

1 See, for example, James and Prout (1990), James et al. (1998) and Qvortrup (1994).

9

THINKING ABOUT ETHICS IN RESEARCH

Questions of ethics are embedded in every aspect of the process of research for development work. However, while some issues are traditionally discussed as ethical dilemmas specific to research (meaningful consent to participation, confidentiality of data), ethics are relevant to a much wider field of concern. Every chapter of this manual has an ethical dimension: Is the research worthwhile? Have community members had a say in its focus and conduct? Is it well defined and carefully planned? Is the sample appropriate, including everyone it should? It is not possible to make research ethical by abiding by a particular set of rules of procedure – you have to consider the ethical aspects of the whole undertaking.

As a researcher, you cannot always foresee what harm may occur as a result of your work, but respondents often can. An open and responsive process is important, but you also need to take care of dull administrative matters like never writing people's names on data and keeping data secure.

This chapter starts with a brief consideration of existing codes of ethics, then moves on to cover responsibilities to respondents, wider accountability and responsibilities to colleagues.

9.1 Codes of ethics

The professional associations for different types of research, including the Social Research Association (www.the-sra.org.uk/guidelines.htm), the Association of Social Anthropologists of the Commonwealth (www.theasa.org/ethics.shtml), the British Sociological Association (www.britsoc.co.uk/equality/Statement+Ethical+Practice. htm) and the British Psychological Society (www.bps.org.uk/the-society/code-of-conduct/code-of-conduct_home.cfm), have produced a variety of statements of ethical practice which govern their professions. However, ethical guidelines frequently raise more questions than they answer. Ethical practice in research is generally a matter of finding a balance between a number of principles, and is highly dependent on specific context. As a researcher, demonstrating that potential ethical problems have been considered and addressed will create greater confidence than simply referring to a standard code.

You should also be aware that new standards in research ethics emerge continually, and it is your responsibility to keep up with current best practice. This means also recognizing the existence of a wide range of occasionally contrasting perspectives – feminist perspectives, for example, offer valuable critiques of mainstream practices which too often omit important considerations of gender.[1]

9.2 Responsibilities towards respondents: some ethical issues to consider

This section discusses the following principles:

- avoiding harm to respondents;
- avoiding undue intrusion;
- communicating information and obtaining informed consent;
- rights to confidentiality and anonymity;
- fair return for assistance;
- respondents' rights in data and publications;
- respondents' involvement in research.

9.2.1 Avoiding harm to respondents

As a researcher, your paramount obligation is to ensure you protect the physical, social and psychological wellbeing and the rights, interests and privacy of those you study. You need to assess the possible risks or costs to respondents of taking part in your research, try to minimize these and weigh them up against the benefits to individuals and wider groups. It is difficult to judge the ultimate impact of any research you undertake, and any benefit from it may not accrue to the respondents themselves. If you fear people may be harmed, do not continue. If you have concerns, at the very least ensure you have direct discussions with representatives of the group to be researched. The following case study shows consideration of various ethical issues arising in a specific research project.

FOR EXAMPLE

Mental Health and Justice

Mental Health and Justice is a research project in London funded by the Big Lottery Fund involving a collaboration of academic (Institute of Psychiatry, Kings College, University College London, St George's and Kingston University) and voluntary organizations (Victim Support and Mind). It involved a prevalence survey of people with mental health problems, and qualitative interviews about their experience of the criminal justice system. The research project was scrutinized by a National Health Service Research Ethics Committee. The respondents faced multiple vulnerabilities, in terms of both their own mental health and the fact that they had been victims of crime. The following issues were considered and addressed:

Distress: revisiting and discussing distressing experiences could 're-traumatize' the participants, be upsetting at the time and have a negative impact on their mental health. Support mechanisms were set up to minimize distress during the interview. Experienced researchers would stop and offer support during the interview, and finish the interview on a positive note. Before the interview, they asked the individual about their support network and suggested they bring a supportive carer with them if appropriate (and offered to pay their expenses). A list of helpful agencies was given to the interviewees, and the researchers offered to contact agencies on their behalf.

Increased risk of victimization: many participants could still be in a vulnerable situation, for example those experiencing domestic violence. If the perpetrator discovered they were discussing the issues, they could be at greater risk. Interviews were taking place at regular health service or the organizational offices rather than at homes, and rigorous data protection and confidentiality measures are being set up to protect anonymity. Researchers were careful to describe the research in broader terms such as 'health' when contacting the participants and not to disclose the content of the research when leaving messages, for example.

Capacity to consent: some people with mental health problems may lack the capacity to make an informed decision to take part in the research, and this could vary according to their mental state at different times. They were approached via support services, and could have worried that the support would be withdrawn if they had said no. Most participants were approached via a mental health professional who could make an assessment about the individual's capacity to consent. Clear written information sheets were provided, and the researchers checked whether they understood and consented throughout the process, stopping at any point if they felt consent was withdrawn. In the qualitative research, the interviewee was offered the opportunity to see a transcript and to change or withdraw their consent.

Disclosure of risk: given the issues discussed, it was reasonably likely that the participants might disclose that someone else was at risk, for example children or other vulnerable adults, or potentially their own offending behaviour. Where this occurred, referrals would be made to appropriate organizations.

Anticipating harm

While potential respondents may be aware of risks to themselves, you may sometimes be better placed to guess at the possible consequences of participation. Even if respondents consent, it is still your duty to protect them as far as possible from any potentially harmful effects, whether these relate to individuals or whole social groups. Groups that face prejudice and discrimination, such as ethnic minorities, may be particularly vulnerable.

Wasting people's time

When you involve people in research, you are often taking time they would otherwise spend contributing to the household income. You may want to give some recompense for this, but it is also important to make sure your research is necessary. Be certain no one has already gathered the evidence you need before embarking on fieldwork. There are impoverished communities in the North and the South, conveniently placed for researchers, which receive a steady flow of researchers enquiring about one thing or another, and whose situation has not been transformed by over-researching.

Raising expectations

A related issue is that of raising expectations inappropriately. It is very difficult for people in need to understand that a researcher is interested in them only for the purposes of broader study and will not bring any assistance in their wake. This is especially true of community-level efforts like Participatory Learning in Action exercises, which explicitly ask people to prioritize issues for action. They may have beneficial effects in themselves, but most people want direct assistance, not just 'facilitation'.

On the other hand, if we worried too much about raising expectations, we would do nothing. And, at times, expectations are so low they should be raised. The issue is complex, but it must be thought through. In research for development work, the most practical response is to do everything possible to ensure any work is embedded within a programme of practical work and advocacy, and to be honest with respondents about likely outcomes.

Working with particularly vulnerable respondents

The issues discussed in this chapter are particularly pertinent where respondents are especially vulnerable, perhaps politically; perhaps because they are refugees who feel unwelcome in the country they have fled to; or perhaps because of power imbalances of other kinds: they are children, have learning difficulties or disabilities which impair communication or simply cannot read or write. With such groups, your duty to think ahead about the impact of your work is greater, and in terms of the process you need to pay extra attention to good communication with respondents. More time will be needed to gain valid consent and to build trust among particularly disempowered people.

In planning research, it is a good idea to assess the particular risks of your specific piece of work. There are a wide range of vulnerable groups – children; women; disabled people; lesbian, gay, bisexual and transgender people; victims of violence; among others – and each demands careful consideration regarding the unique set of potential risks your research may raise. Thinking systematically through strategies for minimizing such vulnerabilities is critical from the outset, as is revisiting them throughout the evolving research project. You have a responsibility to familiarize yourself with the particular vulnerabilities of the research group in question, both in general terms and with regard to the community you will engage. Obviously, the risks of different research projects vary widely in nature and intensity – each needs to be assessed specifically.

In terms of dealing with vulnerable individuals, researchers need guidance on what to do if, for example, a respondent talks about suicide or harm to others. Guidance within professional ethics guidelines is a starting point here. You should be very clear on any legal obligations regarding disclosure of such information – for instance, under subpoena or as mandated by child abuse legislation – both in the country where you are based and in those in which your field research is being conducted. At the end of an interview, researchers should talk directly to the person about their concerns and discuss with them what should be done. They should also have available on-the-spot information about possible sources of help. In some projects, researchers routinely leave behind a package of information for respondents. It is always appropriate to share such issues with a research supervisor who can advise on the basis of wider experience.

Child protection

Because of children's relative powerlessness, researchers have a particular responsibility for their protection. This obviously includes preventing any harm to children caused by the research itself, but also giving thought to what you will do if a child takes the opportunity of a research interview to disclose current or past abuse.

Organizations need to discuss this difficult issue and agree a policy, to support individual researchers in any action they take. For example, the UK National Children's Bureau has the following policy guidelines on this matter (Shaw et al., 2011):

> As far as possible, children and young people participating in research should be afforded the same degree of protection regarding confidentiality, anonymity and data protection as adult participants. However, when it comes to matters of child protection, there is clearly a duty to ensure the safety of children and young people over our responsibility as researchers to guarantee confidentiality.
>
> Any organisation wishing to involve children and young people in research should have policies in place to address safeguarding issues; specifically setting out the circumstances under which information given by a child would be disclosed in the interests of their safety (or that of another child).
>
> The limits to confidentiality must be explained clearly to potential research participants through information provided about the research and reinforced during the consent process. [...]
>
> The researcher should also make sure that they are in a position to assist children and young people who have participated in research to access appropriate help or support, if required. (However, it is important that researchers maintain their professional boundaries and recognise the limits of their own expertise, signposting to external sources of support rather than attempting to provide support or counselling themselves.)

As with adults, where disclosure of harm or risk of harm is made, the first priority is to have a direct discussion with the young respondent about what they think should be done about the abuse. Often, they will know what action they would prefer. It may be helpful if the child can be persuaded to tell someone else they trust, who can help to support them and address the situation.

FOR EXAMPLE

Reports of child abuse: children on commercial farms in Zimbabwe

A project investigating the needs of children on commercial farms in Zimbabwe found several instances where abuse was indicated. One group reported 'we are physically and mentally abused by our stepmothers. They always accuse us of something we have not done. If anything is missing at home, we are always blamed. Some of us girls are given men, whom we do not want. If the men we are given become broke, our stepmothers usually look for another man with money. Some children are abused by stepfathers, when their mothers are away.'

Some children also wanted to report their own physical abuse. These were referred on to a professional counsellor or to members in the community who were judged to be competent and better placed to deal with the issue. One of the adult coordinators of the project said 'the subject of child abuse has not been easy to deal with. [...] Unless services, professional counselling and legal protection are available, a child who reports abuse can be placed in an even worse situation. There is need to establish an education, protection and care programme in these communities if this problem is to be adequately addressed.'

Source: McCartney (2000)

In many (or perhaps most) parts of the world, reporting child abuse by no means guarantees a sensitive and positive response from the authorities. This is of course a huge problem, but is not a good enough reason to turn a blind eye to what a child is telling you. And while you cannot guarantee a wholly appropriate response from others, it is also true that a researcher by herself is most unlikely to have suitable skills to assist a child who is in an abusive situation. The child will need help from others, and you should facilitate this, involving the child as far as possible in any decisions you make (see Section 8.4.5 on working with children for a fuller discussion of ensuring quality in data collection during research with children).

Meanwhile, remember also that it is possible for research staff to take advantage of their position to abuse children. If researchers are working closely with children and building up trusting relationships, and especially in the rare cases where the research requires significant unsupervised one-to-one contact, there need to be checks to ensure the risk of abuse is minimized. Every effort should be made to obtain official confirmation of the candidate's integrity in this regard, with police checks carried out on anyone in this position. Where police checks cannot be done, or are likely to be ineffective, organizations employing researchers need to be more vigilant themselves.

Check on the identity of those applying for (or holding) such posts by asking to see documents such as a birth certificate or passport and by following up references offered. Asking to see qualifications is a simple but practical and effective vetting measure. Reference requests should seek specific information on the candidate's suitability to work with children. Select referees who have experience of the candidate's work with children and ask for further information from them.

Unless it is essential to the research, you should avoid making plans which involve researchers being alone with children. These issues are discussed further in guidance produced for the UN Study on Violence against Children (Laws and Mann, 2004).

9.2.2 Avoiding undue intrusion

It is easy as researchers to get very excited about how important our research is, but remember that respondents have other priorities. You need to consider how potentially intrusive your research is, and whether this is necessary and justifiable. You have no special entitlement to study all phenomena, and the pursuit of information is not in itself a justification for overriding other social and cultural values.

Having said that, as noted in the example above, many violations of women's and children's rights take place within what is seen as the 'private sphere' of the family. Regard for the privacy of family life cannot be allowed to block all research which aims to open up these issues. Nevertheless, these sensitivities need to be considered in the choice of methods and sampling and in numerous other research decisions. Informal research methods may be more effective than more structured approaches.

9.2.3 Communicating information and obtaining informed consent

Giving information is closely tied up with the process of getting consent from respondents in an appropriate way. Research needs the freely given informed consent of its respondents to be ethical. It is therefore essential that researchers work out effective ways of ensuring respondents understand what the research is about: its purpose(s); the anticipated consequences; the funders and sponsors; anticipated uses of the data; possible benefits and possible harm or discomfort that might affect participants; how much of respondents' time you require and whether you will provide any incentives or reimbursement; how data will be recorded and stored; and the degree of anonymity and confidentiality that can be afforded to respondents. Information sheets can include photos of interviewers, to help put a human face to the process. It is worth having a checklist of the things you need to say to each respondent!

Some researchers give respondents an information sheet and ask them to sign a form stating that they have read it and consent to participating in the research. This is good practice where respondents can read and understand such materials, and where having evidence that respondents gave their consent is felt to be important. A clear, simple information sheet can also help respondents if they think of questions about the research after the researcher has left. But this approach has its problems. You don't want respondents to feel that, because they have signed a piece of paper, they are obliged to take part in the whole research process, if it later strays into areas they are not happy with. And, of course, it is inappropriate if respondents can't read or understand what is written.

It is best to think of consent as an ongoing process, in which you remind respondents of the possible future uses of the information they give you as appropriate, and in which respondents can opt out whenever they wish. With children in particular, who are often given little choice about participating in processes, such as schooling, it is important to show them they do have a choice. One approach is to tell children that whenever they say 'stop' the interview will stop, and show them that this is so.

It can be difficult for potential respondents to understand what is meant by 'research'. People may naturally tend to assume that, if you are approaching them with a lot of questions, there is some particular reason why they have been chosen. You need to explain particularly clearly that they will not benefit or suffer personally, regardless of whether or not they take part in the research (see also Section 8.5.1, which discusses some practical steps to take in relation to obtaining consent).

ACTIVITY 9.1

Gaining informed consent

Practise explaining about your research, including all the issues you need to cover, and asking for people's consent to participate, in a role-play exercise with colleagues. Think about the particular people you will be researching with, and explain as you would to them. Have the person playing the respondent ask some awkward questions. You can try out draft information sheets at the same time, where appropriate.

FOR EXAMPLE

Informed consent from children with communication difficulties: the UK

A joint project between Hammersmith and Fulham Social Services (London) and Save the Children looked at ways of consulting children and young people with disabilities about services. The children were aged between four and 14 and had a range of disabilities and communication needs. The researchers had a number of concerns about how to get valid consent from them and how to assure confidentiality. Working closely with practitioners from a day centre the children used was very helpful in encouraging parents and children to agree to take part, but did it make it difficult for them to decline? It was hard to maintain the anonymity of respondents with this high level of staff involvement, and on one occasion confidentiality was broken (a staff member told a parent something that a child had said).

Gaining consent was satisfactory in some cases, as shown in the following account:

> I said, 'shall I tell you a bit about why I'm here?' She signalled, 'yes'. I got out the leaflet. I read it through to her, showed her the picture, explained that what she says will go in a book but not her name. I said you don't have to say anything you don't want to, I said you can stop when you want. I asked if it was OK to talk to her about [the centre]. She signalled 'yes'.

In other cases, it was less clear that the child understood what was being said, and they were not included in the research.

Ongoing consent was also felt to be important. One researcher established a means for a child to indicate that they wished to stop:

> I got out the 'stop' sign, gave it to [child] and explained that if he wanted to stop for a short while, to stop to eat or drink, or just to rest, or stop for today, or stop altogether, he could let me know by holding up the stop sign. I said, 'how will you let me know if you want to stop?' and he put up the sign and smiled.

Source: Lewis and Kirby (2001)

9.2.4 Rights to confidentiality and anonymity

Respondents should have the right to remain anonymous and to have their rights to privacy and confidentiality respected. You should make every effort to protect the identities of those from whom you collect data. There are a number of steps you need to take in putting this guidance into practice. As well as changing individuals' names, you may need to protect the identities of villages or other geographical areas.

In some situations (such as participatory work within small communities), it is not realistic to undertake to protect the identities of those taking part; in this case, of course, you should not suggest that you could. Then people can decide for themselves what they say and what they don't say, knowing that their neighbours or local government officials, for instance, may find out what they said.

It is important to be specific about what confidentiality means in any particular study.

Consent and confidentiality: studying the problems girls face in Surkhet, Nepal

A study of the difficulties girls face in families in villages of Surkhet district, Nepal, produced a video documentary of girls' voices and a Safe Environment for Girls project. Informed consent was obtained from village development committees, teachers and non-governmental organizations (NGOs) before undertaking any fieldwork. The objectives of the research were outlined before starting the discussion with the various groups. Individual interviews with adolescent girls were kept confidential and not disclosed in their village, and the names of the informants were not given in the report. The individual girls for case study were chosen by the girls themselves, with reasons explained in the group before choosing them, to reduce the group's expectations.

To protect the girls, the draft video was shown to the children whose ideas were documented in filming. Once it was shown to the children, they requested and were excited to show the video to their parents too. The researchers returned to the village and filmed the parents talking about the girls' difficulties and then showed them the film. In the video, lots of views were raised against parents' behaviour towards daughters. Surprisingly, brothers and parents were convinced and agreed that what they said was indeed happening in their village. They then agreed to the video being shown to any audience.

FOR EXAMPLE

As part of their responsibility to avoid doing harm to respondents, the researcher has a duty to anticipate ways in which confidentiality may be compromised. For example, it is not enough just to change names, if people remain identifiable from their characteristics or the story – the only male teacher in the school, or whatever. Where this problem is difficult to overcome, it can be useful to discuss with the respondent in question what to do for the best. They may want to withdraw consent to use their data, or they may decide they are happy to be identifiable.

In participatory projects, respondents may want to use their real names, getting acknowledgement for their work. Researchers need to think this through, as respondents may not be aware of all the possible consequences of publishing their views or experience openly. Again, it is essential to explain the possible effects of such an action in detail to all those concerned. One option to consider is for respondents to choose their own pseudonym for use in reports, so they can recognize their own words.

There are, however, limits to any guarantee of confidentiality in situations where the person may be at risk. See above, on child protection.

9.2.5 Fair return for assistance

There should be no exploitation of respondents, as individuals or as groups (for example a village used for an exercise when training in Participatory Learning and Action techniques), and fair return should be made for any help. Why should people spend their time helping you when they could be doing work to put food on the table? Chapter 10 discusses this issue in relation to sampling. Particular issues are raised by peer research, where participants may put large amounts of work into a project (see Section 12.2).

9.2.6 Respondents' rights in data and publications

It is important to recognize the rights of respondents over data and publications you produce. It is good practice, where possible, to allow respondents to see transcripts of interviews and field notes, and to alter the content, withdraw statements and provide additional information if they wish. The same process can be carried out verbally, explaining what you understood the person to say. However upsetting it is to the researcher to lose good data, if a respondent does not want you to publish them, that's that.

The question of feedback and consultation on action or publications arising from the research is also an ethical one. Respondents are entitled to know what you are saying about them!

9.2.7 Respondents' involvement in research

This manual emphasizes the value of respondents' participation. Perhaps the most difficult, and the most crucial, point where this should be followed through on is at the end of the project. People need to be involved in the process of deciding what will and will not happen as a result of the research project.

Meanwhile, the right to active involvement should extend to all members of the community. It is easy to perpetuate discrimination against groups of people by taking the easy way out and ignoring those the majority routinely exclude. Development researchers need to ask questions about, and endeavour to involve, people who are not readily visible, as well as those who are.

Another issue to consider in the conduct of your fieldwork is how you as researchers will respond if you hear prejudiced or degrading comments about discriminated-against groups. Traditionally, a researcher should not put forward their own view in any circumstances, staying outside the issue. But if you ignore such comments, you can seem to collude with these attitudes. If you intervene, you can alienate your respondents or get sidetracked. It is useful for an organization to consider these issues, so fieldworkers know what kind of action they should take.

Dealing with equality issues

Consider the following situation:

You are running a focus group discussion, and right at the beginning two participants make strongly prejudiced negative comments about ethnic minority people in their area, blaming them for all kinds of social problems. Only one other participant appears to disagree, and he is intimidated.

Discuss within your research team what you should do.

ACTIVITY 9.2

9.3 Wider accountability

If you aim to study powerful people, such as directors of multinational companies, you can be sure you will be made accountable for your work in a variety of ways. The same does not necessarily apply to those in poverty. Researchers may need to set up structures to assist in making themselves accountable for their actions. An advisory group for the research, involving key stakeholders, is a good start.

9.3.1 At national level

It is important to be aware of national laws or administrative regulations that may affect your research. You should also remember that, in most cases, social research data are not privileged under law, and may be subject to legal subpoena.

Research conducted outside one's own country raises special ethical and political issues, relating to personal and national disparities in power, political interest and national political systems (Mabry, 2008) . In some countries, the government requires that researchers from other countries affiliate themselves with a local research institution before consenting to their work. This is in any case good practice, as it ensures the researchers of the country have a chance to contribute to and learn from the research.

In projects planned from one country and conducted in others, it can be a good idea to set up a research advisory or reference group within any country where fieldwork takes place, perhaps in addition to an advisory group for the whole project. This can have all kinds of benefits, including useful advice on local conditions, building wider ownership of the issues the research is addressing and perhaps empowering 'the researched'.

9.3.2 At community level

This manual has focused on researchers' relationship with the community throughout the research process. Development work aims to empower communities, and research needs to work in the same direction. This often means an increasing level of participation in research processes, but this needs to be appropriate to the particular situation (see Chapter 12). Participation in research processes cannot be assumed to be beneficial.

9.3.3   Research ethics committees

Because of the particular risks of medical research, there is a well-developed approach within health care to the scrutiny of research proposals for their ethical implications. In the UK, research proposals in the health or social care fields usually need to be submitted to a research ethics committee for approval before staff will be able to assist in contacting service users or staff. If the research requires access to health service records, or if patients are to be contacted through such records, the project needs to go through this process.

Ethics committees – also known as institutional research boards – look at the overall quality and relevance of the research as well as direct risks to respondents. They have a governance role for organizations (deciding whether research is worthwhile to support) as well as considering ethical issues that arise from how it is conducted. These committees were originally constructed with clinical research and all the risks it brings with it in mind, and social researchers have at times met with lack of understanding of qualitative research (Tolich and Fitzgerald, 2006). Nonetheless, as universities and other organizations implement referral to research ethics committees as standard practice in response to public concern about the need for scrutiny of research practice, learning how to manage a committee's role in one's research project has become an important skill for any social researcher.[2] It may be necessary to get agreement from both a university research ethics committee and a committee that governs access to particular respondents – these have different roles and responsibilities.

There are some practical issues you should always anticipate when dealing with a research ethics committee. First, committees may work to a fixed timetable, and their deliberations may well cause disruptions and delays to your schedule – to save yourself unnecessary frustrations, maintain good communication, be clear about deadlines and budget your time accordingly at the outset for such contingencies. (See Section 4.4 for more on timeframes.) Second, the committee will generally have a set of recommendations and criticisms of your project you will be expected to respond to. It is worth approaching this feedback with the same openness to constructive criticism you might expect at the final stages of work following the publication of your research.

Third, the proliferation of research ethics committees worldwide has led to a rise in the practice of formal ethical review committees across Southern research institutions. Such institutions may have practices distinct from their Northern counterparts, as well as more stringent limitations in terms of financial and material resources for reviewing proposals. You should anticipate these challenges and plan accordingly, contacting the institution you will be working with directly for any clarification.[3] A good starting point, given the wide variation in emerging practice across the South, is to seek guidance from any colleagues who have had past experience working with ethics committees in the country (and, ideally, with the institution) in question.

There are a number of additional tips for dealing with research ethics committees which you may want to familiarize yourself with – a useful starting resource is the website Research Ethics Guidebook (www.ethicsguidebook.ac.uk).

9.3.4   Making information available

If anyone is to learn from your work, it is essential that findings and information about the methodology be published or otherwise made available to others. One way of helping to prevent the waste of resources involved in duplicate studies of the same issues and groups is to ensure key findings are available for future researchers to read.

It is also important to publish within the country or area where the data are collected, for the same reasons, and to publish in the language/s of that country, so your findings are made available to those they concern most.

Failure to publish, or deliberate suppression of information, can be unethical, if you think of the waste of resources and broken promises involved. It is worrying when data are treated as private property and people are prevented from publishing by those who commissioned the research.

9.4   Responsibilities to colleagues

Research for development work is often very much a team effort. As well as experienced staff, there may be research assistants, interpreters and community workers, working in various capacities. All those involved should be treated with respect, and efforts made to ensure less experienced staff gain the maximum possible benefit from their involvement (see also Chapter 6).

Northern researchers should take account of the interests and needs of Southern colleagues, considering the disparity in resources available to them. Development research organizations should make every effort to invest in Southern research institutions.

The safety of researchers while undertaking fieldwork should be given explicit consideration, with discussion encouraged among the research team. Researchers should be told that their own safety is more important than the successful completion of research tasks. Assess the risks of your particular project, plan ahead and avoid danger as far as possible. In some environments, researchers share some risks simply by being there – organizations should have their own procedures for protecting all staff in insecure situations, and these should be applied equally to researchers. A specific code of practice on safety for researchers has been developed by the Social Research Association, and can be found on their website.

Some risks will be specific to the topics under investigation, but a few guidelines apply to many situations:

- Make sure a research colleague *and* a trusted friend/family member knows where you are and what you are doing each day, and when you expect to return. Let them know when you have returned.

- Consider working in pairs – this has other benefits in terms of quality of data collection and opportunities to learn.
- In countries where it is possible, a mobile phone is useful for keeping in touch, should plans change, and for calling help if you should need it.
- Think about what will be the safest transport option.
- Ensure your dress is appropriate. Avoid carrying anything of value with you.
- Carry documentation establishing your identity as a researcher.
- Stay aware at all times of changing political/security developments during the course of your research.
- Appropriate debriefing for immediate action should be conducted if any security threat is encountered, using a chain of communication which needs to be established at the project's start.

 ## Key points from this chapter

Checklist: ethical issues to consider in research for development work

- ☑ Is the research necessary?
- ☑ Is the research well planned as a project, and integrated into a programme of practical work?
- ☑ Have you considered the specific ethical issues the project raises, and how to address them?
- ☑ How will informed consent be obtained from respondents?
- ☑ Are you providing accessible information about your project?
- ☑ What level of confidentiality and anonymity can you offer to participants, and how can they be informed of this effectively?
- ☑ Is there appropriate stakeholder participation in the project?
- ☑ Are you offering appropriate returns for assistance?
- ☑ Are respondents able to check your version of the information they have given you?
- ☑ How will you ensure information is fed back appropriately to those who were researched?
- ☑ What systems are in place to ensure you learn from your experience?
- ☑ How are respondents to be informed of, or consulted on, the results of the research?
- ☑ Assess any risks to field researchers and work out ways to minimize them.

 ## Further reading

Alderson, P. and Morrow, V. (2004) *Ethics, Social Research and Consulting with Children and Young People*. Barkingside: Barnardo's.

Commissioned by Barnardo's, this is a thorough consideration of the ethical issues involved in research with children. It looks at each stage of the research process as well as at questions like what research is done and what is not. Includes a useful summary of ten topics in ethical research.

Association of Social Anthropologists of the Commonwealth (revised 1999) 'Ethical Guidelines for Good Practice'. Available online at www.theasa.org/ethics.shtml.

Christensen, P. and James, A. (2008) *Research with Children: Perspectives and Practices,* 2nd edn. London: Jessica Kingsley.

A clear guide on ethics regarding children in development research across different social and cultural contexts. Includes discussions of ethics and reflexivity in research; quantitative and qualitative approaches; and dealing with children as researchers.

Economic and Social Research Council (ESRC). *The Research Ethics Guidebook.* Available online at www.ethicsguidebook.ac.uk.

An extremely accessible online resource, with an emphasis on outlining regulatory processes and procedures that can apply to social research. A good source for practical, straightforward explanations of how research ethics committees function in contemporary academia. See in particular advice on dealing with research ethics committees in social research.

Mertens, D. and Guinsberg, P. (eds) (2009) *Handbook of Social Research Ethics.* New Delhi, Thousand Oaks, CA, London: Sage.

Authoritative source on the full range of issues to consider in research ethics, updated with current best practice and written specifically with social researchers in mind. Provides a particularly good look at emerging trends in codes of conduct across social and behavioural research, as well as chapters dedicated to discussing research approaches for specific vulnerable groups. See also chapter by Mabry, 'Governmental Regulation in Social Science', for a discussion of several common ethical dilemmas researchers should be aware of when confronting the issue of government regulation in research.

Liamputtong, P. (2006) *Researching the Vulnerable: A Guide to Sensitive Research Methods.* New Delhi, Thousand Oaks, CA, London: Sage.

Well-organized, clear and accessible work dedicated to the specific ethical and methodological issues raised in researching the vulnerable. Draws on global examples and addresses children, women, disabled people, elderly people, lesbian, gay, bisexual and transgender people and a range of other groups of vulnerable subjects in depth.

Social Research Association *Ethical Guidelines.* Published annually in its Directory of Members. Available online at www.the-sra.org.uk/guidelines.htm.

World Health Organization (2005) *Multi-country Study on Women's Health and Domestic Violence against Women.* Geneva: World Health Organization. Available online at www.who.int/gender/violence/who_multicountry_study/en.

The detailed methodology (Annex 1 of the report) provides an informative example of sensitive research practice as followed by a large-scale project centred on female victims of violence.

Notes

1 For a good introduction, see Brabeck and Brabeck (2009).
2 In the UK, for instance, the Economic and Social Research Council's (ESRC's) recently updated Research Ethics Framework represents an important shift in promoting formal ethical review in British universities and research organizations (ESRC, 2010).
3 For a discussion of the African context, see Kass (2007).

10

CHOOSING A SAMPLE

This chapter explains different ways of approaching sampling for various types of research. Quantitative research and qualitative research have different requirements in terms of sampling, but a good sample is a key criterion for quality research of any sort. It is always important to look carefully at the sample involved when you are evaluating a piece of research someone else has done – and you can be sure readers will do the same with your research.

We first discuss a variety of different types of sample, which fall into two groups – probability samples and non-probability samples. Sampling for qualitative research is discussed next. The chapter concentrates mainly on sampling people, but also looks briefly at choosing time, places and events for study. A short section looks specifically at site selection for participatory policy research. Then we look at a number of ways of increasing your response rate – the proportion of those you approach who agree to take part. In particular, we consider ways of including traditionally 'hard-to-reach' groups. Finally, the question of whether or not to use incentives is discussed.

Assessing levels of need: refugees in Rwanda

In 1982, when 50,000 displaced people from Uganda arrived in neighbouring Rwanda, the Red Cross reported that 20 per cent of children under five were in a state of serious malnutrition. This figure was accepted by the UN High Commission for Refugees and the government, neither of which had reason to doubt it. The data were transmitted to non-governmental organizations (NGOs), and plans were made for a massive response based on emergency feeding procedures.

An Oxfam doctor managed to reach the camp within a couple of days and pointed out that the figure was unusually high and, if it were true, was an indicator that the whole refugee population was in a very bad way indeed.

Further enquiries revealed that the Red Cross data had been collected at the emergency health post in the camp. In other words, the sample was biased because the only children to be taken to the health post were children who were already ill, many of them with intestinal complaints. A random nutritional survey was put into operation, and within a short time reliable data were available which put the nutritional status of under-fives at a figure which was normal for southern Uganda at that time of year. The nutritional status of the whole population was therefore not of acute concern. Plans for emergency feeding were scrapped.

Source: Pratt and Loizos (1992)

FOR EXAMPLE

Table 10.1 Some terminology

Technical term	Definition	Examples
Population	The complete set of cases about which generalizations are to be made. Theoretical concept, not an explicit list.	• All adults in Peru; • All villages in a district; • Children attending a school; • All possible welfare policy reforms in a country.
Sampling frame	The specific set of all cases from which the sample can be selected. The sampling frame makes the population tangible so sampling can be carried out. It is a list or rule that determines which particular cases form part of the population.	• Electoral register for Peru; • List of villages in a district; • School register; • List of all actual welfare policy reforms in a country.
Sample size	The total number of units selected from the population.	A sample of 60 students drawn from a school register of 400 registered students – sample size = 60.
Response rate	The proportion of all sampled individuals who actually respond.	Of a sample of 100 households, 27 households returned a paper questionnaire – a response rate of 27 per cent.
Non-response	Failure to obtain data from some of those in the sample because they do not respond or cannot be contacted. May cause bias in the achieved sample if non-respondents are different from respondents.	Respondent is out when you call at their house. (Bias may be created when calling at houses only during the daytime for example, because you will not be able to speak to people who are out working all day.) Person is unwilling to take part in your research. (Bias may be created when a certain group of people is more likely to refuse to take part.)

Source: Singleton and Straits (1999)

10.1 What does sampling mean?

Researchers talk about sampling on the principle that you usually cannot gather data from everyone you are interested in. Studying an entire group of people takes time, is costly and is often plagued by other practical considerations (such as accessibility). A sample can represent the larger group (the population), which is essentially the universe of your units of analysis (such as all people, villages or regions) and will be indicated by your research purpose. (Table 10.1 gives some other useful definitions of terms used in this chapter.) The image this description of sampling conjures up may seem rather remote from your experience. Frequently, development workers are interested in groups not listed tidily anywhere, possibly without fixed addresses and often not appearing in official counts, for a variety of reasons. You might feel your sample has chosen you rather than the other way around. But however the process of selecting respondents is done, it is still called sampling, and it requires clarity about what can be claimed for what type of sample. The next section discusses the choice between quantitative and qualitative sampling in more detail.

Whatever the approach, it is likely some negotiation will be needed to get access to respondents. This may mean talking to the chief of a village, writing formal proposals to public bodies or meeting with a hospital manager or head teacher. This process comes before choosing a sample, although it is involved with it.

We talk first of all about sampling people, which is what the term is usually used for, but remember there may also be sampling issues in relation to location, time and events that you study – see Section 10.5.

10.2 Quantitative or qualitative sampling?

There are essentially two main types of sample: probability or random samples and non-probability or purposive samples. Basically, if you want to claim your data are statistically representative of a larger population, you need a probability sample. To be convincing, quantitative research requires a reasonably representative sample of units from all possible units. Purposive samples are more likely to be appropriate to qualitative approaches. The term 'purposive' refers to a particular group of people being sampled to obtain specific information about that group. For example, if your research is about the needs of HIV-positive mothers of young children, no one is going to give you a list of all these people, but you can build up a sample by working through service providers and direct appeals to the community. Those you are able to contact may differ in some important respects from those you cannot, but you will still learn a great deal from them in relation to your research questions.

The choice between a quantitative and a qualitative sample depends ultimately on the research purpose, the topic and the expertise of the researcher, among other issues (see Chapters 2 and 7). As always, the point is to consider all the advantages and disadvantages of each type of sampling and then make a conscious decision.

More generally, quantitative sampling consists of a set of procedures to achieve statistical representativeness, and always involves probability sampling. By selecting cases randomly (or with a certain known probability) from the population with the help of the sampling frame, generalizations about the population can be made, based on the information from the sample and using probability theory.

However, in some circumstances, it is not feasible, practical or desirable to use probability sampling, such as if you specifically want to study only a subset of the population without generalizing, when you are studying unique events or a very small group of people or when the population cannot be defined, for example when you are investigating something often hidden or little understood. Qualitative sampling has its own sampling logic and procedures. We cannot make the same kind of generalization about a population using the rationale of probability theory. However, this does not mean that purposive sampling, for example, is unrepresentative or haphazard.

Meanwhile, qualitative sampling also has some advantages of its own, and it is not the case that it is appropriate only when quantitative sampling is unfeasible. Often, research for development work sets out to explore issues which are not at all well understood. Sections of the population that face particularly acute problems are involved. Purposive sampling is perfectly acceptable when it enables the investigation of issues about which little is known. As long as you explain clearly exactly how sampling has been done, and acknowledge any sources of bias you are aware of, the reader is able to judge for herself what weight to give your findings. The danger with small purposive samples is that your evidence may be dismissed as merely anecdotal.

The following list presents some reasons why the idea of a sample that represents a population can be inappropriate or impossible (Thomas and Mohan, 2007):

- There is no enumerable population from which to sample (for example historical events such as civil wars cannot be sampled from a population – they happen or they do not happen).
- You may not know enough about the units of analysis in the 'universe' to be able to define a sample (for example you undertake the study to identify differences you do not know about at the start).
- You may not have access to part of the population (for example when studying the clients of sex workers or a group of activists).
- You may be interested in rare or unique phenomena – when you have only one or a few examples, you cannot use statistical techniques.
- The phenomena you are interested in studying may also be observable, but rare enough to require an unfeasibly large probability sample in order to say anything representative of the population (for example a rare health condition only observable in one out of 100,000 people). Here, the feasibility of the sample size will depend on the resources and time you have available for your project.

The most common types of sample can be grouped as follows.

Probability samples:

- simple random sampling;
- systematic sampling;
- stratified random sampling;
- cluster sampling.

Non-probability or purposive samples:

- quota sampling;
- snowball sampling;
- judgement (purposive/theoretical) sampling;
- convenience sampling.

Different types of samples can also be combined. In large-scale surveys, for example, sampling methods are often mixed in what is called multi-stage samples.

10.3 Probability or random sampling

Probability or random samples are central to quantitative sampling and analysis. Only when the cases are sampled at random can probability theory be used to make generalizations about the population. How to select these is discussed in more detail below.

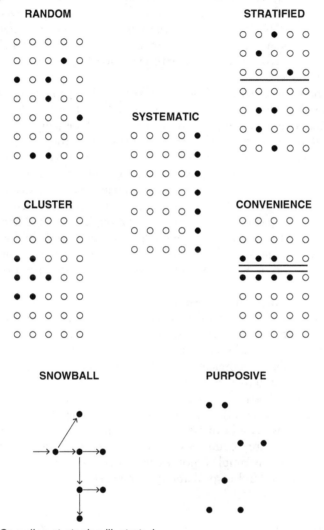

Figure 10.1 Sampling strategies illustrated

Source: Blaxter, L., Hughes, C. and Tight, M. (2010) *How to Research*, 3rd edn. Maidenhead: Open University Press ©. Reproduced with the kind permission of Open University Press. All rights reserved.

10.3.1 How to take a simple random sample

As mentioned above, the first thing to get clear is that a random sample is not the same as a haphazard, arbitrary or careless sample. A simple random sample is designed so each combination of units in the population has an equal chance (probability) of selection. This can be visualized as similar to drawing raffle tickets out of a hat. The units are selected randomly for the sample to avoid biasing it. The sample needs to be large enough to be able to use statistical techniques to analyse it at a later stage and generalize the results to the population using probability theory.

If a sample is truly random, it will usually be unbiased. This requires the sampling frame to list the complete target population, every combination of units to have an equal chance of being selected and there to be few refusals or missed contacts. It is important to ensure fieldworkers make every effort to contact the person or household who actually falls into the sample, otherwise you may get bias towards types of people who are for some reason easier to make contact with. And, unfortunately, it is not acceptable to avoid households with large dogs, up steep hills or with other unattractive characteristics!

You could be very unlucky and pick only very similar people, but the chance of this declines as you select more and more people. A random sample from a general population that is large enough will automatically include people from the important subgroups within it, in roughly the proportion that they are present. So you should get a spread by, for example, educational experience, economic category, ethnic group or whatever, without specifically selecting for this. Unfortunately, it also means that, unless your sample is very large, you may miss some small minorities. If you are particularly interested in a small group (for example elderly people over a certain age or from a particular minority ethnic group), you could first draw a random sample and then check you have enough respondents who fall into the categories you are interested in. If need be, carry out some extra purposive quota sampling at that juncture (see Section 10.4). Stratified sampling is another alternative approach (Section 10.3.3).

If you are undertaking a major research project for which you want a good random sample, it is worth getting advice from an experienced researcher, probably a statistician, on exactly what issues to consider, and in particular how large a sample you need. Don't leave it until it is too late to adjust your strategy in light of advice.

Sometimes, compiling a complete list of all possible units in the population, drawing a random sample and then collecting information for this can require quite a bit of work. In a city with a population of more than 1 million people, for example, listing all people and randomly selecting and visiting some of them can be difficult and costly. In other cases, for example when you want to make generalizations about the population of an entire country, you may not have a very reliable list. When drawing a simple random sample is not feasible or even possible, it is sometimes still possible to draw some kind of probability sample, such as a systematic, stratified random or cluster sample (see below).

10.3.2   Taking a systematic sample from a list

A systematic sample is a version of simple random sampling in which only one unit from the sampling frame is randomly selected and then every nth unit from that unit onwards is also selected. Every unit in the sampling frame still has an equal probability of being selected (because the first unit is randomly selected), but certain combinations of units will no longer be possible.

If the list of all units can be ordered in a meaningful way, a systematic sample could ensure you include examples from each category. For example, if you could arrange a list of villages in order of size, using census data, a systematic sample of villages will ensure you include examples for each category of village size. In this way, you can avoid biasing your sample towards small or large villages. However, if the list is poorly arranged, your sample could become biased. Here, it is important that the interval you choose between data points does reproduce a periodic trait in the population. For example, you may wish to study economic indicators within a community over a period of several years, subdivided by seasonal quarters (autumn, winter, spring, summer). If you select points from this list at a fixed interval of four, you will draw samples only from a single season. Given that household income often fluctuates between seasons, your sample may well be biased.

A disadvantage of systematic sampling is that, as in random sampling, you need a detailed, accurate sampling frame for the full target population. However, unlike in simple random sampling, you cannot be certain your sample is unbiased, because you exclude the selection of certain combinations of cases. You can also still get a sample of widely dispersed units, making fieldwork expensive. However, in certain cases, systematic sampling can be easier to carry out than random sampling, and also ensure a more balanced sample, for example when you have only a printed list of villages ordered according to population size.

10.3.3 How to take a stratified random sample

In some situations, you do not want to take a simple random sample because you want to be certain your sample contains people from certain subgroups. A simple random sample can fail to select people from important subgroups, especially if the population is large and the sample size small. One solution is to increase the sample size of the simple random sample, but obviously this is costly. Other types of samples have been developed that aim to deal with this problem more efficiently. One solution is the stratified random sample.

First, the population is divided into non-overlapping subgroups of similar people, called strata, using existing information. For instance, a group of people in a village could be subdivided into a group of men and a group of women. Then, a random sample from each of the subgroups is taken. Together, these samples make up the stratified random sample. The researcher can be certain this final sample contains people from both groups. Some characteristics researchers often use to divide up a population are settlement size, ecological zone, housing area, distance from a central point, presence or absence of key facilities (such as a health centre); many more are possible.

Again, you need a list and a great deal of information about your target population to divide it into subgroups of similar people. However, selecting people from all possible strata ensures the sample is not biased along the criteria you used to define the strata (for example it will not be biased towards men or women if gender was a criterion in defining strata). This is a much more efficient way of ensuring an unbiased sample than increasing the sample size in the simple random sample. However, as in the systematic sample, you exclude certain combinations of people and therefore can't be certain your sample is not unbiased with respect to criteria you did not take into account.

10.3.4 How to take a cluster sample

This method is the only probability sampling method that does not rely on a complete list of the population – but the more information you have, the better. First, the population needs to be broken down into natural groups or clusters. In contrast with strata in the stratified random sample, clusters need not be groups of similar units, but are often natural groups, such as regions, cities or villages in a country, and these groups may be dissimilar in many respects.

For example, you could select villages (clusters) randomly from a census list and hold all your interviews only in these selected villages with people you have selected randomly within these clusters. By focusing on only a small number of villages, you spend less time and money travelling than you do if you use a simple random sample. You can identify clusters within clusters and sample only these lower-level clusters. You can also combine elements of stratified random sampling and cluster sampling, for instance by stratifying the list of clusters before you select areas for interview. If you select clusters of villages not randomly but by size after stratifying the clusters accordingly, and then select one or more villages randomly from each size grouping, you avoid biasing your sample to large or small villages.

The following list provides some useful rules for cluster sampling (Nichols, 1991):

- Before you choose the sample, arrange a list of clusters into similar subgroups of about the same size.
- Use many small clusters rather than a few large ones.
- Number each cluster.
- Using random numbers, select a sample of complete clusters. The exact total sample size depends on the clusters selected, but if clusters are roughly equal in size this is not a problem.
- Fieldworkers interview every household/individual in the selected clusters.

Keeping these rules in mind, you can combine cluster sampling with elements of stratified random sampling or other probability samples to creatively tackle the problems in drawing a probability sample in your specific research situation. You will need to clarify the procedure you followed to your research audience.

Let us consider a hypothetical example. Suppose you want to interview women living in rural Indian villages in Uttar Pradesh. Using a list or map of villages in Uttar Pradesh (for example employing the data from the recent Indian census), randomly select a number of villages (the clusters). Then, within the selected villages, randomly select households from a list, if you can find one. It is likely you will have to use your imagination! For example, you could use maps of the villages to make new clusters, such as of streets or neighbourhoods, and sample randomly from these again. Or, you could first use the more general information about the population of the villages that will be available from the recent census to divide the clusters of all villages in the region into strata of similar population size (say, small, medium and large). Then, select villages randomly from each of these three groups and try to speak to a 'randomly selected woman', for example by stopping at every fifth house in the selected streets, maybe even throwing a dice to decide which one of all the women living at the address to interview. By using an imaginative yet systematic approach to probability sampling, you can try to produce a sample which avoids the most obvious sources of bias. Or it may be better to accept you need to work with a purposive sample. It is a matter of doing the best you can in the circumstances.

Off the map in Israel

Within Israel's agreed borders are Arab villages which are not recognized by the government. These lack basic services like water and sanitation, which are supplied to other villages, often on the next hill. If you took a sample from a government list of villages, you would inevitably exclude the inhabitants of these villages. Your sample would be biased in a particular way, as the experiences of these villagers will be systematically different from those of people living in recognized settlements.

FOR EXAMPLE

10.3.5 Panel studies

Panel studies are surveys where information is collected from the sample units two or more times. This type of research lends itself to studying changes over time. For example, the UK National Child Development Study has conducted studies of a sample of people at seven-year intervals, asking a wide range of questions about health, education, employment and so on. The children of the original sample are now being studied. Panel studies show how individuals change over time and can therefore be useful to understand the causal processes of change. However, they are often expensive, because the survey has to be repeated at regular intervals. Also, the same people have to be contacted over and over again. The sample therefore necessarily becomes smaller as a proportion of people will always drop out of the study.

10.3.6 How large a sample do you need?

This definitely counts as a 'frequently asked question' in social research! And wouldn't you know it, there is no simple answer. How large your sample size should be depends on a number of things, such as how heterogeneous the population under study is, how much precision is desired in the statistical analysis, the sampling design and, of course, costs. What is important is not only the total number of respondents, but also how many people would be found in any subgroup of respondents – and then how much those subgroups matter to the issue in question.

For example, in parts of North London, any study where ethnic origin is an important factor would find a very diverse population yielding small numbers of people of more than 25 different backgrounds. Then there are gender and age. To do a statistically valid study, for example of access to health care for people of different backgrounds, in each subcategory the numbers would become very small. Your main sample might be 100, but there could be only two women of Somali or Bangladeshi background between 16 and 45. And any differences found would be based on too small a number to be meaningful. (Not to say that data from such a study would not be valuable – just not statistically representative.)

How large your sample size is also depends on the type of sample you have chosen (simple random, stratified random, cluster or multi-stage sample designs). Cluster sampling, for example, requires a larger sample to achieve the same precision as a simple random sample, because cases within clusters tend to be similar. In general, the larger the sample size is, the greater the precision of your estimates in the statistical analysis will be. As an absolute minimum to be able to use statistical data analysis, your sample should include 15–30 cases (this number depends on many things, and we refer the reader to more specialist readings at the end of this chapter). The precision you gain by adding more cases is very large when you increase the sample from, say, 30 to 100, but becomes smaller and smaller as your sample size increases. Regardless of the size of your population, the precision of your sample will increase only very slightly when you include more than a few thousand cases in your sample.

There are obvious costs associated with collecting so much information, so a trade-off must be made. There are mathematical formulas that can help you to calculate the size your sample should be, based on the desirable level of precision, but these are beyond the scope of this text. If you want to collect a statistically reliable sample, it makes sense to ask expert advice about your particular sampling design, including the sample size.

10.3.7   Response rates

It is important to realize that it is not enough to declare that you will work with a large sample, and attempt to include them, for example by posting out a questionnaire to 3,000 households, if very few are actually returned. This is what is referred to as your response rate – the proportion of respondents who actually take part in your research, relative to those you approached.

A very low response rate casts doubt on the quality of your research, because there may be systematic differences between those who took part in the research and those who did not. It is worth putting quite a lot of work into getting a good response rate: expect to call back, send reminders, make new appointments to replace missed ones, etc.

10.4   Purposive or non-random sampling

A good random sample enables you to claim with some confidence that your data are representative of the wider population. However, in many situations, the sampling frame is simply not available. Sometimes, a study is not so much interested in counting how many people hold a certain opinion, but more in finding out what these opinions are. Or a researcher may be interested in interactions among people. Cost may also be a factor.

Non-random sampling is the term used to describe all sampling methods that are not based on random selection. For this reason, these methods can produce bias and the analysis of non-probability samples cannot rely on the rationale of probability theory. That does not mean this type of sampling is unrepresentative or haphazard. Qualitative sampling has its own procedures and quality criteria.

10.4.1   Sampling for qualitative research

Most of our ideas about sampling relate to quantitative research, where claims about statistical representativeness are central to its validity. Qualitative research works to different priorities: there is no single standard of sampling as there is for quantitative samples. Which type of sample is used usually depends on the aims of the study. The purpose might be to explore a relatively understudied or unique issue, or to test a certain theoretical hypothesis. Qualitative research sometimes employs procedures of which random sampling is part, such as quota sampling (discussed below), but often purposive or theoretical sampling is more appropriate, for example when a study aims to understand the opinions or experiences of a particular vulnerable group or when the impact of a new NGO programme on a particular community needs to be assessed.

Theoretical sampling is

> [...] the process of data collection for generating theory whereby the analyst jointly collects, codes, and analyses his [sic] data and decides what data to collect next and where to find them, in order to develop his theory as it emerges. This process of data collection is *controlled* by the emerging theory. (Glaser and Strauss, 1967)

The initial decision on where to begin collecting data is not based on a preconceived theoretical framework but on a general sociological perspective on a subject area. When a category emerges from the data, the researcher looks for information that would elaborate the category further. This process continues until no new aspects of the category emerge. The category is then said to be saturated (like a sponge full of water). So, in theoretical sampling, data are collected as long as they are adding to the development of a particular category. Unlike statistical sampling, the sample cannot be predetermined numerically – it has to be worked through.

A study of a new issue, such as how young people use social media such as Facebook and Twitter, might see its purpose as to generate hypotheses (ideas) about the important issues in this field. Such a study may entail observation in a number of different sites; seek out young people to talk to through a snowball sample, moving through informal networks; or carry out group discussions in schools and other settings or on blogs. Ideas would be generated, perhaps that social media give young people the freedom to express their ideas, which could then be tested by targeted observation and discussion. Fieldwork would cease at the point when it seems to the researchers that they are not hearing anything new from their respondents.

10.4.2 How to draw a quota sample

First, decide what characteristics dividing the population are important in relation to the aims of your study. You can really only use features that can be observed, such as age, sex, location, etc. Remember that getting a balanced sample for some characteristics does not guarantee there will be a representative sample on other factors, such as social and economic differences. For example, a quota sample of fathers of teenagers in an inner-city part of London could end up including no minority ethnic men and no unemployed men, if the fieldworkers have not been instructed to take account of these factors. While the sample obtained in this way may include fathers from each area, for example, it could still be considerably biased in terms of the ethnic or socioeconomic background characteristics of the respondents. So you must consider carefully what the dimensions relevant to your research question are so you can take these into account when drawing a quota sample.

To design a quota sample, you must know, at least approximately, how the target population is divided up according to the factors you are concerned with. You must check against census or other data what proportion of each 'quota' you need in order to reflect the make-up of the broader population.

Quota samples are quick and cheap to organize. However, the method can produce bias, and you should clearly state that the representativeness of such a sample cannot be relied on. Quota samples are different from stratified samples, in that they are not drawn randomly from a known population. Therefore, they are not a probability or random type of sample.

> **Tip**
>
> Remember you may need to use more than one type of sample within your research project, just as you may use more than one data collection technique.

Table 10.2 Some types of purposive sample

Type of sample	Definition	Example
Judgement (purposive/ theoretical) sample	The researcher chooses respondents, trying to obtain as wide a representation as possible, taking account of likely sources of difference between individuals. The danger is you have no way of knowing how typical your sample is.	In a small rural case study, choose one or two villages with 'typical' health problems.
Quota sample	Uses information about the target population to describe the types of units to be included in the sample. Individuals are then sought who fit these characteristics, for example by age, sex, housing type or location.	In a study of informal water sellers, specify a small quota of informal sellers in each housing area, based on the number of on-plot water supplies (available from water authority records). Fieldworkers locate their quota through talking to those carrying water.
Snowball sample	Start with one or two respondents, and ask them to refer to you others who share characteristics with them. And so on.	A study of illicit drug use started with a few contacts and asked them to invite friends who also use drugs to take part.
Matched sample	To compare two subgroups which are similar in some way. Units (whether a whole settlement or an individual) are matched to share as many relevant characteristics as possible.	Choose a matched pair of villages with similar populations and services, where only one of the pair experiences a new project, and look at changes in both villages.
Convenience sample	Sample includes whoever happens to be around at the time. Not possible to generalize from.	Clinic users attending on a particular day.

10.5   How to sample for cases, location, time and events

Sometimes, the aim of a study is to select not people but some typical, unique or distinctly different cases. Sometimes, sampling has to take into account important differences not just among people but also across location, time and events.

10.5.1   Selecting case studies

Where your project consists of a group of case studies, you need to think of their selection in a different way again. Case studies cannot be, and do not claim to be, representative of the wider situation in any statistical sense. You cannot usually know to what extent they may be representative, because you do not have information about the whole 'population' of cases that is out there. See Part 3 on case studies for a discussion on how to choose cases for a multiple case study.

10.5.2   Selection of location

Sites for study obviously need to be selected in light of the aims of the research. In addition to seeking some sort of representativeness (see above), you need to take account of:

- accessibility – in the sense of the degree of access/entry given to the researcher;
- unobtrusiveness – with the researcher able to take a relatively unobtrusive role.

Remember your choice of site is likely to determine many other things about the research process, and don't jump to conclusions about what is possible or desirable.

Often with participatory research, the project grows out of the site, rather than there being any selection by an outside agency. However, in wider exercises such as Participatory Poverty Assessments, a balance has to be struck between working in areas where there is some infrastructure, so as to facilitate ongoing participation, and the claims that action research needs to make about the applicability of its findings to a wider area (see Chapter 12).

Holland and Munro (1997) suggest that it may be helpful to think in terms of 'nesting' potential areas within a cascading series of spatial levels, from the national down to the sample site. You then try to reconcile diversity with representativeness at each level by

- Selecting a small, but sufficient, number of regions: small in order to retain richness and depth of analysis, but sufficient to arrive at a range of regional profiles that are representative of national-level diversity. Extreme cases should be avoided – that is, regions from which insights could not be transferred to any larger area – unless they are specifically needed as a contrast.
- Within each sampled region, purposively sampling a small number of sub-regions that represent a range of contexts that can be pre-identified in the region, again avoiding extremes.

- Selecting a 'typical' site profile in order to provide a regional-level reference point for examining the implications (for analysis and policy recommendations) of the diverse elements within each site profile. In other words, a control group-type population with which the analysis of the diverse profiles can be compared.

So you could represent a profile of the areas involved at each spatial level in a matrix, setting out various community characteristics. This then makes it possible to see where the sites you study fit into the wider picture. You will build confidence in the importance of your findings by putting the particular communities you work with into this wider context.

10.5.3 Selection of time

If you are studying a community or an organization, it is important to understand its rhythm, by looking at:

- the range of activities/events over a 24-hour period;
- the activities that take place during the day as opposed to the night; the week as opposed to weekends; any day of rest or prayer as opposed to ordinary days;
- seasonal changes in activity;
- imposed patterns, like shift systems for work.

10.5.4 Selection of events

Events can be classified as:

- routine – situations that occur regularly;
- special but anticipated, for example Christmas, Ramadan, etc.;
- untoward – emergencies, crises.

The researcher aims to observe a spread of events over a timescale which takes account of important variations in activity. In research that makes great demands on respondents, for example participatory assessments, it is essential to schedule the work at times of year and day when hard-pressed people are most able to spend time on it.

10.6 Including 'hard-to-reach' people

In planning your sampling strategy, remember some kinds of people may be systematically easier to contact than others. Having power in a society gives people greater ability to choose to participate or avoid participation in public processes like research. You will probably need to make special efforts to talk to some of the people who most need to get their voices heard.

If you work primarily through public group discussions, women may simply be absent in many cultures; in others, they will be expected not to speak. Equally, if you

visit households and do not specify who in the family you want to talk to, male family members will probably present themselves first – depending on the subject of your enquiries. In most cultures, to enable women to be able to get their views heard, it is a good idea to hold separate group discussions, and separate interviews, with women.

Disabled people are also often excluded from public discussions. Unless you specifically ask, you may not meet disabled people at all, even if they are living nearby – it will not be assumed that their views are of interest. Where disabled people are in institutions, you will need to make particular efforts to include their perspective.

Children's and older people's views are also often not considered important. On the other hand, in some cultures, where elders are highly respected, younger people may not be comfortable giving their views in front of them. Other groups likely to be excluded are people belonging to ethnic minority groups and those with a lower educational achievement than average. Think about the community you are interested in, and the particular inequalities that affect it. For example, take advice from local women on how you handle gender issues. You need not settle for accepting the status quo. See also Chapters 8, 11 and 12 on improving communication with respondents.

Achieving the 'impossible'

A woman evaluator from India, who was used to working with women in a semi-closed society, was able to achieve in Sudan what she was told would be impossible. She succeeded in holding meetings with large numbers of poor women, and getting them to speak openly about their views on their economic role. Previously, women project staff had accepted the traditional view that women would not and could not meet for such discussions, because they were themselves part of the same tradition, despite their professional roles.

Source: Pratt and Loizos (1992)

FOR EXAMPLE

Some interesting approaches have been developed by those addressing the HIV/AIDS epidemic with communities around the world. To tackle this obviously sensitive topic, one programme in Ghana started with focus groups using action research, in single-sex groups of six to 12 married or unmarried people. The groups later suggested that women and men meet together as well.

The use of participatory learning approaches in exploring sexual health concerns can radically change the development programmes in the villages concerned in a number of ways. For the first time groups of men and women, older and younger people are sitting together to talk about sexual issues of great importance to them. People can communicate more easily with their spouses and men in particular are pleased and relieved to be involved in what has been seen as 'women's business'. (Save the Children, 1997b)

Checklist: improving response rates

- ☑ Get the backing of people or organizations who are known and respected by the community you wish to work with.
- ☑ Get groups of 'the researched' actively involved at the start of the study.
- ☑ Consider whether you will need to use interpreters or advocates to overcome language or cultural barriers or serve as a point of contact.
- ☑ Make any direct approaches to people personalized – address them by name.
- ☑ Explain clearly the aims of the study and why it is important that people participate.
- ☑ Make sure you give a contact name and a way of contacting them to potential respondents.
- ☑ Ensure information about the study is presented appropriately, taking into account problems with literacy, language barriers and disabilities – expect to repeat verbal information many times.
- ☑ Give respondents a choice of ways of participating – some may lack the confidence to take part in a group discussion, for example.
- ☑ Choose accessible neutral venues for fieldwork, away from service provision (for example hospitals) – somewhere people will feel at home.
- ☑ Consider employing outreach workers who know the community you wish to work with to recruit participants and publicize your research.
- ☑ Think creatively about recruiting participants – for example go to relevant work places, places of worship, community centres, etc.
- ☑ Consider using researchers from the community to collect data face-to-face.
- ☑ Use pre-existing groups to recruit participants where appropriate – for example tenants' associations, self-help groups, etc.
- ☑ Consider offering some incentive to those who participate – at least meet their expenses and offer some refreshment.
- ☑ Expect to have to ask some people more than once.

Source: Craig (1998)

10.7 Incentives: what are the issues?

One way of increasing your response rate is to offer some kind of incentive to respondents to take part in the research. This is a hotly debated issue, with some saying it is unethical to offer incentives under any circumstances and others arguing it is unethical not to! Increasingly, researchers are offering some kind of vouchers, or even cash, to people who take part in interviews or focus groups, although incentives are not allowed in health services research. However, problems of sustainability and creating expectations exist, and international researchers should check local protocols so as not to undermine local research initiatives, as local researchers are likely to work over the longer term in the same context, whereas many international researchers cover a number of country contexts.

Many different types of incentives can be used. Researchers should expect to meet expenses people incur in taking part, and assistance with travel costs, for example, will often make a key difference with regard to whether or not people can take part. Offering food and drink creates a comfortable atmosphere. Sometimes, a local business will donate vouchers for this purpose.

Some types of incentive are as follows:

- food and drink;
- expenses repaid for travel, child care or replacement care for disabled people, for example;
- useful information offered at the end of the session;
- telephone cards (especially useful for homeless people);
- gift vouchers for the cinema, shops, etc.;
- goods relevant to the project, for example seeds for farmers, pencils for children;
- gifts to a community organization rather than to individuals, such as a blackboard for a school;
- cash equivalent to a day's wages to compensate for lost opportunity costs.

Table 10.3 Pros and cons of incentives in social research

Benefits of paying incentives	Drawbacks of paying incentives
• Avoids sample being distorted by people being unable to take part if they don't gain any financial benefit. • Can encourage more people to take part. • Recognizes the value of respondents' time and contribution.	• Sample may be distorted by people taking part to gain financial benefits. • Could create a sense of obligation, and hence compromise informed consent. • Can create expectations of recompense for other participation in the future. • People might take part for the money and then answer with a view to pleasing you. • And of course cost!

Views are mixed on the payment of incentives, although there is no doubt it increases response rates in market research – this is why the practice is spreading. One study looks at the issue in research with injecting drug users, and emphasizes that, for all respondents, there are many motivations behind participation – especially seeing the research as interesting, relevant and worthwhile. The study quotes some respondents' different views (Hughes, 1999):

Phil: [...] 'when you said you get a five pound voucher that's why I said [yes]. It was for the money but not only that – it helps you doesn't it [...] To be honest mate if I hadn't have had that [...] I wouldn't come, because I've got to go ahead and make some money.' [...]

Kieran: 'yeah, it's all right but I'd do it for nothing. It doesn't really bother me talking about it.' [...]

Robert: 'I mean I didn't come here knowing that. You've just told me today. I will accept it, thanks a lot. I'll get something for the little lass, thanks very much.'

An incentive payment will likely make only a marginal difference to people's decision whether or not to participate in research, but it may tip the balance for some people, perhaps especially those under financial pressure.

FOR EXAMPLE

Not offering incentives has costs too: young people and mental health services in the UK

In a peer research project with young people using mental health services in Bolton in England (Laws et al., 1999), unforeseen difficulties arose when recruiting respondents for interview. It had been assumed the peer researchers would be in touch with others 'like them', but in fact they did not have friends who were also users of mental health services. Thus recruitment to the study was slow, and the peer researchers advised that, if incentives had been offered, more young people might participate, greatly improving the scope of the research. Any cost incurred would easily have outweighed the wasted costs of staff time spent failing to recruit respondents.

Issues to consider in deciding on use of incentives include the following:

- What is the state of the local economy?
- What is standard practice for research in your area?
- How much trouble are you putting people to? For example, a focus group takes more effort than an interview in your own home.
- How important is the issue to your respondents?
- Will respondents have to forgo any income in order to take part in your research?

A related set of dilemmas presents itself in peer research projects in relation to the question of whether or not to pay people who actually carry out research alongside professional researchers. This issue is explored in Section 12.2 on peer research.

 ## Key points from this chapter

Sampling is one of the most important decisions you will have to make in your research. It is perhaps also one of the choices that will attract most criticism from readers, so be prepared to justify yourself. However, it isn't rocket science – it just needs careful consideration.

> ### Checklist: sampling in research for development work
>
> ☑ Make a clear decision as to whether you are going for a random/probability sample or a purposive/non-probability one.
> ☑ Expect to spend time and effort negotiating access to your sample.
> ☑ Be clear whether you are sampling for quantitative or qualitative research.
> ☑ Once you have chosen a sampling method, stick to it and carry out selection of respondents in a consistent way.
> ☑ In choosing an appropriate sample, consider:
>
>   ☑ how good a sampling frame you have available;
>   ☑ what response rate you anticipate;
>   ☑ logistical problems;
>   ☑ costs; and, as ever,
>   ☑ the purpose of the research and its audiences.
>
> ☑ Make a special effort to reach out to those normally excluded from research processes.

Further reading

Agresti, A. and Finlay, B. (2009) *Statistical Methods for the Social Sciences*. Upper Saddle River, NJ: Pearson Education Inc.

Clear overview of quantitative sampling types and strategies, as well as help in calculating required sample size and further references.

Blaxter, L., Hughes, C. and Tight, M. (2010) *How to Research,* 3rd edn. Buckingham: Open University.

Clear account of all types of sampling.

Craig, G. (1998) *Women's Views Count: Building Responsive Maternity Services.* London: College of Health.

Written to assist in identifying appropriate methods for assessing satisfaction with UK maternity services, this is a very thorough and helpful presentation of a range of different research methods.

Nichols, P. (1991) 'Social survey methods: a field guide for development workers', *Development Guidelines* 6. Oxford: Oxfam.

Strong on sampling methods for surveys in the South.

11

COLLECTING DATA

This chapter focuses on five of the most widely used methods in research for development work. It needs to be read alongside chapters on how to choose a method (7), sampling (10) and contacting respondents (4). As ever, it is important to make sure you are clear on the aims, objectives, focus and key research questions for your study before you begin to choose methods for it (see Chapter 7). There is no 'ideal method', just methods fit for their purpose.

After a short general section on how to ask questions, the chapter gives guidance on key research techniques: interviews, focus groups, questionnaires, secondary research/ using documentary sources and observation. Chapter 12 describes methods that facilitate participation, such as ranking and scoring techniques, visual methods like drawing, mapping and video and drama and role play. Since many other books give detailed guidance on methods, each technique is described only briefly, along with comments on its strengths and limitations. The manual aims to recommend tried and tested approaches, rather than emphasizing new and experimental ways of working. There are many, many others, but you can get a long way with these few techniques. Learn to do an effective interview and you will be a good way along the path to becoming a competent researcher.

11.1 How to ask questions

This section offers guidance on how to develop good questions for use in research, whether they are for an interview, a focus group discussion or a questionnaire. Specific guidelines for the particular techniques are given in the different sections, but there is much in common, and these core rules are described here.

Checklist: writing good questions

Questions need to be:

☑   related to the research questions – therefore to the overarching research focus;
☑   clear and unambiguous;

☑ simple – one thing at a time;
☑ in everyday language – no jargon, no technical language;
☑ about things respondents will have information about;
☑ directed to the respondent – usually best not to ask one person to answer for others;
☑ asked in a neutral way – see below for types of question to avoid;
☑ ask about concrete events, not unspecified general experiences.

11.1.1 Types of questions to avoid

There are a number of types of questions to avoid:

- Leading questions – 'Would you agree that education should have high priority for government spending?'
- Vague questions – 'What do you think about the education you have received?'
- 'Presuming' questions – 'What qualifications did you leave school with?'
- Multiple questions (two or more questions in one) – 'Why did you leave school and what have you done since?'
- Hypothetical questions – 'If you had been able to complete your schooling, what would you be doing today?'
- Questions which contain value judgements – 'Were you forced to drop out of school at an early age?'
- Offensive, irritating or insensitive questions – 'Why do you not think it important to pay for your child's schooling?'

Leading questions encourage the respondent to answer in a particular way, making it difficult for them to disagree. For example, asked in a group setting, 'Who agrees that capital punishment is wrong?' is a leading question. Questions must be reworded in a more neutral way, for example, 'Do you have an opinion on capital punishment?' could still lead to yes or no answers. If you wanted to hear more about the respondents' views, you could ask, 'What do you think about capital punishment?'

Using leading questions makes it easy for opponents of your point of view to discredit your work. It can be surprisingly difficult to spot them on issues close to your heart, so ask someone who is not involved to check your questions with this in mind.

11.1.2 The process of generating questions

Questions need to be placed in a logical order. Start with an interesting but straightforward question to which everyone will have some answer. This helps respondents to feel confident. For the same reason, the first questions should not challenge or embarrass the respondent (if you really need to ask such questions, use them later and introduce them gently).

In terms of the process, the most important thing is to think about how you are going to analyse any answers, and change the questions if this throws up problems. Draft your questions early, and expect to redraft them many times. Consider whether to collect 'boring details' at the beginning or end. Doing it at the beginning has its pros and cons: it can remind people of 'official', assessment-type interviews and put them on the defensive. But it can also signal that this is a non-threatening questionnaire. No matter what you do, remember to collect all details you will need.

You must also pilot test your questions – first by asking a number of people to read them over, and then, with corrections made, by getting some people to work through them and try to answer them. Finally, test them on a small group from your final sample to see how they work in 'real life'. Each of these stages can reveal major issues which can then be sorted out.

11.1.3 Evaluating your draft questions

It is easy to get carried away with all the interesting things you could ask, and it can be surprisingly difficult to work out how to ask the questions that will really answer your key research questions. But it is important to ensure you include only those questions that will be key in shedding light on your research problem. When you critically read your draft questions, think about the following points:

- Look back at your research focus and key research questions (see Chapter 3) and check that you can get answers to these.
- Think about what kinds of replies you might get, and imagine how you will use these in the final report – what is the story you want to tell? Will this material enable you to do so?
- Read Chapter 13 before finalizing your questions, and think how the replies to each question will be analysed. Consult anyone you hope will help you in the analysis at this stage.
- Analyse which type of question each one on your questionnaire/topic guide is, and check it is right for its purpose.
- And just check – you are asking the right group of people, aren't you? Sometimes we assume we must research the powerless, when actually our problems lie in understanding the thinking and behaviour of the more powerful.
- Experienced researchers get skilled at seeing which are good and which are bad questions for a particular purpose: it is always worthwhile showing a draft to at least one researcher.

11.2 Interviews

11.2.1 What is an interview?

This section looks at one-to-one interviews, where a series of questions are addressed to an informant and their responses recorded. Group interviews (focus groups) are considered separately, as are self-completion questionnaires. For a general discussion on how to achieve effective communication in research, especially relevant to interviews perhaps, see Chapter 8.

All sorts of professional workers undertake interviews as part of their daily work, but a research interview follows quite different rules from these. It may be necessary to consciously 'un-learn' some of the habits you have developed for interviewing in other contexts. As we shall see, the 'rules' for research interviews also depend on the type of interviewing involved.

The rest of this section focuses on individual semi-structured and in-depth interviews. Guidelines for highly structured interviews are more akin to those for questionnaires (see Section 11.4).

11.2.2 How many people are involved?

Often, a research interview is literally one-to-one. However, there may good reasons to have a third person present (although too many people can also be intimidating for the interviewee):

- At times an interpreter is required.
- A second researcher can write notes while the first interviewer concentrates on asking questions.
- If you are learning to do interviews, it helps you to observe and improve.
- Some research teams have members with different perspectives who might ask different types of question.

11.2.3 When should you use interviews for research?

Interviews are most useful when:

- You need to know about people's experiences or views in some depth.
- You are able to rely on information from a fairly small number of respondents.
- The issue is sensitive and people may not be able to speak freely in groups.
- Your respondents would not be able to express themselves fully through a written questionnaire.
- You do not yet know much about the details of the phenomena you are investigating, but can identify 'experts'.

11.2.4 Conducting an interview

Preparing for the interview

- Ensure your recording method (note taking, audio recording) is workable in the context of the interview.
- Eliminate all but the absolutely necessary questions – and then go back and eliminate some more!

- Some respondents will not be free when you want to interview them – expect to have to call back. Their time is pressured too.
- Send your questions or at least some of them to the respondent before to allow her to get an understanding of what to expect – unless you have reason to expect that providing the questions early will introduce biases.
- Think about the environment you are interviewing in and what can and cannot be talked about in it.
- Especially for long interviews, get some water and maybe even snacks for you and your respondent.
- Send a reminder the day before the interview and express that you are looking forward to it.

Table 11.1　Some types of interview

Structured	Semi-structured	Depth/unstructured
• Useful when research questions are very precise and quantified answers are needed • Questions must be asked in a standard way • All questions in the interview guide should be asked • Most questions have pre-set answers to choose between • Results are easy to analyse as long as you do the bulk the of work beforehand (for example pilot the questionnaire) and carefully consider each question and how you are going to analyse it • Follow many of the same rules as questionnaires	• Useful where some quantitative and some qualitative information is needed • Questions may be asked in different ways, but some questions can be standard • Questions can be left out and others added • Include a mix of types of question – some open, some closed	• Useful to help set research focus, or to explore new or sensitive topics in depth • More like a conversation – no standard questions, just topic areas • Follow (or ask) respondents to establish what is important to discuss • Avoid questions which can be answered by 'yes' or 'no' • Analysis can be time consuming • Follow many of the same rules as focus groups

Continuum of structure in interviewing

Opening up the interview

- Begin with an appropriate greeting and suitable small talk.
- Introduce the research properly and encourage discussion of its purpose. This is often not as simple as it sounds and is well worth rehearsing in advance.

- Give respondents another opportunity to withdraw their consent if they wish to. Be clear with people that they will not directly benefit from participating in the research, nor will they suffer any adverse consequence by not participating.
- Early questions should be straightforward and not threaten or challenge the respondents.

Monitoring progress

- Keep an appropriate level of eye contact, and note any non-verbal signals which might help in understanding what has been said.
- Encourage the interviewee to tell their story the way they want to, only later checking to make sure their account contains the information you need.
- Look for the underlying logic of what the respondent is telling you.
- Ask sensitive questions only when the person seems to be at ease with you.
- Look for apparent inconsistencies and probe to discover the thinking behind them.
- Be on the lookout for answers which seem designed to distract you – probe further if you are unconvinced, although beware of seeming to interrogate your interviewee.
- Keep a discreet eye on the time.
- Be aware of your own body language and try to keep it neutral.
- Give people time to respond – especially with sensitive matters. There is often an urge to jump in to fill the gap, but often very good/interesting points come up only when you give the respondent time.

Closing down the interview

- Perhaps ask how the respondent feels about the interview, and if there is anything else they would like to say.
- Perhaps summarize the gist of what you think the person is saying back to them, so they can check you have got it right. This takes extra time from the interviewee and is less feasible if they are very time constrained.
- Repeat assurances of confidentiality.
- Give sincere thanks for the time the respondent has spent talking to you.
- Afterwards, make notes for yourself about the context (for example small children present, respondent feeling unwell) and of any non-verbal communication you observed.

You might wish to interview a person alone, but this is not always appropriate. It may be best to accept this, or you can try and find a time when others may not be around, if your respondent is happy with this.

11.2.5 Telephone interviews

Where respondents have a reasonably reliable telephone service, using the phone for interviews reduces the costs in terms of researcher time enormously. The problems are, of course, that, even in relatively well-off communities, not everyone has a

Table 11.2   Strengths and limitations – interviews

Interviews – strengths	Interviews – limitations
• Depth of information – you can gain insights into people's rationale for acting as they do, and the feelings behind an issue • Individual respondents can tell their own story in their own way • Can reach people who would not be happy to take part in groups or fill in questionnaires • Respondents usually enjoy interviews – people like the rare opportunity to be listened to at length	• Time consuming • Analysis can be difficult with less-structured interview data • Who the interviewer is will have an effect on the responses you get • Interview data tell you what people *say* they do – you may need to check how this relates to what they can be observed to actually do • A group setting may give more confidence and an interplay of ideas which is not available in a one-to-one situation • There is potential for invasion of privacy – tactless interviewing can be upsetting for respondents

phone, so you must not exclude some respondents on this basis. In addition, you cannot build rapport as easily as you can face-to-face, and there may be confidentiality issues. But for some purposes, for example in collecting reasonably straightforward information from professionals, using the phone is a very efficient method. It is used more and more as telephone use increases.

11.3   Focus groups

11.3.1   What is a focus group?

A focus group is a group interview which brings together six to 12 people, who may be strangers to each other or drawn from an existing community group. Interaction between group members is part of the process and should be encouraged: unlike interviews, focus groups aim to understand social sense-making/opinion-forming processes about a particular issue, so the unit of analysis is not the number of individuals but one group. It is important to do more than one focus group wherever possible because group processes can lead to extreme positions that are not representative.

In planning focus group work, it is important to distinguish between groups in which the participants share some important characteristics or experience and those where they do not – perhaps to represent a wider population. Political parties often use the latter type to test their 'messages'; this process is sometimes criticized as leading to 'lowest common denominator' responses. However, being with people who are similar in relation to the subject under discussion – for example they all farm similar land, they have all had breast cancer, whatever – can give respondents confidence to speak about their experiences in a way that may not be possible in one-to-one interviews, especially, perhaps, when the subject under discussion is stigmatizing in some way.

11.3.2 How many people are involved?

A focus group requires an experienced facilitator who can enable everyone to talk and not be tempted to join in the argument. Someone not directly involved in the issue under discussion is best.

Many researchers also work with an observer, which has several benefits. The observer can take notes, deal with the audio recorder, observe non-verbal communication and help the facilitator in putting people at ease before and after the session. This frees the facilitator to concentrate on listening to and steering the group.

11.3.3 When should you use focus groups for research?

Focus groups are useful when:

- You need in-depth information about how groups think about an issue – their reasoning about why things are as they are, why they hold the views they do.
- You need guidance in setting a framework for some larger-scale research, about what groups see as the issues for them.
- You want people's ideas about what would be better.

A process where all stakeholders participate in one focus group session is very different from one where each group (for example service users; those who refer people into a service; commissioners) meet separately, and will produce very different findings.

Because focus groups sometimes make participants aware that they are not alone with their problem, they can encourage individuals to take part in political processes. Consultation expands on this idea and combines several such methods to create an interface between research and political process.

Consultation: combining research and political process

In the UK, some methods have been developed to assist public bodies to consult the public on public policy issues more effectively – driven by government's concern to be seen to be more answerable to the public in its decision making. Consultation is a directly political process – it should have a life of its own and not be constrained by the conventions of research. There may also be a wish to engage the public more deeply in the problems of prioritization of spending, for example in relation to health services, in the hope of reducing demands on them. There are many ways of consulting

(Continued)

(Continued)

communities which are more familiar as part of the community development worker's repertoire.

Some principles for community consultation:

- Recognize community members' competence.
- Allow enough time to build up trust and to carry out the consultation work.
- Be flexible about the process you follow.
- Find a balance between collecting information and a positive process for community members.
- Ensure all sections of the community are consulted, taking account of factors which mute some voices.
- Engage other agencies in the consultation process.
- Involve people who are good at communicating with the group in question.
- Ensure you have the support you need.
- Ensure community members' views are heard.

Source: Laws (1998)

11.3.4 Conducting a focus group

Please also refer to the guidelines on individual interviews in Section 11.2 – many points are relevant – and also Section 11.1, on how to ask questions.

Preparing for the focus group

- Prepare a topic guide well ahead of time, with up to ten questions to focus the discussion.
- Ensure questions are open and straightforward – closed questions will stop the group dead.
- Test the topic guide out on a pilot group of colleagues or friends – this will also give practice in facilitating.
- Consider combining your focus groups with more creative techniques (see Chapter 12).

Opening up the focus group

- Brief the group that they do not need to come to any agreement, and that everyone's views are valued.
- Perhaps agree some ground rules with the group at the start, by asking them for suggestions and writing them up, to engage members with the issues of confidentiality, not interrupting and so on.

- Make sure your first question encourages everyone to speak – it should be straightforward but open, for example 'What were your first impressions when you arrived in this area?'
- Ask 'how' questions first; move on to any 'why' questions after the group has got going.

Monitoring progress

- Be attentive to everyone, and try to draw out in a sensitive way those who are quiet.
- Do not allow individuals to dominate.
- Check whether group members are in agreement with statements being made, 'Is that what everyone thinks?' 'Does everyone agree that xyz?'

Closing down the focus group

- Towards the end, summarize what you have heard and check with the group whether this is what they thought was said (the observer can do this if you have one).
- Thank people for their time – coming to a focus group is quite a commitment.
- Ask if participants have any questions – they will often ask what will be done with the findings, so have your reply prepared!
- Ask how people have felt about taking part in the focus group.

Table 11.3 Strengths and limitations – focus groups

Focus groups – strengths	Focus groups – limitations
• Group interaction can produce invaluable data on how people think about an issue – their own explanations and understandings • Accessible to people who cannot read or write • Particularly good when you want people to think about what changes they would like to see – support from others like them can enable people to think more creatively • Can reduce the power of the researcher, with participants feeling some 'strength in numbers' and having greater control of the process • Enjoyable for participants • Very rich data generated • Sometimes group members are motivated to take action as a result of sharing their stories	• Do not produce statistics • Data can be complex to analyse • Can be 'led' by dominating individuals, with controversial or different views suppressed • A skilled (preferably independent) facilitator is needed • May be difficult to recruit to – asks a lot of the respondents in terms of time and effort • Can exclude people who are not comfortable (or accepted) speaking in public, so minority voices may not be heard • More difficult to coordinate, especially if you want specific participants, as a date has to be found that fits everybody's schedule

> ### Checklist: conducting focus groups
>
> ☑ Find a suitable location for the group – somewhere quiet and comfortable.
> ☑ Put people at ease with an informal, open approach – ensure they do not feel they are under scrutiny.
> ☑ Make sure everyone gets a fair chance to speak.
> ☑ Encourage interaction between group members, but keep them on the subject.
> ☑ Prevent group members from pressuring others to agree with them.
> ☑ Do not rely on one focus group to represent a whole group of people's point of view – do more to guard against a 'rogue' group going off at a tangent.
> ☑ Remember the data collected relate to the group, not the individuals in it.
> ☑ Invite enough people: sometimes it is a good idea to overbook, especially when you expect some of them not to show up. There is a window within the ideal number of participants of about six to 12.

11.4 Questionnaires

11.4.1 What is a questionnaire?

A questionnaire is a written list of questions, either given or posted to respondents, who fill it in themselves (this is called a 'self-completion questionnaire'). Many of the questions are likely to offer the respondent some possible ('pre-coded') replies to tick.

Sometimes, researchers ask questions from questionnaires verbally, and then fill in the answers – the process then becomes a type of interview, although the questionnaire itself may look very similar to a self-completion questionnaire. This is a more common practice in the South, owing to low literacy rates. For this type of research, much in this section will be relevant, but see also Section 11.2 on interviews.

11.4.2 When should you use a questionnaire for research?

Questionnaires are useful when:

- You need information from large numbers of respondents.
- You know exactly what data you need.
- The information you need is fairly straightforward, and you want it in a standardized format.
- Your respondents can read and write and are comfortable filling in a questionnaire.

11.4.3 Online surveys

Where people have reasonable internet access, online surveys using programs such as SurveyMonkey are becoming increasingly popular. Much of the process of set-up, data entry and analysis is automated within the website of the provider. Of course, the sample is restricted to those who have internet access, although special arrangements can be made to log onto a survey while a researcher is sitting beside the respondent. This can be a very efficient means of collecting data, but beware – it is easy to put questions into the system, but there is still the need to be very careful as to how questions are worded if you want answers that are meaningful.

Online evaluation for health education in schools

Coram Life Education provides high-quality, interactive health education in more than 3,500 primary schools across the UK, with an emphasis on substance misuse prevention. The organization renewed its materials for evaluating children's response to the lessons it provides, and introduced a consistent set of questionnaires for feedback from children and teachers. Using SurveyMonkey, it was possible to set up a system where data could be entered online locally either by the children and teachers themselves, where they had adequate access, or by an administrator. Then each local centre around the country can do its own analysis and print off the results of its own surveys. Both quantitative and qualitative information is included. Reports can also be provided to individual schools, as well as bringing together the evidence at national level. This is a far more efficient system than was previously possible. For more information, see www.coram.org.uk/section/coram-life-education.

FOR EXAMPLE

11.4.4 Omnibus surveys

Another approach that can be efficient is to work with a survey research company to include some questions in what is called an omnibus survey. This means your question is included alongside commercial market research questions, and will be put to a potentially large sample, drawn to represent a segment of the general population.

An omnibus survey on school violence

One of the projects to measure how successful Plan's Learn Without Fear has been in promoting debate, challenging violent attitudes and reducing school violence in different populations consists of an omnibus survey. This aims to assess the general population's understanding of and attitudes towards school violence by using opinion polls at various stages of the campaign.

For the pilot study, colleagues in Plan Peru and Plan Kenya inserted five questions into two national opinion polls, which reached a randomly selected representative sample of households across each country.

On a scale of 1 to 7, where 1 means a very small problem and 7 means a very big problem at national level, Kenyans scored school violence at on average 4.7 and Peruvians 5.7. Taking into account these very high scores, and that the large majority of Kenyans (70.9 per cent) and Peruvians (93.9 per cent) think governments should outlaw school violence, Plan has a clear mandate in both countries to work with the authorities to improve and enforce laws to protect schoolchildren.

FOR EXAMPLE

(Continued)

(Continued)

The study also found that, if Kenyans see an adult beating a schoolchild, 12 per cent would do nothing. Equally worrying is that one in two Peruvians would call authorities before trying to stop the situation of abuse. The situation changes dramatically when people see one child beating another child: 69.4 per cent of Peruvians and 50.7 per cent of Kenyans would talk to the abuser and around one in five (22.3 per cent and 18.5 per cent, respectively) would try to stop the abuse by physically stopping the abuser.

At the time of writing, Plan had completed data collection in two further countries (Liberia and Pakistan) and was planning the second wave of data collection to compare results and inform a multinational response against school violence.

11.4.5   Conducting a questionnaire survey

Hang on! Make sure before you start drafting a questionnaire that the aims and objectives, focus and questions for your study are clear and agreed (see Chapter 3).

Preparing the questionnaire

Please also see Section 11.1 on how to ask questions.

- Prepare questionnaires very carefully – small mistakes in wording a question can make the response useless, and you have only one chance to get your replies. The actual questions are commanded by the research matrix (see Chapter 7). Don't ask 'bonus' questions.
- Consider carefully the order of the questions.
- Ask around to see copies of questionnaires people have used in your agency or on the subject area you are working in.
- Pilot any questionnaire carefully, including timing how long it takes to answer.
- Give information on the questionnaire as to who you are and the purpose of the research.
- Choose the sample with care (see Chapter 10).

Pre-coded questions

When researchers talk about 'coding', they are referring to the process of assigning categories to data. Pre-coded questions give the respondent a choice between a set of categories determined by the researcher. Open questions allow the respondent to write whatever they please. For example, an open question might ask

How long have you lived in this area?

Whereas a pre-coded question would ask,

Have you lived in this area for

Less than six months?

Between six months and one year?

Between one year and five years?

More than five years?

Pre-coded questions are much easier to analyse than open questions. However, using them does mean you are obliging respondents to fit their reply into your categories, so you need to make sure the categories you offer are right. For example, if you used the open question in the example above, some answers might mirror the options we thought of, for example 'four months'. But others might say 'since my child was born', or 'since the earthquake in my home village' or 'all my life'. With open questions, you allow the respondent to use their own categories – these are less easily comparable, and are usually not quantifiable, but may be more meaningful. You could use both, even in a single question (for example by including a 'comments' option).

Table 11.4 Types of question that can be used in a questionnaire

Verbal or open	The expected response is a word, phrase or extended comment. Responses can produce useful information but analysis can present problems. Gives respondents a chance to give their own views on the issue.
More structured questions are easier to analyse. Youngman suggests the following broad types (1986):	
List	A list of items is offered, any of which may be selected. For example, a question may ask about types of crop grown and the respondent may grow several types of crop.
Category	The response is one only of a given set of categories. For example, if age categories are provided (20–9, 30–9, etc.), the respondent can only fit into one category – so categories have to be mutually exclusive.
Ranking	The respondent is asked to place something in rank order. For example, they might be asked to place qualities or characteristics in order of importance to them.
Quantity	The response is a number (exact or approximate), giving the amount of some characteristics.
Grid	Records answers to two or more questions at the same time.

Source: Youngman (1986), in Bell (2010).

If you used the pre-coded example, and many respondents replied, 'less than six months', you can't find out whether that means two weeks or five months – which are very different in terms of how a person feels. You also can't find out whether they moved before or after an event you later think may have had an impact.

If you use open questions, you have to 'code' the replies – group them into categories – after the event, as part of your analysis. This is worthwhile for important questions where detailed qualitative information is needed, but very time consuming compared with the simplicity of adding up replies to a pre-coded question.

See Section 11.1 above for guidance on how to evaluate a draft set of questions.

Table 11.5   Strengths and limitations – questionnaire surveys

Questionnaires – strengths	Questionnaires – limitations
• Relatively cheap way of collecting information from large numbers of people • Easy to analyse if mainly pre-coded questions are used • Self-completion questionnaires remove any 'interviewer effect' from the picture, so respondents are reacting to a standard package • Quick for the respondent to complete • Some people find 'tick boxes' easy to deal with and more attractive than other research approaches	• Response rates can be low • Pre-coded questions can slant findings towards the researcher's view of the world rather than the respondents' • 'Tick boxes' can frustrate respondents and put them off participating • Can take substantial time to draft and pilot and for people to complete and return • People who can't read or write can be included only by making special arrangements • Little opportunity to check the truthfulness of responses, especially with postal or online questionnaires • As opposed to interviews, questionnaires are a 'one-shot exercise'; they cannot be improved as you go along

Setting up the survey

Preparing a survey questionnaire is a major administrative task: it requires organization, persistence and attention to detail. Some essential matters to consider are:

• Include background information: whose research is this; any official backing you have; the purpose of the research; return address and date; confidentiality; voluntary response (that is, there is no obligation on the respondent to complete the questionnaire); thanks.
• Give very exact instructions to the respondent, and preferably an example, to show how to fill in the questionnaire.
• A serial number can be used to distinguish date and place of distribution, etc., to establish which questionnaires are returned. But if data are to be anonymous, ensure that any coding system does not compromise this by identifying the individual.
• Ensure you include 'don't know' as an option (missing answers should be recorded as such).
• Make sure the questionnaire is as attractive and well set out as you can make it – this will increase the response rate. It will also help you when you analyse the data.

Carrying out the survey

• Make sure you are meticulous in keeping track of paperwork – keep a record of what goes out and what comes in.

- Plan to follow up on people who have not been contacted – this will increase your response rate.
- Think about anything else you can do to improve the response rate (see Chapter 8 on increasing response rates among hard-to-reach groups).
- Keep it short!

Checklist: questionnaire survey research

☑ Allow enough time to:
  ☑ plan and design a first draft of the questionnaire;
  ☑ show it to people;
  ☑ revise it;
  ☑ pilot it;
  ☑ revise it again in light of the pilot; and then
  ☑ print and distribute the final version.
☑ Consider from the beginning the implication the design has for the analysis.
☑ Make sure you obtain any official approval you need to distribute the questionnaire (see Chapter 8 on contacting respondents).
☑ Allow resources for the production and distribution of the questionnaire.
☑ Carry out follow-up on people who have not responded to increase your response rate – this takes time and effort.
☑ If you plan to analyse the responses on a computer, think about how you are going to prepare the data for this.

11.5 Use of documentary sources and secondary data analysis

11.5.1 What is research using documentary sources?

Most research projects require some sort of literature review (see Chapter 5). But sometimes a study of documents is central to the research, either by itself or combined with other methods. Documents are treated as sources of data in their own right. A systematic review is a special type of study of existing research following rigorous procedures, usually applied to health care issues (Antman, 1992 and Oxman, 1993, in Higgins and Green, 2011).

It is sometimes possible to reanalyse existing datasets to ask new questions (known as secondary analysis). For example, the UK's data archive (http://www.data-archive.ac.uk/home) makes much valuable data potentially available for secondary analysis. It is really worth considering this, as it could save massively on costs, while often drawing on strong sampling techniques. This type of analysis is pretty technical, and development agencies would be well advised to commission experienced researchers.

11.5.2 When should you use documentary sources?

Documentary research is useful/possible when:

- It is one element of a larger study.
- Some of your research questions may be (even partially) answered by existing data.
- Reasonably reliable data exist on the population you are interested in.

11.5.3 Conducting a study of documentary sources

Please see also Chapter 5, which gives detailed guidance on locating and working with documents of every kind, since this is also needed for a literature review.

Locating relevant documents

- Much important material may be unpublished – ask people what exists and seek it out.
- Be persistent: part of the ethos of academic research is to make material publicly available in order to allow others to replicate the results. Make guesses about what 'ought' to be available, and see if you can find it.

Analysing the documents

- Once you locate a document, always make full notes, especially of its bibliographic details, before you hand it back – you may never see it again.
- If you want to use statistics quoted in documents, note down full details of exactly how, when and by whom the data were gathered, and what definitions were used.
- With important figures, if possible, talk to those who produced them to get further insight into their status (for example how much weight can be put on them).
- Read critically, keeping your own questions in mind.

Table 11.6   Strengths and limitations – using documents

Using documents – strengths	Using documents – limitations
• Can add authority to your study • Can avoid wasteful duplication of research that has already been done • To influence policy, you need to show you are aware of current work in the field, especially any which appears to contradict your argument	• Usefulness depends on the quality of information available for your area • Data will have been produced for another purpose than yours, so will rarely fully meet the objectives of your own study • Can be difficult to keep a clear focus on your own research questions • Documents cannot be treated as objective representations of reality – they represent the point of view of those who produced them • You need to ascertain whether participants who provided the data for the original research agree their information be used in the secondary analysis

Writing up your study

- Give complete references for all sources (see Chapter 5).
- If citing others' figures, note any obvious criticisms that could be made of them, and explain what level of credibility you would give them.

Checklist: using documents

☑ Keep your own research focus clearly in mind as you work on the documents.
☑ Assess all information for credibility – look for possible sources of bias or error.
☑ Look out for what is not there: gaps are often very revealing.
☑ Any reanalysis of existing data should be undertaken with advice from a statistician in the case of figures, and an experienced researcher in the case of qualitative data.

11.6   Observation

11.6.1   What is observation?

Observation plays a role in all research. For example, noticing children drinking from a stream when there is a well nearby, or recently destroyed areas of forest, might suggest questions to ask. By directly observing what happens, the researcher can check whether what people say they do or think is reflected in their actual behaviour. The two main types of observation research, systematic observation and participant observation, are very different from each other.

Table 11.7   Some types of observation

Systematic observation	Participant observation
• Observers look for specified behaviour at specific times and places	• Observers learn about the inside-out perspective and not the outside-in perspective often adopted by researchers. This allows them to appreciate evaluation criteria used within a community and the meaning of activities situated in a cultural context for those who perform them
• A checklist of items to be observed is required	
• Quantitative data are generated	
• Observers are open but unobtrusive in making their observations	• The observer notes everything they can
	• Qualitative data are generated in large quantities
	• Consent can be an issue, if people forget you are a researcher

11.6.2   Systematic observation

Systematic observation involves observing objects, processes, relationships or people and recording these observations. You need to identify indicators that are important to your research questions and can be assessed by direct observation. For example, if you are studying an institution caring for disabled people, you could observe numbers of interactions between residents and staff, between different residents and between staff members themselves. A study of access to clean water might involve observations of how people use different water sources.

When should you use systematic observation for research?

Observation is useful when:

- The information you want is about observable things.
- You need to cross-check people's account of what happens.

Conducting a systematic observation study

Preparing for the study

- Draft an observation checklist which identifies the indicators to be sought.
- Pilot checklists and procedures (times of day chosen, etc.).
- When observing a complex event, for example a local celebration, have different observers concentrate on observing different groups of people (women, men, children, tourists).

Carrying out the systematic observation

- Work in a systematic, consistent way, to allow comparisons across time and sites.
- Disturb the setting as little as possible, by placing yourself somewhere unobtrusive and avoiding interaction with people (can be easier said than done!).
- If you have several observers, train them to ensure they code their observations the same way. It can be useful to have several observers code the same situation and to compare the data they collect.

Table 11.8 Strengths and limitations – systematic observation

Observation – strengths	Systematic observation – limitations
• Directly records what people do, as distinct from what they say they do • Can be systematic and rigorous • Can produce large amounts of data in a fairly short time • Can generate data which can then form the basis for discussion with those observed	• Focuses on observable behaviour and therefore sheds no light on people's motivations • Danger of leading to over-simplification or distortion of the meaning of a situation, especially in cross-cultural contexts • Presence of an observer cannot help but influence the setting they are observing to some extent

Checklist: systematic observation

- ☑ Use observation alongside other method/s – the meaning of observed behaviour can't be assumed to be obvious; people should be asked to interpret it themselves.
- ☑ Observations can be based on:
  - ☑ Frequency of events – how often does the event on the checklist occur?
  - ☑ Events at a given point in time – observer logs what is happening, for example every 30 seconds or every 20 minutes.
  - ☑ Duration of events – instances are timed as they occur.
  - ☑ Sample of people – individuals can be observed for predetermined periods of time, after which attention switches to another person.
- ☑ Items may be included in the checklist if they are:
  - ☑ overt – observable in a direct manner;
  - ☑ obvious;
  - ☑ context-independent – context does not affect interpretation;
  - ☑ relevant;
  - ☑ complete – should cover all possibilities;
  - ☑ precise – no ambiguity between the categories;
  - ☑ easy to record.

Source: Denscombe (2010)

11.6.3 Participant observation

Participant observation has its roots in traditional ethnographic studies which aim to gain an insider's perspective of a study community. It always takes place in community settings, that is, in locations relevant to the research study, and requires the researcher to become directly involved in the community's daily life. Participant observation is a useful way of gaining an understanding of the social, cultural, economic and physical context of a study community, the relationships between people and their behaviours, interactions and activities.

Participant observation should not be seen as a single method or technique that can be used in isolation from other methods and procedures. Rather, it should be regarded as a combination of methods and techniques: it might involve some social interaction with people in their own setting, some direct observation of relevant events, some formal and a great deal of informal interviewing, some collection of documents. In large part, it consists of the researcher writing and reflecting on detailed field notes acquired using some of these methods.

It is important to stress that participation observation, as exciting or inspiring as it can be, can also be very difficult. Articles, conference presentations and specialized textbooks are full of warning messages on the importance of thorough methodological, logistical and psychological preparation. The following summarizes the main issues to address if you decide to embark on such a project.

When should you use participant observation for research?

Participant observation is useful when:

- Your research is of an exploratory and descriptive nature.
- Your research is concerned with exploring from an insider's perspective human behaviour, relationships and interactions on a daily basis.
- You are able to gain entry and access to the community field setting.
- You have some knowledge of the language, customs and culture of the setting.
- You can rely on information by observing one or a small number of respondents.
- You are able to gather qualitative data through direct observation, informal interviews and other such techniques pertinent to the setting.

Undertaking participant observation in research

Some guidelines to help you to carry out participant observation in your research are as follows.

Planning the field research

- Have a clear understanding of your research focus so you can determine specific objectives for the participant observation research.
- Use the work of authors who have used participant observation to answer questions related to yours and identify key issues.
- Choose a site that is easy to enter, that is, one where accessing data will be easy.
- Determine the population(s) to be observed and contact relevant people in the community.
- Get permission to stay in the study site.
- Inform the community how long you intend to stay.
- Plan how you will take notes during research. It may be useful to prepare a checklist of things to pay attention to.

Entering the study site

- Bring as much documentation about yourself and the research project as possible to ensure maximum transparency.
- Be prepared for questions about yourself and your assignment. You can practise explaining yourself and your study before entering the field – be sure you are able to do so in easily accessible language.
- Get to know the physical and social layout of the study site.

Becoming part of the community

- Talk to as many people in the community as possible.
- Take a keen interest in the daily life, special events and culture of the community.
- Engage to some extent in the activities taking place, either to learn more about the study community or so as to not to draw too much attention to yourself. For example, eat what local community members eat and participate in social activities.

Carrying out participant observation research in the study site

- Keep a record of what is happening in a notebook: events; how people behave; their body language, attitudes, physical gestures, conversations and interactions; their comings and goings; the general environment. Begin each entry with the date, time, place, event/activity taking place, number of people present.
- Write field notes either during participant observation or following the activity.
- Remember to be discreet when taking notes: try not to stand out or disrupt the natural flow of social activity.
- If you decide to take notes following the activity, do so as soon as possible so your memory of the details does not fade.
- Check your notes regularly. Look for entries that need clarification or follow-up.
- It is most likely you will be able to make only brief notes during data collection. You should therefore keep time aside at regular intervals (preferably within 24 hours) to expand the notes you have taken into a descriptive narrative.
- Avoid reporting your interpretations rather than an objective account of all that is happening around you.
- Draw a map of your study site that marks important places, places where certain activities are taking place and places where follow-up observation is needed.

Departing from the field

- Depart in a way that is appropriate to the culture of the study community.
- Type your notes onto the computer as per the study format.

Analysing your observations

- Go back to the literature: what did you know about your subject before collecting new data?
- Present the main findings of your study, emphasizing comparisons of what is found to happen in one place but not in another.

FOR EXAMPLE

Social responses to the integrated control of tropical diseases: Uganda

To investigate the case for the development of national programmes for the integrated control of tropical diseases in Africa in the early 2000s, researchers at Brunel University and the London School of Economics studied social responses in Uganda to a programme dealing with two such tropical diseases: schistosomiasis and soil-transmitted helminths.

Fieldwork involved participant observation in a wide range of settings in Panyimur subcounty. This included 300 open-ended, unstructured interviews, visits to homesteads, talking to fishermen at landing sites on the shores of Lake Albert, 'hanging out' in one of the lodges in Panyimur town and talking to people as they passed through the markets. Those interviewed also included 20 local healing specialists, 9 village elders, 15 health care providers, 10 schoolteachers and 12 political figureheads. Wherever possible, interviews were undertaken in a relaxed and open manner, with a great deal of emphasis given to establishing trust and rapport with informants.

Findings showed that adults were increasingly rejecting free treatment owing to a subjective fear of side-effects as well as inappropriate and inadequate health education. In addition, current procedures for distributing drugs at a district level were found to be problematic. The research study therefore recommended strongly that education materials be made increasingly available, that some existing procedures for disseminating information be revised and that serious efforts be made to communicate with local people in local languages, so as to make the programme work and ensure adults seek treatment on a regular basis.

Source: Parker et al. (2008)

FOR EXAMPLE

Participant observation in action: the US

In the early 1990s, sharing needles during drug use was a known risk factor for HIV acquisition in the US. After educational campaigns informed injecting drug users about the importance of using clean needles, surveys indicated that needle sharing had declined. High rates of HIV transmission persisted among this population, however. An anthropologist's observation of heroin users in one state confirmed that users were not sharing needles. In observing the preparation process leading up to injection, however, the anthropologist noticed numerous opportunities for cross-contamination of the instruments shared in cooking and distributing the heroin (such as cooking pots, cotton, and needles), and of the liquid heroin itself. Discovery of this phenomenon through participant observation constituted an important contribution to understanding injecting drug use behaviour as related to HIV acquisition.

Source: Mack et al. (2005)

Table 11.9   Strengths and limitations – participant observation

Participant observation – strengths	Participant observation – limitations
• Documentation relies on first-hand information • Allows the researcher to gain insights into contexts, relationships and behaviours that are beyond the scope of more distant surveys and document searches	• Documentation relies on memory, personal discipline and diligence of researcher • The method is inherently subjective • Time consuming

Participant observation – strengths	Participant observation – limitations
• Some behaviours and beliefs can be understood only in more intimate, day-to-day relationships or by being there when things happen • Generates a rich source of highly detailed, in-depth information about people's behaviour and the study group/community	• Restricted to fairly small-scale studies carried out over a long period, and the group/community being studied is unlikely to be representative of any other social group

Key points from this chapter

This chapter has introduced a number of key research methods used in development work. Such a selection will unavoidably leave some gaps, but all of the methods presented here are widely employed and will provide you with a good starting point. The aim is not to explain the methods comprehensively but to enable you to make an informed judgement about their relative strengths and weaknesses and, in conjunction with other chapters, to decide which method is the most likely to address your research problem in the specific context you are facing.

Further reading

General

These texts provide introductions to different, mostly qualitative, research methods. As they are written mostly for social science students, they are more exhaustive in the selection of methods they present and the theoretical rationale they provide.

Bauer, M. and Gaskell, G. (eds) (2000) *Qualitative Researching with Text, Image and Sound*. New Delhi, Thousand Oaks, CA, London: Sage.

Also explores methods to analyse more unconventional forms of data such as images and sound.

Creswell, J.W. (2009) *Research Design: Qualitative, Quantitative and Mixed Method Approaches*, 3rd edn. New Delhi, Thousand Oaks, CA, London: Sage.

Foundational text in social research design, providing more theoretical grounding for the methods presented in this chapter.

Mikkelsen, B. (2005) *Methods for Development Work and Research: A New Guide for Practitioners*, 2nd edn. New Delhi, Thousand Oaks, CA, London: Sage.

Critical and extensive guide on development research focusing on qualitative research.

Singleton R. and Straits, B. (1999) *Approaches to Social Research*, 3rd edn. Oxford: Oxford University Press.

A balanced treatment of four major research approaches: experimentation, survey research, field research and use of available data.

Tashakkori, A. and Teddlie, C. (2003) *Handbook of Mixed Methods in Social and Behavioral Research*. New Delhi, Thousand Oaks, CA, London: Sage.

Focuses particularly on the theoretical rationale and practical application of the mixed method paradigm.

Interviews

Denscombe, M. (2010) *The Good Research Guide for Small-scale Social Research Projects*, 4th edn. Maidenhead and Philadelphia, PA: Open University Press.

Has a chapter covering interviews in detail.

Theis, J. and Grady, H.M. (1991) *Participatory Rapid Appraisal for Community Development*. London: International Institute for Environment and Development and Save the Children Federation.

Has a good section on semi-structured interviewing.

See also further reading recommended in Chapter 8 on communication, especially for work with children.

Focus groups

Barbour, R. (2007) *Doing Focus Groups*. New Delhi, Thousand Oaks, CA, London: Sage.

Bloor, M., Frankland, J., Thomas, M. and Robson, K. (2001) *Focus Groups in Social Research*. New Delhi, London, Thousand Oaks, CA: Sage.

Hennink, M.M. (2007) *International Focus Group Research: A Handbook for the Health and Social Sciences*. Cambridge: Cambridge University Press.

Jowett, M. and O'Toole, G. (2006) 'Focusing researchers' minds: contrasting experiences of using focus groups in feminist qualitative research', *Qualitative Research*, 6 (4): 453–72.

Documentary sources

Levitas, R. and Guy, W. (eds) (1996) *Interpreting Official Statistics*. London: Routledge.

Interesting collection of essays, looking at the issues in relation to a range of UK official statistics.

Pratt, B. and Loizos, P. (1992) 'Choosing research methods: data collection for development workers'. *Oxfam Development Guidelines* 7. Oxford: Oxfam.

Includes a discussion of the use of secondary sources in development work.

May, T. (2003) *Social Research: Issues, Methods and Process*, 3rd edn. Buckingham: Open University Press.

Includes two relevant chapters: 'Official statistics: topic and resource' and 'Documentary research: excavations and evidence'. UK oriented, but the general approaches discussed are relevant anywhere.

Observation

These texts focus on observational research in the form of systematic as well as participant observation.

Cohen, A. (2004) *Custom and Politics in Urban Africa: A Study of Hausa Migrants in Yoruba Towns*. London: Routledge.

Denscombe, M. (2010) (see above).

Saukko, P. (2003) *Doing Research in Cultural Studies: An Introduction to Classical and New Methodological Approaches*. New Delhi, Thousand Oaks, CA, London: Sage.

Outlines methodological approaches to the study of lived experience, texts and social contexts within the field of cultural studies.

This section has also drawn on Theis and Grady (1991) (see above).

Questionnaires

Guidance on questionnaire design and administration is in most books on how to do research. If you need detailed guidance for a major questionnaire exercise, Oppenheim and Moser and Kalton are classic textbooks, and still useful. For simpler exercises, Denscombe (see above for reference, drawn on in writing this section) and Bell give excellent advice.

Bell, J. (2010) *Doing Your Research Project: A Guide for First-time Researchers in Education, Health and Social Science*, 5th edn. Maidenhead: Open University Press.
Bulmer, M. (1998) 'The problem of exporting social survey research', *The American Behavioral Scientist*, 42 (2): 153–67.

Helpful advice for designing simple questionnaires. Also drawn on in preparing this section.

Escobar, A. and Roberts, B. (1998) 'Surveys as instruments of modernization: the case of Mexico', *The American Behavioral Scientist*, 42 (2): 237–51.
Moser, C.A. and Kalton, G. (1971) *Survey Methods in Social Investigation*, 2nd edn. London: Heinemann.
Oppenheim, A.N. (1992) *Questionnaire Design, Interviewing and Attitude Measurement*, 2nd edn. London: Pinter.
Weisberg, H., Krosnick, J.A. and Bowen, B. (1996) *Introduction to Survey Research, Polling, and Data Analysis*. New Delhi, Thousand Oaks, CA, London: Sage.

12

PARTICIPATORY RESEARCH

Participatory research has become established in recent years as a powerful tool for development workers. This kind of research aims to enable people who traditionally have been merely the 'subjects' of research to take an active part in making their own voices heard. Participatory research may be embedded within a process of development work in a way traditional research would not be.

Here, we first present some of the main principles underpinning participatory research, then describe some typical methods used and finally focus on some practical issues that arise and challenges to this approach.

What is called participatory research covers a wide range of practices and derives from a number of different sources in both the North and the South (Harper, 1997; Reason, 1998). This type of work goes by many names in different parts of the world – action research, practitioner research, participatory inquiry, Participatory Learning and Action/Participatory Rural Appraisal (PLA/PRA), Participatory Action and Research (PAR). It is widely recognized as a powerful way of making change in complex situations, and has emerged as a new 'mainstream paradigm' (way of thinking) in development studies (Mikkelsen, 2005). The core process is to enable participants to share their perceptions of a problem, to find common ground and then to engage a variety of people in identifying and testing out some possible solutions. There is a process of shared learning for all concerned. This can be particularly useful in situations where local professionals have not felt empowered to take action on an issue. This type of work may or may not involve community members, the 'end users' of services.

However, participatory research of all sorts follows some unifying principles. At its heart is the validation of the knowledge and intelligence of ordinary people. Research and learning are seen as essentially intertwined, and attention is focused on the processes by which people actually learn, rather than on an idea of facts or truth as something that exist in the abstract. The other key common thread is an orientation to action. Participatory research may have a better chance of leading to solutions to problems, because it actively involves those who best understand, and have the greatest stake in, the issues – community members themselves. The research process itself may be seen as more important than its outputs, in the sense of written reports and so on.

Participatory research takes a facilitative approach to respondents, rather than aiming to extract information from them. Researchers need to be conscious of the impact of their own attitudes, behaviour and feelings and to have a commitment to hand over power and initiative to others. A very wide range of different methods are used in participatory research, including pretty much the full range of methods used in the social sciences, adapted to a participatory approach. Large-scale surveys can feed into a participatory process. PLA, developed for work in the South, uses an eclectic collection of methods, specializing in ones which enable people without literacy skills to express their views and knowledge.

From the perspective of development workers, participatory research is one of a range of methods used to facilitate community members' greater participation in decision making. It will not always be the best method to empower community members, since a research orientation (that is, towards finding out information) brings with it some difficulties as well as some opportunities.

Participatory research has influenced and been influenced by civil rights and anti-racism, feminism and community development approaches, and has contributed to the development of such social movements (Gustavsen, 2003).

Next, we look briefly at the purposes of participatory research, who is involved and what exactly it is that people participate in.

12.1 Participation for ...?

Like policy-focused research, participatory research explicitly aims to make change in society. But the way change takes place is seen differently. Community members' own learning and growth in self-confidence is seen as crucial to enabling them to act more effectively on their own behalf. The key outcomes of such research may relate more to the empowerment of those concerned than to formal reports or high-level policy change – but often both types of outcomes are desired.

Since the overall aim is empowerment, it is key to participatory research processes to seek to make links between local communities and the larger policy framework – to influence the forces that structure people's lives. The study of the contribution of older people to development in Ghana and South Africa described in Chapter 1 is an example of a highly participatory process linked to policy change at the national level.

PLA has been very important internationally (Gosling, 2003; Theis and Grady, 1991). It developed out of Rapid Rural Appraisal, which was oriented towards local needs assessment processes. It was then used to build up broader policy-oriented processes, such as national Participatory Poverty Assessments (PPAs) (Holland, 1998). Participation may also simply help in gathering more accurate information.

The impact of HIV and AIDS on children in New Delhi, India

FOR EXAMPLE

In research by Save the Children in New Delhi on the impact of HIV and AIDS on children, the involvement of children and practitioners from partner agencies helped in obtaining richer information. For example, a female street educator provided information on the sexual behaviour of girls living on the streets and what sex means for them. Street boys helped in finding out how information about HIV and AIDS does not translate to behaviour change, because boys lack control over these behaviours (for example condom use in commercial sex) and over the circumstances they live in. Some of this information had never been documented before. The children were involved in getting access to other children, collecting information and framing questions to be asked to other children.

12.2 Participation by ...?

Often, when people refer to participatory research, they are talking about community members – who might be villagers, street children, people with experience of mental health services or women traders, for example. But it is also important to foster participation in research for development work by people whose support would be needed to find a solution to a problem. These may be local or national government agencies; local non-governmental organizations (NGOs); professionals like doctors, nurses or teachers; politicians.

One of the major issues for participatory research is that the inequalities of power between different groups within the community in question need to be handled with care. In any community, it is likely that women, children and disabled people will have difficulty in getting their point of view heard. The poorest people out of any group will be in the same position. It is crucial that specific measures are taken to counterbalance social inequalities, or else participation can simply mean that those with the loudest voices get their way once again.

12.3 Participation in ...?

Participatory research is not a method but more an approach, a way of working. It can involve the use of a wide range of methods, qualitative and quantitative. Participation can occur in a number of different ways, such as:

- setting the broad agenda for the research;
- clarifying the detailed research focus;
- responding to research which uses interactive methods;
- undertaking fieldwork – interviews, group discussions;
- analysis of data, making sense of findings;
- promotion of findings;
- appointing researchers;
- managing the research, for example membership of advisory groups;
- advocacy using the results of the research.

Involvement of each type has different consequences for the way in which the research needs to be conducted, for example in terms of the support offered to participating people. There is no one recipe for successful participatory research. Judgements must be made with knowledge of the purpose of the exercise, the resources available, the skills of those involved and the nature of the issue in question.

12.4 Some participatory research methods

This section describes some methods typically used in participatory research, but note that all those described in the last chapter should also be considered. There is no formula for finding the best methods to use. Chambers (1996) makes the need for flexibility very clear in calling for an 'eclectic pluralism [which] means that branding, labels, ownership and ego give way to sharing, borrowing, improvisation and creativity, all these complemented by mutual and critical reflective learning and personal responsibility for good practice'.

The four types of methods introduced here are presented by order of 'intensity' on the participatory scale: we first look at ranking and scoring techniques, which require relatively 'light' involvement by participants, then visual techniques, before moving on to describe how to use drama and role plays for research purposes. A final subsection deals with peer research, which gives communities a particularly prominent role.

Checklist: Participatory research

☑ A reversal of learning – 'experts' learn from ordinary people;
☑ Learning rapidly and progressively;
☑ Offsetting biases;
☑ Optimizing trade-offs – 'optimal ignorance' – knowing what is not worth knowing and 'appropriate imprecision';
☑ Triangulating – using a range of methods to cross-check information;
☑ Seeking diversity;
☑ Facilitating – 'they [community members] do it', 'handing over the stick';
☑ Self-critical awareness and responsibility – welcoming error as an opportunity to learn to do better; using one's own best judgement at all times;
☑ Sharing of information, ideas, resources.

Source: Chambers (1992)

12.4.1 Ranking and scoring

Ranking and scoring are useful to learn about the categories people use to understand their worlds and the values they place on things. Ranking means putting things in order; scoring relates to the weight people give to different items (Mikkelsen, 2005; Theis and Grady, 1991), done as part of an interview or separately, or in some cases as the basis of a group discussion. Visual images can be used to represent the items to be ranked, or people can 'vote' with stones or beans.

These techniques are an accessible way of initiating discussion of possibilities in the local situation. Ranking exercises are also used widely in more traditional research, again with either individuals or groups.

Wealth ranking, for example, has been used widely in research for development. You might ask a number of individuals to carry out the ranking of community members' wealth independently, and then put the results together in a table. You then discuss the results, without revealing who gave which scores, with a group of community members. It is quicker, but perhaps less reliable, to go straight to the group setting.

Ranking and scoring exercises are most useful when you want to engage with community members in deciding priorities for action, or when you need to understand community members' ways of categorizing things.

Generally, ranking and scoring exercises involve four steps:

1 A set of problems or preferences is prioritized, for example farming problems or preferences for tree species.
2 The interviewee is asked to give her favoured items in this set, in order of priority. A list of three to six items from each interviewee is thus obtained.
3 The exercise is repeated as many times as there are people to interview.
4 A table of responses is drawn up (see Table 12.1).

Table 12.1   Example of preference ranking

Constraints to agricultural production

Problem	A	B	C	D	E	F	Total score	Ranking
			Respondents					
Drought	5	5	3	5	4	5	27	1st
Pests	4	3	5	4	5	4	25	2nd
Weeds	3	4	4	1	3	3	18	3rd
Costs of inputs	2	1	2	2	2	2	11	4th
Labour shortage	1	2	1	3	1	1	9	5th

Reproduced with permission from Theis and Grady (1991)

This exercise needs to be adapted carefully to the local situation. This may happen naturally through other fieldwork, but it will often be a good idea to start the process with a brainstorming discussion about what items should be included – in Table 12.1's case, what are the main problems for farmers here? You could also work in a large group, which has the advantage that you will also learn by hearing people debating the relative importance of different factors or items.

Choosing priorities is obviously a key step in the move from research to action – this exercise can be used to structure that process. But again, remember that, if you work in a large group, less powerful members may find it difficult to get their priorities heard.

Checklist: Ranking and scoring exercises

☑ As the first step, discover and learn to use community members' own ways of categorizing things – their own units of measurement and names for things.
☑ Discuss any ideas you have about what to focus on with knowledgeable people first.
☑ Let people do it their own way.
☑ Make sure you get the perspectives of different groups of people on any ranking process you do: women, men, young, old, etc., will have different points of view.
☑ Probe people's reasons for the order of the ranking and their criteria in giving importance to items.

12.4.2 Visual methods

A wide variety of visual methods have been used in research for development work. They are an important feature of participatory research, enabling participation by all types of people, including children. They can be used with either individuals or groups – where the group draws a map based on suggestions from all participants – for example of a typical home–school journey or of a neighbourhood or a workplace. Such tools can then be used as stimulus material in subsequent interviews.

These methods need to be used creatively and adapted to find the information you need. The options are many: the next subsections discuss the following:

- drawings, including draw and write technique, body mapping;
- maps, including participatory mapping, social network maps (highlighting the number and intensity of interactions in a community), mobility maps, transects (walking across an area with residents and systematically recording their observations about, for example, safety, waste management or access to public buildings);
- photographs;
- videos.

Visual methods are most useful when

- You want to learn quickly about how things work.
- A focus is needed to encourage group discussion of the issues.
- You are trying to open up sensitive or embarrassing topics (use with care).
- People relate better to visual representations than to verbal discussions.
- You are interested in issues relating to the physical environment, for example farming problems or access to water, and how they relate to social issues.

Drawings as research tools

There are many ways of using drawing to learn from people. They have been widely used with children, but with different disciplines taking very different approaches. Challenges relate to consent, ownership of drawings and interpretation (Morrow, 1999; Pridmore and Bendelow, 1995).

In research, it is always critical to record what people say about their drawings, not to try to interpret them yourself. Figure 12.1 below, drawn by a 12-year-old street boy in Addis Ababa, is difficult to interpret without the boy's own explanation. An adult might not see the significance of the most important feature – the hat. The boy explained that he had drawn himself eating rotten fruit and was wearing a hat because he was ashamed of being seen by other people.

The 'draw and write' technique was developed within health research as a way of learning about children's perceptions of health and ill-health issues. For example, children in inner-city Manchester in England were asked first to draw something – for example 'you find a bag with drugs in it – draw what you found'. Then they were asked to write around and alongside it about what their picture showed. They were then given a short series of tasks, drawing and writing in response to different

Figure 12.1   Drawing by a street boy in Addis Ababa

Source: Boyden and Ennew (1997)

suggestions. The study on drugs went on to ask the children to draw the person who might have lost the bag they had found, and then to write what you would like to say to them. Some of the children drew a drug dealer looking good in his designer-label clothes and trainers.

Body mapping has been used internationally to get people to draw their images of how bodies work. It can be used to find out people's names for different parts and functions within the body, and to open up discussion of all kinds of health-related issues. For example, women can be asked to draw their own reproductive organs and discuss their drawings, which can produce useful information about how they understand them to work (Johnson and Mayoux, 1998). However, it should not be assumed that drawing is familiar to people – in the example from Zimbabwe quoted by Johnson and Mayoux (in Cornwall, 1992), several of the women had never drawn anything before.

Maps as research tools

In participatory research, maps and diagrams are often drawn on the ground, using locally available materials to build up the picture. This means everyone can see what is being made and can chip in with their ideas, using familiar things to show what they mean. The discussion around the mapping process is part of the data.

This technique allows you to discover the 'mental maps' of community members. It is usual to get more than one group of people (women/men, old/young) to draw a map and then compare them. Mapping usually involves the following steps:

- Decide what sort of map should be drawn (social, natural resources, farm, etc.).
- Find people who know the area and the topic of the mapping exercise and who are willing to share their knowledge.
- Choose a suitable place (ground, floor, paper) and medium (sticks, stones, seeds, pens, pencils).
- Help people to get started but let them draw the map by themselves. Be patient and do not interrupt. It is *their* map.
- Sit back and watch, or go away!
- Keep a permanent (paper) record, including the mappers' names to give them credit.

Maps can be very useful in some circumstances, for example when studying issues such as territoriality, land use or mobility. For instance, a mobility map can show a person's contact with, and knowledge of, the outside world and her authority in the community. It may also indicate freedom, wealth, empowerment, education, consciousness and many other notions yet to be discovered.

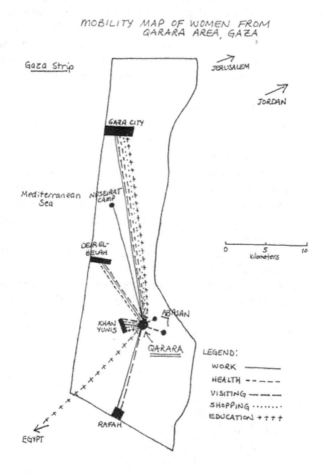

Figure 12.2   Example of a mobility map

Reproduced with permission from Theis and Grady (1991)

People being asked to draw mobility maps need to be given a certain time period to which it should relate (week, month or year). Maps could be drawn individually, and then compared, or drawn as a group exercise. Different colours could be used to show different activities, and different frequencies of journeys could be shown with thicker and thinner lines.

Photographs as research tools

Photo research is a relatively recent approach to participatory research. Extensively used only since the 1990s, digital cameras have now made it even easier and cheaper. The principle is to look *into* sets of images rather than *at* them (Harper, 2002). Its objective is to record unarticulated perspectives on specific issues; indeed, it is more fruitful as a group exercise. Photographs taken can raise consciousness through small group discussion and are often used to represent the concerns of the powerless to policymakers.

Typically, in the vein of other action research methods, photo research can be used to empower communities and give them greater autonomy in their daily lives. For instance, it can be an opportunity for young people to learn the basics of photojournalism or simply to use cameras to build skills and self-esteem. Photo research training places a great emphasis on teaching photographic techniques, setting up exhibitions and communicating with policymakers and the public at large.

Photo research involves the following steps:

- Recruiting participants: if potential participants think it sounds time-consuming, emphasize the new skills they might get out of the experience.
- Preliminary training: both theoretical (how cameras work, power and ethics, etiquette and safety when using cameras, including consideration, permission, reactions, etc.) and practical (how to make a meaningful and aesthetic photograph).
- Definition of a research question: What is the situation to be described?
- Fieldwork: photo reportage.
- Discussion of pictures: free discussion or use of a structured, theory-based framework (Bauer and Gaskell, 2000).
- Sharing information with the wider community and policymakers through photoboards, captions, articles, exhibitions or public presentations.

Typical questions in photo research include:

- Who/what is in the photo?
- Who/what is missing?
- What does it represent/symbolize?
- Whose perspective is represented?
- Who is the intended audience?
- What can be done about it?

As with any other research method, photo research should be done ethically: always ask for permission to take a photograph of someone and restrain yourself if you feel the photograph is humiliating or could be used against the participant.

See It Our Way: a PhotoVoice project on child trafficking in Eastern Europe and the Middle East, 2010

The 50 young people trained in photography by PhotoVoice through the See It Our Way project live in communities that are source, transit and destination communities for human trafficking across the Middle East and Eastern Europe. Between August and December 2010, PhotoVoice delivered courses of 10 workshops with young people in Albania, Armenia, Lebanon, Pakistan and Romania and supported them to explore the risks and root causes of child trafficking in their communities through photographs and words. The resulting body of work provides a revealing picture of the underlying causes and impact of the lucrative exploitation of children and adults.

Photographs taken by the young people reveal ground-level issues from the unique, inside perspective of young people particularly vulnerable to trafficking. The training has enabled these at-risk young people to consider the issues more carefully themselves, while playing an active role in informing and guiding peers in their communities who are also at risk of falling prey to traffickers. Their work is informing future prevention and campaign activities by local World Vision teams and partners.

In 2010, to coincide with Human Rights Day on 10 December, exhibitions and campaigns were held in each participating country with targeted messages identified by the young people to address the issues most important to their communities. A selection of photographs in Armenia, Albania and Lebanon were shown at the European Union Summit on human trafficking in Brussels in November 2010, where significant steps were taken to change policy to tackle human trafficking more effectively.

Work from all five participating countries is feeding into the Human Wrong campaign in the US, aimed at bringing the exploitative trade in human beings to an end.

Work is continuing in each country around this issue as a result of the PhotoVoice process. World Vision Armenia, for example, has been consulting with Gyumri Police Underage and Passport Departments and field NGOs to prioritize a second awareness raising campaign, focusing mainly on child and labour abuse.

Source: www.photovoice.org

Videos as research tools

Just like photographs, videos can be used as a research method and serve a number of purposes, including stimulating a group discussion or simply recording an event. As with other participatory research tools, the process of filming is as important as the film itself. A normally 'extractive' process of recording others becomes a tool for research respondents themselves to take control of the filming process. In this way, researchers can gather insights through analysis of valuable primary source data, promote the sharing of local knowledge and help to impart research skills to participants.

Video has an obvious interest whenever a situation or a human interaction is too complex for a single researcher to describe comprehensively while it unfolds. Traditional events and celebrations are excellent candidates, although the technique has also been used recently in a policy context, for example to evaluate the implementation of a European programme in the area of agricultural development (www.methodspace.com/video/what-is-participatory-video-by). A good practice is to consider how the multimedia component will add significant value. Are there particular

'Sweet sixteen in my country': 'I took this picture of Mehak behind the fence because it shows how young girls like us aren't allowed out and how we are locked all the time. It feels like a prison, it's like we're behind bars all the time' (© Amjad/World Vision/PhotoVoice).

Figure 12.3

PhotoVoice workshop in action, led by photographer Jenny Matthews, in Rawalpindi, Pakistan, as part of the See it Our Way project. © Matt Daw/PhotoVoice

aspects of your research a donor has requested be represented in video? Have you identified a gap in data which can be best expressed through this medium?

Most of the advice given earlier for photographs applies to videos. On the technical side, significant consideration needs to be given to the filming devices themselves. A few key points:

- USB outputs are important, so footage can be recorded directly to a computer while filming, or at least transferred later.
- Video files can become quite large – measured in hundreds of megabytes or even gigabytes – so be sure you have enough space for storage of longer footage. External hard drives might be a good idea.
- It is also important to standardize settings across multiple recording devices (date and time, frame rates, sound quality and 'folders' within the devices themselves for organizing recorded data).
- Bring along spare batteries, USB cables for laptop charging and, ideally, an adapter/charger that can be charged via a car cigarette lighter.
- Always run the equipment through a spot-check to ensure sound and image quality. Otherwise, entire interviews can be inadvertently lost owing to poor sound/vision quality which becomes apparent only later.

Before you begin filming, make sure researchers and field support staff are properly trained. This means knowing, for instance, when to step in during recording and when to remain silent. Do not underestimate your staff's familiarity with the recording devices (many are quite user friendly), but do ensure everyone has at least a basic degree of acquaintance with the equipment and some fundamental filming techniques. The best time to impart these skills is during capacity-building workshops and in the pilot phase.

From a process point of view, one of the main differences between photo research and video research is that the latter involves substantially more work in the post-production phase, as a film is made of thousands of pictures that all convey some information.

First, you need to choose a unit of analysis, be it a camera shot (each new camera frame as a new unit) or a line of speech (each new piece of dialogue as a new unit). Second, you need to transcribe the information contained in a relevant selection of units, that is, to generate a dataset amenable to coding and analysis. The transcription includes both visual and verbal information. The result is called a 'verbatim' (see Table 12.2 for an example). Alternatively, the selected units could be used as supporting

Table 12.2 Example of verbatim

Unit	Timing	Visual information	Verbal information
Frame 1	00:01:26	Character A looking up	A: 'Though this be madness …'
Frame 2	00:01:28	Character A looking straight	A: '… yet there is method in it'

material in an interview with the individual or group of individuals filmed. The researcher might then ask why the action unfolded the way it did in the film.

The information contained in the verbatim can then be analysed either qualitatively or quantitatively (Bauer and Gaskell, 2000).

One word of caution: videos can also be used to open up sensitive areas for discussion but their use in this way should be piloted carefully so as not to cause distress. It is also important to provide feedback to the individual and/or community on the material provided. Show materials to others only if consent has been acquired from individuals who wish to share sensitive or confidential information that might have been revealed during conversations. Check local referral processes for incriminating evidence as well – declarations of legal or rights violations captured on video can, in certain circumstances, be considered evidence. And child protection issues should always be considered when participatory filming involves children as either subjects or as videographers themselves.

In editing the finished product, be aware that professional editing is very expensive, and prone to inputs from stakeholders who often hold strong feelings on how ideas and experiences are represented. Resources for these discussions, and for potential re-editing, should be agreed and allocated in advance.

Finally, in dissemination of video, it is very important that multimedia files be compressed, so they can be uploaded online and, if possible, included as email attachments. A note of warning about video dissemination on public sites such as You-Tube, Vimeo or even your project webpage: multimedia, once public, has a greater probability of going 'viral' very quickly. If your project is popular (and/or controversial) enough, you should be prepared to handle the possibility, and consequent risks, of a larger-than-expected response.

FOR EXAMPLE

Using video to conduct research on childhood poverty in Uganda

The use of video was one of the approaches used as part of the multimedia package to capture childhood poverty in Uganda. All multimedia tools used aimed to listen to children's own voices and perspectives about their lives and their own point of view about how they experience poverty. These participatory research methods included, among others, for those three to six years old and seven to thirteen years old, drawing and painting as a means to convey what made them happy and unhappy in life. This was extremely revealing on their fears and dreams: the young ones drew cockroaches in urban areas and snakes in rural areas as part of the threats they disliked in relation to their housing conditions; the older ones drew about more complex fears such as sexual assault (defilement).

In the specific case of participatory videos, a couple of adolescents (male and female) were selected based on their level of participation in a previous focus group discussion with children to show their experiences of poverty and express their views and thoughts on the subject. The team leader was asked to observe not only the level of participation but also how determined the boy or girl seemed to be to share their opinions on different matters. Then they were asked about their interest in being part of the exercise. If they agreed, they were given a consent form to be signed by their parents before starting.

The exercise started with a brief training on how to use the camera and the objective of the exercise, which was to allow them to talk about what was important to them and what they really cared about. Following these general guidelines, we were taken to different settings, such as their houses, neighbourhoods, the University of Makerere (and the faculty where they wanted to study and why). In the case of more rural locations, they filmed their houses and took us to the field or showed us locations children use to fetch water, etc. They were asked to narrate while they were shooting with minimal intervention from any adult present (usually one who sometimes made short questions to clarify the scene or gave technical instructions to handle the camera).

All participants were given total freedom to decide on locations to talk about, for about one to two hours. All this video material from five sites around Uganda was collected and edited for the purpose of enriching the written report. In several cases, children talked about issues hard to capture through indicators or a literature review, or with a different emphasis, which made the experience quite unique to complement the written reports. The 25-minute video was also used as an effective advocacy material in a public event (children's conference) for the UN Children's Fund (UNICEF) in Uganda to sensitize national authorities on childhood poverty and, more importantly, to create a space on the public agenda to listen to what they have to say and acknowledge their right to be heard.

Source: Villar (2012), personal communication

Table 12.3   Strengths and limitations

Visual methods – strengths	Visual methods – limitations
• Most people enjoy taking part in research using visual methods • Mapping or drawing can create a good focus for group interaction • Some people may find it easier to communicate if they do not have to use words	• Interpretation is inherently tricky with visual images – there is a danger of misinterpreting what is meant • It may not be culturally appropriate and you need to be familiar with local 'ways of seeing' to make sense of images • Some people may see the use of visual methods as patronizing, or be inhibited by the method, for a variety of reasons • It is crucial that there is opportunity for respondents to explain or interpret the images they have produced – this should not be rushed • There can be problems about ownership and reproduction of image • Equipment cost

Checklist: Using visual methods

☑ Interpret pictures – listening to and recording what people say about the images they make is as important as the images themselves.

☑ Do not comment on the artistic merit of any product – that's not the point.

☑ People own their drawings or maps – ask permission if you want to take them away or use them in a larger group, and make copies for yourself if people want to keep the original.

☑ Do not assume all children, especially older children and young people, will be happy to express themselves through drawing – some will see it as more for younger children and be insulted; others may never have learnt how to draw and not have the ability to do so.

12.4.3 Performing techniques

There are many ways in which drama, music and performance can be used in research. Songs, dances and ritual processes can be rich repositories of local knowledge about a community's history and its relation to nature or other communities. Ethnomusicology, a relatively recent and highly multidisciplinary approach to social research, tries to assess the whole process and contexts through and within which music is imagined, discussed and made. The approach has also been used for advocacy purposes, for instance in South Africa, to promote environmental conservation and sustainable development (Impey, 2005).

In other contexts, performing techniques such as singing and acting can be used with children and young people when the researcher wishes to tackle contentious or sensitive issues. They have also proved more effective than traditional research methods for engaging adults in discussions on moral dilemmas to do with conflict and violence, gender relations, the care of children and sexual health and HIV.

Music can also be a wonderful ice breaker, for example in work with children. Some children may find it more comfortable to sing songs than to immediately start to talk to a researcher. Making up your own songs can be a good way of expressing difficult feelings in many cultures.

Drama can be used with groups to draw out and illustrate what is important to community members.

FOR EXAMPLE

Using performing arts to promote sexual health: Papua New Guinea

Life Drama supports community leaders in Papua New Guinea in using drama and performance techniques to explore issues important to the community, such as sexual health. For example, the two-week Theatre Exchange Laboratory held in Madang in February 2010 included the performance of traditional songs and dances by ex-members of Raun Raun Theatre and current members of the National Performing Arts Troupe; excerpts from folk operas and village plays devised by Raun Raun Theatre and performed by members; and examples of Life Drama forms. These practices were examined and discussed by a cross-cultural group comprising representatives with expertise in the area of theatre for development from a number of organizations.

In another project activity, the evaluation team was able to video the work of one participant, a Sunday school teacher, as she conducted Life Drama activities with her Sunday school class. One member of the group, the participant's father, volunteered the information that he had previously been fearful of people who were HIV positive and discriminated against them. He stated that he had changed his attitude as a result of his daughter's teaching, and now accepted that people with HIV should be accepted as equal members of the community.

Source: www.lifedrama.net

Yet another way in which drama can be used in research is to show, rather than tell, people about things on which you want their opinion. In the following case study, drama was used to explain to respondents about things that were at that point outside of their experience.

Use of drama: eliciting design ideas from elderly people

FOR EXAMPLE

Research from Dundee University Computing Department used video clips to elicit design ideas from elderly people in relation to ways of monitoring falls where elderly people are living alone. It is often hard to get feedback from potential users of new technology before it is finally designed, especially older people. This study aimed to find out what older people and their carers thought about a potential new support system using technology. Focus groups were run to get ideas and user stories. These ideas and stories were turned into scenarios and acted out by a theatre group specializing in interactive theatre. The scenarios were filmed and shown to three groups of older people (eight to fifteen people in each) and two groups of carers (fifteen to eighteen participants).

Each scenario was designed to provoke discussion of slightly different aspects of the system. Groups were encouraged to discuss issues that occurred to them following each separate scenario and these discussions were also recorded on video. The research found that older people, when presented with new technological possibilities in an appropriate form, were very capable of considering and discussing desired functionality. They provided extremely useful and interesting suggestions about what would make such a system useful to them, and had strong views about what they did not want. They also asked very relevant and interesting questions about the system, and often unexpected topics were raised that the researchers had not predicted. Following this study, using the information from discussions, another set of scenarios is being developed to explore particular aspects of the system.

Source: www.computing.dundee.ac.uk/staff/stephen/HCIInt2003.pdf. For more information: Contact Professor Alan Newell: afn@computing.dundee.ac.uk. Also see Newell (2011)

12.4.4 Peer research

Peer research has developed in recent years as a valuable tool for development work in both the North and the South (Kirby, 1999; Treseder, 1997). People from the group in question – street children, users of mental health services, disabled people – are engaged as researchers to work alongside professional researchers to investigate their own situation. They are offered training in research methods and work together to identify key issues, develop research tools (questionnaires, focus group topic guides, etc.) and carry out fieldwork. They are usually paid for their time.

Peer research has been particularly at the fore in work with children and young people, perhaps because young people can feel a greater distance from older researchers. It may be particularly useful as an approach to work with people who share some sort of minority, stigmatized status, because of the bonds between 'people like us' where there is an assumption that their experience is outside the mainstream.

Peer research approaches are attractive to development workers, as they build the skills of community members in a number of areas, as well as producing a piece of work which is fully informed and owned by them. It can be a good way of showing what community members can do and also yields at the end informed and motivated people who are excellent advocates to promote the findings of the research.

However, remember peer researchers will require considerable support throughout the life of the project if they are to participate fully in the decisions that are made. Research can be a drawn-out process, and this can create problems for people with busy or unstable lives – it may be worth trying to concentrate the work into a short period. It is also true that 'people problems' affect all types of research. Don't assume peer researchers will naturally find it easy to show empathy with others like themselves.

Meanwhile, the training needed to produce research of reasonable quality is considerable. No one wants to see people used as tokens, sent out to undertake work they do not fully understand. If other community members are to be enabled to give their views in an open way, peer researchers need time to learn the relatively complex skills involved in qualitative fieldwork.

Particularly where the issues being researched are sensitive and personal, it is important to remember the needs and rights of the respondent as well as those of the peer researcher (Laws et al., 1999). Some respondents will be encouraged to participate by the fact that it is 'someone like them' doing the research. However, for others, the loss of privacy involved in talking to someone from their own community will be a problem. Traditional 'neutral' researchers who are distanced from the community may in fact be easier to trust with very personal information. Accordingly, it may be appropriate to offer a choice of interviewers, rather than assuming peer researchers are the best for all respondents.

Importantly, the decision to use peer research should be justified by a genuine and intrinsic interest of peer researchers themselves – be it in the study or in the experience they hope to get from it. Local stakeholders might give you some guidance here.

FOR EXAMPLE

Women prisoners as peer researchers to explore needs of female (ex) offenders

The Hallam Centre for Community Justice, a UK university-based research centre, in collaboration with SOVA – a national volunteer and mentoring organization – used a peer research approach to explore the barriers to employment, training and education for women (ex) offenders. They employed 3 full-time peer researchers and 25 'sessional' workers and interviewed a total of 346 women both in prison and in the community. Some of the researchers were currently serving prisoners. Peer researchers were involved in the whole research process, including research design, conducting interviews, data analysis and report writing. The full-time peer researchers received seven days' training in the practicalities of conducting peer research, research design and qualitative data analysis, as well as ongoing formal supervision from the programme manager. The sessional workers received a two-day training programme on the practicalities of conducting research, especially interviewing skills. The full-time workers were allocated a personal mentor from an outside organization, and also adopted the role of mentor for some of the sessional workers. They did interviews alongside professional researchers at first, then alone or in pairs. They had an important role in developing the interview schedules, making sure the wording was appropriate. They devised information sheets and promotional material using images and words they knew women offenders would relate to.

The benefits of peer involvement in the research process identified included the following:

- Peers were able to recruit participants for interview more easily than academic staff, especially in prisons.

- Peers have extensive knowledge of the subject being researched, which positively influenced the research design and also provided valuable learning experiences for members of the research team with a non-offending background.
- Employing peers facilitated interview situations which were relaxed and informal.
- The use of peers enabled interviews to have multiple functions (for example information/ experience exchange between researcher and researched as well as gathering the required data), and this proved empowering for women.
- Peer researchers provided positive role models for the women they interviewed.

As a result of the research, pilot projects were developed to address the needs identified by women offenders. Several peer researchers went on to have full-time paid employment as support workers in these projects. The research report 'Moving Mountains' had an impact on the development of UK government policy on the resettlement of women offenders.

Inevitably, significant challenges were also encountered:

- Training and support needs for peer researchers are often intensive, and this needs careful consideration when planning budgets.
- Peer researchers need to be given clear guidance about the implications of disclosing their own status (for example ex-prisoners) to those they are interviewing.
- Peers are more likely to have their own agenda and therefore ask more leading questions than non-peers and impose their own views on the research.
- Peer researchers often had their own personal barriers to overcome to be involved in the study – particularly those women who went back into prisons where they once resided to conduct the research.

Source: O'Keeffe (2004)

Checklist: Peer research

☑ Recruit peer researchers with appropriate skills and attitudes – research is demanding and responsible work.
☑ Recruit enough peer researchers to allow for some to drop out as time goes on.
☑ Consider carefully how peer researchers will be recompensed for their time, in light of their existing situation.
☑ Ensure enough time is spent on the training to enable peer researchers to make genuine choices about the research focus and methods.
☑ Include ethical issues of consent and confidentiality in the training process.
☑ Provide easy access to support and supervision during fieldwork.
☑ Work out ways of involving peer researchers more fully in analysis and writing processes.

12.5   Practical challenges in participatory research

Development workers have several major advantages in undertaking participatory research; in many ways, such approaches are a natural group of methods for them to use. They are likely to be skilled in working with people in a facilitative way. Their orientation, too, is towards action for change. Indeed, another way of looking at this area is to consider participatory research as one of a range of methods used to facilitate community members' greater participation in decision making.

That said, there are a number of important challenges to consider.

12.5.1 How much participation?

Much writing about participation refers to the concept of a 'ladder of participation' (Arnstein, 1969; Hart, 1992), which starts from decorative or tokenistic participation and rises to the group in question initiating and being fully in charge of a process. The virtue of this image is that it demonstrates how some processes that claim to be participatory involve minimal or no change in power relations. However, this imagery tends to suggest that, whatever the situation, greater participation is desirable, with the final goal being autonomous organizing by the group in question. But there are many situations where this would be an entirely unrealistic goal. Many valuable pieces of work facilitate participation in one or two aspects of a process,

Figure 12.4 The wheel of community participation in research

and this may be all stakeholders want. It should not be assumed that participating in every aspect is necessarily a desired goal for community members.

Consider instead a wheel of participatory research (see Figure 12.4), whereby participation in different aspects of a piece of work is given value as appropriate within any particular piece of work. The key reason participation is important is that there is some transfer of control of decision making. Important participation can take place in a number of different ways, at different stages in a process.

A community group might request that a piece of research be done (perhaps an investigation of pollution to their water source), but not want to take much role in the details of the process. Or, in another project (perhaps a needs assessment to set priorities with people with AIDS), researchers might use strongly qualitative methods which would enable respondents to consider very fully their responses and to get their own questions answered. This can enable those individuals to 'have their say' and be heard more fully. A third project might involve community members as researchers, using a simple self-completion questionnaire. This might give respondents less space to put forward their views, but would engage community members in actively investigating an issue, building their confidence to take action. These different types of participation should not be seen as more or less valuable, but each as valid in its place.

The wheel also suggests the idea of travel, and reminds us that research is a means to an end and not generally an end in itself. It is also important to acknowledge that the practice of participatory research is evolving as people learn more about how it works.

What factors to take into account in deciding the level and type of participation appropriate to a particular project is a complex matter, one which can't easily be reduced to a checklist. Development workers will have experience of assessing situations to make decisions about what is possible with a particular group, but a few points are worth making here.

First of all, don't make too many assumptions about what people are capable of – try and check this by undertaking some exploratory exercises. The questions to ask may be more about what you are able to support them to do, and what they might *want* to do.

Another key factor is your organization's existing relationship with potential participants. It is much more difficult to start out on participatory research 'cold' than it is where some trust already exists between the community and the agency. This is usually based on some kind of service provision, some sort of positive, practical engagement with the community.

Time is often the central factor in deciding these questions. A very short timescale inevitably limits participation. Wherever possible, negotiate to extend deadlines to enable greater participation to take place.

Factors to consider in deciding appropriate types of participation in research include:

- community members' wishes and level of commitment in relation to participation;
- the issue the agency wants to investigate and its match with local concerns;
- existing relationships with stakeholders – is there some trust already there?
- time available (both worker time day by day and the deadline);
- level of support available;
- skills of those working with community members;
- current skills and experience of community members.

Table 12.4 could form the basis for a discussion with community members about which elements of a research process they wish to be involved in.

Table 12.4 Guidelines on planning how community members will participate in a research project

Stages in the research	1. Level of involvement	2. Who will carry out the process
	• None	• Community members
	• Being informed	• Staff
	• Expressing a view	• Partner agency
	• Shared decision	
	• Main decider	
Initiate research		
Set budgets		
Decide the research topic		
Set aims and objectives		
Recruit researchers/other workers		
Advisory group		
Choose research methods		
Create research tools		
Collect information (fieldwork)		
Data from community		
Data from professionals		
Data from existing material		
Provide research data (own experience/views)		
Analysis		
Choose recommendations		
Write report		
Produce other product (presentation, video)		
Disseminate research findings		
Access to research findings		
Development and campaigning		

Source: Adapted from Kirby (1999)

12.5.2 Compensating participants in peer research

A major reason for non-cooperation – or less than enthusiastic cooperation – is a sense that those being asked to cooperate will get no benefits from the exercise. There are many strategies to help you to overcome this. As we have seen, one of these is to make sure there is adequate involvement of communities and stakeholders in the design stages of the overall research and in designing and piloting instruments. This will ensure that, for example, community leaders, head teachers or local business people see their own questions included in the research agenda and therefore see the results as relevant.

Another easy and cost-effective way of encouraging participation is a commitment to sharing the findings of the research with those who participated. This can take the form of a publicly available report, a feedback letter containing an executive summary or an invitation to a feedback meeting once the research is complete. The information generated during the project might be of interest to a number of professional organizations and policymakers eager to get a better understanding of the needs and preferences of local communities.

Finally, when the research project gives a prominent role to local communities – as in peer research, for instance – you might want to compensate those involved for their time. After all, if peer researchers are working alongside professional researchers or development workers, carrying responsibility for the outcomes of the research project, why shouldn't they be paid for their work? Practice varies. Some projects pay a weekly wage for a short period, others pay expenses at a good level, others give a grant to the peer researcher for the project and others do not pay at all. There are many issues to consider. Where the peer researchers are children, there are further issues. For example, are we encouraging child labour if we pay street children who work with us on research projects to compensate for lost earnings?

In deciding on this matter, you obviously need to take account of your context. Employment opportunities are valuable to people, but you need to think through exactly what is entailed in setting up the peer research in this way. It increases the distance between the peer researchers and other participants considerably, but also creates a deeper level of engagement from a small group of people. Projects have grappled with these issues in different ways (Boyden and Ennew, 1997; Kirby, 1999).

See also Chapters 9 and 10, which discuss broader issues in paying incentives to respondents in research.

Issues in paying peer researchers: street children in Dhaka, Bangladesh

A peer research project with street children who had been incarcerated, carried out in Dhaka by Save the Children, found it was making increasing demands on children's time. The girls especially mentioned that they had to have regular paid work to survive. It was decided to offer children a daily amount equivalent to the average income of a street child, to be paid only for the days the children worked on the research. After some days, some difficulties emerged, with children asking to be paid for days when they were not working. The issue was taken to the group of children to discuss. They agreed they should be paid only for days they worked. In favour of their decision, they mentioned that Save the Children or the partner agency Moitree Parishad would not support them for their whole life. Before the research they were on their own and they would be on their own after the research also.

Source: Khan (1997)

FOR EXAMPLE

12.6   Critical perspectives on participatory research

Despite the strengths of participatory research, critics of the approach identify several potential limitations which should be kept in mind when considering how such methods might be incorporated into your own research. For example, as they tend to deal with 'the community' as a group, poorly implemented participatory methods have the potential to perpetuate power differences. This may mean those with more power – men, adults, majority ethnic groups – or those who know what they want, perhaps the somewhat better-off farmers for instance (Ashby and Sperling, 1995), are more able to get their issues taken seriously (Mosse, 1994).

PLA practitioners often make efforts to enable women's and children's voices to be heard, for example by meeting separately with them. But the essentially public process of the PLA means individuals can sometimes feel less confident to speak about their situation. Here, a high level of community participation can occasionally make it *more* difficult for those with less power to raise issues which may be seen as 'private' – for example concerns relating to inequalities within households or violence against women or children.

The PLA type of process, which emphasizes open discussion within a local community, is therefore likely to be most suitable to investigate issues already identified as shared community problems. Conversely, more formal research methods can have the virtue of distancing the respondent from the findings, so issues can be raised in a generalized way without people being obliged to 'own' a particular experience. As always, it is up to you, as the researcher, to fit your approach to the research context in question – more often than not, a balance must be struck between empowerment of the participant through ownership of the participatory research process and sensitivity to issues of confidentiality and anonymity.

Finally, some critics have questioned the deeper theoretical foundations of participatory research. They argue that well-intentioned promotion of empowerment and ownership through local participation, and the takeover of the external 'expert's' role as change agent, is a refined and accelerating – yet unconscious – process for 'colonizing the life worlds of villagers' (Cooke and Kothari, 2000; Rahnema, 1992).

This can be a particular issue where the intention is to use a participatory process to develop research aimed at policy influence. The imperatives involved in policy-focused work to be very clear about audience and message are hard to follow if you are also working with a community-led agenda. However, a middle way can generally be found, as community members are realists too. Enabling the participating group to set the research agenda means there is usually a need to reconcile stakeholder priorities with your own practice and research priorities.

Methodologists continue to debate the degree to which such issues are inherent in the participatory research processes. It

is, however, still critical for development research to engage with grassroots experiences and to do so in a way that allows ample space for ordinary people's voices to be reflected. So participatory research is valuable – it just has to be well informed and self-reflective, with a clear understanding of how much participation is being used and to what end. For this reason, it is always important to maintain and cultivate a strong awareness of social inequalities and how they work within the local context when conducting participatory research.

 ## Key points from this chapter

Any effort to undertake participatory
research needs to consider the following

- Participatory research approaches can reveal more about an issue.
- Participatory research is oriented to finding solutions.
- Careful thought needs to be given to involving a range of people, including community members themselves and local service providers.

- Community participation is possible at many different points in the research process, from identifying the focus, to doing interviews, to promoting the findings – consideration needs to go to how much participation is appropriate and at what point/s in the process.
- A balance needs to be struck between community priorities and agency agendas.
- It should not be assumed that the participation of some community members, for example in fieldwork, will automatically facilitate full participation by others.
- Participatory research requires strong facilitation skills, an interest in research rigour and an interest in solutions.

Further reading

General

Mikkelsen, B. (2005) *Methods for Development Work and Research: A New Guide for Practitioners,* 2nd edn. New Delhi, Thousand Oaks, CA, London: Sage.

Mukherjee, N. (2002) *Participatory Learning and Action – With 100 Field Methods.* New Delhi: Concept Publishing Company.

Reason, P. and Bradbury, H. (eds) (2008) *The Sage Handbook of Action Research, Participatory Inquiry and Practice.* New Delhi, Thousand Oaks, CA, London: Sage.

Theis, J. and Grady, H.M. (1991) *Participatory Rapid Appraisal for Community Development.* London: International Institute for Environment and Development and Save the Children Federation.

Covers one group of methods. Enthusiastic and clearly written. Includes useful guidance on general training approaches and techniques. Lots of individual methods simply explained, including in-depth interviews.

Websites

Cornell University PAR Network

http://cornellparnetwork.blogspot.com/2011/02/cornell-participatory-action-research.html

Eldis

www.eldis.org/participation/index.htm

World Bank

www.worldbank.org/participation /

David Wilcox's 'Guide to Effective Participation'

www.partnerships.org.uk/guide/index.htm

US Agency for International Development

http://rmportal.net/tools/biodiversity-conservation-tools/putting-conservation-incontext-cd/participatory-approaches-resources/1-c.pdf/view

Websites

Life Drama www.lifedrama.net

PhotoVoice www.Photovoice.org

'What is Participatory Video?' A video by Chris High. Available online at www.methodspace.com/video/what-is-participatory-video-by

Peer research

Kirby, P. (1999) *Involving Young Researchers: How to Enable Young People to Design and Conduct Research*. York: Joseph Rowntree Foundation.

Practical guide to peer research with young people, based on a group of nine projects undertaken in England by Save the Children.

Treseder, P. (1997) *Empowering Children and Young People: Promoting Involvement in Decision-making*. London: Save the Children.

Worrall, S. (2000) *Young People as Researchers: A Learning Resource Pack*. London: Save the Children.

Training pack linked to the Kirby manual.

Website

The Wellesley Institute – Peer Research in Action. Available online at www.wellesleyinstitute.com/uncategorized/peer-research-in-action/

PART 3

ANALYSIS AND RESEARCH COMMUNICATION

13

UNDERTAKING RESEARCH ANALYSIS

Analysing data can be very interesting and rewarding but can also be overwhelming: facing a huge heap of data can lead development research projects to grind to a halt. However, although it has traditionally been seen as the lonely burden of a single researcher, it can also be done in a team. Involving stakeholders here as in other stages of the research process is important, given that this stage determines what research findings are presented.

This chapter helps you to analyse your data in the most convenient way for you and to an adequate standard for your project. We begin by discussing how to get organized, as well as the core principles underlying analysis. We then discuss methods for qualitative and quantitative data, emphasizing straightforward techniques inexperienced researchers can use with confidence, also covering computerized data analysis packages. The final section looks at synthesis – the process of drawing out the key important points from your findings. Your analysis is not finished until you have answered the question 'So what?'

13.1 Getting organized

The first phase is all about getting the paperwork (field notes, notes from interviews, surveys) under control. As it comes in, make sure you list it so you know exactly what you have. If questionnaires do not already have codes, add them now and record these along with the date they arrived in the office and any other information. Table 13.1 gives an example of a recording sheet.

Table 13.1 An example of a recording sheet

Date received	Code number	Type of data	Area data originate from	Other key factors
	1	(Interview by x; notes of observation of y; focus group transcript)		
	2			
	3			

Don't put this off! In fact, you should do it as you go along: if everything is numbered and dated, you will be able to trace any missing material.

Also, make sure all data are page numbered, so you will be able to identify where someone said something by a page reference. If transcripts are lengthy, you may also want to number the lines – word-processing packages can do this. Catalogue all photos, drawings, etc., as well.

Common pitfall

Letting a huge pile of disorganized paper accumulate, with no record of what is (or should be) there

FOR EXAMPLE

Thinking about your data

What forms of data have you collected?

- Questionnaires?
- Interview notes, recordings, transcripts?
- Notes of reading?
- Copies of documents?
- Notes or videotapes of observations?
- Measurements of behaviour?
- Charts, maps, tables, diagrams?
- Photographs?
- Art work?
- Notes in your research diary?
- Other forms of data?

Work out roughly the amount of each you have. Think about where they have come from, how they have been collected or produced and how reliable they are. Think also about how much you will need to reduce the volume to fit the space available.

Source: Blaxter et al. (1996)

Table 13.2 Is it worth putting data on a computer?

	Pro	Con
General	Speed	Requires access
	Flexible handling of large quantities	Can exclude others from analysis
	You can return to data repeatedly, to find things and try different ideas	Learning to use programs may require time
	May impress people	May create an illusion of accuracy
Quantitative analysis	You can recalculate easily if changes are made	If you lack experience, can lead to a feeling of losing control
	You can draw graphs directly from data	
	Better control of human error, although you still have to get data entry right	
Qualitative analysis	Enables handling of large quantities of data	May require typing of a lot of text
	Easy to recode data when you change categories, encouraging a flexible approach	

13.2 What is analysis?

Data analysis means taking things apart and putting them together again, to work out the links between respondents' inputs and your original questions. What does it all mean?

This is not a new trick you have to learn. For example, suppose a colleague doesn't turn up for work one morning. People begin to guess (hypothesize) why this might be. Have they gone to a meeting? Are they ill? Have they overslept?

These guesses are tested when the person turns up, or when new evidence comes to light, such as someone arriving for a meeting arranged with the missing person. Or we make decisions based on our hypotheses, knowing there are uncertainties, such as on what to tell the person who expects to meet our colleague.

It is the same with data analysis. Using all your knowledge, you guess at links between data – always keeping in mind that new data may change your conclusions. The central task is to seek out patterns – trends. Are different people telling you the same thing? Or are there clear patterns of difference, for example women with one point of view and men another? At times, you have to actively pull the meaning out of the data – it may not jump out by itself. What findings surprise you? What patterns are missing that you expected to find? (For example do data show unexpected conformity of opinion between men and women around an issue you thought would be more contentious?)

After identifying patterns, check what data fit these and whether there are exceptions. If some women did agree with the men, what might explain this? Were the men present during interviews? Do these women come from a different income group from other women?

At the same time, you need to be questioning the data, to make sure you can have confidence in it.

Check the trends (where the same information appears in different places)

- Do they fit in with what you expect?
- Are they surprising? Do they contradict your expectations?
- Could they be the result of researcher bias?
- Do they reflect the way the methods were used?
- Does this mean the research has uncovered new information and ideas?

Check the contradictions – are they the result of

- Working with different groups?
- Using different methods?
- External factors affecting data collection at different times?

Check the gaps (where information you expected to see is missing)

- Did you forget to collect some important information? If so, is it possible to return to the field, or use secondary data?
- Is there a social silence about this topic? If so, why?

Source: Adapted from Boyden and Ennew (1997)

For example, if observation findings conflict with what people said, what does this mean? If you used a small number of key informants, how much weight can you give their views? How representative are they? Why do they see things like this? Can you base an argument on these data? How able were people to say exactly what they thought during data collection?

Gaps in water and sanitation in Ethiopia

FOR EXAMPLE

Research carried out by WaterAid Ethiopia and its partner ZemaSef found that Ethiopia's water and sanitation sector had neglected to focus on people with disabilities while considering ways to expand services to marginalized populations. The team also identified a gap in the international research literature on disability issues, which had largely ignored the global importance of water and sanitation issues. The result was a severe neglect of disabled people in Ethiopia in terms of access.

Source: Tesfu and Magrath (2007)

There is no universally correct approach to analysing research data: you need to find a process you are comfortable with, given your skills, phobias and general disposition. Having said that, there *are* wrong ways of doing it. Perhaps the greatest temptation is to claim more than the data really justify – that is, over-interpreting the material. Question the meaning of the data at every level, and don't allow preconceived expectations and

Tip

Look for patterns, develop ideas about trends, but keep in mind that your ideas are provisional, for testing against the data as a whole and others' interpretations.

your own inherent 'confirmation bias' to guide your analysis. Be aware of the distinction between correlation and causation (see below), and take particular care in drawing conclusions: while some degree of speculation is fine (and often very useful), it is wise to be conservative. Your credibility relies on how well your claims are supported by the data – be clear in your mind what is description and what is conjecture, and offer only analysis that you can back up with facts. Having an external perspective from other researchers, colleagues and local communities can help to guard against over-interpretation.

Avoid jumping to conclusions: the UK

FOR EXAMPLE

A training exercise with UK health service staff learning qualitative analysis asked them to analyse statements from patients about their experience of services. Trainees often produced a category of 'staff shortages', into which they sorted some of these statements. In doing this, they were bringing in their own assumptions about why any problems occurred: no statements referred to staff shortages. Introducing such categories at this stage in the analysis in fact blocked off consideration of exactly why problems occurred, when there may have been all kinds of other explanations.

13.2.1 When to start carrying out analysis

You can think about how to organize your material and what themes to look for as you design your research although, again, remember initial ideas will need to be revised in light of what you go on to learn.

Analysis can begin *during an interview or focus group discussion*:

- Check your understanding of what a respondent really means.
- Check one person's experience or views against another's.
- Ask for explanations where people's views diverge.

Or *at the end of an interview or focus group*:

- Ask respondents to identify their main topics of concern.
- Summarize what has been said and ask for confirmation.

This ensures you are assessing respondents' priorities rather than your own. It also enables them to further explain any ambiguous comments they may have made.

Immediately after the interview or focus group:

- Ensure you have full notes or a recording; if not, write notes as soon as possible.
- Write down your thoughts: main themes, surprises, expected responses.
- For researchers in a team, discuss observations made and record conclusions.

After a few interviews, you can begin to build a theory as to what is happening. You may change this as time goes on, or you may not.

13.2.2 Styles of analysis

Many texts describing research data analysis are impenetrable, and many describe extremely complex processes. Don't be put off. Think of your audience and ensure your approach makes sense to them and meets your project aims. It needs to have integrity and be convincing to others: keeping it simple is the best approach.

Most academic approaches see analysis as essentially about assessing theory through data. This is often also the case in research for development. For example, we might want to know what impact a change in policy has had on people's behaviour and views – and we have some kind of theory about what this might be at the start of the project.

However, sometimes analysis just describes what was found. For example, in consulting a group of people about their views on a government service, it would be inappropriate for you to bring in your own theories to make sense of what they have said, at least when you first report it. In many cases, the analysis you require is quite straightforward.

13.3 Interpretation

As we have seen, interpretation is central to the quality of your analysis. Sometimes, research is carried out to 'prove a point' – but be careful: 'do not claim that your data prove something – this makes your use of data much easier to attack' (Mayer, 1998). You can never convince everyone of the truth of any statement. This is not to say evidence is not important – just we have to be very wary about the claims we make.

A 'rigorous approach' is one where you consider alternative explanations for anything you claim to be true, and where you show you have done this. Imagine how a critic would challenge your interpretation, then, in a group, have a good argument, with someone 'playing devil's advocate', to check you can defend your position.

It is important to avoid claiming a causal relationship between things, when in reality what you are showing is that the two appear to relate to each other in some way. For example, if long-standing illness is found to be more common among unemployed people, does illness and the resultant inability to work lead to unemployment, or did unemployment itself lead to illness?

Cause or effect? Size of landholding and household size in Tanzania

Collier et al. (1986) argue that 'other than their own labour, Tanzanian peasant households have only a limited range of assets', mainly land and livestock. But 'land is abundant and so we would expect distribution to be determined predominantly by the availability of household labour'. In light of their evidence, this view seems reasonable.

However, the authors do not explore other possible explanations: they merely give evidence in support of their hypothesis. They assume household size is fixed and, hence, land size adapts to the number of members. But is it correct to do this? Perhaps they reason that household size depends on the number of children. However, children may leave a household; others may join it. What then determines household size? Is it just a matter of chance? Or, for example, is a poor household (with fewer assets) more subject to fragmentation? Is a rich household not only more cohesive but also more able to draw on the labour of poorer relatives? Assets (including, but not only, land) are very likely to matter, even if most Tanzanian peasants have few at their disposal. Differences in asset ownership may well help determine differences in household size.

The authors' evidence supports this hypothesis also and hence you can't decide between these rival explanations. To do so, you need additional data, possibly including qualitative evidence on individual cases.

FOR EXAMPLE

It is in fact quite common to see a correlation but not be able to tell which factor is causing the other. Here, you need to leave open the chance that another explanation could be better than yours. The more evidence you can show for your point of view, the more likely you are to convince others.

Guarding against a biased interpretation is the reason researchers are always keen to make detailed notes that are close to what the person actually said. There is a risk of introducing bias as soon as you start to summarize. Be very aware when you are making your own interpretation, and ensure the data are available in their 'raw' state, so you can make checks as to when any interpretation came in.

13.3.1 Getting others' perspectives on the data

Everyone with any involvement in your research will be making their own interpretations of what you have found. This is a rich resource to draw on: learning from others' ideas improves the quality of your analysis. It also lets everyone feel their contribution is valued, which increases their commitment to implementing any action that may arise from the results. Moreover, it can help you to take account of alternative approaches to interpreting the data and to show why you have decided on yours.

You might ask others to do some of the analysis in parallel with you. This is one way of checking whether personal bias is being introduced into the process. If you work alongside others when collecting data, they will be part of the ongoing process of analysis that naturally accompanies data gathering.

You may want to hold workshops, first among core team members, then with the wider team, perhaps including partner agencies. At a later stage, it is useful to ask an expert to read a draft to check how your conclusions fit in with existing knowledge. How strong is your evidence, if it is unexpected?

Checklist: principles of data analysis

☑ Ensure interpretation is accurate and honestly reported.
☑ Avoid introducing your own preconceptions into the data.
☑ Take into account all possible explanations, including those which conflict with your own.
☑ Avoid generalizations which cannot be supported by the data.
☑ Where appropriate, strengthen your analysis by reference to other existing research findings.

13.4 The process of data analysis

13.4.1 What is the process of analysis like?

Analysis processes are very diverse. If your project is straightforward and entirely quantitative, analysis may require just counting up totals or feeding figures into a computer and then reading the results. You still need to decide how meaningful these results are, but basic data sorting can be very swift. Most of the thinking is done at an earlier stage, when you set the questions. Some projects will require more complex quantitative analysis (see Section 13.8).

Few development-related research projects, however, depend only on numbers, and qualitative analysis is a very different process. It can be difficult to get on top of the information you have collected: some researchers say you will spend as long doing the analysis as you did collecting the data. And no one has ever said their analysis went more smoothly than they expected!

A warning: it will be very difficult to get the analysis done if you can't concentrate solely on this task. It is too complex to do in fits and starts – you lose a lot every time that you have to start again. Your brain is your essential tool – no amount of card indexes, tables or computer files can substitute for your overall grasp of what is significant.

13.4.2   Who should do the analysis?

In qualitative analysis, it is best for those who undertook the fieldwork to analyse the data: their direct learning from the field will help in a variety of ways, especially in understanding what was most important to respondents. If they are not experienced in analysis, they should get help from someone who is.

Some quantitative development research projects hand over data to a consultant for analysis. This is only a good idea where:

- They have been involved in designing the study.
- They have a good understanding of the aims and ethos of the study.
- The analysis required is quantitative and straightforward but involves big numbers.

Generally, it is best either to contract out the whole project or to do it all in-house.

Checklist: 'farming out' your data analysis

If you really do need to get help with your analysis, here is some advice:

- ☑ Write down a list of the questions you want answered by the data.
- ☑ Consider asking up to three people/organizations how they would handle this task (that is, tender for it informally) before you decide who should do it.
- ☑ Get a clear explanation of any method or computer program the consultant intends to use, what it does and why they think it is suitable.
- ☑ Find out what experience they have of analysing other similar datasets.
- ☑ At the outset, make sure the agreement you set up is clear in all its details and written down.
- ☑ Who is responsible for entering the data – you or them?
- ☑ Who of their team will actually do the work?
- ☑ What format will the analysis be in (what will it look like and can they give you a disk and printout)?
- ☑ Can they provide graphs, charts?
- ☑ If you will need assistance to interpret their work, will they be willing to walk you through their data or analysis – either written or verbally?
- ☑ Are you willing for them to use your data for any purpose other than your project?
- ☑ Ensure there is clear agreement about the confidentiality and ownership of the data.
- ☑ If possible, keep a copy of the whole dataset.

13.5   Participation in the analysis process

Participation often breaks down at the point of data analysis. How can we involve a wider group of people in this stage? There are a number of models to draw on here.

To create a robust process, and to increase the chances of action following on from your research, you may want to engage not only communities but also co-researchers or staff from agencies that will be involved in implementing findings. Be prepared to mediate between different views and remember to avoid putting disadvantaged people in a difficult position.

The Participatory Learning and Action (PLA) approach integrates data collection with analysis. As local people take part in exercises, they are asked to identify their key issues and to draw conclusions. Meanwhile, it is possible to check on apparent contradictions. For example, if people say time spent fetching water is not a problem, but women and children are observed spending a great deal of time doing this work, it will be possible to ask what this means. Participatory research also means emerging theories can be shared with community members for immediate feedback. Action may be taken as a result of understandings gained while the process is underway; it may in fact be necessary to guard against people doing so too quickly. Meanwhile, this approach relies on it being easy to assemble the research team in one place, and on community members being readily available. This is not always the case.

Other projects have involved participants in analysis in a variety of ways.

FOR EXAMPLE

Local women carry out quantitative analysis: Newcastle-upon-Tyne, England

In a large quantitative study of local people's experiences of health services in Newcastle in 1999, local women researchers did much of the work themselves. Having gathered data from all households in a small area (500 questionnaires were returned), they did the coding and data entry. This meant community members dealt with all the small decisions that are part of the analysis process, which was demanding and at times tedious but gave them a great sense of pride in the work and of course ownership of the findings. They later used them to campaign successfully for changes in health service provision for their area.

It may be worth considering what impact the techniques and technology you use will have on your ability to involve a wider group of people in it. For example, unless there is good access to computers, using simpler technology may be helpful (not if the dataset is large, however!).

It is more difficult to share qualitative analysis, but by no means impossible. One approach, when working with a group of community members, is for one person to identify key themes and any interpretation problems they see and then to feedback verbally to the group. Everyone can then discuss these issues, using their own as well as their fieldwork experiences.

Another way, more demanding, is to decide on the key themes together and then organize the material relating to each theme. Each participant takes a theme and looks at the key issues emerging from the data relating to it. A lead researcher may need to coordinate this process.

Many people find the process of commenting on long documents daunting (and tedious!). It is all the more difficult for those whose education is more limited: while it is important to show drafts of reports to participants, work may need to be done to encourage comment – for example pointing out the particularly important parts.

Participatory analysis in Tanzania

FOR EXAMPLE

After conducting eight Participatory Poverty Appraisals (PPAs) across Tanzania (Gaventa and Attwood, 1998), 18 staff members worked on a synthesis report to make recommendations at national level.

At a workshop, each participant was asked to list the most important things they saw, felt and learnt in the fieldwork, as if they were sharing the experience with close friends, to give 'a certain feeling to the analysis'.

On subsequent days, groups of participants took turns to present case studies and take questions. Other participants had to write down key themes on cards. The over 800 cards produced were then sorted and categories developed. Eventually, groups identified chapter headings and a report structure, which they presented back to the whole group for discussion. Each report was indexed using the categories that had been developed, and a smaller team was identified to finish writing up the synthesis.

This process not only produced quality analysis but also engaged participants in complex debate about the issues. This was of great value, as many of them were government employees with a real influence on policy.

You could also ask people who have just undertaken fieldwork to present their impressions back to the core team as a basis for discussion. This process encourages reflection on how an interview has gone. In this, a framework of categories can be developed to test against the detail of the data at a later stage.

Checklist: participation in data analysis

☑   Ask participants how they would like to be involved, offering some ideas.
☑   During data collection, ask community members to prioritize issues, explain contradictions you find in your data, etc.

(Continued)

(Continued)

- ☑ Co-researchers can give verbal presentations and other research group members can identify themes from these – or brainstorm initial categories together.
- ☑ Make sure techniques and the technology you use do not unnecessarily exclude wider participation.
- ☑ Discuss possible explanations for the findings – what causes what?
- ☑ Don't impose your own categories or explanations without good reason, but at the same time situate the analysis within a broader framework where appropriate.

13.6 Methods of analysis

The processes you follow to analyse quantitative and qualitative data are very different. It is helpful to be clear what kind of information you are looking for, and to separate out the material into the two types.

For example, semi-structured questionnaires include both quantitative and qualitative questions: 'How long have you used xyz service?' might be followed by 'What have you found helpful about xyz service?' You will have numbers in answer to the first question, and words – perhaps whole paragraphs – in answer to the second.

Quantitative data include all yes/no questions and also rating scales, for example 'How satisfied were you with xyz service?' with a pre-coded set of simple and predetermined answers, such as 'not satisfied/somewhat dissatisfied/somewhat satisfied/satisfied'. In the latter case, you might then ask 'Why?' leading to a set of qualitative responses.

You may also want to quantify qualitative data to some extent. For instance, you might analyse the answers to this type of 'why' question by making a set of categories from the various answers you receive and counting how many respondents gave each answer. However, don't place too much reliance on this type of figure. In mentioning one answer, a respondent is not necessarily denying the veracity of the others. For example, responding to the question 'Why were you satisfied with xyz service?' by mentioning its location and friendly staff, a respondent has not disagreed that other factors may be important, such as cost. They may just not have thought of them at that moment. If you offered a list of possible reasons for satisfaction or dissatisfaction, the numbers would have more meaning.

In general, the power of qualitative data is in the concepts they convey – their inherent meaning. It is best to think in terms of emerging themes and not worry too much about how many respondents said one thing or another. However, you do need to distinguish a single anecdote from themes that are meaningful for many people, and also to take note of what kinds of people bring up what kinds of issue.

Having dealt separately with the two kinds of data, you can then process each in a different way without getting confused. You will then need to reintegrate them so you can report the findings as a whole.

13.7   Qualitative analysis

13.7.1   The core process

Essentially, the task is to draw out a set of key themes that summarize the important categories within the data, and to look at how these relate to each other. However you plan to handle the data, the following steps will be needed:

- Familiarize yourself with the data: read and reread notes, interview schedules and transcripts.
- Make a preliminary list of themes or categories you can see in the data.
- Go through the data again, making notes in the margins as you go along as to what theme is being dealt with where.
- Look at your list of categories before, during and after this second reading, and make changes as problems emerge.
- Set out your list of categories in a clear format (separate sheets, charts, cards – see below) so you can link them directly with notes, quotes or references in the data.
- Go through the data again and note all material relating to each category under its heading (make sure you make detailed references to the data with any quotes or notes so you can trace them back). Researchers often call this process 'coding' – that is, locating material in the data that relates to the codes, or categories, you are using to analyse them. It is best to work through the material looking for all your categories at one time – searching for each category in turn is too slow.
- Then look at each category and see what you have got, and it will be easy to make sense of the material you have collected.

Your categories will come out of your specific project. For example, a study of a lesbian and gay youth group had comments on the group itself (positive and negative); other sources of advice and information; overcoming isolation; experiences of prejudice from others; coming out to parents; coming out to friends; and self-esteem issues. A further categorization within the comments about the group itself concerned the issues young people identified as important to them.

> **Tip**
> As you analyse qualitative data, many ideas will occur to you – keep track of these as some of them will be useful. Write yourself memos, and read them over at intervals while you are working on the analysis.

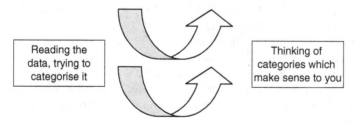

| Reading the data, trying to categorise it | | Thinking of categories which make sense to you |

Figure 13.1   The iterative process

Common pitfall

Before you start analysing, but after you have put the material in good order and put codes on it, photo-copy the whole of your dataset and put away the original. Loss of data would be a disaster.

Tip

Always keep a code number and page or line number alongside any quote or other direct references to the data – you will soon forget who said what.

As Figure 13.1 shows, it is crucial not to set out a rigid set of categories and then stick to them through thick and thin. You want the data to help you to form the categories you use. They should arise from the data, not be imposed on them.[1]

One issue relates to deciding how your different categories link to each other. Is one a subcategory of another or a separate category? You will probably change your mind on this a couple of times. Some people find it helpful to draw a diagram of their categories to see how they fit together.

For example, in a study of the experiences of women who have reported a rape to the police, respondents identified attitudes of health service staff as a problem. Do you create a category relating to health care, or do you include this material within a category covering attitudes of all professional staff types? Or one covering stigma towards rape victims more generally? Or does this issue require a category of its own?

If you can, the best way of checking on your categories and how you see them relating to each other is to go back and do some more fieldwork, perhaps directly asking people's views on the framework you are developing.

Note that, if you simply group the answers to the questions you asked under a heading of each question, you will find a good deal of repetition and overlap in the themes emerging. For example, what people say when you ask 'What did you find helpful in the way in which xyz authority dealt with you?' might overlap with what they say when you ask 'What advice would you give xyz authority to improve their services?' It is better to draw themes from both sets of replies and use these as your headings.

13.7.2 Analysing focus group data

In some ways, focus group data look much like qualitative data drawn from individuals. But the great strength is in the interaction between participants – the way people work together, or argue with each other, to make sense of an issue. You can try to preserve this in the analysis, perhaps by quoting a discussion between participants.

Focus groups should not be analysed as if they were a series of individual interviews: it is generally inappropriate to add up responses from individuals to a question asked during a group discussion. The group process often influences people, meaning only limited confidence can be had in these figures. For example, some people may not speak about a certain issue simply because someone else has already made the point. Another approach, perhaps more appropriate, takes the group as the unit of analysis, and looks at how many different groups an issue comes up in.

Adding up focus group data: the Child Labour Project, Sialkot, Pakistan

In Sialkot, 46 focus groups were held with a range of people. Researchers counted how many of the groups mentioned issues like poverty, education or concerns about unemployed young people running wild, etc. They could then report, for example, that 75 per cent of groups mentioned improving quality of education as an important step in improving quality of life for these communities.

13.7.3 Some techniques for qualitative analysis

Some ways of setting about qualitative analysis are quite crude; others enable very subtle and careful handling of the material. This section and Table 13.3 list some common techniques, which can be suitable for different types of project.

Table 13.3 Techniques for qualitative analysis

Technique	Can it be done by hand?	Can a computer help?	Suitable for?
Cut and paste	Yes	Yes, word-processing	Small, simple projects
Charting	Yes, this is the usual method	Yes, tables in word-processing program or on a spreadsheet	Any size project
Card index	Yes	No	Any size project, when you have time for careful analysis
Computer programs	No	Essential – needs a special program	Projects requiring detailed analysis of large quantities of textual data

Cut and paste

This is a crude approach but perfectly effective when you are in a hurry, your study is small and your data are pretty simple. It can be done by hand or using a word-processing package.

By hand

Here, you absolutely must photocopy the whole of your dataset, as you are going to literally cut it up. Using an A4 sheet for each of your categories, cut out all the important material from your data and stick it on the various sheets – with Blu-Tack or paperclips, so you can move things around easily. Be careful to write on each note or quote where the item comes from, so you can trace it back – to be sure all your quotes do not come from one person for example.

You could just write a very short note and a reference to the data on each sheet, but actually taking whole statements means the material is in a very handy form to work from. However, this is possible only with small datasets.

What you end up with is a set of sheets with a jumble of statements for each category. You need to organize these carefully, as new sub-categories may emerge. Once this is done, you can look within each category for the themes of people's statements about it.

Cut and paste by computer

This is essentially the same process but carried out on the computer. Type the data into the computer, then either make a word-processing file for each category or give each category a page in one large file. Copy and paste data to the analysis files. Again, keep track of which item comes from which interview or set of notes, and copy and paste rather than cut and paste, so you retain a complete dataset in the original file.

Doing this on the computer allows you to move the material about in a very flexible way. Also, importantly, you can put the same material under more than one heading, which may be helpful where there is overlap.

Charting (by hand)

This method, known as 'Framework', is particularly well suited to research for applied policy research (Ritchie and Spencer, 1994). It was developed in part to formalize qualitative data analysis in order to build confidence in the validity of its results. It is not as technical as the name might suggest – you can do it by hand on big pieces of paper! – but it does enable you to handle much bigger datasets. There is now an online version available (www.framework-natcen.co.uk/). You don't directly sort quotes, but rather create a set of codes that enable you to map all the data onto a series of charts.

Again, follow the same core process: in familiarizing yourself with the data, look at only a sample if there is a lot. Then set up a framework of categories, referred to as an index. Some researchers give each category and subcategory numbers, others make short descriptive textual 'labels' to apply to the text. Now go through the data and label them in the margins with these codes. Some passages may relate to a number of codes.

Next, create a number of charts, using large sheets of paper (at least A3), with your categories and subcategories along the top and your cases (interviews, focus group transcripts, observation notes) down the side, always in the same order. This enables you to see the whole story for each case easily – which is often essential in making sense of what people have said, even if you do not intend to report cases individually. If you like, you can group your cases in such a way as to make it easy to investigate differences between groups. For example, you could enter information from people living in different geographical areas together. It is worth giving some thought to the way you arrange the categories, as this will either help or hinder you in writing up the material.

Table 13.4 gives an example of the way a subject chart is built up, looking at what women disliked about UK maternity services during labour and delivery. The study also had charts covering antenatal and postnatal care. For each of the three stages of the childbirth process, there were three subcategory charts: for things women liked, for things they disliked and for suggested improvements.

Table 13.4   What women particularly disliked about labour and delivery services

	(I) Information	(F) Facilities	(M) Monitoring	(SS) Staff busy/ shortage/no staff to assist/left alone
Group 1	• Conflicting information because of busy period (276–9) • Conflicting advice/ information from doctors (333–8)	• Theatre cramped (286–8) • Beds too high (297–307) • Lack of privacy (309–26)	• Frequent monitoring (241–6)	• Too busy compared with previous birth (235–40) • Have to ask for assistance (240–1) • Have to get your own tea (252–3)
Group 2	• Lack of information when in labour (134–6)	• Lack of privacy in delivery rooms (199–216)		• Staff rushed 'conveyor belt' delivery (283–4) • Midwives running between delivery rooms (222–34)

Source: Gill Craig/The College of Health (2001) personal communication

Once the charting is complete, you need to look down each column and decide what you need to report from the data in each category. You can also read across, to check how an individual respondent's answers fit together. This makes it easier to write your report.

Card index

A more traditional approach in some disciplines is to use index cards. A card is allocated to each category, on which you write notes of material you have collected relating to this, including cross-reference information. It is best not to write on the back, so you can lay out the cards and see their contents easily.

The joy of index cards is that they are small, so it is easy to try out different ways of organizing your material. However, they also show only limited information before getting full. It is also tempting to keep adding more cards, for more categories, without checking how they relate to each other. To stop things getting out of hand, review your categories regularly and either merge some or divide some.

Example of index card used for qualitative data analysis

Sources of income: trading by women.

Interviews with women: earn 'own' money – int.5 p.9 [interview 5, page 9]; took over selling cloth from mother – int.21 p.4; sells farm produce – int.23 p.6.
Observation notes: market in town (detailed notes) 5 May; also 12 May; stalls by roadside – 2 July.
Interviews with men: useful contribution to family income – int.3 p.10.
See also: Markets.

Again, to locate direct quotes, you need to go back to the data, directed by your references on the card.

When you come to writing up, you can arrange and rearrange your cards into whatever patterns you like, maybe laying them out on the floor to do so.

Data analysis software

Standard programs such as Microsoft Word and Excel can be relied on for basic analysis of both qualitative and quantitative data, helping you to move, order or copy text, add up or compare figures, prepare diagrams and more. There are also software packages dedicated to qualitative analysis, as well as numerous options for quantitative work. These tools can add greatly to the depth of your analysis while making the task less time consuming. However, they can also add to its costs, and it can often take extra time to learn how to use them. Decide early on which software you will use, as the way you prepare your data for analysis will depend on the method you to use to analyse it.

If you expect to go on doing research in your professional life, it is worth getting access to, and learning to use, certain packages. Also, entering data into a computer allows you to access the editing and storage advantages software packages have over paper documents. This is particularly useful if you want a number of people (community members, staff) to participate in the analysis process – as long as they have adequate access to computers. No matter what software you choose, computers are of course 'very high speed idiots' – they can organize and reorganize large quantities of data very quickly but can't think for you.

FOR EXAMPLE

Combining by hand and software methods

Qualitative data can be entered into common software programs to aid in analysis. Here, Microsoft's word-processor program Word and its spreadsheet program Excel have been used to organize and analyse data from Overseas Development Institute focus groups conducted with farmers in Vietnam in 2010.

In the first example, content from in-depth interviews has been separated thematically and typed into a custom table in Word. Researchers have used Word's editing features to distinguish groups by bold and italic typefaces.

Focus Group Discussion Findings – Vietnam 2010 fieldwork (characters in black is from women's, underlined is from men's group, **bold** is for female adolescents group, *italics* is for male adolescents group)

	Ha Giang Site 1	Ha Giang Site 2	An Giang Site 3	An Giang Site 4
HH Food security	-	-		
HH food access	- **Have 3 meals a day but sometimes miss meals. Eat more and better at school than at home (at school: veg, meat, fish or eggs, with 2-3 bowls of rice. At home: rice with veg soup and 1–2 bowls of rice).** - **3–4 months of food shortage per year (April–July)** - **Drank Milk when they were young. Most cannot afford to eat chicken, only occasionally.** - Rice grains are too flat. Some was women-eaten. Corn is normal this year. - Meals are better, and the food shortage lasts only a short time. Cultivate enough to eat. - *This year have less corn and rice.* - *Don't always eat breakfast. Don't always eat their fill.* - *Meals at home are better than at the school.*	- **Eat less because of poverty, harvests reduced from weather and rice infected by insects.** - **Eat 3 meals, but don't have breakfast at boarding school (only a small rice cake). Just eat vegetables, every meal has broccoli. Have meat 3 times per week.** - This year the productivity of corn increases, while rice reduces by half (probably because of seeds), Quality of rice is not good. - May be in hunger for 3 months this year because of crop failure. - School serves more food than at home. - *Normally eat rice with veg. Sometimes fish, pork. Never have milk.* - *Foods considered good are porridge with beef, fruits, milk.*	- **Families are not hungry, but food is still lacking (eat less). Eat 2 meals a day.** - **Food is often in short supply in the rainy season and they can't work on the mountain. Richer people have higher ground they can cultivate on even in rainy season.** - **One is fed at her employer's house.** - *Sometimes lack rice. Often eat fish, porridge for breakfast. Best is fish sour soup.* - Rice is more expensive this year. - Still have enough food, eat 2 meals. Eat crab often and meat occasionally. Can't afford to eat many dishes in a meal. - Sometimes don't have enough food (when can't find work).	- **This year rice is more. Rice is lacking at times. Eat 2 meals a day. Buy/catch fish, buy pork or chicken, and add veg.** - **Many would like to be able to drink milk.** - *Beef and pork are available now (not in the past), eat it now and then. Have mostly 2 meals.* - *Hungry sometimes and feel stomach ache.* - Work for hire in agricultural sector. Lack food for 2–15 days per year. Have smaller meals when in shortage. - Water level is low so impossible to catch fish. Impossible to buy it so meals become simpler. - Don't have money for meat and vegetable. - In recent years, rice is bit inadequate but they are not hungry. This year market price hasn't increased for rice. - *Eat 2 meals a day and vary.*

Example 13.1

In a second example, a simple Excel matrix keeps track of in-depth interview data collected from the same project, with particularly relevant observations noted in **bold** (red may be used as an alternative to **bold**).

Interview	Province	Commune	Gender	Age	Marital Status	Occupation	Vulnerabilities faces by men/women in community	Risks faced over last five years and coping strategies used	Risks faced in distant past and coping strategies used	Current challenges and extent to which govt programmmes are helping	Future ambitions	Notes
LH11	HG	Lo Va Chai	F	44	widow with 5 kids	She has some livestock that she breeds. She seems to also have fields where she grows rice and vegetables. She works all the time: "I am so sad but I have to do the best for mt two children."	**When the Mong people let their daughter to get married, it means that they have lost a person to help, then they are sad.** Another case is that when they have a daughter-in-law, but they are separated. Moreover the mother had to pay a lot of money to get her daughter-in-law, so she cannot be happy. Women work much harder than men, they have to raise children and work. Men do not do housework. **Before her husband died he made all the decisions. Women are more likely to not speak Vietnamese. This makes it very hard for them.**	Last year her home was damaged in a flood. She prays about it but doesn't know how to fix it. "As a woman living alone I did not know how to overcome it". Her husband dies 2 years ago - the family has been poor since. She had to take out loans for the funeral. She has almost paid them back. They sometimes don't have enough to eat - they have no money for fertilizer.	Nine years ago one of her sons died at the age of 2. Five years ago her oldest son got married, that was very expensive. The family took out large loans from relatives for the wedding. **She grew up wealthy, but did not go to school because girls did not go to school.**	Her husband got free medical care when he was sick, but meals were expensive. The family gets free tuition, free medical care and provides seed. She took out a state loan that she used to pay off an older loan.	She would really like the State to build her a house. She would like to have more land for farming - and fertilizer.	
LH12	HG	not listed	M	18	single	Student in grade 9	His mother is teh breadwiner in the family. She raises livestock, rice and corn. **Hmong girls do not go to school past 8th grade, they get married. His class is mostly boys (18 to 4). He wants to marry a girl less educated than him-**	The subject goes to school in the morning and then goes home in the afternoon to do chores for his mother before returning to school to study again in	**His father died when he was 2. One of his sisters has never been to school so that she can work at**	he goes to boarding school for free, the family must contribute rice. He works for the school gathering wood and cleaning. He gets free medical	He wants to pass entrance exams for boarding school so that he can	

Example 13.2

FOR EXAMPLE

Why choose a dedicated package over Excel and Word?

Excel is ideal for basic data analysis tasks such as data entry and storage, and can run elementary statistical analysis. It is also ubiquitous and user friendly. However, it can have difficulties coping with more advanced statistical tasks. Dedicated statistics packages such as Statistical Package for the Social Sciences (SPSS) and Stata (see below) take longer to learn and cost more, but provide a much more robust range of technical functions in quantitative analysis.

Similarly, Word is a versatile program for data entry and editing. However, when you need to group and link concepts, dedicated computer-assisted qualitative data analysis software (CAQDAS) programs such as NVivo 8 (formerly NUD*IST) and HyperRESEARCH offer greater flexibility. Other popular programs are Transana and The Ethnograph. There are many others on the market – including a few free, open source options, such as the Coding Analysis Toolkit, a web-based suite of CAQDAS tools developed by the University of Pittsburgh (http://cat.ucsur.pitt.edu). In particular, these programs make it easier to change categories and re-label data, which can save a lot of time and energy.

With very large projects, it could be madness not to use computer technology. With very small ones, it may not be worth learning new tricks, although you could use a computer for a simple project as a way of learning the ropes. You can teach yourself to use these packages, or else you can go on a course run by the manufacturers or a university.

For more guidance, it is worth contacting Qualitative Innovations in CAQDAS (QUIC) at the University of Surrey.[2] There is also good information on each of the companies' websites. You can also get help from Sage, which distributes much qualitative data analysis software.[3]

13.7.4   Rigour in qualitative analysis

Qualitative research does not aim to provide statistically reliable information for which representativeness can be claimed. However, it is important to show your methods and conclusions are justifiable. To do this, you need to give as much information as possible to enable readers to understand how the research has been carried out, through a full account of data collection and analysis, sometimes referred to as an 'audit trail'.

It is also very important to keep track of all the codes used in your analysis process to present as a 'codebook'. The idea is that another researcher should be able to follow your process and see where decisions were made and why.

As we have seen, identity inevitably has an impact. For example, a European man researcher would have a different perspective from an Angolan woman researcher in a study of the effects on children of the conflict in Angola. So it may be appropriate to give some biographical details about the researcher as part of the analysis. You can say in what ways you feel your own background, values and experience may have influenced the research, so the reader can judge how reasonable the writer's claims are. This is referred to as 'reflexivity' – rather than claiming to have no 'vested interests', we declare them and let the reader make their own judgement.

Validity

Denscombe (2010) suggests the following checks to assess the validity of the findings:

- Do the conclusions do justice to the complexity of the phenomenon and avoid 'oversimplifications' while also offering internal consistency?
- Has the researcher's 'self' been recognized as an influence in the research, but guarded against causing biased reporting? This is a difficult tightrope to walk.
- Have the instances selected for investigation been chosen on explicit and reasonable grounds as far as the research aims are concerned?
- Have alternative explanations been explored?
- Have the findings been triangulated with alternative sources as a way of bolstering confidence in their validity?
- Have the findings been fed back to informants to get their opinion on the proposed explanation?
- How far do the findings and conclusion fit with existing knowledge on the area, and how far do they translate to other comparable situations?

It is important in qualitative work to present findings in context – and avoid, for example, taking 'quotes' from an interview in such a way as to twist their original meaning. The context includes not only the words on either side of a particular statement but also the situation in which the words were produced. Was it said in a public group setting? In front of the respondent's family or her boss? The day after some significant event?

Checklist: qualitative analysis

- ☑ Do the categories or themes reflect the research questions and the data?
- ☑ Has the topic been approached with an open mind?
- ☑ Have alternative explanations been explored?
- ☑ Have the data been presented in context?
- ☑ Are the findings of one technique or group of respondents triangulated with those from another technique or group?
- ☑ Have the conclusions been checked back with respondents?
- ☑ Have existing relevant research findings been used to support your data?
- ☑ Has the process followed in the research and the analysis been made explicit?

13.8   Quantitative analysis

If you are doing complex work, such as tests of significance (only appropriate with large representative samples), get advice from an experienced researcher, preferably a statistician. But most research for development needs only a few procedures.

13.8.1 Some techniques for quantitative analysis

The data matrix

You may find it helpful to think of the data you have collected in terms of a matrix – a table with rows and columns. Set out all the information from each respondent along one row, with a column for each question.

With small simple questionnaires, it may be possible to do your calculations directly from a data matrix. Usually, though, things get too complicated, and you need to work on each question on a separate sheet. This is similar to the charting method for qualitative analysis described in Section 13.7, but entering numbers rather than words.

Coding

Some data naturally present themselves in the form of figures, but often the first process is that of turning the information into figures from words. With luck, most of your questions contain pre-coded answers (see Section 11.4 on questionnaires). This means you decide before you ask the questions what groups of answers you expect, and give respondents limited options. You now need to group and code your questionnaires – meaning, here, assigning numbers to the different answers you received.

Missing data and 'other'

It is important to record missing answers clearly. There is a difference between people who gave no reply to a question, for whatever reason, and those who said they did not know, which is a meaningful response. Include a category for missing data in all your coding schemes. Where appropriate, 'don't know' and 'other' should also be included. Traditionally, researchers use 8 or 88 for 'other' and 9 or 99 for 'answer missing'.

Counting up the totals

The most common calculation involves simply adding up how many people answered in which way to closed questions. Researchers call these 'frequency counts'. The most straightforward way of doing this by hand is to set out a tally (reckoning, counting) sheet like that in Table 13.5A (Hall and Hall, 1996). For this, you can use a blank questionnaire, if there is space, or else a separate sheet for each question. Go through the questionnaires and enter a *mark* in the correct category for each answer.

Table 13.5A   Simple tally sheet for the question 'Do you own a refrigerator?'

Response		Number
Yes	ЦН I	6
No	ЦН ЦН ЦН II	17
No answer	III	3
Total		26

A refinement, enabling you to go back and check your information, is to enter onto your tally sheet the *code number* for each questionnaire (Table 13.5B). You can still count them up in the same way.

Table 13.5B Simple tally sheet using code numbers for the question 'Do you own a radio?'

Response		Number
Yes	①⑥⑧⑩	4
No	②③⑤⑦⑨	5
No answer	④	1
Total		10

This method also means that, if you have qualitative data too, for example about why people said they did or did not own a radio, you can turn to the material directly from your tally sheet.

Percentages

Table 13.5C shows how much easier it is to get the basic gist of the information contained in numbers when they are worked out as percentages. This is one convention for presenting actual numbers and percentages. You then could write in the text, for example, 'six (26 per cent) said they owned a refrigerator'.

However, percentages can be misleading, especially if the total number of respondents is low (certainly if it is fewer than 40), when one individual can make a big difference to how the figures look. For example, if your sample is only 25, each individual accounts for 4 per cent of the total. In this case, always give the actual number as well.

Percentages are calculated after excluding missing answers – this is why there is no percentage shown in the row for 'no answer' in Table 13.5C. It may be

> **Tip**
> This method is really useful – consider using it BEFORE you spend days using the simple counting method only to find you have one missing answer and don't know where it should have come from.

> **Tip**
> To handle percentages confidently, make sure you understand how they relate to fractions. When you are using a calculator, make a guess first to check that your answer is in the right general area.

Table 13.5C Simple tally sheet with percentages for the question 'Do you own a refrigerator?'

Response		Number	(%)
Yes	ⅬⅯ I	6	(26)
No	ⅬⅯ ⅬⅯ ⅬⅯ II	17	(74)
No answer	III	3	
Total		26	
Total valid replies		23	(100)

important to show actual numbers as well, so the reader can decide what importance to put on your figures, knowing exactly how many people were involved. What you are reporting is the *percentage of those who gave a reply*, and you need to make this clear.

FOR EXAMPLE

Identifying meaningful figures: maternal and child health in Liberia

A Save the Children study of maternal and child health in Liberia asked about families' experiences of diarrhoeal illnesses in children, and mothers' knowledge of how to make a rehydration solution using sugar and salt. It was more meaningful to report percentages in relation to the knowledge of mothers whose children had experienced diarrhoea than in relation to the whole sample, which included a lot of missing answers. About 40 per cent of the sample had experience of diarrhoea in their children. Only a small proportion of these mothers (15 per cent) gave correct information, and this was an important clue that health workers needed better communication training.

It is best with small samples not to present calculations to one or more decimal points, as this gives a false impression of precision. Round numbers up or down as appropriate. For example, if 9 out of 17 people said 'x', round the answer up from 54.94 to 55 per cent. With very small numbers, perhaps in this example, it may be best not to give percentages at all, to avoid seeming to try to make wider claims than your data support.

To find a percentage of a number

It is best to ignore the % button on your calculator. To answer the question 'What is *something* per cent of *something else*?' remember x per cent of y simply means x divided by 100 multiplied by y.

Example: find 15 per cent of 240

Rewrite it like this: 15/100 × 240

And calculate: 15÷100 × 240 = 36

To express something as a percentage

This is where we change a fraction or a ratio into a percentage. Use this technique when you are trying to answer a question which basically says 'What is *something* as a percentage of *something else*?' The answer is always a percentage. The basic technique is to divide the top by the bottom and multiply the result by 100.

Example: 60 out of 130 students on the course are female. What percentage is this?

Rewrite the question as: 60/130 × 100

And calculate: 60÷130 × 100 = 46.1538

Give the answer as 46 per cent, since a whole number is probably accurate enough.

Grouped data

It is often useful to put raw data into groups. For example, it would be tedious to present all ages in your sample in turn, so you might consider grouping them into, for example, 0–18, 19–29, 30–59, 60 plus or some such. Be careful when you do this. Offering your respondents only a set of groups to tick leaves you stuck with the groupings for any analysis you may want to do. If you later decide that under and over 16 would have been a better grouping, you do not have the information. You could group it later during the analysis, which leaves you more flexibility. In doing this, it may be helpful to list all the data for one variable in order, to see where natural groupings arise. This will also be apparent if you look at the basic frequencies for the variable.

Analysis of open-ended questions in a questionnaire

This common task falls between qualitative and quantitative analysis. You ask a question which invites comments, and then want to make categories within the replies and add up how many respondents made a comment within each. You may also want to quote typical comments for some categories, for example what school children taking part in a particular programme hope to gain from it.

The first process is similar to the core process for qualitative analysis described in Section 13.7. Bring together all the responses, perhaps taking a sample if you have a very large dataset (for example every nth questionnaire). As ever, keep track of which statements come from which questionnaire – put the code number beside each comment. Some respondents may have made several comments and their code number will appear repeatedly.

Then make a suitable set of categories for the data, for revision as necessary. On another sheet of paper, write these categories along one side. Then enter under each category the code number for each questionnaire where this type of comment was made. You can add up numbers for who made each type of comment.

It is also important to keep track of how many respondents answered these questions at all. You might create a table (on paper or the computer) which just notes 'comment' or 'no comment' against questions which ask for this sort of response. This information could be kept with your main quantitative analysis.

13.8.2 Describing the data statistically

Averages

It is often useful to find the midpoint or average of a set of values. There are three types of average in mathematics, known together as 'measures of central tendency'. Each is useful for a different purpose (Denscombe, 2010).

The mean

The mean is what most people are talking about when they refer to 'the average'. Add up all the values given then divide them by the number of respondents (excluding those for whom there is a missing answer). For example,

```
Number of children in family
2  1  4  3  2  9  3  2  10  1  1
1  Add them all together (38)
2  Divide by the total number of cases (÷11)
Mean number of children in a family = 3.45
```

The mean describes what would result if there were an equal distribution of values – if the total were spread evenly. How well it can represent a set of values therefore depends on how spread out or dispersed the values are around the mean. In addition, it is affected strongly by any extremely large or small numbers: where this happens, the distribution is said to be skewed – as in our example where, apart from the two large ones, most families are quite small. Another example is income distribution, where a mean can present a false picture for the majority if one or two very high earners pull the figure up.

The median (middle point)

The median is the middle value of a set, when the values are arranged in order of size. Using the dataset discussed above, place the numbers in ascending order. The number falling halfway between the highest and the lowest values is 2. This is the median.

```
1  1  1  2  2  2  3  3  4  9  10
```

If there is an even number of cases, the median falls between the two middle numbers, and the convention is to take the mean of the two. The median here is the mean of 2 and 3, so 2.5.

```
1  1  1  2  2  2  3  3  3  4  9  10
```

The median can be useful when your data are skewed, and also works better than the mean with small numbers of values. Meanwhile, it is easy to understand what it is: half the values in the set are above it and half below. In the example, half the families have more children and the other half fewer children than the median number.

The mode

The third type of average is the mode, and there can be two or more. You find it by counting the number of times each value occurs. It can be used with any kind of data and, like the median, is not affected by extreme values. Going back to our example:

2   1   4   3   2   9   3   2   10   1   1

Both 1 and 2 occur thrice, so these are the modes.

Measures of spread

Measures of spread are logically linked to averages. They describe the way the data are arranged around the midpoint. The range is the simplest measure and is very easy to work out. Subtract the lowest value from the highest one. In our example, the smallest families had one child and the largest had ten, so the range is nine.

However, as with the mean, the range is affected strongly by extreme values. If only one family has nine children and all the rest have one or two, the range is still nine.

There are a number of other ways of describing spread, including by the shape of the distribution in relation to the standard deviation. While for large datasets these may be relevant, you should get help from a statistician in making such calculations and explaining their relevance. You also need to be sure your audience will understand the meaning of any statistics you use.

Some terms

Beyond measures of central tendency and of spread, a number of additional technical terms arise in quantitative analysis. These may appear intimidating at first glance, but knowing a few 'basics' of these can be very helpful in your work.

A **variable** is any characteristic of a number of individuals which has different degrees of magnitude or different categories, so individuals vary in the extent to which they possess this quality or fall into each category. In effect, each question you ask usually relates to one variable.

Continuous variables are those which can represent any range of real number values (for example weight, height). *Discrete variables* can represent only finite, indivisible values (for example number of children). *Nominal variables* divide data

(Continued)

(Continued)

into non-numerical categories (for example village, gender, occupation). If these categories have a clear, hierarchical ordering (for example 'small', 'medium' and 'large' villages), they are *ordinal variables*. If they refer to a range (for example villages with '100–200', '200–300' and '300–400' people), they are *interval variables.*

When you study just one variable (for example income), this is *univariate analysis.* When you study the relationship between two variables simultaneously (for example income by gender), it is *bivariate analysis.* More than two (for example the relationship between income, gender and age) is *multivariate analysis.*

Correlation is the degree to which change in one variable is related to changes in another variable. This is typically presented as a number (the *correlation coefficient*) between -1.0 and +1.0. A *positive* correlation coefficient means increases in one variable tend to be associated (correlated) with increases in the other. A *negative* correlation coefficient sees increases in one variable paired with decreases in the other. For example, if your data show a rise in local household income every time investment increases, you might determine that investment and household income have a positive correlation. Conversely, in a negative correlation, your data might show that drought-hit households have a corresponding decrease in household income.

Causation is the causal relationship between two or more variables. Be very careful in distinguishing between causation and correlation – they are not the same thing. Your data might show a positive *relationship* between investment and household income but you cannot necessarily prove those investments caused the rise in income. The correlation between the two might be pure coincidence, and the change in income could be the result of something else entirely.

Standard deviation relates to how much the data you collect deviate from the mean (that is, from the value you expect to see). Lower standard deviations confirm what you might expect – the data point you have collected does not stray far from the expected mean value. Higher standard deviations imply your data are more diversified. This is expressed by the Greek letter σ.

In terms of **statistical confidence,** a result is deemed *statistically significant* if it is unlikely to have occurred by chance. *Confidence intervals* and *significance levels* (also known as *p-values*) require more complicated explanations (see Further reading below), but you should recognize them as the tools for determining statistical significance.

13.8.3   Finding connections: tests for correlation

Cross-tabulation shows the number of cases that occur jointly in each combination of categories of the variables under investigation. It answers the questions:

- Is there any association or relationship between two variables?
- If there is, how strong is it?

For example, you want to know whether people on low incomes are more likely than people on higher incomes to have problems of access to clean water, or whether men are more likely than women to hold a certain view. This is called a correlation or cross-tabulation.

Having got advice, you need to think about which cross-tabulations you want to look at. What statistics you can use for your project depends on the size and type of sample you used.[4] Even with quite a small dataset (not too many respondents or too many questions), a vast number of cross-tabulations could be run. You need to go back to your theories about what is going on and see what relationships you would expect to see in the data, then look for them. And then question any you find!

> **Tip**
> Consult a statistician or quantitative researcher now.

A correlation that might be expected but is *not* found may be important too. For example, most people would expect gender to affect school examination performance in different ways in relation to each subject – or that girls (or indeed boys) would simply do worse at everything. If girls and boys do equally well, this could be important.

Table 13.6   Cross-tabulation of illness during last four weeks by age (adults)

Health status	Age	18–40	40–60	Over 60	Total
Yes (illness present)		10 (17%)	8 (15%)	14 (47%)	32 (23%)
No illness		50 (83%)	44 (85%)	16 (53%)	110 (77%)
Total		60 (100%)	52 (100%)	30 (100%)	142 (100%)

You can work out basic cross-tabulations by hand. Set out a large table like Table 13.6, with lots of space in the boxes, and go through the data, entering code numbers as in Table 13.5B. Then add up the totals for each box.

Using a computer is a much easier way of working out cross-tabulations for large datasets. SPSS does this easily (see below). Such software also allows you to easily convert your cross-tabulations into attractive charts, graphs and tables (see Figure 13.2 for an example).

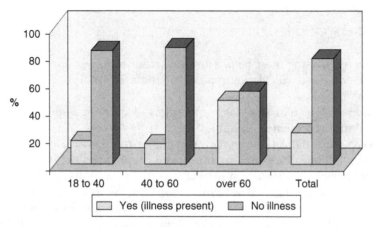

Figure 13.2   Illness during the past four weeks by age group

A very important note of caution

You cannot be sure, even if you find a correlation that is statistically significant, which way causation goes (what is the cause and what is the effect). For example, if more charges are brought in areas where there are more police officers, is a higher level of crime the explanation or are more officers simply able to prosecute more cases?

Another very important note of caution

When we set up cross-tabulations, we usually have an idea in our minds about what the relationship between the data means. But there is always a possibility that any relationship is simply the result of chance, that is, it would not recur if you did the research again. This is why tests of significance are used: to help us see how reliable our findings are (see box explaining terms above).

However, unless you are working with a large, reasonably representative sample, it is unlikely that any correlation will be statistically significant. It is bad practice to publish correlation data unless they reach a reasonable level of significance – you can seem to be misleading readers. Consult an expert to test significance: SPSS will calculate some tests for you automatically, and many others on request, but you still need to be able to interpret the information correctly.

Common pitfalls

Wasting time running dozens of cross-tabulations when your dataset is not big enough to have confidence in any statistics generated

13.8.4   Data analysis software

A number of options are available in terms of computer software for quantitative analysis.

Specialist statistical packages

These will give you the most help. They are set up to expect survey data and will easily carry out all the calculations you need (and many more).

- SPSS allows you to analyse large quantities of data. In a spreadsheet format, each column represents a variable and each row a case. You can put in labels that keep information about the meaning of the data close to the numbers involved. SPSS produces quality tables and graphs, and the latest versions are quite user friendly. It is worth buying if you expect to do more than one substantial survey (perhaps 60 or more respondents) with a quantitative element.[5]
- Stata is a popular alternative to SPSS. It has equivalent functionality and is generally as widely used in academic institutions around the world. It features a relatively straightforward, user-friendly interface.[6]

- PSPP is an open source substitute for commercial statistics programs – particularly SPSS, whose interface it intentionally mimics. It offers a strong set of basic capabilities, including frequencies, cross-tabs, comparison of means, linear regression and others.[7] In recent years, PSPP has proven popular in the South.[8]
- Epi-Info is a series of microcomputer programs for word-processing, data management and epidemiological analysis, designed for analysing public health data and widely used in the South. Although its reference point is medical, it can be used for other kinds of survey. It is easy to use, but also offers programming languages for both data input and analysis, so permanent health information systems can be developed. It can generate a questionnaire as well as analyse the results.[9]
- Kwikstat is a shareware package running on PCs which does more than enough to analyse your data. Shareware is free software which can be downloaded from the internet. Search for 'shareware' and you should find it.

Spreadsheets

Microsoft Excel, Lotus 1-2-3 and Quattro Pro can be used for laying out tables and producing graphs to present your data. You could set up a data matrix on one. Data are entered as one huge table, with each row containing a case and each column a single variable. You can then apply various formulae to the data: they do everything a calculator does and a lot more. But spreadsheets are not designed to analyse research data, and some tasks, like cross-tabulation, though possible using pivot tables, can be a struggle.

An easy-to-use statistical analysis package is more helpful for these purposes. You can generally export data from a spreadsheet directly to such packages, which allows you to use the spreadsheet for easier data entry and statistical software for data manipulation and analysis (refer to your spreadsheet software's specific documentation for guidance on this process).

Database packages

Database software packages can be useful in data entry. Popular programs such as Microsoft Access or the open source MySQL (www.mysql.com) can design a set of data entry tables that match your questionnaire closely, so reducing the risk of mistakes. Data can then be exported to other packages for analysis. But databases are of limited value in research, as they cannot carry out the analyses you will need.

Online research packages

Online survey packages such as SurveyMonkey make analysis very easy – you undertake the analysis of your survey results inside their package. The most basic packages will undertake simple quantitative analysis for you and, if you pay a fee, you can get access to software that helps analyse qualitative responses as well.

13.8.5 Rigour in quantitative analysis

Essentially, this is common sense: to be satisfied with the honesty of the findings, the reader needs access to enough information to see what has been done and how. You need to describe fully the methods you used to reach your conclusions so another researcher can do what you did and get the same results.

Two key concepts need to be understood (Denscombe, 2010):

- In relation to research data, *validity* refers to whether or not the data reflect reality and cover the crucial matters. The question is 'Are we measuring what we intended to measure [are the right indicators being used] and are we getting accurate results?'
- Researchers need to feel confident their measurements are not affected by a research instrument (such as a questionnaire) that gives one reading on one occasion and a different one on the next, when there has been no real change in the item being measured. A good level of *reliability* means the research instrument produces the same data on each occasion it is used, and that any variation in the results reflects real variations in the thing being measured.

The techniques for piloting questionnaires (see Chapter 11) are important to increase confidence in the validity and reliability of your instruments. Your report should describe the piloting you did. Did respondents understand your questions as expected?

Response rates

You have to report what proportion of your original sample actually took part in the research. If the proportion is very small, it can undermine confidence in the findings' representativeness (see Chapter 10). It may be worth checking to see if those who took part reflect the sample you aimed to include. You could look at some obvious sources of bias, for example gender, area of origin, language spoken or income level.

You should describe any sources of bias you are aware of, and discuss how important you consider them to be. Equally, you should be honest about any problems you see with any analytical procedures you have undertaken. This will not undermine your work; on the contrary, it will show you understand its limitations.

Chapter 14, on how to write an effective research report, describes ways to present quantitative data images.

13.9 So what does it all mean?

During analysis, it is easy to lose sight of the bigger picture and imagine people will be interested in every detail of your findings. Sadly, they will not. It is now up to you to identify the most important aspects of your research in relation to what was previously known and the questions you were setting out to answer.

This step underscores the vital importance of careful thought at the design phase. Recall that, in Chapter 3, you established key questions and objectives to address throughout the research project. Analysis is always a taxing process, and one inevitably wants to collapse at the point when the data have been organized into a coherent picture. But this is when you need to find some new energy and look around you again.

There are sure to be lots of fascinating details, but what really is the significance of this work? What key evidence have you produced, and what exactly can it be said to show? Do your findings answer your key research questions? If so, to what degree? Do the answers confirm or diverge from what you expected to find? How have you contributed to and challenged existing knowledge? What are the implications for programme or policy change? Have you achieved your objectives? If not, why? Is more work needed?

If analysis is a process of breaking things down, then this is a process of synthesis – bringing them together again, but in a new form. For example, you may be able to bring together quantitative and qualitative information in a new way.

Meet those who have worked with you – co-researchers, community members, perhaps even funders – and brainstorm the key points you think are emerging. You might find it useful at this point to talk to a press officer or a friendly journalist. Journalists have a 'So what?' mentality: they want you to summarize the point in at most three sentences. This is always agonizing for the researcher, but is a good thing to learn to do. You may conclude that your research is aimed more at a knowledgeable audience who will make the effort to understand your more technical version of the findings, but at least have a go at producing a plain-language short statement.

It may be important at this stage to bring in data from other studies, or information from other sources – government statistics, newspaper reports (see Chapter 5). You can build confidence in the trustworthiness of your data by setting alongside it findings of other studies with similar findings. If your work appears to challenge the findings of other studies, it needs to discuss potential reasons for these differences.

Next, test the points you want to make by playing devil's advocate. Question and criticize your own conclusions and assumptions from the point of view of those you need to influence. You need to cover your back by anticipating and refuting the arguments that will be made against you. Give evidence – you can't ask your readers to make any leaps of faith. They may not share your value base, so why should they take your word for anything?

13.9.1   Writing recommendations

Practical research usually aims to produce recommendations for action based on its findings. Sometimes, ideas for action arise directly from the research process, and action may start at an early stage, especially in PLA-type projects. However, although respondents sometimes describe the problems well, they sometimes don't have much inspiration as to solutions.

At this point, you need to be very clear about the status of the research and your role in relation to making recommendations. If your research aims to 'give voice' to a group of people, it may be a good idea to ask community members what recommendations they think you should make. Group work can be better than individual interviews at helping people think into the future and be imaginative. People can build on each other's ideas and gain confidence from the group process.

You may also want to consult relevant implementing agencies, including any that have already been involved with the project. It is far more likely the research will have an impact if those who need to put recommendations into practice feel some ownership of it. It may be helpful to present key findings to a group of managers and practitioners, asking them to work out what should be done about problems identified. This could be done alongside consultation with community members.

However, you need to be clear whether your findings actually support any recommendations they are suggesting. There is no problem with agencies publishing their own response to your research, which can bring in new ideas, but these should not be presented as recommendations *of the research*. Your own recommendations must be linked directly to the data you have presented.

 # Key points from this chapter

Checklist: bringing it all together

- ☑ Consider the question – so what does this mean?
- ☑ Look at the bigger picture – what is important about this study in relation to key questions in this field?
- ☑ Look at your findings in relation to other important research in the field – does it support or challenge it?
- ☑ Ensure your data genuinely give evidence for your arguments.
- ☑ Test the claims you want to make, to cover your back.
- ☑ Consult respondents, community members and partner agencies about recommendations, but remember your findings must support these.

Further reading

The best two general accounts we have found of data analysis for practical small projects are:

Denscombe, M. (2010) *The Good Research Guide for Small-scale Social Research Projects*, 4th edn. Maidenhead and Philadelphia, PA: Open University Press.
Hall, D. and Hall, I. (1996) *Practical Social Research: Project Work in the Community*. Basingstoke: Macmillan.

More specialized texts

Agresti, A. and Finlay, B. (2009) *Statistical Methods for the Social Sciences, International Edition*. Upper Saddle River, NJ: Prentice Hall International.

A well-established, accessible introductory text for learning basic statistics, written for undergraduates and non-academics in a very clear, organized structure. Includes self-directed exercises at the end of each chapter to help test understanding.

Flick, U. (2009) *An Introduction to Qualitative Research*, 4th edn. New Delhi, Thousand Oaks, CA, London: Sage.

An excellent, succinct and very accessible overview of CAQDAS in Chapter 26, and good practical advice on both qualitative and quantitative analysis throughout.

Gilbert, N. (ed.) 'Social research update'. Available online at http://sru.soc.surrey.ac.uk.

A quarterly series of short papers on practical research issues, for example analysing qualitative data by computer and secondary analysis of qualitative data. Subscriptions free to researchers with addresses in the UK. All back issues available on the internet.

Golafshani, N. (2003) 'Understanding reliability and validity in qualitative research', *Qualitative Report*, 8 (4): 597–607.

Accessible academic article on reliability and validity in qualitative research.

Krueger, R. and Casey, M. (2000) *Focus Groups: A Practical Guide for Applied research*, 3rd edn. New Delhi, Thousand Oaks, CA, London: Sage.

Practical, friendly and thorough text on focus group research, with a deep but clear overview of analysing focus group data.

Nichols, P. (1991) 'Social survey methods: a field guide for development workers', *Development Guidelines* 6. Oxford: Oxfam.

On the analysis of quantitative research in developing countries.

Patton, M. (2001) *Qualitative Research and Evaluation Methods*, 3rd edn. New Delhi, Thousand Oaks, CA, London: Sage.

Very strong text on qualitative analysis, particularly Part 3 (qualitative analysis and interpretation and enhancing the quality and credibility of qualitative research). Addresses computer-assisted qualitative analysis, offers numerous strategic themes and criteria-based frameworks for analysis and is written clearly for a broad audience.

Notes

1 Some approaches preset categories at the start. These generally emphasize the use of quantitative methods and make for weak qualitative research.

2 CAQDAS Networking Project, Department of Sociology, University of Surrey, Guildford, GU2 7XH. Tel: +44 (0)1483 683053. Email: z.tenger@surrey.ac.uk. The website (http://caqdas.soc.surrey.ac.uk) includes discussion groups, lists of software, demo software that can be downloaded, etc., and has links to companies that produce this kind of software, a guide to choosing the right software package and up-to-date comparative reviews of the leading programs. This is a very good place to start.

3 Tel: +44 (0)845 111 5555 (a Sage helpline number for all its software). Email at support@sage.com. Website: www.sage.co.uk/contact_us.aspx.

4 See Chapter 10 on sampling for more on this.

5 For guidance on how to use SPSS, see, for example, Argyrous (2005). SPSS is available from SPSS UK Ltd, St Andrews House, West Street, Woking, Surrey, GU21 1EB. Tel: +44 (0)1483 71920, IBM worldwide and sales offices located in a number of countries, listed at www.spss.com/worldwide/.

6 The University of California, Los Angeles, maintains a useful website for guidance and links on using Stata at www.ats.ucla.edu/stat/stata. Stata is available through a number of global distributors, listed at www.stata.com/worldwide.

7 PSPP can be downloaded for free at www.gnu.org/software/pspp.

8 The South African Statistical Association, for instance, presented a 2006 conference which included an analysis of how PSPP can be used as a free replacement to SPSS.

9 Epi-Info is public domain software and is distributed free by the Centers for Disease Control (CDC) and the World Health Organization. The CDC's Epi-Info home page is at www.cdc.gov/epo/epi/epiinfo.htm. You can download the software from there, in a vast range of languages (the website gives addresses to write to for the translated materials). Alternatively, you can purchase it from the suppliers, which also includes the users' manual (which is of course helpful): Public Health Foundation, PO Box 753, Waldorf, MD, 20604, US. Tel: +1301 645 7773. Email: info@phf.org. Or you can copy it legally from someone else's computer.

14

WRITING EFFECTIVELY

This chapter helps you to write about your research – especially to write reports, press releases and policy briefs, which are usually necessary to present your findings. We start by giving some guidance about writing style, what you need to include and what you can leave out, and then discuss how to go about the task of writing. Not all research must be presented in report format: as Chapter 15 on promoting research uptake will show, other measures can be more effective, including, for example, face-to-face feedback to communities and/or decision makers. Sometimes, findings begin to have influence long before any report is written – when key stakeholders take action as a result of information they themselves generate.

Learning about poverty in Mozambique

The Mozambique Participatory Poverty Assessment (PPA) team took a long time to produce an overall poverty assessment for the country, but in the meantime achieved purposeful collaboration among many organizations and government agencies. Two types of policy-relevant information were apparent:

- Outputs from wealth-ranking and problem-ranking exercises were immediately impressive, and were put to direct policy use, even in rough form and with little analysis. They helped to identify priority problems as perceived by those concerned.
- Equally important, but more complex, were findings derived from the aggregation (adding together) of livelihood analyses. These touched on many areas of life, and had the potential to illuminate the collective and multidimensional causes and consequences of poverty. Achieving this required more complex, sustained analysis and study.

Source: Owen (1998)

FOR EXAMPLE

Reports and related short written products are not an end in themselves, and collaborative working should not be sacrificed to achieve tidy outputs on paper. Nevertheless, for most substantial pieces of research, it will be necessary to write a report of some kind, if only to decide for yourselves what your findings mean. Once you have done this, it becomes much easier to write short summaries, policy briefs or articles, and to publicize your message through verbal presentations, press releases and so on. Reports are also important to create a permanent record of the information collected and to prevent future duplication of effort.

ACTIVITY 14.1

What makes a good research report?

Brainstorm with a group of colleagues what you look for in a research report. Try to think of real examples you have admired, and identify why they were effective.

14.1　What to write

It is important to tailor reports and articles to their audience, and for them to be part of a wider promotional strategy.

14.1.1　Style of writing

Your style should be determined by your own natural way of expressing yourself and the needs of your audience. However, while some audiences might be impressed by a complex way of writing, the main purpose of the exercise is to convey information. The crucial thing is to encourage people to actually read it. Clear and simple expression will help people to make sense of the material you present, and therefore to act on it.

The plain English/plain writing movement

In 2010, the US government instituted regulations forcing official documentation to comply with standards in line with a broader 'plain English' movement, which has been adopted throughout the US legal and academic sectors. This demands writing which is accessible, understandable and appropriate to the reading level and knowledge base of a specific audience. (These principles apply to all languages, although certain specific grammatical points may vary.)
Documents written in plain English

- are organized to serve the reader's needs, including useful headings;
- use short sections and sentences;
- use the simplest tense possible;
- omit excess words;
- use concrete, familiar words;

- use 'must' to express requirements;
- use lists and tables to simplify complex material;
- use no more than two or three subordinate levels;
- use the active voice.

This before and after example, drawn from a US Environmental Protection Agency campaign to lower water usage, demonstrates how effective plain language can be in improving conciseness and clarity.

Before: 'This program promotes efficient water use in homes and businesses throughout the country by offering a simple way to make purchasing decisions that conserve water without sacrificing quality or product performance.'

After: 'This program helps homeowners and businesses buy products that use less water without sacrificing quality or performance.'

Source: www.plainlanguage.gov/howto/index.cfm.

Style of writing

In a group discussion, the facilitator should write the following statements on a flip chart for participants (individually, in pairs or altogether) to criticize. (Here, they have been written with the problem words or phrases underlined; on the flip chart, the underlining should not be shown.)

- Ribero says that half the children in Peru work.
- Many Ethiopian elderly people suffer from malnutrition.
- UNICEF says that urbanization in Africa is increasing. More women and children are migrating from rural areas to towns, and this 'contributes to the lack of housing infrastructure' (Smithson). NGOs are also concerned about growing numbers of CEDC and delinquents. The resulting misery can only be eradicated by drastic government action and should be supported by international aid agencies.

Source: Boyden and Ennew (1997)

ACTIVITY 14.2

If you are presenting a lot of quantitative data, use charts and diagrams to make it easier to understand (see below for guidance). Some people find flowcharts helpful in understanding how systems work. But do not let charts get too complicated – present only essential data in this way. You can use appendices for those which include necessary information but would disrupt the flow of your argument if included in the main body of the text.

14.2 What not to write

What you leave out is as important as what you put in. Don't attempt to include all of your data: include only the minimum necessary to fulfil the aims of your

project. If you did some fieldwork which was not very helpful or relevant, you might refer to it in an appendix, but you need not describe it or its findings in your main report.

Plagiarism – the unattributed theft of another author's words or ideas to present as your own – is totally unacceptable in any form of published research. Most often, however, plagiarism occurs because of carelessness on the part of well-meaning researchers or lack of clarity regarding proper citation procedure. It is therefore very important to know the key rules in this regard, which means using footnotes or in-text citations and quote marks appropriately. First, when using someone else's exact words, always use quote marks and follow the quote immediately with a citation to the original work. Data which are not your own also require reference to the origin. Second, if paraphrasing someone else's ideas or arguments, provide acknowledgement of ownership in the same text, along with a citation. When in doubt, cite.

14.3 What must be included

Checklist: what to include in your report

- ☑ Contents list;
- ☑ Summary;
- ☑ Introduction giving background and rationale – why did you undertake this study?
- ☑ Details of funding and partner agencies (with brief descriptions);
- ☑ Original aims and objectives;
- ☑ Brief literature review (see Chapter 5);
- ☑ Account of the methods you used (for analysis as well as for data collection) – can go in an appendix;
- ☑ Description of the sample, how it was drawn and any problems you see with it;
- ☑ Presentation of your findings;
- ☑ Conclusion – overall value of the study;
- ☑ Policy and/or practice recommendations, where appropriate – already discussed with key players;
- ☑ Full references for any research you cite.

We are not advising you to create a section headed 'discussion', 'analysis' or 'synthesis', as is usual in some academic traditions. Chapter 13 emphasized the importance of bringing your ideas together, but this process should inform the whole approach to presenting your findings, and should not necessarily form a separate section set out alongside the data.

The most effective research reports in terms of having an influence weave new findings with information about the context of the research and data from existing research. Headings should be relevant to the questions the reader has in her mind – or to the way respondents think about the issues. This is not a report on a scientific experiment where methods, data and discussion are set out separately. Remember to include information about issues you looked for but did not find, for example issues you expected community members to be concerned about but which they did not bring forward.

14.3.1 Summaries

Many people will read only your summary, so it is worth spending some time getting it right. This means it should be very short (maximum three pages and preferably one) and straightforward, using plain language. Different types of summary are needed for different purposes. An executive summary is addressed to an agency that commissioned it and will use it directly to take decisions, so just call it a summary if what it does is summarize the contents of the report. Obviously, the key findings are its core, but you also need to include some contextual information, research aims and objectives, perhaps a few short quotes if this will show the strength of your research and any key recommendations.

Academic articles traditionally have a type of summary called an abstract, which is typically 100–500 words long. (Individual journals and research institutes have differing requirements.) An abstract should include the topic or research question, theories and methods used, details of the sample and conclusions reached.

14.3.2 Forewords or prefaces

When you want to add authority to your publication, you might ask someone to write a foreword to it. This lends their support to your message and may help politically as well as perhaps encouraging people to read it. Who you ask depends on what you need: you could ask a well-known person with an interest in your field, a senior manager of your own organization or someone who represents the community you have worked with.

14.3.3 Introductions

The introduction is very important, as some readers may never get any further – it needs to draw them in. By this point you are over-familiar with the issues, and probably rather tired of the data. But you need to start at the beginning for the reader, and take them through the logic that led you to design your project as you did. Aim to interest them in the questions you were interested in. Include some contextual information, perhaps about the area you are working in, your own programme or broader initiatives relevant to this one. But make sure this is carefully chosen and relevant – too many reports start with context of the 'Mali is a country in West Africa' kind – any reader interested in your findings will already know this. Get quickly to the point of this report, giving broader background later, if necessary. State your ultimate research objectives and expectations clearly here, to prepare readers for the following discussion. Provide a brief background on funding and partner agency details.

FOR EXAMPLE

Ask someone who knows: the case of the UK Chapter for Learning

A Charter for Learning for people with learning difficulties in UK adult education was produced with strong participation by people with learning difficulties themselves. It had a preface by Eve Rank-Petruzziello, who was a member of the government's Disability Rights Commission and was the first person with learning difficulties to sit on this kind of important committee. The editor of the report worked with her to get on paper what she wanted to say about the Charter.

Source: Jacobsen (2000)

14.3.4 Literature reviews

Literature reviews should show the reader how you are adding to an existing body of knowledge, and what your conceptual framework or approach is. Does other research support or contradict your findings? What light does it throw on them, or they on it? The literature review is a critical component of the report, but you have some choices in how you present it. The most common way is to dedicate a section of the report at the outset to reviewing existing research. Other researchers prefer to weave insights from the wider literature throughout the text, supporting the discussion of their findings in a more organic way. While we generally recommend the latter approach, the choice is up to you. Chapter 5 discusses literature reviews in fuller depth.

14.3.5 Describing the methods

A brief but complete account of the methods used is part of researchers' accountability for their work. It enables readers to decide for themselves how much weight to put on findings and how to interpret them. But how much emphasis to put on process as opposed to findings is something to judge in relation to the particular project. If the methods are particularly interesting, write them up fully – but people who are interested in the findings may be different to those who are interested in the methodology. Even if your methods were not innovative, it can save future researchers huge amounts of trouble if you describe clearly what you did and any problems and how you solved them. You could write two different kinds of report, one for each audience.

At a minimum, you should include the approaches and techniques you used and why, whether ethical clearance was required and obtained, sample size and how it was drawn, how people were approached and response rates. Say how well you felt your methods worked, and whether you would do it differently another time. You should also explain how you analysed the data. Did you do quantitative analysis by hand or on a computer (which software)? Why do you have confidence in your analysis? (See also Chapter 13.)

14.3.6 Presenting findings

You have to think carefully about how to present your findings to the reader. There are important differences involved in presenting quantitative and qualitative data, as well as specific considerations to take into account when discussing particularly sensitive or controversial issues. This section offers advice on how to present all three types of data.

Presenting quantitative data

Some ways of presenting quantitative data are better than others. Most importantly, try to present your data in visual form – many people find diagrams and charts much easier to learn from than figures typed in the text. Statistical programs but also spreadsheets and even word-processing packages can easily produce all kinds of diagrams and charts (see Section 13.8 on this topic). But you still need to make sure you use them in a way that makes sense. It is easy to get carried away or overwhelmed!

Note that the way you present graphs and charts can mislead the reader. Keep control of the scales on both axes of a chart throughout your document to ensure you do not distort the way data should be understood. It is fine to add footnotes to tables if you think they are needed.

Charts

If you are presenting your data in charts, the text can discuss just the key material from these – you do not need to describe the complete dataset in the text as well as visually. The important general rules are to:

- keep it simple.
- avoid including so many data the reader is unable to make sense of them.
- choose an appropriate type of table or chart for your purpose.
- always give the total number of cases you are reporting on: n = ?
- help the reader with visual clues and clear presentation.

Tables

People often present tables without all the information you need to understand them. Usually, this is because the writer is over-familiar with the information – but it may be entirely unknown to the reader, so tables need to include the following information:

- a title, fully explaining the point of the table;
- a number, for reference and to show where it goes in relation to the text;
- the name of the column variable (for example income), and its categories or values (perhaps income bands), especially any unit they come in (£, $, etc.);
- the name of the row variable, to the left of the table reading across, and its categories or values and the unit they come in;
- the actual number for respondents who fall into the relevant categories, in each 'cell' of the table – and for the total sample involved;
- totals for both rows and columns;
- percentage figures alongside the actual number, clearly labelled as such – also show the percentage total of 100 for clarity;
- statistical information such as significance test figures, where appropriate;
- the source of the data, if they were originally produced elsewhere.

Bar charts

Bar charts are a good way of presenting simple information about frequencies. The bars should be of equal width, with their height representing frequency or amount for each separate category. The item on the horizontal axis (the independent variable) is usually discrete or categorical – it falls into distinct groups such as countries. Bar charts are easy to read providing you do not include too many categories (beyond 10).

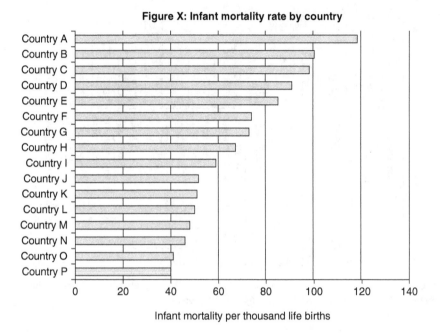

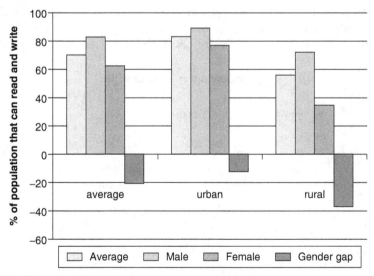

Figure 14.1   Example of bar charts

Source: http://web.worldbank.org/WBSITE/EXTERNAL/TOPICS/EXTCY/EXTECD/0,,contentMDK:202 16717~menuPK:524407~pagePK:148956~piPK:216618~theSitePK:344939,00.html

Stacked bar charts make it possible to show the component elements of the total within a category.

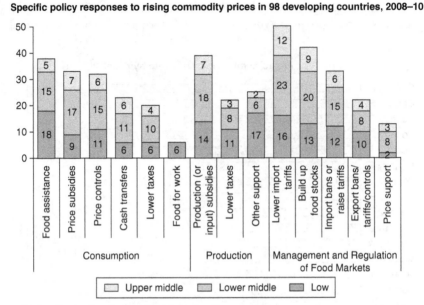

Figure 14.2   Example of a stacked bar chart

Sources: Demeke et al. (2009), FAO (2009a; 2010a, K and I) and International Monetary Fund country reports (2009–10) in www.oxfamblogs.org/fp2p/?tag=unicef.

Line graphs

A line graph is used to depict development or progression in a sequence of data. It is most commonly used to show change over time, with time plotted from left to right on the horizontal axis. Line graphs work best with large datasets and big variations.

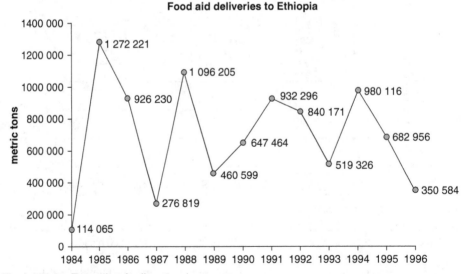

Figure 14.3   Example of a line graph

Source: http://reliefweb.int/node/70175.

Pie charts

Pie charts present data as segments of a whole pie. They show clearly the proportions of each category that make up the total. Usually, the segments are presented as percentages. To highlight a particular segment, for example the proportion of government expenditure invested in health from a pie chart illustrating expenditure allocations across sectors, it can be helpful to separate out that segment from the rest of the pie.

Pie charts are visually powerful, but they can't be used to compare two values, as with the other charts described above. However, it is possible to use two or more pie charts, perhaps of different sizes, in proportion to the absolute figures expressed, to make comparisons. It is good practice to show the figure for the percentages, where possible within the segments.

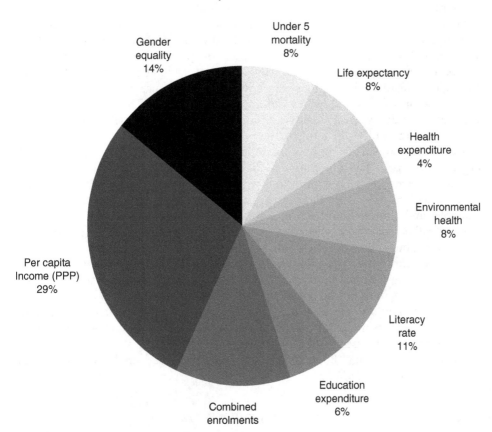

Investing in people: expenditure allocated to different aspects of human welfare

Figure 14.4 Example of a pie chart

Source: www.usaid.gov/locations/europe_eurasia/wp/MCP_Methodology.html.

Checklist: presenting quantitative data

- ☑ Choose an appropriate way of presenting the data – make sure they make sense.
- ☑ Keep it simple – don't include too much data in one chart.
- ☑ Don't go mad with the charts and diagrams – present only important data in this form, and only those you have reasonable confidence in.
- ☑ Make sure tables and charts have informative titles and labels for all their content.
- ☑ Include clear information about the units of measurement for each category.
- ☑ Make sure the source of any information from another study is given clearly.

Presenting qualitative data

Qualitative data – in the form of written or recorded transcripts, subjective observations, recorded responses, texts, etc. – tend to be densely packed, with multiple themes and avenues of analysis. Their rich multidimensional nature can also present a real challenge in terms of knowing where to begin with presentation, which often demands both writing and analysis skills. Some basic guidelines are as follows.

First, decide on a basic framework for organizing your qualitative findings to help guide the reader through your discussion. Much of this structure is already waiting for you – work done in your methodology preparation and subsequent data analysis should have given you an idea of an outline. Individual or groups of questions from your semi-structured interviews, focus groups or questionnaires can form natural subsections of discussion (Chenail, 1995). However, don't just organize a report through the headings of the interview schedule – make sure your reporting makes sense in terms of how the reader will approach the issues. The key themes which emerged from across your qualitative data provide a readymade template of individual headings under which to structure the content and flow of your discussion.

Second, as you will always have limitations in terms of page length (and the reader's attention span), it is important to be as strategic as possible about the most effective and efficient way to juxtapose your written analysis with actual examples pulled from your data (Chenail, 1995). This often means being strict about how many examples and quotes you include in each section, and knowing when to summarize findings rather than 'show' them. Excerpts from interviews might be fascinating and informative, but if they are overly long and break up the flow of your writing, they can bore or completely lose your reader. This material can always be moved to an appendix if you feel it is too important to leave out, or even made available as a separate document or posted online.

Third, you have a tremendous degree of flexibility and space for creativity in how you approach presentation of your data. A conventional layout addresses the major themes or questions raised in the research, supported by both illustrative examples and references to key findings. But there are many ways to frame such discussions (see, for example, Chenail 1995).

Presenting sensitive or controversial issues

Sometimes, the process of analysis and writing makes issues clear – and sometimes it identifies areas where there are real contradictions between different points of view.

When you have conflicting data, one response is simply to set these out, perhaps side-by-side in two or more columns, and let the readers see the tensions for themselves. Perhaps a group of parents and a group of teenagers have produced entirely different perspectives on the same issue. It is not your role to sit in judgement on them, although you could put people's views into context by giving information about the situations they face. It is fine to describe dilemmas or tensions as well as to lay out recommendations. This can give a framework for discussing difficult issues tactfully.

While we are on this subject, there is the question of what to do when your findings are strongly critical of the government or some other agency. This book urges you to involve key players in your project from the start, to avoid your research report becoming a site of confrontation. Assuming your aim is to change the behaviour of the criticized agency, rather than to confront it, it is best to approach it directly, before publication, and let people see what you are saying. It may be appropriate to give them some way of responding publicly to your findings, perhaps by speaking at your launch event, or writing a short statement of response you can include in your report.

However, you should not compromise honest presentation of your findings. There may be times when criticism is justified and necessary. If this makes you uncomfortable, keep in mind that the practice has a strong tradition within academic scholarship, where it is seen as an opportunity to engage with wider research debates and advance knowledge. Furthermore, if you can't involve your audience in the process of the research, then publishing the report has to be seen as part of a campaigning process. Unless it is absolutely unavoidable, though, do not criticize any individuals by name. Be aware of the law on libel, as well as the danger of diverting attention from the issues.

Don't feel it is necessarily your responsibility to find a solution to the problems your research exposes. Take the analysis as far as you can, and reflect carefully on whether or not you can give guidance for action. Sometimes, the best we can do is present problems clearly, in context, and invite others to engage with us in addressing them.

Finally, be very careful to maintain in the final write-up any anonymity you promised your participants during data collection. Keep an eye out for anything that might jeopardize this and err on the side of caution.

14.4 How to write: the process

The task of writing a major report can loom large, and you have to make space for it.

- Get started – don't put it off. Decide on the day and time you will start, and start then, whatever excuses present themselves!
- Don't leave all the analysis and writing to the last minute. Aim to start the final report with lots of materials to work from. The worst thing is facing a blank sheet with your data disorganized and no part of the material already written up. You should already have:
  - o organized and analysed your data;
  - o drafted some sections, for example your survey of existing information or reports on elements of the data collection (a set of focus groups, some observations);
  - o worked on a synthesis – bringing it together, asking what it means (see Chapter 13).
- Draft an outline early on – you can always change it later. This is a working document: it can include just headings or have some phrases to help you

remember what needs to go in each section. You might consult colleagues on your outline.

- Break down the task. Doing an outline will help you with this.
- Start wherever seems easiest (often in the middle), working from some data you are interested in. It is never a good idea to try to write a report from beginning to end. These are the most difficult parts to write, and the most likely to be read. Write them when you are well into your flow and know what needs to go into them.
- Think of it as a draft, and learn to accept others' criticisms and suggestions: rewriting is very valuable. Occasionally, people make comments that are impossible to make use of, but usually asking colleagues or other knowledgeable people to read and comment will improve your text hugely. You don't have to incorporate everything everyone says, but do think about why they have made their suggestions.
- Write as directly and clearly as possible.
- Keep your audience in mind. Choose someone you want to address – not someone hostile, but someone who needs to know what this research says and is interested – and write for them.
- Remember where your readers are. Explain why you decided to do this research in the first place, why it is important.

14.4.1   Dealing with procrastination

Procrastination affects even the most experienced writers, and there may be points at which you or your team of researchers find yourselves suffering from lack of motivation. Often, such frustrating delays stem not from laziness but from a fear your work might not be good enough; sometimes, the task ahead seems unmanageable. Luckily, there are several strategies for overcoming procrastination. Perhaps the best is to divide a large task into smaller, more manageable subtasks, and begin working on them right away to get back into the writing process.

Blaxter et al. (2010) offer a useful checklist of additional 'emergency' steps you can take to restart your productivity:

- Take notes on reading materials, interviews and discussions with supervisors and managers.
- Do smaller, more approachable tasks to get back into writing: type up references, quotes you might use, points you will refer to or chapter or section structures.
- Set a daily or weekly word target.
- Record your thoughts, then transcribe them.
- Work out how many words you will devote to each chapter, section or subsection.
- Set yourself a word limit, then edit what you have written.
- Think about all the other times you have procrastinated and what you did about it.
- Don't allow yourself to do anything else until you have written something.
- Give someone else the responsibility to oversee your writing.
- Talk it through with someone else.
- Try writing at a different time of the day or the week.
- Just write anything.

14.4.2 After the first complete draft

A lot of work remains to be done even after you have written your first full draft. If you are involved in any sort of collaborative process, you must show the draft to others. It may be that community members are involved and you want to hear their comments, probably also setting up a verbal presentation of the main points to enable those who will not read complex written materials to have a say.

Editing processes can be quite problematic when many interests are at work. Sometimes, it is only at this point that different participants' expectations are declared, and this can be difficult to handle. In our experience, most authors can improve a document by about 25 per cent in light of comments at this point – not more. If a great transformation is required, think again about how to achieve this – and whether it is wise to try. Go back to the brief and see what it says.

Support and supervision need to be sustained into the writing-up and editing periods. Sometimes, what seems to be writer's block really points to issues within the work which need further discussion.

Also, consider the possibility of presenting an adapted version of your rough draft as an unofficial working paper to an academic or professional audience. This would offer an opportunity to pilot the actual release of your report in a professionally safe environment, and to elicit critical feedback when it matters most – before the final draft and publication. It would also give you a chance to build potential networks which might be called on in the research promotion stage. To do this, you can look for calls for papers for academic workshops and conferences, or organize your own informal event with colleagues or the local community.

14.4.3 After the final draft

Even after you have sent your text off to be published there will be further work to do. It is very important to thoroughly proofread text, tables and diagrams, making sure spelling and grammar are correct. It is easy for mistakes to creep in, even though printed text is usually taken directly from the author's digital file. For example, a paragraph can simply be lost if it doesn't fit on a page and someone loses concentration. (You may have one last chance to review the document in the form of page proofs – a final copy of the manuscript which has been edited and formatted carefully by the publisher.) Have a good check at the last minute, before the report is printed.

Checklist: before sending a publication to the printer's

☑ All the text is where it should be.
☑ The credits and acknowledgements include everyone they should.
☑ The publication is dated and an address is included.
☑ The title is interesting and communicative – avoid 'Final Report of Long and Complicated Project in Obscure Place by Five Organizations with Long Names' syndrome.
☑ Anonymity of respondents is maintained effectively.
☑ There is a blurb (short advertising paragraph) on the back to tell readers what the report is about and who it is for.
☑ Tables, charts and diagrams are complete and properly labelled.
☑ References are complete.
☑ There is an International Standard Book Number (ISBN) (see Chapter 5).

You may think of these as technical tasks for someone else, but nowadays, with desktop publishing software, there are often no technical experts involved in producing a report. In any case, researchers need to remain involved to ensure the message does not get distorted further along the chain. For example, people may be tempted to try to spread the word further by introducing titles or publicity materials which make generalizations and in effect claim more than the report can properly support.

Checklist: writing effective research reports

☑ Write in your own voice, adapted to your audience.
☑ Present information in an unemotional way, but let respondents' voices come through.
☑ Make it as short and simple as possible.
☑ Start by planning an outline, giving the report a logical structure.

☑ Include:

 ☑ an appropriate summary;
 ☑ a brief description of the methods used and how well these worked;
 ☑ an account of the sample, how people were contacted and any problems you see with it.

☑ Expect to rewrite several times – consult partners, including community members, on drafts.

14.5 Writing press releases, policy briefs or journal articles

In order to influence your target audience, it is critical to devise a research communication strategy that sets out how you will use your report to communicate its key findings (see Chapter 15). As part of this process, it may be advantageous to produce a press release and/or policy brief to accompany the release of the final report. These two formats are very different, and each has certain features to consider: a press release is designed to announce a research project's findings to the media, whereas a policy brief is written with a targeted audience of policymakers in mind. However, both rely on your ability to relate your key points clearly and succinctly to very busy people (journalists and policymakers), and both require forethought in terms of considering your target.

14.5.1 Press releases

Writing a press release to attract media attention to your research ties into broader research promotion strategies, as outlined in Chapter 15. If you or your organization has access to a press office, you should always try to involve a press officer at the first opportunity, as they are well practised in this task. Key points are as follows (adapted from: www.esrc.ac.uk/_images/Guide_to_publicising_your_event_tcm8-5093.pdf):

- Keep the document brief: press releases are typically around 500 words long.
- Begin with an attention-grabbing headline.
- Follow the inverted pyramid rule of journalism and answer the 'five w's' (who, what, when, where, why) in the first paragraph to ensure information is imparted even to readers who do not read to the very end.
- Remember the layout is the inverse of an academic report: to catch the attention of journalists, present the conclusions and implications first, not last.
- Avoid technical jargon and write in a simple, easy-to-understand style (see above on 'plain writing'). Explain any necessary technical terms at the outset.
- Include quotes – ideally from local community members and/or authoritative figures in your field – which can easily be 'pulled' for use by journalists.
- Always include contact details.

FOR EXAMPLE

Overseas Development Institute press release

The following is a recent online press release from ODI. It is designed to communicate the main research findings, even for those who read only the first paragraph. It includes quotes from relevant experts and answers the 'five w's'. It ends with a direct hyperlink to the report in question, as well as relevant work by ODI on the same issue.

New analysis reveals African countries are making progress towards the MDGs, 22 June 2010

As G-8 and G-20 leaders prepare to gather in Canada, new analysis issued by the Overseas Development Institute (ODI) and the UN Millennium Campaign finds that, in absolute terms, many of the world's poorest countries are making the most overall progress towards achieving the Millennium Development Goals (MDGs) – the set of promises world leaders made to significantly reduce extreme poverty, illiteracy and disease by 2015. Eleven of the 20 countries making the most absolute progress on the MDGs are amongst the poorest countries in Africa; half of African countries are on track to meet the target of halving poverty by 2015.

'This study decisively establishes with hard evidence that much of the negative reporting on progress on the MDGs is misleading,' said Salil Shetty, Director of the UN Millennium Campaign. 'Instead of lamenting that Africa might miss the MDG targets, we should be celebrating the real changes that have happened in the lives of millions of poor people, not least because of the unified effort between governments and citizens, supported by donors.'

'This study seeks to broaden the debate about MDG progress. The first findings show that progress is taking place, sometimes in unexpected places,' said ODI Director Dr. Alison Evans. 'In a world where support for development is under increasing scrutiny, we hope that this work will contribute to a broader appreciation of how we assess progress to date.'

The analysis focused on progress on Goal 1, which seeks to eradicate extreme poverty and hunger; Goal 4, to reduce child mortality; and Goal 5, to improve maternal health – all issues on the agenda of this week's G-8. Amongst the findings:

- The largest number of reductions of deaths of children under the age of five occurred in regions with the highest initial levels of such deaths, such as sub-Saharan Africa and South Asia.
- Even though the Goal of reducing maternal mortality has seen the least progress, access to maternal health services has improved in 80 per cent of countries.
- Countries making the most relative progress tend to be middle income countries, such as Ecuador, China, Thailand, Brazil and Egypt.

The research was funded by the Bill & Melinda Gates Foundation and the UN Millennium Campaign. The analysis is based on the MDG database, with the exception of income poverty data for Africa, which are based on the ReSAKSS database. The data on equity – the distribution of progress within a country – are based on household Demographic Health Surveys and Multiple Indicator Cluster Surveys. Where the available data permit, countries have been compared over the same time period against average annual rates of progress, irrespective of population size.

Source: ODI (2010)

14.5.2   Policy briefs

A policy brief is a short document presenting the key findings and recommendations of your research to a non-specialist audience, and represents an important tool in communicating research findings to policy audiences (Young and Quinn, 2002). It should be a standalone document focused on a single topic, typically 1,500 words (that is, two to four pages), supported by both text and graphics.

Presenting your evidence in the form of an argument policymakers will find persuasive is at the core of a good policy brief. This must be tailored to the specific policy context: address the needs of the target audience, link the information presented to specific policy processes and provide clear and feasible recommendations on policy steps to take. If you have the opportunity, you could tailor policy briefs to different policy actors. Make sure recommendations are actionable and clearly connected to specific decision-making junctures in the policymaking process – a critical consideration for policymakers under pressure to deliver rapid and visible impacts. Wherever possible, include a Southern component to your evidence-informed opinions.

Recommendations must also take into account underlying power relations impacting the policy analysis – for particularly controversial recommendations, you need to find a delicate balance between advocating change and avoiding alienating your readers. That being said, don't shy away from opinion and value judgements. You are absolutely justified in offering your own perspective on the policy implications of your research, although you should do so in a way that clearly differentiates those aspects of your argument which are opinion based from those which are evidence based.

For this reason, it is a good idea to sit down and think strategically about how best to target your brief before you begin writing. Here, ODI (2009) suggests several useful questions to ask yourself and your colleagues.

• Which stage(s) in the policymaking process are you trying to influence?
• Which stakeholders have been/are involved at each stage of the policymaking process?
• Have you identified a clear problem to address? Can you summarize it in two sentences?
• Do you have sufficiently comprehensive evidence to support your claim that a problem exists?
• Have you outlined and evaluated possible policy options that could solve this problem? What evaluation criteria did you use?

- Have you decided on a preferred alternative?
- Do you have sufficient evidence to argue effectively for your chosen policy alternative over the others?

Once you have considered these questions carefully, it is time to write. Here, you want to use as clear language as possible in distilling your main points down to essential information. Policymakers tend to be generalists, so it is especially important to keep your language clear, jargon-free and pitched towards educated non-specialists. You will also want to follow a general outline based on the following:

1 The *title* should be of immediate interest to the reader, as with a newspaper headline. Consider using verbs in the title to make it more dynamic, or phrasing it in the form of a question – for example 'How effective have new aid modalities been in Africa?' – to raise curiosity.

2 A very short *executive summary* is an overview which serves to distil the essence of the brief for busy readers, while at the same time acting as a 'hook' to entice them to read further. It should appear on the cover, or at the top of the first page, and contain the overarching message of the study.

3 A good *introduction* answers the central question 'Why is this research important?' It should describe your research objective, provide a general overview of your findings and conclusions and generate curiosity about the rest of the brief.

4 In describing your research *approach*, you should offer the reader a concise summary of the background and context to your investigation, and describe the research and analysis that took place – including a review of your methodology and who specifically undertook data collection and analysis. This is an important opportunity to ensure transparency while simultaneously highlighting the strengths and contribution of your research.

5 What did you learn? The *results* section should include a summary of the key findings, beginning with a broad overview and moving from general to specific details as space allows. It is very important here to focus on making content as easy to follow and understand for the reader as possible.

6 In the *conclusion*, interpret your data for the reader, aiming for concrete conclusions they can consider. Here is where you make your strongest assertions, but at the same time the ideas you raise need to be balanced, defensible and grounded in your data.

7 Flowing directly from the conclusion are the *implications* you draw out of your findings: What policy changes or actions do the results of your study point to? What do you believe will be the natural consequences of your findings? The *recommendations* are the actionable steps you personally suggest policymakers take next. You need to decide whether to provide implications, recommendations or both: if you decide to call for policy recommendations, make sure they are actionable, as precise as possible, credible, feasible and relevant to the context.

Finally, your policy paper needs to be visually engaging and attractively formatted, with information presented in charts, graphs, explanatory diagrams, photos and easily digestible bullet points. A visually as well as conceptually engaging document is critically important to hold a policymaker's interest: it is well worth devoting careful thought to graphics and layout. One common visual tool is the sidebar or textbox, a short insert examining a specific aspect of the research. This breaks up the main text and can hook the reader's attention very effectively.

Checklist: writing effective policy briefs

A good policy paper should:

- ☑ define and detail an urgent policy issue or issues within the current policy framework which needs to be addressed;
- ☑ outline the possible means by which this issue could be acted on immediately;
- ☑ provide an evaluation of the probable outcomes of these options based on an outlined framework of analysis and the evidence from the current policy framework;
- ☑ choose a preferred alternative (policy recommendation) and provide a strong argument to establish why your choice is the best possible policy option;
- ☑ be tailored to the specific policy context and policymaking audience you are trying to influence;
- ☑ be written with an awareness of underlying power relations and political sensitivities, while also presenting your opinions and forcefully advocating for change;
- ☑ be visually engaging and attractively formatted;
- ☑ be short – 2–4 pages maximum.

Source: Jones and Walsh (2008); Start and Hovland (2007)

14.5.3 Professional and academic journal articles

Finally, you may also want to publish your findings in a professional or peer-reviewed academic journal – this process can lend both visibility and an additional level of scholarly legitimacy to your research. It is likely that a development worker would need help from someone with more academic training to get such an article published. A journal article is a fairly short format – often between 5,000 and 10,000 words – but at the same time may prove attractive in allowing you the freedom to dig a bit more deeply into some of the theoretical issues that need too much discussion for a press release or policy brief. You should consider carefully whether you intend your discussion to focus on theory or empirical data, and whether the article itself will represent a broad summary of your research or a more detailed look at one aspect of it. Often, choosing one theme, case study or dimension of your argument to consider in detail is a better idea than trying to summarize the full scope of a research project – but either option is perfectly viable, as long as you pay careful attention to the word count.

Writing an article requires you to submit your written work first to the journal's editors for consideration – be aware this process can often be a slow one, and also involves the potential for rewrites. Some journals have submissions read by independent referees before deciding on which to publish. Keep in mind that journals' stylistic conventions vary. It is wise to check first to see the format and length they demand before writing.

 ## Key points from this chapter

Communicating your findings in writing is a critical part of the research process and one where a strategic approach can reap important dividends. This checklist recaps the key points in the chapter to guide you in this process:

Checklist

Find a writing style which balances your own natural way of expressing yourself with the needs of your audience. Always write in a clear and simple manner that allows your reader to understand, and act upon, the material you present.

- ☑ Refer to the checklist on p. 291 for what to include in your report.
- ☑ Pay careful attention to your introduction and summary, which may often be the only part of your report people read.
- ☑ Use charts and diagrams to make quantitative data easier to understand. Clearly title all charts, tables and graphs with proper titles and units of measurements.
- ☑ In presenting qualitative data, be strict about the number of anecdotes and quotes you include. Know when to summarize data instead of 'showing' it.
- ☑ Avoid procrastination when writing: set deadlines and hold yourself accountable to others. Break larger writing task down into smaller, more manageable steps, and begin wherever it is easiest.
- ☑ Leave time and energy for the editing process (particularly if the work is collaborative). Consider presenting early rough drafts to academic or professional audiences for feedback.
- ☑ Refer to the checklist on p. 302 for final steps before sending a publication to the printers.
- ☑ For press releases, avoid technical jargon, follow the 'inverted pyramid rule' of journalism, answer the 'five w's', and always include your personal contact details.
- ☑ Refer to the checklist on p. 306 for key ingredients of an effective policy brief.
- ☑ Professional and academic journal articles provide the chance to develop the theoretical themes of your research. Keep in mind that the journals submission process can be slow.

 ## Further reading

General writing/communication guidance

Babbie, E. (2009) *The Practice of Social Research*, 12th edn. Belmont, CA: Wadsworth.

Chapter 17 of this authoritative text, 'Reading and writing social research', is excellent, and provides a good central text to consult for writing advice.

Berry, R. (2004) *The Research Project: How to Write It,* 5th edn. London, Routledge.

Well-presented, straightforward description of the elements of writing a dissertation, research project or paper. Suggested for those with little prior experience in research writing.

Bigwood, S. and Spore, M. (2003) *Presenting Numbers, Tables, and Charts.* Oxford: Oxford University Press.

For readers who are particularly concerned with presenting quantitative data, an in-depth resource which focuses on presenting numerical information in the clearest and most effective way. Divided into two sections: what to consider when preparing numerical information for presentation, including standards for presenting tables and graphs to the public; and a collection of useful checklists, case studies and exercises to aid the writer, as well as a helpful glossary.

Morse, S. (2006) 'Writing an effective research report or dissertation', in V. Desai and R. Potter (eds), *Doing Development Research.* New Delhi, Thousand Oaks, CA, London: Sage.

Offers a concise review of the writing process from a development research perspective, covering issues of writing for an audience, the importance of clear writing and structure and how to best present both qualitative and quantitative data. Clearly written, to the point and not overly technical.

The Economist *The Economist Style Guide.* Available online at www.economist.com/research/styleguide

One of the more widely used sources in UK writing, accessible online. Covers all aspects of grammar, alongside practical 'dos and don'ts' of writing.

University of Chicago Press (2010) *The Chicago Manual of Style,* 16th edn. Chicago, IL: University of Chicago Press.

The source text for the American Anthropological Association, the Organization of American Historians and most US social scientists. Includes chapters relevant to book publishers and journal editors as well as writers, and offers multiple style formats which it advocates mixing, provided the results are consistent. Excellent sections on grammar, punctuation, academic citation formats, endnotes/footnotes, etc., as well as a good overview of the central elements of a book and the broader process of editing.

Press releases/policy briefs

Gainsbury, S. and Brown, C. (2006) 'How is research communicated professionally?', in V. Desai and R. Potter (eds), *Doing Development Research.* New Delhi, Thousand Oaks, CA, London: Sage.

Very useful dissection, paragraph-by-paragraph, of a 500-word sample press release for reference.

Economic and Social Research Council *Guide to Publicizing Your Event.* Available on line at www.esrc.ac.uk/_images/Guide_to_publicising_your_event_tcm8-5093.pdf

Advice on writing a press release

Jones, N and Walsh, C. (2008) 'Policy briefs as a communication tool for development research', *Background Note*. London: ODI.

A very comprehensive overview of policy briefs in concept and practice, including a review of the divides between the policy and research communities, key obstacles to policy uptake and best practice derived from seven case studies and an international survey.

15

PROMOTING RESEARCH UPTAKE

We all hope our research will have an impact of its own accord, and that the power of its findings will speak for itself. But this often does not happen (Finch, 1986). You need to take the information to those you hope to influence, and it is essential to plan this work in light of clear thinking about who your key audience is.

The chances of your research being used will increase if you:

- develop a systematic communications strategy for reaching different audiences;
- write timely reports in direct, non-technical language, using a style appropriate to various potential users;
- use a wide range of tools and techniques for promotion – including individual and group briefings, policy briefs, web-based platforms and media engagement.

Promotional work tends to have different priorities depending on whether the research aims primarily to inform the programme in which you are working or to influence policy more broadly. This chapter discusses these, and ways of reaching the various audiences involved, including those who were the focus of the research. There may well be some overlap, in that research for a programme may have implications for policy more broadly (and vice versa), but practical decisions have to be made about where to direct the greatest promotional effort. It is important to list all the audiences you would like to reach, but then to prioritize the two or three groups you think are most important and you also have a good chance of influencing in some way.

Below, each arm of Figure 15.1 – influencing programmes and influencing policy more broadly – is explored in turn. First, however, this chapter teaches you how to develop an overarching communications strategy to guide both approaches.

Referring back to Chapters 2 and 3, we next offer guidelines on presenting reports and on promotional work 'beyond The Report', as well as on dealing with the media and building capacity among knowledge intermediaries with whom you may work in partnership. Chapter 14 discussed how to a write the actual research report.

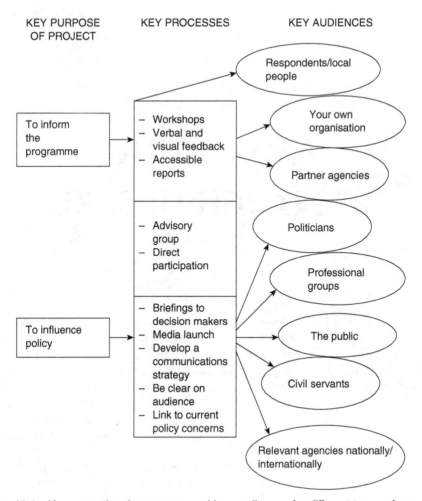

Figure 15.1   Key promotional processes and key audiences for different types of research

Managers are advised to plan for promotion right from the start of the project and to continually refine their strategy as the research evolves. While research and other staff obviously need to be involved in the promotion of results, it should not be left to them to carry out in isolation. A few researchers are excellent at this, but many are diffident about this process or lack experience. If your organization has a press or communication office, seek support at the earliest stage from press officers and communication managers. It is also important to budget for the costs involved in promotional work.

15.1   Building a successful communications strategy

Whether pursuing programme or policy change, you will need a communications strategy to guide your research promotion efforts. Chapter 3 identified a communications strategy as an integral aspect of your research project's lifecycle. Here, we cover in greater detail the key ingredients necessary to establish a successful communications strategy at the outset of your research.

A communications strategy, in brief, is a plan to aid you in systematically thinking through the full communication cycle of a research project or programme. It enables you to set concrete communication goals for your project, map how these are to be achieved,

Common pitfalls

Forgetting to plan or budget for any work to promote the findings of the research

consider the internal and external challenges and opportunities for maximizing overall impact and establish feedback mechanisms to learn from the experience. It is also inherently scalable: your strategy can involve the demands of a single report, an entire project or even an entire organization, and can include general or detailed guidance.

A basic communications strategy can be formed by asking eight broad questions during the project planning stage:

1   What are your *objectives*? What do you want your communication activities to achieve in relation to your project? Goals should be reasonable and realistic in light of project size, scope and timeframe.
2   Who is your *audience*? Who are you trying to reach? Who are your obvious targets? Who among these possible audiences are most strategically important? Tools introduced in Chapter 3 – such as stakeholder analysis – help here.
3   What are the *issues*? What challenges and opportunities are involved in achieving your objectives? Strategically assess the full range of factors, both internally and externally, that you and your colleagues face.
4   What are your *messages*? What do you want to say, and to whom? Break down messages into 'background messages' and 'key messages' to help to show how a specific project fits into a larger programme. Limit key messages to a maximum of three and tailor all of them to the specific audience. All should be memorable (simple, limited in number), engaging and – if a background message – answer the questions 'who', 'what' and 'how'. Remember the SUCCESS criteria: you want to present Simple, Unexpected, Concrete, Credible, Emotional Stories.
5   What *tools and activities* will you use to deliver your messages to the target audience? See below – communication tools are highly specific to the audience you want to reach, ranging from policy briefs to the full range of media interviews, etc.
6   What *resources* do you have? What materials, skills, knowledge, time and funding are available to help achieve the communications objectives? A realistic appraisal here can save you major challenges later – and help you to see what you need now.
7   What are your *timescales*? How long will activities take to accomplish? When and in what order will they take place? Consider drawing up a calendar of activities, with a realistic, conservative appraisal of how long it will really take.
8   Evaluation and learning – what has worked and what hasn't? See Chapter 16 on assessment for an overview of some key tools here.

It is very important to see the integration of a communications strategy into your work as an inherently iterative *process* rather than a 'one-time' step. The strategy you decide on will become a reference point to continually return to, update and adapt as your research project evolves and new challenges arise.

FOR EXAMPLE

Designing a communications strategy for International Migrants Day

International Migrants Day is an annual event sponsored by the UN in recognition of the growing number of migrants around the world. In response to the UN's invitation to 'disseminate information on the human rights and fundamental freedoms of migrants' in advance of the event, the Overseas Development Institute (ODI) designed a communications strategy to help raise awareness among key stakeholders. Below are some sample components of this strategy.

Objectives

- Organizations working on migration and remittances are made aware of, and read, the latest briefing papers and blogs from ODI on International Migrants Day.
- Media picks up and profiles ODI work.
- ODI staff know what has been released for International Migrants Day.

Audience

- UK and international organizations working on migration;
- international media;
- ODI staff and partners;
- key policymakers, practitioners and opinion formers on migration and remittances.

Messages

Background messages:

- 'Due to the unprecedented increase in migration (both within countries and across borders) over the last decade, migration has become a major policy priority in many countries.'
- 'International Migrants Day is an annual event to recognise the enormous role that migrant workers play in the global economy and to share experiences to ensure their continued protection.'

Key messages

- 'ODI is among a number of UK organisations contributing to policy discussions on migration – especially as it relates to poverty and development.'
- 'Short-term, non-permanent migration from under-developed regions to more prosperous regions can offer people an important opportunity to diversify and exit from poverty. However, current policy and institutional structures allow neither the sending area nor the receiving one to maximise the benefits from migration.'
- 'ODI is developing social protection measures for poor and vulnerable migrants especially women, girls, children and ethnic minorities; and developing safe and efficient remittance mechanisms.'

Issues identified for strategic consideration in translating this message to the target audiences

What challenges and opportunities exist in achieving the objectives, both internally and externally? ('Issues' raised here could be big or small, positive or negative or even just background information.)

Also established at this stage was a place to list known constraints and opportunities, so everyone involved in a project team was 'on the same page'.

Tools

- a front page notice on ODI's website;
- a blog and accompanying blog media release;
- an ODI newsletter article.

15.2 Promotion for implementation: influencing programmes

With a communications strategy in hand, you can begin to think about the specific factors involved in research promotion. First, where the research has aimed primarily at informing the practical work of an organization, promotion of findings will concentrate on feedback to four main groups:

- staff directly involved with the programme in question;
- relevant senior managers and others working with you in different parts of the agency;
- community members/potential users of the programme;
- managers and practitioners in partner agencies locally and perhaps more broadly.

If you haven't done Activity 2.2 in Section 2.6, which asks you to reflect on which research projects have influenced you, you might like to do it now. When groups of managers and practitioners undertake this exercise, people often identify research projects they have been directly involved in. This lends weight to the importance of stakeholder participation in research processes.

It is absolutely crucial in this type of work to identify the stakeholders in the issue you are investigating as early in the process as possible. These may include government ministries, local government departments or perhaps other non-governmental organizations (NGOs) – the issue is the same. People will not be interested in the results of research in which they have had no direct involvement; building up a sense of ownership early on makes it much more likely they will act on the findings. (See Chapter 3's discussion of stakeholder analysis for more.)

It is helpful in the planning stages to consult widely on the brief, asking advice of those you want to influence, to build a sense of the research as a shared enterprise. Once the research is underway, invite relevant people to be on the advisory group so they will see the process unfold over time. Decision makers may also be respondents in your research process. You could even ask partner agencies to allow staff to participate in data collection and/or analysis, where appropriate.

A useful way of encouraging relevant agencies to get involved is to hold a workshop or seminar to present the findings. It is best to avoid focusing exclusively on the research itself, but to use it to open up discussion on the issues it raises. It may be wise to give the floor to key agencies at some point in the day, to give them time to make a response.

Common pitfalls

Not involving partner agencies that will need to implement your findings until the research is complete

You may like to organize such a workshop in the middle of the project, after some data collection but well before the final report is written, to present 'early findings' and ask for discussion of their significance. This engages other agencies with you as partners in understanding the meaning of your work. This can be very helpful in working towards recommendations and will also act as a form of validation – checking that the findings make sense to others with a good knowledge of the field.

Checklist: feedback to other professionals/partner agencies

- ☑ Directly involve those you hope to influence throughout the life of the research and take advice from them on how to reach others.
- ☑ Hold events like seminars or workshops to enable people to ask questions and make their own contribution – invite representatives of key agencies to speak alongside you, to respond to your findings.
- ☑ Consider how your target audience usually receives information – professional journals may be important.
- ☑ Don't forget your own agency – use its communications systems to let people know about the research.

15.2.1   Taking findings back to 'the researched'

It is also extremely important to feed findings back appropriately to your research participants and the general population groups from which they were drawn. This may come naturally to participatory projects but it is equally important to inform local people of the findings of other kinds of research, which may have been quite technical and carried out at a distance from community members. Likewise, it is commonly expected of researchers to send finished research publications to individuals, institutions and communities with which they worked or studied – an act of reciprocity which Hertl et al. (2009) call a 'hallmark of socially conscious research'.

FOR EXAMPLE

Making the South African Children's Budget accessible

The South African Children's Budget Project developed a popular version of the Children's Budget in recognition of the need to disseminate the information to a broader range of children's rights advocacy and service organizations. It was written in easily accessible language, used an innovative layout and designs to represent technical statistics and was compiled as a loose set of information sheets that could be used separately. This increased the accessibility and affordability of the information, which enabled smaller children's rights organizations across the country to obtain and use it.

> ### Checklist: feedback to community members/respondents
>
> ☑ Consult people from the respondent group about how best to inform their community of your findings.
> ☑ Perhaps involve them in a working group to promote the research messages.
> ☑ Plan your strategy to fit in with the ways in which your target group normally communicate – go to them, ask for some space in their events.
> ☑ Provide access to the written final report. Expect to include some direct verbal feedback as well to those who are most interested – literacy may be an issue in any group of people: don't make assumptions.
> ☑ Consider asking some community members to lead the feedback to their community.
> ☑ Write clear simple summaries, and draw out the implications for the real world as fully as possible.

Finally, at all levels of promotion, you should consider presenting your findings alongside good practice examples and evidence drawn from other cases and contexts. This can add weight and credibility to your conclusions and recommendations, for instance if you add a persuasive argument that similar approaches have been tried successfully elsewhere already.

As there is often overlap in terms of promotional work between programme- and policy-focused research, it might help you to read the next section as well.

15.3 Promotion for policy influence

Policymakers increasingly draw on research evidence in developing new policies. Chapter 2 briefly introduced the concept of the 'research–policy interface', that is, the point at which policymakers receive, process and, ideally, make use of research to improve and adapt a particular policy or change the broader policy environment. Good research can significantly influence the actual practice of development policy and bring about positive change.

However, promoting your research within the policy community is rarely straightforward. Perhaps the most significant barrier is the fact that policymakers and researchers differ greatly in their incentives, priorities and approaches to knowledge and research-based evidence. Jones et al. (2009) point to several key differences:

1 Policymakers have to contend with a number of practicalities that researchers don't. They operate under very tight schedules, whereas researchers typically enjoy (comparatively) longer timeframes, and are almost always under pressure to produce actionable results as quickly as possible. This is exacerbated by limited money, time and political capital, all of which the policymaker must spend sooner rather than later. Policymakers therefore tend to place a premium on knowledge that is timely and can be digested quickly to be used to inform a decision – sometimes even at the expense of waiting for more credible and accurate evidence. They often lack the luxury of waiting for long-term research projects to conclude.

2 Policymakers may be experts in their fields, but they often lack the degree of technical knowledge a dedicated researcher may possess regarding the same issues. Terms and concepts which are second nature to you by the end of a

long research project can come across as obscure, overly technical jargon to a policymaker. Also, as the tools of research promotion continue to evolve, more researchers are producing and making their research available in journals and online. This offers a wider pool of sources to draw evidence from, but this very diversity can overwhelm policymakers, who find themselves with *too much* research at their fingertips. Indeed, when they have to sift through a wide range of – sometimes conflicting – data, they are often strongly prone to selecting evidence which conforms most closely to their own biases and political leanings.

3 Policymakers are often beholden to a range of additional interests which dictate the policies they pursue and the sources of knowledge they employ. The demands of political superiors, of the broader policy context and of lobby and pressure groups – among others – influence, direct and constrain their decisions. So do the policymaker's own experience, judgement, values and ideological tilt. (Jones et al., 2012)

These differences in incentives and decision-making priorities mean even the best research can have a hard time achieving a direct impact on the policy environment. Recall that Chapter 2 identified three main factors as influencing the utilization of research: political context, quality of evidence and 'links'– the pre-existing and working relationships between all the actors involved in the research. Indeed, keep in mind that, very often, the choice to pursue policy change is based on a number of competing factors, of which the evidence your research provides may be only one of many.

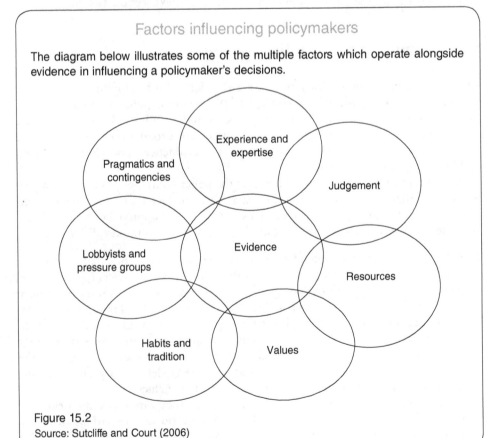

Factors influencing policymakers

The diagram below illustrates some of the multiple factors which operate alongside evidence in influencing a policymaker's decisions.

Figure 15.2
Source: Sutcliffe and Court (2006)

15.3.1 Bridging the divide – some key tools

Fortunately, there are a number of very effective strategies you can use to maximize the potential of your research communication and help to bridge the divide between researcher and policymaker.

Perhaps the single most effective way to ensure effective communication of your research to policymakers, though, is to start planning for policy impact from Day 1. Chapters 2 and 3 drew your attention to this need – and the fact that sometimes it is a new way of defining a question that influences people's thinking, rather than the findings themselves. Here are several concrete steps you can take during research design and throughout the project lifecycle to maximize utilization by policymakers.

Understand how your research can affect the policy environment

Start and Hovland (2004) outline three basic steps in planning and implementing a policy-influencing strategy for your research project: to identify the central policy objective you are pursuing; to consider the target audience; and to focus on how you will promote your message.

Around each of these steps are a number of specific planning tools you may find helpful in establishing a plan for promotion. One of the most comprehensive starting tools is the Context, Evidence and Links framework you were introduced to in Chapter 2. Developed by ODI's Research and Policy in Development (RAPID) programme, this framework contains a set of specific questions you and your research team can ask throughout the research lifecycle to gain a better understanding of how to best influence key stakeholders on the other side of the research–policy interface (www.odi.org.uk/rapid/tools/toolkits/policy_impact/Framework_qus.html).

Context

- Who are the key policy actors (including policymakers)?
- Is there a demand for research and new ideas among policymakers?
- What are the sources of resistance to evidence-based policymaking?
- What is the policy environment?
- What are the policymaking structures?
- What are the policymaking processes?
- What is the relevant legal/policy framework?
- What are the opportunities and timing for input into formal processes?
- How do global, national and community-level political, social and economic structures and interests affect the room for manoeuvre of policymakers?
- Who shapes the aims and outputs of policies?
- How do assumptions and prevailing narratives (which ones?) influence policy-making; to what extent are decisions routine, incremental, fundamental or emergent; and who supports or resists change?

Evidence

- What is the current theory or prevailing narrative?
- Is there enough evidence (research-based, experience and statistics)?
- How divergent is the evidence?
- What type of evidence exists?
- What type convinces policymakers?
- How is evidence presented?
- Is the evidence relevant? Is it accurate and applicable?
- How was the information gathered and by whom?
- Do policy actors perceive the evidence and source as credible and trustworthy?
- Has any information or research been ignored, and why?

Links

- Who are the key stakeholders?
- Who are the experts?
- What links and networks exist between them?
- What roles do they play? Are they intermediaries between research and policy?
- Whose evidence and research do they communicate?
- Which individuals or institutions have significant power to influence policy?
- Are these policy actors and networks legitimate? Do they have support among the poor?

External environment

- Who are the main international actors in the policy process?
- What influence do they have? Who influences them?
- What are their aid priorities and policy agendas?
- What are their research priorities and mechanisms?
- How do social structures and customs affect the policy process?
- Are there any overarching economic, political or social processes and trends?
- Are there external shocks and trends that affect the policy process?

These questions are intended as a very flexible guide: it is up to you which ones you ask. Taken individually or as a whole, they represent a useful starting exercise in thinking strategically about how evidence can best be used to affect policy change.

Force field analysis

With a good working knowledge of the policy process you want your research to influence, and a general idea of the key points raised by questions such as these, you can begin designing a research plan which emphasizes policy impact from its earliest stages.

Here, a range of more specific strategic planning tools are available. You were introduced to strengths, weaknesses, opportunities, threats (SWOT) analysis and stakeholder analysis in Chapter 3 – both are particularly important in designing research for policy influence.

Don't miss the boat

An additional tool you may find helpful is force field analysis, a technique for visualizing the various forces influencing a policy issue and understanding their relative strengths (Start and Hovland, 2004).

In a small group, establish the policy goal or objective you want to achieve. Write this inside a long vertical column on a flip chart. Next, on the left of the column, list all the forces driving this change forward; on the right, list all those holding back the desired change. Each force should be evaluated according to the magnitude of its influence – from 1 (weak) to 5 (strong). It may also help to use different colour pens.

Figure 15.2 shows this process in action.

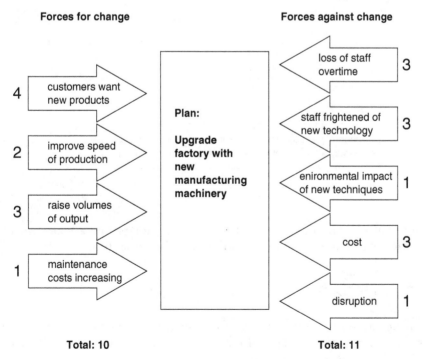

Figure 15.3   Force field analysis example

Completing a force field analysis will inevitably generate dialogue and group analysis which feeds directly into the planning process, while at the same time enriching parallel exercises like SWOT and stakeholder analysis.

Influence mapping

As we have seen, involving people early on in an advisory group, or presenting interim findings informally to small groups, can develop a sense of ownership of the research during its development. Stakeholder analysis, first introduced in Chapter 3, is very helpful in identifying these key actors for initial outreach.

A second useful tool here is influence mapping, which explores individuals and groups identified through stakeholder analysis as holding the power to effect key policy decisions. This helps you to better anticipate the steps needed to fine-tune and market your message to a specific audience.

First, divide your group of stakeholders into *decision makers* – those who hold ultimate responsibility for making the policy decisions under consideration – and *opinion leaders* – who can influence them. Opinion leaders are almost always more accessible than decision makers themselves. Both groups are accountable to a wide number of interest groups and lobbies.

Then construct a pyramid of influencing factors and forces leading up to the chief decision maker. In the process, further detail the key stakeholders and identify specific targets.

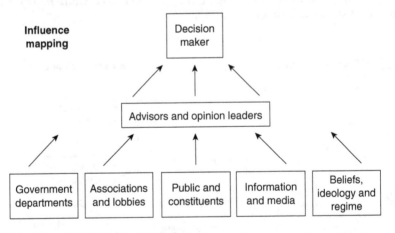

Figure 15.4   Example of influence mapping

These are just several of the many tools available for planning your research to maximize policy influence – see the further reading section below for more.

15.3.2   The right kind of evidence

Section 2.6 introduced specific factors related to the post-planning phases to give your work the best chance of being used for policy change. You must ensure throughout the research process that your data:

- are of high quality – accurate, credible and objective;
- challenge the status quo;
- are clear in their implications for action – contain practical, realistic recommendations;
- are relevant to their audience;
- are timely and topical;
- are clearly expressed and well promoted;
- involve the researched 'speaking for themselves';
- are accessible and easily available to policymakers.

15.3.3 Employ a communications strategy and specific tools

Finally, once your research findings have been framed in a way that resonates with current policy debates and you have a good understanding of the policymaking environment, a range of specific communication tools and techniques can assist you greatly in delivering your findings to the right people. The next section presents some of these.

15.4 Some tools for communication

The messages of research carried out as part of development work usually need to reach many people who will never read a full report of a project, however well written it is. It is important to think creatively about how to reach these people.

Again, a press officer or journalist may be better able to draw out the key points of a report for a lay audience than its author, although it is always important that the researcher checks any summary to ensure the work maintains its integrity.

Using different dissemination strategies to publicize research findings

We understood a long time ago in Plan that, in order to create opportunities for researchers and the general public to connect and collaborate, we needed to translate strong evidence into powerful stories that give authentic voice to real people.

In the context of the Learn Without Fear campaign, whose vision is of a world where children can go to school in safety and expect a quality learning experience without fear or threats of violence, we commissioned ODI to write a report on the economic impact of school violence. (http://plan-international.org/learnwithoutfear/economic-impact-of-school-violence-report).

Normally, campaigners choose the best bits of a report and put them into a press release. In order to publicize this research project, however, we went further and decided to make the report more accessible.

For example, rather than describing methods for quantifying school violence-related costs and showing multivariate equations, we decided to present ODI findings through illustrative stories and analogies such as the following:

FOR EXAMPLE

(Continued)

(Continued)

- The total cost of school violence in social benefits lost (in just 13 countries for which information is available) equates to almost $60 billion – that is equivalent to the World Bank's estimate of additional foreign aid needed to achieve every Millennium Development Goal by 2015.
- The national cost of violence in schools in Brazil was estimated at $943 million per year. The cost of running a national (already proven effective) Making Room Programme would be $16 million per year. The programme costs between $0.30 and $0.70 per participant per month, which covers workshop running costs and providing a meal. In comparison, the cost of jailing a young offender for a month is $1,500.
- School violence – predominantly corporal punishment – costs India up to $7.4 billion in foregone social benefits. Running the Learn Without Fear campaign for every schoolchild for a year would cost just over $67.4 million.
- After receiving several threatening letters and texts, Maria was attacked by one of her classmates who cut her face with a razor blade hidden between her fingers. A worker at the school took her to the local medical centre but her father, a cobbler, couldn't afford the immediate or long-term medical costs – equivalent to 20 times their weekly household income – and relied on the support of family and friends. Maria's parents reported the case to the police who took the case to court, even though this cost the family the equivalent of Maria's father's monthly income.

As a result, the report (http://plan-international.org/learnwithoutfear/prevention-pays-the-economic-benefits-of-ending-violence-in-schools-1) was widely disseminated through the BBC, CNN and a few other international news channels, attracting a very broad audience that goes beyond the usual audience for such reports.

Source: Cesar Bazan (2011) personal communication

Reaching policymakers at different levels: child wellbeing in Andhra Pradesh, India

FOR EXAMPLE

Research findings are often relevant to multiple, interacting communities of policymakers. Careful mapping of policy networks, and a dissemination strategy tailored to multiple stakeholder levels, can help to maximize impact and uptake.

In 2005, researchers with Save the Children UK and the Hyderabad-based Centre for Economic and Social Justice (CESJ) conducted a UN Children's Fund (UNICEF)-funded study into decentralized user committees in Andhra Pradesh state in India. Their goal was to explore and assess how these newly introduced community mechanisms were helping to improve the service delivery of children's education and nutritional services. The study identified a number of good practice features which had contributed to improvements in child wellbeing and encouraged greater representation and empowerment of local community members. However, it also drew attention to several impediments to fuller participation in committees, related to issues of inclusivity and socioeconomic, gender and caste barriers.

These findings were relevant to multiple policy communities spread across national, subnational and local levels. In order to promote their evidence-based findings to best effect, Save and CESJ planned a comprehensive dissemination and communications approach to target each level of policymakers with a tailored policy narrative. At the national and state levels, researchers published and disseminated in-depth reports to high-level stakeholders in Hyderabad and Delhi through seminars and small face-to-face meetings. In interacting with national-level policymakers, the researchers chose to frame their findings in the context of broader debates and discussions surrounding decentralized service provision, with an emphasis on how observations drawn from Andhra Pradesh might be applicable to child wellbeing initiatives in other Indian states and across the South Asian region. State-level policymakers were made aware of the promising aspects of parental user committees in Andhra Pradesh, in order to help to preserve and promote stakeholders' faith in the model, despite some observed access limitations the research had identified.

At the district- and sub-district levels, targeted policy briefs were designed for local decision makers, and cartoon-based brochures helped to encourage community feedback sessions on the project. These sessions were used to disseminate the research findings, and also fulfilled the project's commitment to principles of community reciprocity and an equal exchange of information. Within these sessions, the policy narrative was simplified, stressing the tangible community benefits of service monitoring committees and raising awareness of existing child wellbeing services.

Lastly, the researchers presented their findings at conferences in America and Norway, engaging with policy communities at the international level to encourage the development of a stronger evidence base regarding decentralized social policy worldwide and implications for child poverty and wellbeing.

As a result of this multi-tiered approach, the project team was asked by the Andhra Pradesh Department of Women and Children to contribute to the design of a State Action Plan for Children, thus contributing directly towards improved policies aimed at child wellbeing.

Source: Jones and Sumner (2011)

In addition to specific, focused efforts to promote the results of a particular piece of research, agencies can spread the word by producing materials which integrate a number of different research findings to make an argument. Often, a project can look at only some aspects of an issue, and the significance of its findings are clear only when this evidence is set alongside other information. Below, we review several of the more common tools and techniques for communication.

15.4.1   Individual and group briefings for key decision makers

Personal briefings on your findings and recommendations create a forum for discussion – they are highly visible, allow intensive interaction and encourage action. They can be tailored to a specific decision maker or decision. Briefings need to clearly convey research results, answer questions and offer recommendations oriented towards concrete action. Decision makers are usually far less interested in the details of your data and their analysis, although they want assurance that the research is of good quality.

Checklist: personal briefings

☑ Understand the audience – find out their particular concerns and the questions they are likely to ask.

☑ Summarize findings in a one-page briefing summary, identifying three key messages.

(Continued)

(Continued)

☑ Carefully select the information to present – include only those research results that really matter to the audience.

☑ Provide concrete, specific recommendations on what is to be done, by whom and when.

☑ Choose skilled presenters and involve people who have a relationship with those you are presenting to.

☑ For PowerPoint presentations, ensure your slides are uncluttered and concise, with no more than seven lines each. They should never distract the audience from your words.

☑ Bring findings to life with quotes, personal stories and accounts of particular situations, as appropriate.

☑ Rehearse your presentation and make sure it fits the time you have been given.

15.4.2 Policy briefs

A policy brief is a short document presenting the key findings and recommendations of your research to a non-specialist audience (Young and Quinn, 2002). Chapter 14 provides more detailed guidance on the process of writing policy briefs.

15.4.3 Academic and professional journals

Professional groups have their own journals, which are often an effective way of reaching them. In the eye of the reader, the information is given status simply by appearing in such journals – which are seen as containing what they 'need to know'. Likewise, academic journals are often read widely by both policymakers and programme directors – publishing your results there can draw attention and add additional credibility to your findings. See Chapter 14 on writing journal articles.

15.4.4 Websites

The most obvious advantages of promoting your research through a website are coverage and cost: you can provide information easily and instantaneously to a massive audience, avoiding the costs of printing, mailing and so on. Websites can also keep people updated on your research throughout its life. They allow use of a wide range of media – including pictures, audio and video – in addition to text. And you can link to other sources, communities and networks relevant to your research.[1]

On the other hand, web access is limited in many parts of the world, particularly in the South. People with internet access may not be web literate – they may be unfamiliar with logging on or using search engines, web-based software and social media. Older computers and/or slow connections may make it difficult to access media-rich webpages using lots of megabytes. Therefore, it is well worth trading some of the more elaborate features of modern web design (particularly fancy graphics and streaming media such as videos and audio) for quick-loading, accessible sites. Avoid creating difficult-to-navigate sites packed with too much material – users can easily grow frustrated with 'information overload' and confusing layouts. (For more on web design guidance – a very large topic in its own right – see Further reading suggestions at the end of this chapter.)

Also, don't forget to use existing websites to promote your research. One way of reaching development practitioners, for instance, is through *Insights* – a free e-journal offering periodic thematic overviews of policy-relevant research findings on international development, distributed free to policymakers and practitioners globally via the development research portal Eldis (www.eldis.com/http://www.eldis.org/insights). Similarly, the UK Department for International Development (DFID)'s Research for Development (r4d) website provides updated information about DFID-funded research programmes, including news, case studies and information on current and past research (www.dfid.gov.uk/r4d).

Finally, whenever possible, ensure there are channels for those without an internet connection to access your web-based work. Circulate phone numbers and postal information widely to let people know how to acquire printed copies of your report, press release, article or brief through the mail. If you have a press office at your organization, they should be able to help to provide logistical support in this regard.

15.4.5 Blogs

A 'weblog', or 'blog', is a type of online journal on which you can post brief informal updates, short essays and comments – typically supplemented with external links relevant to the topic under discussion. Like any webpage, the blog itself must be hosted online in order to be accessible. You can set up your own blog either through your own organization's website (consult an IT officer or web-hosting service for guidance here) or using free web-hosted blogging software such as WordPress (www.wordpress.com). Blog posts are easy to write, and can be used to advertise the release of your material, update on your progress or provide a space for deeper engagement with themes and topics you feel are relevant to your research. Furthermore, the emphasis on informal writing can help to reduce jargon and communicate your research message more clearly to policymakers.

Blogs can also be a great way to encourage feedback and develop networks. Most blogs allow a comments section, where readers can offer responses to your post and to each other. Policymakers, practitioners and other researchers can take part in discussion and debate. As such, blogs can also serve as a forum to elicit commentary and analysis on relevant topics from experts – this interaction can lead to new audiences and the possibility of collaborative networking (Start and Hovland, 2004).

Some useful tips for blog writing you may wish to follow are:

- Stick to writing on a single topic per post.
- Match your style and tone to your subject material. Over time, try to develop a distinctive 'voice'.
- Maintain regular posts, even short ones, to keep the blog active. Frequent updates attract more readers.

- Allow comments on your posts to foster discussion, although you may have to monitor for inappropriate/offensive material and remove it.
- Always respect copyright laws and fair use of copyrighted materials. The rules for plagiarism apply also to blogging: always follow proper citation procedure and link to another organization or person's work if you're discussing it.
- Separate your own personal opinions from those of your organization. Personal opinions are a fundamental and attractive aspect of blogging – just be sure you make it clear when you are speaking for yourself and not for your organization. (http://stage.esrc.ac.uk/funding-and-guidance/tools-and-resources/impact-toolkit/tools/interactive-media/index.aspx).

15.4.6 Social media

'Social media' is a collective term for the wide assortment of internet-based applications that enable interactive communication in large online user communities. Several offer innovative ways to advertise your research to wider audiences. Websites like Facebook (www.facebook.com) provide popular, and free, forums to post updates, press releases and links to full reports. Twitter (www.twitter.com) allows users in your network to register and receive brief, 150-word text updates that can be useful in keeping others closely in touch with your work. Interviews, recordings of workshops and meetings and edited audio programmes can be shared online as 'podcasts' using a range of dedicated software. By registering with Wikipedia (www.wikipedia.com), you can edit articles on your research topic or relevant issues to help to shape the codification of facts and terminology. There are dozens of additional social networking sites out there to explore; many have features and services you may find valuable in promoting your research to the wider online community.

15.4.7 Don't forget about email

Finally, don't overlook the utility of targeted emails to key audiences to promote your research. Almost everybody who uses the internet – including those who access the internet by phone (for example Blackberries and similar devices) – have email they check regularly. Second, unlike visiting a new webpage with a potentially off-putting new layout to learn, accessing email is typically routine – and people on the whole visit websites far less often than they receive and check their email. Finally, there are unique advantages inherent in how 'personal' emails are: not only can they be addressed directly to someone, but also they are often treated with a degree of professional attention and urgency far greater than a visit to a website.

15.5 Dealing with the media

The media can prove a powerful resource in communicating your work to a wider audience, gaining the attention of policymakers and generating pressure for policy change.

However, it may be difficult at first glance to know where to begin engaging journalists. Below are some practical tips to help to guide you in dealing with the media, which should be equally relevant for Northern, Southern and international media organizations.

First of all, don't assume your research needs to get into the mass media to have been promoted appropriately. Some research is addressed primarily to professional or local audiences, and is simply not of sufficient interest to a wider audience. A good test is to consider what would happen if you started to explain your project's findings in your local bar. Would you have cleared the place by closing time? If it makes a good story, it will make a good story!

Prepare for interest from the media in research you publish even if you do not plan to actively promote it in this way. The press may pick it up from a professional conference, for instance.

Second, it is helpful for the research team to identify a media spokesperson at an early stage. This person should then have media matters in mind as the project progresses. Some large agencies like senior managers to deal with media interest; this can reinforce the importance of the issue, but they may not be familiar with the details of the research. It is extremely embarrassing when a spokesperson cannot answer sharp questions about a piece of research. It may be best to use the most confident speaker directly involved with the research, probably the researcher herself. Representatives of 'the researched' themselves may be also excellent spokespeople on the general issues raised.

Third, keep in mind that the nature of the media environment is highly dependent on context: the degree of press freedom can vary greatly, as can the attitudes and approaches of journalists to their audiences. (One excellent example is radio, a format often far more popular in the South than the North.) Likewise, do not focus exclusively on coverage in the 'serious' press. If you want to have an influence on the public, far more people read local papers and listen to local radio than read the national newspapers. Local media are often short of material and more open to approaches from NGOs. Also remember the Southern media reach millions of people – don't focus just on Northern or international media.

Beyond this general advice, you also need to know the more practical aspects of engaging the media: first, producing a written press release and contacting media outlets directly; and second, conducting interviews.

15.5.1 Preparing a press release and contacting journalists

Preparing a press release

The journalist's focus on the questions 'What's the story?' 'What are we really saying here?' gives helpful sharpness to efforts to promote research results. It is therefore very important to produce a short statement of your key findings, to brief journalists. This may take the form of a press release, or simply be a background paper which can be given to journalists once they contact you. Journalists are lay people and may not have any specialist knowledge of the field you work in – their audience certainly won't have. Reporters frequently take a very short time to work their story up from your briefing material, so you need to make it as short and clear as possible.

If you or your organization has access to a press office, try to involve a press officer in the process at the first opportunity. Also, be sure to check with your organization before sending out the release, as there may be protocols you need to adhere to.

Chapter 14 gives some guidelines on writing press releases. We here include some activities and examples to help you further in this type of writing to promote your research results.

ACTIVITY 15.1

Practise writing for a general audience

Write a draft briefing on your research findings to fit on an A4 page in normal type (about 250 words). Test out your draft on anyone you can get hold of who isn't 'in the business' – friends and relatives, the person in the next office. Get at least two people to read it quickly and then tell you what they think it said. Listen particularly to the questions they ask you about it. Make revisions and try again on someone else.

It is crucial that the meaning of research results is not distorted in pursuit of a good story. It is often tempting to generalize from too little evidence, but NGOs must be very careful not to appear to make claims they cannot substantiate.

FOR EXAMPLE

How many elephants?

The highly charged debate in 1990 around a worldwide ivory ban was confused by contradictions between the Worldwide Fund for Nature's high-profile campaign for elephant protection and its low-profile support to a more complex solution to sustainable wildlife management. This contradiction became public when conservationists aired their disagreements in the British journal, *BBC Wildlife* (Princen and Finger, 1994). A later example of the alleged distortion of facts around the same issue was described in *New Scientist* magazine, when readers were told of an elephant over-population crisis, with statistics apparently based on animals that never existed (Pye-Smith, 1999). The article accused environmental groups of perpetuating the myth of a catastrophic decline in elephant numbers across Africa, not least because 30 organizations were identified as depending on that myth for their financial survival (Harper, 1997).

FOR EXAMPLE

Tripping up on statistics: the UK

Making the results of research meaningful to local media around the country can be a problem for press departments in national charities. Research and development workers in one major UK children's charity were embarrassed in the early 1990s when the results of a national survey were broken down by region in a press statement. The survey had been on parents' views on children's safety and the press office had worked out figures for different regions from the general data in the report. They put out a statement to the effect that 'x per cent of mothers in

Birmingham do not let children play outside because of fears for their safety'. A numerate journalist found that the numbers interviewed in each region were too small to reach significance
and challenged the legitimacy of the claims the agency made. The lessons from this are that
you need to work very closely with your press department or press officers to ensure their
legitimate efforts to get your work into print don't rely on illegitimate means.

The examples included here reflect conflicts which can arise between the need to
present research findings in a compelling enough way to get attention and the need
to be scrupulous in presenting them accurately. Managers need to keep control of
the presentation of findings from research they are responsible for, as they will
undoubtedly be held accountable if there is any negative coverage.

Scandal!

Try to think of incidents of controversy over or misrepresentation of research findings –
perhaps your own agency's or perhaps work you have heard of. Conduct a brief enquiry into
each incident you can think of. Could the challenge have been avoided? What should have
been done?

Compare your thoughts on this with those from Activity 2.2, where you were asked to analyse what enables research to have an influence on you. What conclusions might we draw?

ACTIVITY 15.2

15.5.2 Engaging journalists

Once you and your team have prepared a press release, it is time to reach out to journalists. Like policymakers, journalists are usually extremely busy, and are also often
inundated with similar press releases from any number of sources. Sometimes, they will
respond to your initial release. Other times, you will have to get their attention first.

To increase the likelihood of getting a response from the media:[2]

- Keep an eye out for journalists during research, at events and meetings, etc.
  Introduce yourself, give them your business card and, if possible, cultivate a
  relationship.
- Time the launch carefully: be ready, look for a news 'peg' in timing (for example
  the World Bank annual meeting to release a report on debt).
- Appoint a media spokesperson from your research team. Make sure they are
  fully familiar with the research. Where possible, identify and prepare people who
  represent the participants in the research to talk to journalists – ensure you
  explain how the media works and the risks involved.
- Take particular care in drafting your initial press release email. Include the full
  release in the body of the email, along with a succinct, attention-grabbing 'headline' in the subject line. Contact addresses on newspapers' websites are often
  flooded with nearly identical press releases to your own: it is better to send your
  email to a section editor or a journalist you know personally. If in doubt, call the
  paper's head office to ask for the email address of a specific journalist.

- Make yourself as available as possible for follow-up. In your email, give home and mobile numbers and let journalists know that they can contact you there during work hours. Consider allowing permission to contact you outside regular work hours, as many journalists work odd hours.
- From the moment the press release is sent, be prepared to be interviewed and quoted at short notice. This means staying apprised of your key messages, evolving issues and important facts you may have become rusty on.
- Have information and sources on hand so you can respond quickly to a journalist's requests – in so doing, you can develop your reputation as a valuable source.
- Never pass along information to a journalist unless you know it is true. If in doubt, simply pass on the question.

Once you have the attention of the media, several things may happen. Journalists may copy your press release in whole or part in their article, and possibly contact you to clarify points, confirm facts and solicit quotes. This typically involves an interview in person or by phone. Inquire in advance regarding the questions they expect to ask you. If the journalist calls unexpectedly and you feel unprepared, ask if you can reschedule in a few hours to get a chance to organize your thoughts. Be sure to have to hand your notes, sources and any other materials you need.

If you have contacted a newspaper or magazine with a press release or a direct request to contribute a piece, you may also be asked to write an article or editorial on your research. This is a great opportunity to articulate your points to a wide audience from a position of authority. Often, such opportunities arise from a combination of diligent networking and fortuitous timing, that is, how relevant your research findings are to breaking news. Sometimes, this is a matter of pure luck; other times, you can strategically engage papers during a particularly relevant period. Occasionally, a quiet news period will allow a journalist to revisit your research and request written content.

15.5.3   Broadcast interviews

In the case of radio and TV, you may be interviewed directly on air, in real time, to speak on your research, or as an expert on the broader issue related to your research (http://publicwebsite.idrc.ca/EN/Resources/Tools_and_Training/Pages/Toolkit-for-researchers.aspx).

In undertaking broadcast interviews, remember you may get a very short time to say your piece. Write a 'script' before any interview, summarizing the main points to be made, with reminders of relevant examples to mention. Decide on the one main point to make in case you do not get time to say more. Use the questions you are asked to make sure you get this point across. If you deal with the media regularly, it is a good idea to organize some training, involving real journalists, to help staff improve their skills and understanding of this kind of work.

Margaret Thatcher was noted for saying what she wanted to say regardless of the questions asked of her. She remained Prime Minister for a very long time! Obviously, this policy can be taken to extremes, but it is a good rule of thumb to stick to your script wherever possible.

It is important to be prepared for negative media approaches to your work. It is a common strategy for journalists to identify or generate 'controversy'. This is often not a problem; indeed, we may welcome discussion of the issues. But it is important not to sound defensive in response to hostile questions.

Role play a media interview

ACTIVITY 15.3

In preparing for radio or TV interviews, it is very helpful to role play the process with some colleagues. Find someone to act as the journalist, and ask them to prepare a few tricky questions. They need a general grasp of the subject of your research – not a detailed one. Ask some other colleagues to be your audience and to give you feedback on how you came across. You could tape record or video the role play to review later – or not, if you can't face it! If you can, add realism by involving a real journalist.

These tips apply to both radio and TV broadcasts, as well as to formal interviews which appear in print.

Checklist: successful broadcast interviews

- ☑ Be prepared. Research the media organization and the interviewer, discuss ground rules before going on air, refresh yourself on key facts and practise your answers to anticipated questions.
- ☑ Dress appropriately. Maintain eye contact with the interviewer, sit up straight and avoid nervous fidgeting. Smile, speak slowly and clearly and remember to breathe.
- ☑ Identify the three main points you want to make, and practise making them in one or two minutes – often TV or radio slots are very short. You can always elaborate on specific points later in an interview or question and answer session.
- ☑ Stick to them – do not be diverted onto irrelevant issues.
- ☑ Illustrate the main points with well-chosen, timely examples.
- ☑ Avoid jargon – imagine a friend or neighbour outside your professional field as your audience.
- ☑ Remember people listen to radio or TV individually, and speak as if to one person, not to a public meeting.
- ☑ Actively 'shape' your answers to questions – keep answers brief, consider the impact of each response and remain aware of the overall direction of the interview as it progresses.
- ☑ Deflect difficult questions and try to support your claims whenever possible. Don't feel obliged to fill silences or gaps, and don't try to respond to a question when you don't know the answer.
- ☑ In debates, don't interrupt when your opponent is speaking, but don't allow your opponent to talk over you or dominate when it is your turn.
- ☑ Anticipate potentially confrontational questions, and be aware of interviewers or debating opponents who 'bait' you for reactions. Don't overreact or become angry.

15.6 Capacity building

Finally, your research promotion strategy should include a consideration of how to build capacity among a wide range of people – journalists, academic researchers and policy analysts, local politicians, government staff and even policymakers and legislators themselves – to better access research evidence to contribute to the policy change process more effectively. This might take the form of aiding local journalists to draw on existing evidence to help them to question policymakers, or improving policymakers' ability to access and interpret research in developing new policy. It could involve assisting Southern university research departments and think-tanks to expand their research capacity and better connect to Northern networks from which they may be excluded.

Tools include – at the individual level – hosting workshops and training sessions; sponsoring training, mentoring and coaching; producing materials; offering small research grants; and developing and inviting groups into networks and communities of best practice. At the organizational level, capacity building might involve providing funding, technical support and mentoring to an organization's projects; small grants for staff training or research projects; and staff exchanges and secondments. Strategic capacity strengthening involves building skills in thinking through processes like the systematic planning, management and monitoring of research promotion efforts and policy-influencing strategies (Jones et al., 2009).

FOR EXAMPLE

Strengthening research consumption skills of journalists in Peru

ODI worked in Peru with a local partner, the Economic and Social Research Consortium (CIES), to help journalists to access research evidence and formulate better questions to ask political candidates during an election. This project encouraged a network of 100 development research institutes to make research findings more accessible at the regional level. Researchers first synthesized their findings for the journalists in policy briefs on 10 key areas, and next produced a list of key questions for journalists to ask political candidates about each area. ODI also emphasized the building of linkages, by establishing partnerships with journalists over an 18-month period, holding weekly meetings with parliamentary special subcommittees and hosting public meetings in five key provinces. As a result, journalists became better equipped to ask substantive questions to candidates, and more evidence was included in policy debates in the pre-election period as a result of greater media coverage and public meetings.

Source: Jones et al. (2009)

Key points from this chapter

Checklist: effective promotion of research findings

- ☑ Plan for the promotion of research results from the beginning of the project and allow resources for the work involved.
- ☑ Consider a wide range of possible methods of promoting the results – think about how to reach your target audience.
- ☑ Include the costs of promoting the findings of the research in your budget for any project – for example printing, postage, costs of workshops, etc.
- ☑ Ensure reports meet professional standards for clarity and presentation and include a summary.
- ☑ Involve staff with expertise in promotional/marketing work.
- ☑ Ensure results are presented in such a way as to maintain the integrity of the research findings.

☑ Involve community members in promoting research findings.
☑ Build research promotion capacity among key partners.
☑ Be polite! Make sure those who contributed to, or are directly affected by, the research get to see the results early on in the promotional process.

 # Further reading

Economic and Social Research Council. *Pathways to Impact Toolkit*. Available online at http://stage.esrc.ac.uk/funding-and-guidance/tools-and-resources/impact-toolkit/index.aspx

ESRC's Media Guidelines have been updated with an extensive collection of media impact toolkits designed for use by researchers – including specific web-based packages for developing an impact strategy, promoting knowledge exchange, public engagement and communicating effectively with key stakeholders. Written in clear language and easy to navigate.

International Development Research Centre. *Toolkit for Researchers*. Available online at http://publicwebsite.idrc.ca/EN/Resources/Tools_and_Training/Pages/Toolkit-for-researchers.aspx

IDRC provides a series of web-based training modules on preparing for strategic communication and media engagement, including how to prepare for a TV interview, how to write policy briefs and web content, how to make effective presentations and tips for dealing with the media.

Nutley, S., Walter, I. and Davies, H. (2007) *Using Evidence: How Research Can Inform Public Services*. Bristol: The Policy Press.

Excellent resource for expanding readers' understanding of 'evidence-informed policy'. Highlights best practice and challenges in systematic inquiry around evidence-based policy, including alternative perspectives on the research–practice nexus. Provides practical guidance on improving the policy impact of research – clearly written and very accessible.

ODI RAPID. *Policy Impact Online Toolkit*. Available online at

www.odi.org.uk/rapid/tools/toolkits/policy_impact/Tools.html

Start, D. and Hovland, I. (2004) *Tools for Policy Impact: A Handbook for Researchers*. London: ODI.

ODI's RAPID is a key resource for learning more about policy-focused research promotion. An excellent starting place is Start and Hovland's policy impact toolkit, which provides a succinct review of key concepts and links to additional resources.

Communication tools

ESRC. Developing a Website for Research Promotion, *Impact Toolkit*.

Available online at www.esrc.ac.uk/funding-and-guidance/tools-and-resources/impact-toolkit/tools/interactive-media/website/index.aspx

Global Development Network. *Toolkit on Disseminating Research Online*. Available online at http://cloud2.gdnet.org/cms.php?id=disseminating_research_online

A wide range of resources exist for guidance on web-based promotion techniques: ESRC provides a very clear, unintimidating introduction and GDN another very good guide.

Jones, N. and Walsh, C. (2008) Policy briefs as a communication tool for development research. *Background Note*. London: ODI.

Jones and Walsh provide a comprehensive overview of policy briefs in concept and practice, including a review of the divides between policy and research communities, key obstacles to policy uptake and best practice derived from seven case studies and an international survey.

Social media

Research Information Network. *Social Media: A Guide for Researchers*. Available online at

www.rin.ac.uk/our-work/communicating-and-disseminating-research/social-media-guide-researchers

A general introduction to social media, aimed at researchers and policy analysts. Offers guidance, an introduction to key terms and concepts, links and resources and a helpful series of case studies from researchers who incorporate social media into their work.

Capacity building

Blagescu, M. and Young, J. (2006) 'Capacity development for policy advocacy: current thinking and approaches among agencies supporting civil society organisations', *Working Paper* 260. London: ODI.

Reviews ODI's work as part of the DFID-funded Civil Society Partnerships Programme, which aims to improve the capacity of Southern civil society organizations to influence pro-poor policy. Offers a good general overview of key concepts behind capacity building, illustrated with examples from ODI's recent work.

Capacity.org. www.capacity.org/capacity/opencms/en/index.html

Capacity.org is a resource portal for the practice of capacity development, and hosts the Capacity.org journal. The website provides access to a broad range of related online resources that researchers and practitioners can draw on to improve their own practice, and includes the latest capacity-building research findings, analytical frameworks, policy debates, practical experiences and toolkits.

Notes

1 See http://cloud2.gdnet.org/cms.php?id=disseminating_research_online.
2 See, for example, Gainsbury and Brown (2006) and Start and Hovland (2004).

16

ASSESSING RESEARCH FOR DEVELOPMENT WORK

By the time you complete a research project, there is a natural tendency to heave a sigh of relief and move on to the next thing. But to develop better practice in this area, we really should assess the work we do as we go along. Your assessment effort should be in proportion to the resources spent on the research project. And how you focus the assessment will depend on your key aims for it.

This chapter looks at some common approaches to evaluating research projects and also ways you can assess the uptake of your research by key audiences, as well as how to measure the impact you have achieved at the programme and policy levels. (Note that this discussion is separate from the tools and techniques used for programme monitoring and evaluation – a topic discussed further in the Appendix.)

16.1 What, who and when?

16.1.1 What to assess: output, uptake and impact

Here, there are three broad areas to consider. The first is the quality of your *outputs* – your data, final report, policy briefs, etc. – and the research process itself. The second is the direct *uptake* of your research by others, and their responses to it in policy documents, newspapers, websites, etc. The third is the *impact* your research has on your target audience, and to what degree it leads (either directly or indirectly) to changes in behaviour, knowledge, attitudes, practices, policies and programming.

The quality of a piece of research relates to both its products and the process through which it was carried out. As well as being useful to undertake during its development, Activity 2.3, from Chapter 2, could be used to look at the strength and weaknesses of a piece of work at the end of its life.

16.1.2 Who should be involved in assessment?

While you could undertake this task alone or with a group of immediate colleagues, it is better to find out what a broader group of people thinks of the project. Deciding who to involve depends on the project's central aims – was the aim to have an impact on high-level policymakers, on middle managers or perhaps on local people themselves?

A short interview with representatives of all the main stakeholder groups (including 'the researched') will yield useful information which will usually focus on process more than final impact. You could use the objectives to structure these questions. The research respondents are the least likely to air their views: you will usually have to make a special effort to find out. Where you are relating to a community group with its own structures, one way of doing this is by going along to a community meeting.

You may want to include funders and senior managers who were not directly involved in the project but who should be influenced by it. Their view of its success is likely to be important to the future of your work; even if it is negative, it is better to have this out in the open and discussed. It gives them an opportunity to let you know what they would like to see from you in future.

You may also consider employing an external evaluator in addition to, or instead of, internal staff. This can be a complicated decision: each option has advantages and disadvantages. An external evaluator is often able to bring a fresh eye to the research, can be more critical of programmes and policies than internal staff and, if accountability to donors or governments is a factor, can provide an unbiased voice. On the other hand, internal staff may require less time to familiarize themselves with the material, programme and context, and may also possess insights no one outside the project has developed. A range of additional factors – such as cost, availability and knowledge – also require consideration.

16.1.3 When should assessment take place?

While it is useful to undertake an assessment process at the conclusion of a research project, it is likely to be more helpful still to set up some kind of monitoring system, or 'formative' assessment process. This helps you to 'form' the project by giving ongoing feedback as the process unfolds.

Checklist: ways of getting feedback as a research project develops

- ☑ Research advisory group: monitor the progress and impact of the project.
- ☑ At the end of interviews, etc., ask respondents how they felt about taking part in the research.
- ☑ Build a short evaluation discussion into the end of any group event.
- ☑ Employ an expert advisor/external evaluator to offer an ear and some ongoing assessment input throughout the life of the project.
- ☑ Meet together at intervals as a research team and step back from the day-to-day work to reflect on progress and any difficulties encountered.

16.2 Assessing research output

Here we look at ways to assess research output – in relation to its own objectives and in relation to a set of quality standards.

16.2.1 Did it meet its objectives?

The most straightforward way to assess research projects, as with other kinds of projects, is to look back at the research questions and objectives and consider to what extent they have been addressed. Analysing the problems you met will be helpful when you come to plan the next project.

Measuring success against objectives

The table below may be useful for thinking these issues through.

	Achievements	Limitations	Issues to consider
Objective 1			
Objective 2			
Objective 3			
Objective 4			

ACTIVITY 16.1

In order to assess success against objectives, you may need to identify a number of specific indicators you can use to measure how well you have done. Indicators are objective ways of measuring (indicating) that progress is being achieved. For example, a change in national legislation could indicate policy influence.

One problem with measuring against objectives is that the original objectives may not have been written in such a way as to express clearly all the purposes the project was in fact trying to achieve. For example, while the project's aim may have been to pilot a new type of development intervention such as a cash transfer to promote safe motherhood, a complementary aim may also have been to promote learning and dialogue between communities of development workers and researchers working on social protection issues on the one hand and maternal health issues on the other. In this case, it may be a

ppropriate to add to them or adapt them. Make sure the evaluation process you follow is as relevant as possible, to get the most learning out of it.

In the case of research intended to inform the programme, you might want to work on the assessment process together with colleagues and perhaps community members who cooperated with you on the project. One approach is to set up a workshop to draw out people's views, or to hold a series of short talks to discuss the extent to which each objective has been achieved.

Or you could simply ask people to think about the strengths and weaknesses of the research, both its process and its final products. This asks them to identify the criteria they are using, rather than using those defined at the start of the project when the objectives were written.

Where the work has been participatory, it will be very important to find out community members' criteria for success. As ever, this is best done early on in a project, as it will draw out any differences of understanding between professionals and community members. You have a better chance of succeeding in the eyes of those you work with if you know what they are looking to see done.

The project's objectives may have included some reference to capacity building; whether they did or not, it will be a good idea to consider this aspect as part of your assessment. What learning has occurred? Do people feel more confident about research work? What problems were encountered and how were these overcome? Would you do it differently another time? What could be done to make it easier for more people to learn from research processes as they go along?

To reach beyond those you work with closely, and to give people more space to criticize, you could send out a short questionnaire or conduct face-to-face or telephone interviews with contacts in key agencies. Questions should start by assessing people's knowledge of the work you have done and then move on to find out their opinions of it. Interviews should really be conducted by someone not directly involved in carrying out the research project.

The virtue of conducting some form of assessment of projects like this is that it gives an opportunity to draw out any problems people see with the work, so they can be addressed in the future. It can also be a useful way of starting to engage people in thinking what should happen next on the issues you attempted to address.

Checklist: assessing the outputs of programme-focused research

☑ Ask community members and colleagues about their criteria for success for the project – sooner rather than later.

☑ Structure your assessment around the project's aims and objectives, or ask people to assess the strengths and weaknesses of the project's products and process.

☑ Include questions which invite people to think ahead, to engage with what should happen next.

☑ Do a small survey – on paper or in person – of key people's knowledge of and views on the project.

☑ Look at the learning and development of staff and community members that has occurred through the project, as well as the other outcomes.

16.2.2 Look back at the quality standards

Another way of evaluating a project is to compare its performance with a set of pre-defined standards of good practice. You might want to look at your project's success in relation to the quality standards this manual proposes (Section 3.1 and summarized in Table 16.1). This could be a desk-top exercise to focus your own thoughts or as a basis for formal or informal discussion with others.

Table 16.1 Assessing your project alongside quality standards for research for development work

Standard	Strengths	Weaknesses	Notes for action
Research planning			
• About an important issue			
• Needed			
• Idea came from 'the researched'			
• Clear brief			
• Planned in cooperation with relevant others			
• Transparent organizational structures			
• Developed participants' research skills			
Research processes			
• Questioned the taken-for-granted			
• Respectful interaction with respondents			
• 'The researched' had a say in design			
• Sample appropriate			
• Research tools piloted			
• Data collection systematic and accurate			
• Social inequalities taken into account			
• Ethical issues actively considered			
• Good communication with respondents			
• Reports explain sampling methods fully			
• Open reflection on researchers' impact on process			
• Statistical processes clearly explained			
• In quantitative work – validity and reliability of tools checked			
• For participatory research, increased local empowerment, knowledge and capacity building			
Interpretation and analysis			
• Interpretation accurate and honestly reported			
• Analysis included consideration of alternative interpretations			
• Broader policy context, wider research findings drawn on			
• All claims can be supported by evidence			
Research contribution			
• Adds to new knowledge			
• Employs existing knowledge to improve and deepen understanding of issue or phenomenon			
Financial considerations			
• Balance in terms of costs and benefits? (should not be calculated too early)			
• Any effect on your and others' ability to attract funding for work in this area?			

(Continued)

Table 16.1   (Continued)

Standard	Strengths	Weaknesses	Notes for action
Promoting research findings			
• Reports concise but include adequate information to assess research			
• Appropriate summaries included			
• Recommendations arose from findings			
• Findings fed back to 'the researched' in appropriate ways			
• Findings fed back to partner agencies in appropriate ways			
• Any research quoted was fully referenced			
• Dissemination targeted at those who could make a difference			

16.3   Assessing research uptake

Beyond assessing the quality of your final research output, you will also want to monitor the attention it receives when it is released – within your organization, in the local community or from donors, policymakers, academia, the media or the public in general. Here, both the quality of your research and your promotion efforts will be factors. Some indicators you might use to assess whether the right people are paying attention in the right numbers are as follows:

Monitoring policy/programme language:

- Keep track of references to your research in official policy documents, operational guidelines, training manuals, textbooks and websites in the relevant policy or programme context.
- Look for changes in terminology used in the policy environment, both written and verbal, which reflect the influence of your research.

Monitoring the media:

- Count column inches or airtime dedicated to your issue, the balance of pro and anti comment and the circulation or readership of the newspaper which covers it.
- Count the number of printed mentions for your organization – a task made much easier with the use of online news aggregators and search engines. [1]
- Analyse whether the media are adopting your language.

Monitoring your reputation:

- Record the sources and number of inquiries you receive as a result of your work.
- For reports and content distributed online, review detailed data on the number of people who have downloaded or viewed your work directly through web analytics software.[2]
- Are you getting to the people you wanted to get to?

- How and where have they heard of your work?
- How accurate are their preconceptions about you and your work?

Monitoring public opinion:

- Analyse the popular climate through telephone polling or by commissioning surveys.

One useful way of keeping track of additional feedback is through the use of an 'impact log' – a list of informal comments, anecdotes and other reactions you receive about your research. You can use this as a 'catch-all' for qualitative feedback, to capture miscellaneous information about research uptake which might otherwise be lost. As your impact log expands, however, it becomes increasingly relevant for illustrating trends and emerging themes in the feedback (Hovland, 2007).

16.4 Assessing research impact

Finally, monitoring the actual change brought on by your research is critical in assessing the lasting impact of your work. After all, you initially undertook a research project to address a specific issue – as such, it is important to judge the success of your effort in terms of how the new knowledge you produced has effected real change, whether in programming or in policy. It is of course difficult to disentangle the contribution your work made relative to a range of other interventions and ongoing changes, so it is important to be modest and realistic about the type of change that might be observed, especially in the short term. Some possible indicators of success might be as follows:

Policy/practice change:

- Direct changes in policy – new legislation, new official guidance, revisions to existing policy documents.
- Direct changes in practice and/or language – observable different practice by professionals and/or use of language that is, for example, more inclusive of marginalized social groups, such as ethnic minority groups or female-headed households.
- References made to your research in policy discussions, for example during debates, in official documents, etc.
- The issue appearing on agendas it was previously excluded from.
- Programmes of work changing in light of your findings.
- Your research being reported in relevant publications/programmes.

Strengthening participation in policy processes:

- Your organization/non-governmental organizations (NGOs) generally invited to join in more discussions, or at a higher level.
- Community members/those representing them given greater access to decision-making bodies – for example invited to join important committees.

Institutional learning:

- Learning achieved – about the issue in question and about research.
- Evidence that people have gained in confidence as a result of this project.

Financial:

- The balance in terms of costs and benefits (should not be calculated too early).
- Any effect on your and others' ability to attract funding for work in this area.

With research that aims to influence high-level policy issues, it can be particularly difficult to identify what impact you have had. You may be able to think of other particularly relevant factors for your project, such as changes in processes – for example, greater involvement of communities in programme design or monitoring and evaluation processes.

FOR EXAMPLE

The Sphere Project

The Sphere Project represents a policy milestone for better accountability and practice within the international humanitarian aid community, and was deeply influenced by the findings of a single large-scale evaluation, the Joint Rwanda Review – a research project which dramatically impacted high-level policy formation thanks to its combination of credibility and close links to key policymakers.

Although the international humanitarian aid sector had grown exponentially throughout the early 1990s, it had not paid sufficient attention to questions of behaviour, professional standards or good practice, until a severely mismanaged international humanitarian response in the aftermath of the 1994 Rwandan genocide finally prompted the aid community to confront its own behaviour. During this period of intense community-wide reflection, Niels Dabelstein, head of the Danish International Development Cooperation Agency's Evaluation Secretariat, convinced a broad range of UN agencies, bilateral donors, international organizations and NGOs to launch a multi-stakeholder evaluation of the troubled Rwandan genocide response.

A 20-person Overseas Development Institute (ODI) research team was tasked with conducting Study 3 of the larger Joint Rwanda Evaluation, which entailed an extensive review of NGO performance across the sector. In 1996, Study 3's findings were released, including two sets of recommendations aimed at improving NGO performance through new forms of regulation and accountability, and the development of a set of professional standards. These recommendations were readily adopted by the Sphere Project, a wide consortium of NGO umbrella organizations created in 1995 by InterAction, the International Federation of the Red Cross and Oxfam. Only a year after the release of the Joint Rwanda Evaluation, the Sphere Working Group, comprising 700 people from more than 200 agencies, had drafted the Humanitarian Charter and Minimum Standards for Disaster Response – a document which codified many of the Joint Rwanda Evaluation's proposed standards into sector-wide policy.

As a result of the Sphere Project, the humanitarian aid community now possesses minimum guidelines for five sectors of practice: water supply and sanitation, nutrition, food aid, shelter and site planning and health services. Their uptake by humanitarian organizations marks a fundamental step in the professionalization of international aid accountability and practice.

Sphere's rapid uptake of the Joint Rwandan Evaluation, and the tremendous impact of its findings, was attributable first to the excellent quality and credibility of its research. The researchers themselves possessed a good mix of academic and operational backgrounds, and based their evaluation around a thorough research methodology which combined documentation review with a comprehensive review of 620 individuals from across the aid sector. The final research product was widely commended on its release for the credibility of its evidence.

The evaluators were also very effective in framing individual components of their analysis to different communities within the international aid sector – aided by an impact monitoring group, the Joint Evaluation Follow-up, Monitoring and Facilitation network, which closely followed the evaluation's uptake and policy impact.

Just as critically, the Joint Rwanda Evaluation recognized and took advantage of a rare opportunity, in the immediate aftermath of the Rwandan genocide, to target a policy community at its most eager and with strong motivation to change.

Here, the fact that the Joint Rwanda Evaluation project had been formed in close consultation with the same policy network it was targeting for impact offered a tremendous advantage. Many of the evaluators were former members of key aid agencies, and the team maintained and built on close links with policymakers via a steering committee representing 38 agencies and organizations. These policymakers, who had commissioned the research to begin with and who developed close working relationships with the evaluators, were deeply invested in the project's outcome. A management group was also established to ensure the team retained its objectivity and impartiality, further strengthening credibility.

Source: Buchanan-Smith (2005)

The following monitoring indicators, proposed by BOND (1999), give a practical framework to use in assessing the effectiveness of your advocacy-related research process. It differs from the broader checklist given above in that it offers more direct and specific guidance on how to actually assess the indicators it identifies.

Monitoring your target:

- Record and observe changes in the rhetoric of your target audience. Keep a file of their statements over time.
- What are they saying about you and your campaign?
- Are they moving closer to your position, adapting to or adopting any of your language and philosophy?

Monitoring your relationships:

- Record the frequency and content of conversations with external sources and target audiences.
- Are you discussing new ideas? Are you becoming a confidante or a source of information or advice?

In addition to these indicators, several specific tools and techniques have been developed by the development research community specifically to help in assessing the impact of research projects on policy change. These can be used individually, or to complement each other in the impact assessment process. A brief review of several particularly useful ones is provided here.

16.4.1 Most Significant Change analysis

By asking key stakeholders to identify what they feel to be the most significant change in a policy or policy environment over a period of time, you can collect narratives to provide you with a more complete understanding of the multiple factors influencing policy change, and the degree to which your research was included among them.

Most Significant Change analysis works by bringing together these stories and presenting them for analysis by a series of review panels, who select the most useful examples. After first collecting a wide range of significant change stories from key stakeholders involved in the policy change you wish to examine, create panels comprising project team members and stakeholders from various teams in your organization and/or those of partners. The most junior panel chooses from the total population of stories a selection of particularly useful examples, which are then 'passed up' to the next level, which then repeats the process. The most senior panel selects examples from the remaining vetted stories, which are then used as the basis for a final review. One advantage of this process is that, as it takes place, project and programme staff gain an increased awareness of how the research project has achieved change at all levels of the organization (Hovland, 2007).

16.4.2 Episode Studies

The Episode Studies approach, developed by ODI's Research and Policy in Development (RAPID) programme, is useful for 'tracking back' a particular policy change in order to help to identify the multiple motivating factors which prompted it and how much your research contributed. First construct a narrative timeline of key policy decisions and practices, events and documents leading up to the policy change under review with relevant stakeholders. Then ask how and how much (if at all) research findings shaped the sequence of events.

ODI looked at the evolution of poverty reduction strategy papers (PRSPs), which came to dominate the development landscape in the late 1990s/early 2000s. The team explored how the idea of PRSPs came to challenge the previous macroeconomic austerity focus of the international financial institutions in development circles and concluded that research had an indirect effect by raising attention among policymakers of the crippling effects of debt burdens on Southern government efforts to improve the situation of the poor. However, other critical factors were also involved in bringing about this change: the networking efforts of NGOs around debt relief; internal dissatisfaction with the results of earlier policies within the International Monetary Fund itself; and powerful coalitions of NGO networks and the role of key champions of change in international development, especially in the UK (including Gordon Brown and then-Secretary of State Clare Short).

Note that, while episode studies may help to put the relative contribution of research to policy change into perspective, they do also risk underestimating its role. Key informants might not recognize research as a factor – the ODI team found that people are not used to thinking about the role of knowledge or ideas in social change process, so might tend to overlook their significance (Court et al., 2005). Moreover, in the case of the PRSP policy change, it is worth noting that it took a high-profile evaluation of existing programmes and a substantial body of research built up over at least a decade to tip the scales in favour of a radical shift in the development world. It is important to look for incremental change over time as well as assessing shorter-term impact. Research of this sort is most effective when it is part of an integrated programme of work.

Key points from this chapter

Managers who want to learn more about how to run better research for development work need to make it a habit to assess research projects as they would other development work. This can be done using the project's objectives as a starting point, or by evaluating its strengths and weaknesses against quality standards. Different issues need attention depending on whether the research aims at informing the programme or at influencing policy more broadly. The success of any efforts to encourage participation in the research process should also be carefully considered.

Checklist: ways to assess research for development work

- ☑ Compare achievement to objectives.
- ☑ Assess the quality of the product and the process.
- ☑ Compare your project with quality standards.
- ☑ Ask views of all participants/stakeholders – and let them decide what is important to mention.
- ☑ Ensure the scale of the assessment effort is in keeping with the scale of the original project.

Further reading

Carden, F. (2009) *Knowledge to Policy: Making the Most of Development Research.* New Delhi, Thousand Oaks, CA, London: Sage.

Presents key findings and summaries of 22 case studies from Asia, Africa and Latin America which illustrate how development research influences public policy and decision-making. Written in a reader-friendly, journalistic style.

Hovland, I. (2007) 'Making a difference: M&E of policy research', *Working Paper* 281. London: ODI.

Jones, H. (2011) 'A guide to monitoring and evaluating policy influence', *Background Note.* London: ODI.

Both documents from ODI's RAPID team offer a good introduction to current best practice in research impact assessment, with useful tools and techniques for evaluating research output, uptake and impact.

Spaapen, J., Dijstelbloem, H. and Wamelink, F. (2007) *Evaluating Research in Context: A Method for Comprehensive Assessment,* 2nd edn. The Hague: COS.

A very useful text exploring additional strategies for assessing the impact of research on policy, written from a science perspective but highly relevant.

Stachowiak, S. (2007) *Pathways for Change: Six Theories About How Policy Change Happens.* Seattle: ORS.

This easy-to-read report, written for both funders and evaluators, provides a useful review of six broad theories of policy change drawn from political science, sociology and psychology. Each theory is presented alongside a short summary, review of important underlying concepts, the theory's application to advocacy and an illustrative example. Helpful for contextualizing policy impact frameworks to broader themes.

Notes

1 A 'news aggregator' is a webpage or search engine that searches the internet for media coverage of any topic you indicate. For instance, Google News (one of the fastest and easiest to use options) is a general search engine for media reports containing key words – using it, you can quickly find a detailed record of any coverage which mentions your research, your organization or your topic of interest online (http://news.google.com). Advanced news aggregators and really simple syndication, or RSS, feeds are also available for free, and may be attractive to the more tech-savvy user, allowing for real-time updates every time your research is mentioned online.

2 Google Analytics provides the most popular, and free, web analytic service. It features a user-friendly interface for first-time users that allows identification of page views, number of downloads of a document and geographical origins of visitors – as well as a broader search of 'buzz' surrounding the page on the wider internet (www.google.com/analytics).

APPENDIX 1
MONITORING AND EVALUATION

Monitoring and evaluation (M&E) is an entire field of practice in its own right, with an ever-increasing body of literature, methods and theory overlapping with, but distinct from, the broader research skills introduced in *Research for Development*. Evaluation is an important type of programme-focused research process. However, M&E in development work often looks more like a management process than a research process – and this is as it should be. Programmes that have systematic M&E plans built in from the start are more likely to be effective than those that hire a researcher at the last minute to evaluate the programme retrospectively. Therefore, this appendix aims mainly to offer signposting to other texts and a short guide to some key terminology, as well as directing the reader to material in the rest of the book that will be useful in M&E work. If you are a practitioner looking for guidance on how to conduct M&E, you may wish to consult a dedicated text for your primary reference in addition to this appendix.

What is M&E? A general overview

The twin tasks of 'monitoring' and 'evaluation' refer to overlapping project management tools. Monitoring is the continuous observation and tracking of project/programme performance during a development intervention. It is descriptive in nature, concerned primarily with the recording of key indicators, inputs, activities and project outputs. Evaluation is about making judgements – assessing the changes in targeted results to which the specific project or programme may have contributed. Taken together, M&E can allow development workers to maintain ongoing feedback on progress and challenges during a development intervention's lifecycle, while also generating best practice lessons for future change.

The central contribution of a focus on M&E lies in assisting managers and practitioners to focus on the results ('outcomes', 'impact') of their work rather than only on the activities delivered ('outputs', 'targets'). Attention is directed towards the changes, benefits or learning the work achieves. It is usually important to collect information about both outputs and outcomes/impact, but little new learning will occur unless efforts are made to focus on the desired results of the work and to what extent they have been achieved.

At a very practical level, M&E methods provide regular feedback on programme performance, as well as an 'early warning' function with regard to the challenges which arise. But beyond this, a well-designed M&E effort also produces critically useful strategic guidance on how a particular programme is – or is not – progressing towards its stated objectives. M&E also has long-term implications, drawing out critical best practice lessons for future refinement of development practice. And, importantly, M&E serves a critical purpose in offering accountability and transparency to key stakeholders involved in the process, from donors to local communities.

Different approaches to M&E

There are many schools of thought on M&E, and many of the same controversies exist as in the wider research field, in particular the tension between positivist and social constructionist approaches discussed in Chapter 2. In choosing an approach, ask questions, as advised for research, about what your key aims are in undertaking this task. If you are taking a highly innovative approach in your programme, it may be unwise to use an evaluation approach which is also unusual and which may not be accepted as valid by those to whom you are accountable. On the other hand, it is not uncommon for funders and other stakeholders to seem to require completely unaffordable levels of 'proof' of effectiveness. Negotiation on evaluation processes with funders from the start is highly advisable. If you do not feel on top of the concepts under discussion, seek help from someone who is, but choose carefully (see Chapter 4).

A distinction has traditionally been made between 'formative' and 'summative' evaluation – the first building systems and processes of reflection that enable improvement to a programme as it goes along and the second making judgements when the work is completed. However, many approaches and tools contain elements of both approaches. While a focus on results is very common, it is also important to think about how to capture relevant information on the context of an intervention, and particularly on how to understand why it might be effective or ineffective. Which key components of the programme are effective?

Some key resources on M&E

Research for Development was originally conceived as a companion volume to Save the Children's *Toolkits* guidebook, and this remains an excellent, accessible guide to the core tools for M&E:

Gosling, L. and Edwards, M. (2003) *Toolkits: A Practical Guide to Monitoring, Evaluation and Impact Assessment*. London: Save the Children.

More reflective, but still of particular practical use, are the following books:

Patton, M.Q. (2008) *Utilization-focused Evaluation,* 4th edn. London: Sage.

Pawson, R. and Tilley, N. (1997) *Realistic Evaluation*. London: Sage.

Specific guidance in relation to M&E for international development work:

Department for International Development (DFID) (2003) *Tools for Development: A Handbook for Those Engaged in Development Activity.* Version 15.1. London: DFID.

Available online at: http://webarchive.nationalarchives.gov.uk/+/http://www.dfid.gov.uk/Documents/publications/toolsfordevelopment.pdf

Guijt, I. and Woodhill, J. (2008) "Annex D methods for M&E", in international fund for agricultural development (IFAD)', *Managing for Impact in Rural Development: A Guide for Project M&E.* Rome: Office of Evaluation and Studies, IFAD. Available online at:

www.ifad.org/evaluation/guide/annexd/index.htm

Mikkelsen, B. (2005) *Methods for Development Work and Research: A New Guide for Practitioners,* 2nd edn. New Delhi, Thousand Oaks, CA, and London: Sage.

United Nations Development Programme (UNDP) (2002) *Handbook on Monitoring and Evaluating for Results.* New York: Evaluation Office, UNDP. Available online at:

www.undp.org/evaluation/documents/HandBook/ME-HandBook.pdf

World Bank (2004) *Monitoring and Evaluation: Tools Methods, and Approaches.* Washington, DC: Independent Evaluation Group, World Bank.

The UK-focused Charities Evaluation Services provides very helpful guidance both on its website and through its training, publications and other activities. www.ces-vol.org.uk

Monitoring and Evaluation News is an online news service focusing on developments in M&E methods relevant to development programmes with social development objectives. http://mande.co.uk/

The rest of this appendix is divided into four sections. The first two describe results-oriented and then more participatory and process-oriented approaches (although this is not a hard-and-fast distinction). The third looks at evaluation approaches with an economic focus. The final section links to the rest of the book by mapping out where you can find guidance there on methods that are particularly useful in M&E work. Results-oriented approaches include Logical Framework Analysis, Theory of Change, Impact Evaluation, Randomized Controlled Trials and Results-based Accountability. Participatory and process-oriented approaches include Outcome Mapping, Most Significant Change and Appreciative Inquiry. The economic approaches discussed are Cost Benefit and Cost Effectiveness Analysis and Social Return on Investment.

Results-oriented approaches to M&E

Logical Framework Analysis

The Logical Framework (LogFrame) approach provides a structured and logical means of clarifying objectives, planning, implementing and monitoring and evaluating projects, programmes and policies. It is used to improve the quality of project and programme design through the preparation of detailed operational plans.

The LogFrame is usually presented in a table and summarizes:

1 the *goal* of the project, namely, the long-term vision;
2 the *purpose* of the project, that is, the changes the project is seeking to make;
3 the *inputs* or resources required, such as materials, equipment and financial and human resources;
4 the *activities* or actual tasks required to produce the desired outputs;
5 the *outputs* or specifically intended results of the project activities;
6 the longer-term *outcomes* and *impact* of the project;
7 the *means of verification*, that is, performance indicators to measure the progress and success of the project;
8 the *risks* that might impede the attainment of the objectives.

For more information

Australian Agency for International Development (AusAID) (2005) 'AusGuideline 3.3: the logical framework approach', *AusGuide – A Guide to Program Management*. Canberra: AusAID. Available online at:

www.ausaid.gov.au/ausguide/pdf/ausguideline3.3.pdf

BOND (2003) 'Logical framework analysis', *Guidance Note 04*. London: BOND. Available online at:

www.gdrc.org/ngo/logical-fa.pdf

Department for International Development (DFID) (2003) 'Logical frameworks', *Tools for Development: A Handbook for Those Engaged in Development Activity.* Version 15.1, London: DFID, Chapter 5. Available online at:

http://webarchive.nationalarchives.gov.uk/+/http://www.dfid.gov.uk/Documents/publications/toolsfordevelopment.pdf

---

Theory of Change

Many schools of evaluation use the concept of a Theory of Change (TOC), but the term is also used to refer to an approach used widely in development work. A TOC explains how a group of early and intermediate accomplishments sets the stage for producing long-range results. A more complete TOC articulates the assumptions about the process through which change will occur, and specifies how all of the required early and intermediate outcomes related to achieving the desired long-term change will be brought about and documented as they occur (Anderson, 2005a) A TOC provides an opportunity for stakeholders to assess what they can influence, what impact they can have and whether it is realistic to expect to reach their goal with the time and resources they have available.

Steps to create a TOC:

1 Identify a long-term goal.
2 Conduct 'backwards mapping' to identify the preconditions necessary to achieve that goal.

3   Identify the interventions your initiative will perform to create these preconditions.
4   Develop indicators for each precondition that will be used to assess the performance of the interventions.
5   Write a narrative that can be used to summarize the various moving parts in your theory.

For more information

ACT Development (2009) 'A guide to assessing our contribution to change', ACT Development Impact Project Working Group.

Available online at:

www.actalliance.org/resources/policies-and-guidelines/impact-assessment/IA-Guide-eng-v1.pdf

Anderson, A. (2005a) 'An introduction to theory of change', *Evaluation Exchange/ HFRP*, XI (2).

Available online at:

/www.hfrp.org/evaluation/the-evaluation-exchange/issue-archive/evaluation-methodology/an-introduction-to-theory-of-change

Anderson, A. (2005b) *The Community Builder's Approach to Theory of Change: A Practical Guide to Theory and Development*. New York: The Aspen Institute Roundtable on Community Change. Available online at:

www.aspeninstitute.org/sites/default/files/content/docs/roundtable%20on%20community%20change/rcccommbuildersapproach.pdf

Theory of Change Community. Available online at:

www.theoryofchange.org/

Impact evaluation

Writers on evaluation use the term 'impact' in different ways: at times it is used interchangeably with 'outcome', but frequently it is taken to refer to the wider impact of interventions, beyond outcomes for individuals, for example on policy and practice. Others use it to refer to the longer-term study of the results of interventions, or to studies that analyse results against some kind of comparator (often 'before' and 'after') (see White, 2006).

For more information

Jones, N., Jones, H., Steer, L. and Datta, A. (2009) 'Improving impact evaluations, production and use'. *Working Paper 300*. London: ODI. Available online at:

www.odi.org.uk/resources/download/3177.pdf

(Continued)

(Continued)

White, H. (2006) *Impact Evaluation – the Experience of the Independent Evaluation Group of the World Bank*. Washington, DC: World Bank.

Available online at:

http://lnweb90.worldbank.org/oed/oeddoclib.nsf/DocUNIDViewForJavaSearch/35BC420995BF58F8852571E00068C6BD/$file/impact_evaluation.pdf

White, H. (2009) 'Some reflections on current debates in impact evaluation', *Working Paper 1*. London: International Initiative for Impact Evaluation (3ie).

Available online at:

http://www.3ieimpact.org/admin/pdfs_papers/11.pdf

International Initiative for Impact Evaluation. Available online at:

www.3ieimpact.org/

http://siteresources.worldbank.org/EXTOED/Resources/nonie_guidance.pdf

Randomized Controlled Trials

The primary goal of conducting a Randomized Controlled Trial (RCT) is to test whether an intervention works by comparing it with a control condition, usually either no intervention or an alternative intervention. The key methodological components of an RCT are:

1 Use of a control condition with which the experimental intervention is compared;
2 Random assignment of participants to conditions.

Random assignment ensures that known and unknown person and environment characteristics that could affect the outcome of interest are evenly distributed across conditions. The use of an RCT design gives the investigator confidence that differences in outcome between treatment and control were actually caused by the treatment, since random assignment (theoretically) equalizes the groups on all other variables.

RCTs are regarded as a 'gold standard' evaluation design in much natural scientific, including medical, research. Their use for social programmes is controversial, since so many factors can be involved. However, comparison with a 'control group' produces uniquely persuasive evidence, where feasible.

For more information

Banerjee, A. and Duflo, E. (2011) *Poor Economics: A Radical Rethinking of the Way to Fight Global Poverty*. New York: Perseus Books.

Barahona, C. (2010) 'Randomised control trials for the impact evaluation of development initiatives: a statistician's point of view', *ILAC Working Paper 13*. Rome: Institutional Learning and Change Initiative. Available online at:

www.cgiar-ilac.org/files/publications/working_papers/ILAC_WorkingPaper_No13_Randomised%20Control%20Trials.pdf

Duflo E., Glennersterand R. and Kremer, M. (2006) *Using Randomization in Development Economics Research: A Toolkit*. Boston, MA: Poverty Action Lab, Massachusetts Institute of Technology.

Results-based Accountability

Results-based Accountability is an approach to evaluation embedded in management practice, developed and promoted by Mark Friedman. It has been highly influential in some national and local government quarters. Principles are given as: ‹

1. Start with ends, work backward to means. What do we want? How will we recognize it? What will it take to get there?
2. Be clear and disciplined about language.
3. Use plain language, not exclusionary jargon.
4. Keep accountability for populations separate from accountability for programmes and agencies.
5. Results are end conditions of well-being for populations in a geographic area: children, adults, families and communities. They are the responsibility of partnerships.
6. Define customer or client results as the end conditions of well-being for customers of a programme, agency or service system. They are the responsibility of the managers of the programme or agency.
7. Use data (indicators and performance measures) to gauge success or failure against a baseline.
8. Use data to drive a disciplined business-like decision-making process to get better.
9. Involve a broad set of partners.
10. Get from talk to action as quickly as possible.

For more information

Friedman, M. (2005) *Trying Hard Is Not Good Enough*. New Bern, NC: Trafford Publishing.

Participative and process-focused approaches to M&E

Outcome Mapping

A focus on outcomes is crucial to many approaches to M&E, but Outcome Mapping (OM) refers to a specific tradition within the development community that is proposed as an alternative to LogFrame. OM was developed by the International Development Research Centre (IDRC) in the late 1990s and focuses on measuring development results in terms of changes in behaviour, actions or relationships that can be influenced by the project or programme (Smutylo, 2005) . However, OM is not based on a cause–effect framework; rather, it recognizes that multiple, non-linear events lead to change (Earl et al., 2001). The originality of this approach lies in its shift away from assessing the products of a programme to focusing on behavioural change.

OM is useful and works best when:

1 focusing on learning processes and attitudinal change;
2 working in partnership;
3 building capacity;
4 understanding social factors;
5 tackling complex problems;
6 creating greater reflection, learning and dialogue.

See Jones and Hearn (2009) to learn more about when to use OM. It is not suited to technical and standardized project work or for measuring quantitative objectives.

For more information

ACT Development (2009) 'A guide to assessing our contribution to change'. ACT Development Impact Project Working Group. Available online at:

www.actalliance.org/resources/policies-and-guidelines/impact-assessment/IA-Guide-eng-v1.pdf

Earl, S., Carden, F. and Smutylo, T. (2001) *Outcome Mapping: Building Learning and Reflection into Development Programs*. Ottawa: IDRC.

Jones, H. and Hearn, S. (2009) 'Outcome mapping: a realistic alternative for planning, Monitoring and evaluation', *Background Note*. London: ODI.

Smutylo, T. (2005) 'Outcome mapping: a method for tracking behavioural changes in development programs', *Institutional Learning and Change Brief* 7. Ottawa: IDRC.

Most Significant Change

Most Significant Change (MSC) is a form of participatory M&E. It is more suited to monitoring that focuses on learning rather than just accountability. The process involves collecting significant change (SC) stories from the field, of which the most significant are systematically selected by panels of designated stakeholders or staff. There are several reasons why organizations find MSC monitoring useful. It is a good means of identifying unexpected changes. It requires no special professional skills. Compared with other monitoring approaches, it is easy to communicate across cultures. Everyone can tell stories about events they think were important. It encourages analysis as well as data collection because people have to explain why they believe one change is more important than another. Therefore, MSC is useful for programmes that are complex, focused on social change, participatory in ethos and designed with repeated contact between field staff and participants. It is less suitable for simple programmes with easily defined outcomes, where quantitative monitoring may be sufficient and require less time.

For more information

ACT Development (2009) 'A guide to assessing our contribution to change', ACT Development Impact Project Working Group. Available online at:

www.actalliance.org/resources/policies-and-guidelines/impact-assessment/IA-Guide-eng-v1.pdf

Davies, R. and Dart, J. (2005) *The 'Most Significant Change' (MSC) Technique: A Guide to Its Use*. Available online at:

www.esf-agentschap.be/uploadedFiles/Voor_ESF_promotoren/Zelfevaluatie_ESF-project/MSCGuide.pdf

---

Appreciative Inquiry

Appreciative Inquiry (AI) is an evaluation approach that rejects the common focus on needs and difficulties and focuses instead on identifying points of success and best practice and thereafter generating insights to inform future strategies. In particular, AI is defined by its approach to identifying and amplifying stories of best practice within communities and organizations in order to stimulate behaviour, visions and plans for improving wellbeing (World Bank, 2004). In practice, AI is more narrative based than analytical, allowing a community or organization to think through and make decisions organically, from within.

The AI process has four stages, which are sometimes referred to as the four Ds:

1 Destiny: creating what will be;
2 Discovery: appreciating what is;
3 Dream: imagining what could be;
4 Design: determining what could be.

For more information

ACT Development (2009) 'A guide to assessing our contribution to change', ACT Development Impact Project Working Group. Available online at:

www.actalliance.org/resources/policies-and-guidelines/impact-assessment/IA-Guide-eng-v1.pdf

Cooperrider, D., Whitney, D. and Stavros, J. (2007) *Appreciative Inquiry Handbook*. San Francisco, CA: Berrett-Koehler.

Elliott, C. (1999) *Locating the Energy for Change: An Introduction to Appreciative Inquiry*. Winnipeg: International Institute for Sustainable Development.

Approaches to M&E that include economic evaluation

Cost Benefit and Cost Effectiveness Analysis

Cost Benefit and Cost Effectiveness Analysis are tools for assessing whether or not the costs of an activity can be justified by the outcomes and impacts. Cost Benefit Analysis measures both inputs and outputs in monetary terms. Cost Effectiveness Analysis estimates inputs in monetary terms and outcomes in non-monetary quantitative terms (such as improvements in student reading scores) (World Bank, 2004). Be aware that both demand highly technical skills in economic analysis, and are often better conducted by specifically trained professional evaluators (Belli et al., 2000).

For more information

Belli, P., Anderson, J.R., Barnum, H.N., Dixon, J.A. and Tan, J.-P. (2000) *Economic Analysis of Investment Operations: Analytical Tools and Practical Applications.* Washington, DC: World Bank.

World Bank (2004) *Monitoring and Evaluation: Tools Methods, and Approaches.* Washington, DC: Independent Evaluation Group, World Bank. Available online at:

http://siteresources.worldbank.org/EXTEVACAPDEV/Resources/4585672-1251481378590/MandE_tools_methods_approaches.pdf

---

Social Return on Investment

Social Return on Investment (SROI) is a specific methodology that offers a comprehensive analysis of the changes experienced by service users and also a financial valuation of their worth. By consulting closely with service users, an SROI builds a detailed picture of the changes attributable to a programme and their value. By assessing the total value of benefits against the cost of investment, the final SROI ratio communicates at a glance the net value of a project: for example, for every £1 of money invested £4 worth of outcomes are generated.

According to the SROI network, the approach is based on seven principles:

1 *Involve stakeholders:* understand how the organization creates change through a dialogue with stakeholders.
2 *Understand what changes:* acknowledge and articulate all the values, objectives and stakeholders of the organization before agreeing which aspects of the organization are to be included in the scope; and determine what must be included in the account so stakeholders can make reasonable decisions.
3 *Value the things that matter:* use financial proxies for indicators in order to include the values of those excluded from markets in the same terms as used in markets.

4 *Only include what is material:* articulate clearly how activities create change and evaluate this through the evidence gathered.

5 *Do not over-claim:* make comparisons of performance and impact using appropriate benchmarks, targets and external standards.

6 *Be transparent:* demonstrate the basis on which the findings may be considered accurate and honest; and show they will be reported to and discussed with stakeholders.

7 *Verify the result:* ensure appropriate independent verification of the account.

For more information

SROI Network (2012) *A Guide to Social Return on Investment 2012*, 2nd edn. London: SROI Network.

The SROI network aims to create consistent standards among practitioners of SROI. Available online at www.thesroinetwork.org

---

Different tools and methods used in M&E

M&E draws on a wide range of tools, methods and frameworks for data collection and analysis, many of which are the same as those introduced in this manual. Others are tailored more specifically to M&E roles – there is a large and ever-expanding universe of M&E methods that is continually in the process of being refined.

This section offers a brief summary of M&E methods, pointing out where in the book you might find additional information as well as suggesting some external sources. The list of methods is by no means exhaustive, and you may wish to investigate further on your own in the dedicated M&E literature.

Methods in M&E

Questionnaires and surveys: M&E makes wide use of questionnaires and surveys as key tools for data collection on baseline measures, performance questions and indicators. You were introduced to questionnaire and survey design and concepts in Section 11.4; Section 13.8 showed how to analyse these types of data.

Semi-structured interviews: Another core M&E method is the semi-structured interview, introduced in Section 11.2, with guidance on analysing interview data provided in Chapter 13. Such interviews can elicit useful insights about project progress, outcome, relevance and quality from beneficiaries and stakeholders.

Direct observation: Direct observation is particularly important for grounding and contextualizing collected data and final results. Section 11.6 provides an overview of observation techniques.

Sampling: In gathering data for M&E, you will often not be able to rely on a full census covering an entire population. In such cases, a representative sample will be called for, drawing on the same techniques you learnt in Chapter 10. These include both probability/random sampling (Section 10.3) and purposive/non-random sampling – helpful in evaluation contexts that demand a particular beneficiary perspective (Section 10.4).

Systematic reviews: Systematic reviews attempt to collate all empirical evidence that fits pre-specified eligibility criteria in order to answer a specific research question. They make use of explicit, systematic methods that are reproducible and selected with a view to minimizing bias, thus providing more reliable findings from which conclusions can be drawn and decisions made (Antman, 1992 and Oxman, 1993, in Higgins and Green, 2011; Bergh et al., 2012). The Cochrane Collaboration on health care has standardized procedures for this and the Cochrane Library holds this body of work (www.thecochranelibrary.com/view/0/index.html).

Secondary data analysis review: Documentary review skills are as applicable to M&E as they are to social research, with a tremendous amount of information contained in project documentation collected in written, electronic, photographic or video form. Documentation review is particularly important in offering background information for baseline studies (see below). For guidance on secondary data analysis in general, see Section 11.5, as well as Chapter 5's guidance on how to find published information.

Rapid appraisals: M&E practitioners also often rely on rapid appraisals: short-term studies (typically conducted over four to six weeks) tailored to the needs of decision makers, which are designed to solicit views and feedback from beneficiaries and stakeholders quickly. Rapid appraisals are particularly useful in quickly generating information to inform decision making for project or programme managers and understanding complicated socioeconomic issues. Rapid appraisals are cheap and quick – hence their popularity. For the same reasons, however, they also lack the same validity and generalizability of more in-depth research.

One common variation of rapid appraisal is Participatory Learning and Action (PLA) – formerly known as Rapid Rural Appraisal (RRA). PLA is an important approach to needs assessment and feasibility studies, and constitutes an important alternative to the tradition of big, 'top-down' surveys, placing community participation at the core of the process. For more, see Chapter 12, 'Participatory Research'.

Stakeholder analysis: Identification of key stakeholders is an important step in M&E design, allowing you to identify which actors to consult and incorporate into an M&E system, as well as whose information you need to collect for consideration. You were introduced to stakeholder analysis in Section 3.4.4, and it remains a common ingredient in M&E studies.

Methods for group discussion

Separate sets of methods are also used in M&E for the purposes of gathering data through group-based discussion.

Focus groups: These are introduced in Section 11.3 and are widely used for M&E, where collecting the opinions of beneficiaries and stakeholders is critical to assess change, quality of services and areas for improvement. See also Section 13.7 for analysis of focus group data.

Strengths, weaknesses, opportunities, threats: A second tool used for M&E purpose is SWOT analysis, discussed in Chapter 3. SWOT analysis is useful in strategically considering and assessing provided services, and understanding relationships between key actors for the purposes of monitoring the project throughout its lifecycle.

Dreams realized or visioning: This technique is helpful to encourage people to identify their own visions or aspirations for development projects. To carry out this process, a facilitator asks a group of participants to identify the characteristics of an ideal situation in the future, or their own visions and thoughts on what 'wellbeing' really means. Individual 'dreams' can, in turn, be used as a project indicator, and monitored to gauge whether the project is 'realizing' or deterring this.

Drama and role plays: Section 12.4 also discusses some more creative alternatives for group work via drama and role plays. These can be of great value in M&E: groups can take part in dramatic scenes and role playing in order to allow a better understanding of their perceptions of key issues for subsequent discussion and monitoring. These approaches can also help to identify attitudes towards post-project changes for the purposes of impact evaluation.

APPENDIX 2
USEFUL WEBSITES

General information

Libraries

Based at the Institute of Development Studies (IDS) at the University of Sussex, the *British Library for Development Studies* (BLDS) is Europe's largest research collection on development issues. Its website offers access to its catalogue, information about the library's document delivery service, subject guides, country resources, e-resources including journals and thematic and regional resources and links to other thematic and statistical databases and development-related libraries: http://blds.ids.ac.uk/

The *WorldCat* is a unique search tool providing access to the collections of thousands of libraries worldwide with millions of items; not only does it enable the user to find an item of interest, but also it locates a copy of this item in the nearest library: www.worldcat.org/

The *United Nations Bibliographic Information System* (UNBISnet) is the official online catalogue of UN documents, publications, speeches and voting records: http://unbisnet.un.org/, whereas the *UN Libraries Central Gateway* provides access to the libraries and resources of UN bodies and agencies: www.unsystem.org/en/libraRies/index.html

Copac is an online library catalogue providing reference access to the catalogues of the major British and Irish national, academic and specialist libraries: http://copac.ac.uk/

The online Integrated Catalogue of the *British Library* provides reference access to over 13 million items of its collections: http://catalogue.bl.uk

Newspapers

The Guardian website includes a specific section on international development, with articles on current development debates, case studies tracking progress on the Millennium Development Goals (MDGs), policy papers and global development statistics from international agencies, a very interesting blog and a fortnightly email newsletter with a brief update of what appeared on the website: www.guardian.co.uk/global-development

The *Newspaper Index WorldWide* provides a directory of online newspapers from every country in the world: www.newspaperindex.com/

Media UK offers a constantly updated directory of British online newspapers: www.mediauk.com/newspapers

News sites

Integrated Regional Information Networks (IRIN) is a news service of the UN Office for the Coordination of Humanitarian Affairs (OCHA) with the latest news and reports on major development themes and links to regional and country webpages: www.irinnews.org/. Recommended ☆

Trust.org is the portal of the Thomson Reuters Foundation, providing access to *AlertNet* (AN), the humanitarian news site with the latest news and reports on current emergencies and an additional climate change focus, and to *TrustLaw* (TL), focusing on governance, anti-corruption and women's rights issues: www.trust.org/alertnet/and http://www.trust.org/trustlaw/, respectively.

The website of the *BBC World Service* offers access to the best of BBC international news programmes and resources: http://www.bbc.co.uk/worldservice/programmes/index.shtml

Also administered by OCHA, *ReliefWeb* offers timely, reliable information and analysis about humanitarian crises worldwide, organized by country and theme: http://reliefweb.int/

The *Women News Network* (WNN) offers news and reports about women's lives and issues from around the world: http://womennewsnetwork.net/

Blogs and podcasts

From Poverty to Power is the blog of Duncan Green, head of research for Oxfam UK. His daily posts provide an excellent overview of current key debates, events and publications on development issues: www.oxfamblogs.org/fp2p/ Recommended ☆

Poverty Matters is *The Guardian*'s blog dedicated to global development, with daily posts exploring key aid and development topics: www.guardian.co.uk/global-development/poverty-matters. The website also offers several podcasts with development experts discussing current challenges: www.guardian.co.uk/content/podcast+global-development/global-development

The *Thomson Reuters AlertNet* also offers several regional (Africa, Asia and Latin America) and thematic (such as aid, climate change, health, and women) blogs: www.trust.org/alertnet/blogs/

The *World Bank* website offers a collection of topic-specific blogs from conflict and governance to climate change and African poverty, which are used as forums for the Bank's staff to discuss their ideas with the development community: http://blogs.worldbank.org/blogs

Development Drums offers podcasts on issues of global poverty and international development: http://developmentdrums.org/

Information on specific issues

Please note that this list includes mainly 'official' development websites rather than alternative ones; however, there are innumerable resources on the web and more are constantly added, therefore a good search can satisfy specific user needs.

Africa

The *UN Economic Commission for Africa* (UNECA) website includes news on current continental issues, information about the organization's own initiatives on climate change, gender, women's rights, population, HIV and AIDS, information and communication technologies (ICTs), media and water along with reports and useful links to relevant portals: www.uneca.org/. It also provides access to the ECA online library with UN and African links, and to the *African Centre for Statistics* with the *ECA statistical database* containing financial, social and environment statistics: http://ecastats.uneca.org/acsweb/ and http://ecastats.uneca.org/statbase/, respectively.

The *New Partnership for Africa's Development* (NEPAD), advertised as the African Union's (AU's) new development strategic framework, has a good website with annual reports, policy documents, case studies, videos, useful links of partners and a newsletter covering NEPAD's six thematic areas (agriculture, climate change, infrastructure, human development, governance, gender and capacity development): www.nepad.org/

The *African Development Bank* (AfDB) website includes a helpful guide to all the topics it works on, country strategy papers, programme and evaluation reports, a working paper series presenting findings on major African policy issues, the Bank's annual Statistics Pocketbook with socioeconomic indicators on African countries and a data portal visualizing these indicators: www.afdb.org/en/

Pambazuka News is an African online forum for social justice on the continent, and its website includes newsletters with the latest news, articles and publications on major issues such as human rights, trade, gender, environment, land and food justice and conflict along with relevant multimedia resources: www.pambazuka.org/en/

The *AllAfrica* website provides daily news from all over the African continent from headlines to regional and country stories in English and French: http://allafrica.com/

Ageing

HelpAge International is an international charity working to promote old people's rights and improve their lives. Its website includes some global ageing data, a few related web-links and, most importantly, factsheets, project reports and research papers on ageing, climate change, emergencies, health, work and pensions: www.helpage.org/

The *Oxford Institute of Population Ageing* is an academic centre conducting research on population change with a demographic focus; its website provides access to research and analysis reviews, a related journal, global and regional reports, a working paper series and videos and radio interviews: www.ageing.ox.ac.uk/

The website of *Global Action on Aging* (GAA), a US-based organization, contains articles and reports published by several agencies on ageing issues and policies in the US and worldwide with a special focus on elderly rights, health, pension, rural ageing, armed conflict and related UN activities: www.globalaging.org/

The *UN Programme on Ageing*, part of the Social Policy and Development Division of the UN Department of Economic and Social Affairs (UNDESA), is currently the focal point on ageing issues within the UN system. Its website includes the current international action plan, related UN resolutions, a few web-links and reports and a brief newsletter: http://social.un.org/index/Ageing.aspx

Agriculture and rural development (ARD)

The UN *International Fund for Agricultural Development* (IFAD) works on agriculture and rural poverty, and its website includes policy and strategy documents, useful fact sheets and thematic papers on issues such as gender, natural resource management, remittances and rural finance. It also provides access to the *Rural Poverty Portal* with related resources: www.ifad.org/ and www.ruralpovertyportal.org/web/guest/home, respectively. Recommended ☆

The UN *Food and Agriculture Organization* (FAO) website offers access to various publications on issues of agriculture, fisheries, forests and markets as well as to country profiles, its knowledge forum with best practices and professional networks and specialist databases with statistics on agricultural resources, production and prices: www.fao.org

The *Consultative Group on International Agricultural Research* (CGIAR) is a global partnership of agricultural organizations and includes a consortium of 15 specialist research centres working on biodiversity, forestry, crops, livestock, fish, food security and water. Its website provides links to these centres, their publications and professional databases: www.cgiar.org/

The *Future Agricultures Consortium* (FAC) is a partnership of African and British researchers working on the links between agriculture, climate change, commercialization, social protection, technology, pastoralism, land and youth; its website includes policy briefs, research and working papers on all these issues: www.future-agricultures.org

The website of the *International Land Coalition* (ILC), an alliance for fair access to and control over land, provides reports, reviews and case studies along with access to a database on commercial pressures on land and to the *Land Portal*, a knowledge-sharing platform for land issues: www.landcoalition.org/ and http://landportal.info/, respectively.

Aid and debt

The *Development Assistance Committee* (DAC) of the Organisation for Economic Co-operation and Development (OECD) includes 24 major donors offering *official development assistance* (ODA) to developing and transition countries; its website offers information about annual aid and other resource flows, a few related thematic reports and, most importantly, aid charts and its International Development Statistics (IDS) with two databases: the DAC with comprehensive ODA data by donor, recipient and region, and the Creditor Reporting System (CRS) with more detailed information on aid activities: www.oecd.org/department/0,3355,en_2649_33721_1_1_ 1_1_1,00.html

The *Development Gateway* uses information technologies for improved aid management and transparency, and its website offers access to several related publications, links to country websites and, most importantly, to the *AidData* portal with datasets on global aid flows and activities: www.developmentgateway.org/ and www.aiddata.org/home/index, respectively.

Development Finance International (DFI) is an independent organization working to improve development finance through debt relief, new aid and foreign private capital; its website provides access to research papers, country reports and technical briefings on debt strategy, public finance and private capital flows: www. development-finance.org/

BetterAid is a civil society platform working on aid and development effectiveness, and its website provides information about its initiatives, links to member organizations and a few policy and discussion papers: www.betteraid.org/

The *Global Humanitarian Assistance* (GHA) website provides a comprehensive overview of the key issues in humanitarian financing, from the role of government donors and delivery agencies to domestic actors, and includes donor and recipient profiles, graphs and charts: www.globalhumanitarianassistance.org/

Asia

The *Asian Development Bank* (ADB) website includes information about the current 2020 strategic framework for its core operational areas, and a wealth of resources from project-related documents to monthly electronic reviews of its activities and regional and thematic e-newsletters as well as key social and economic indicators for Asia and the Pacific, books, toolkits in CD-ROM format, research briefs and working papers by ADB's research institute: www.adb.org/

The *UN Economic and Social Commission for Western Asia* (UNESCWA) website contains information about the 14 Arab countries in the region which comprise the organization, and in its publications section includes annual and meeting reports and some research papers with comparative analysis of key issues in the region from displacement to urbanization and climate change: www.escwa.un.org/

The *UN Economic and Social Commission for Asia and the Pacific* (UNESCAP) is the largest UN regional commission, comprising 62 states with an emphasis on investment, transport and infrastructure development; its website includes resolutions, agreements and annual reports along with thematic maps, toolkits, assessment reports, research and policy papers and the statistical yearbook: www.unescap.org/

The *Regional Bureau for Arab States* (RBAS) is a UN Development Programme (UNDP) regional programme covering 18 Arab countries; its website provides access to several regional initiatives such as the Governance Programme (POGAR) and its parliamentary development knowledge portal, as well as to reports on regional key issues such as the MDG challenges and successes, climate change and women's empowerment: http://arabstates.undp.org/

Charities/non-governmental organizations (NGOs)

The *Oxfam International* website contains discussion and research papers, country case studies and humanitarian policy notes; the Oxfam country websites also contain interesting and even more resources on key issues. For example, *Oxfam GB's* website provides access to policy papers, research and evaluation reports, journal articles, books and best practices for development practitioners: www.oxfam.org and www.oxfam.org.uk/, respectively.

The *ActionAid International* website contains thematic newsletters, articles and reports on issues of food security, women's rights, governance, education, health, emergency support and climate change; in addition, country websites provide information about programmes along with related research papers, evaluation reports and briefings: www.actionaid.org and, for example, www.actionaid.or.uk, respectively.

The Bangladesh-based *Building Resources Across Communities* (BRAC) has a Research and Evaluation Division (RED) involved in the design, monitoring and assessment of its development interventions; its website provides access to relevant articles, reports, monographs and working papers: www.bracresearch.org/

The website of *Concern Worldwide* provides access to evaluation papers and best practices, briefs and thematic reports on issues of education, health, livelihoods and emergencies: www.concern.net/

BOND is the British membership body for international development NGOs, and its website provides a useful member directory with links and a few e-bulletins available to subscribers: www.bond.org.uk/

Children and youth

The *UN Children's Fund* (UNICEF) website offers information about its social and economic policies, legislative reform initiatives and country programmes through multiple resources, from its annual flagship publication, the State of the World's Children (SOWC), to report cards, manuals, up-to-date press releases and other publications organized by date, region, subject and title; country-related resources can be better accessed through each country webpages: www.unicef.org/index.php. Recommended ☆

UNICEF Innocenti Research Centre (IRC) is the agency's research and advocacy centre and its website provides high-quality online resources ranging from summaries of current key debates on child rights' issues to case studies, policy reviews and working papers, along with links to major research projects and related resources: www.unicef-irc.org/

The *Child Rights Information Network* (CRIN) is a global network of over 2,200 organizations, and its website contains a wide range of resources from the latest news and a very useful directory of its members to specific sections on violence, discrimination and rights-based programming, and from databases with international and national legal documents and court cases which used the UN Convention on the Rights of the Child (UNCRC) to national plans of action, toolkits, conference papers and official reports: www.crin.org/index.asp

The *Childinfo* website offers global statistics and data collected and analysed by UNICEF, organized by theme and country in the form of key indicators in child and maternal health, education and protection, presented in tables, charts and maps; it also provides access to the *Multiple Indicator Cluster Survey* (MICS) household surveys, and offers the option to compile one's own tables and graphs of interest: www.childinfo.org and www.micscompiler.org/MICS.html, respectively.

The website of the *Office of the Special Representative of the Secretary-General for Children and Armed Conflict* contains related legal documents, including UN Security Council (UNSC) Resolutions for the protection of children in conflict, working papers of the UNSC Working Group on Children and Armed Conflict (CAAC), annual official reports, country visit reports and several links to other agencies working on these issues: www.un.org/children/conflict/english/index.html

Climate change

The *UNEP (UN Environment Programme) Climate Change* website provides the latest news and a large collection of publications on various aspects of climate change: www.unep.org/climatechange/

The website of the *UN Framework Convention on Climate Change* (UNFCCC) provides access to UN decisions and resolutions, national reports and review papers, key links and project databases: http://unfccc.int/2860.php

The *Climate Funds Update* website provides information on finance initiatives helping developing countries to address climate change, a list of such initiatives along with graphs and statistics, project information and relevant publications: http://www.climatefundsupdate.org/

The website of the *Climate and Development Knowledge Network* (CDKN) for climate-compatible development offers a few policy briefs and reports on related projects: www.cdkn.org/

Please see also resources under *Environment*.

Conflict and security

The website of the *International Crisis Group* offers the latest news on conflict situations worldwide, its monthly bulletin with conflict updates, CrisisWatch and a collection of useful reports, briefings and podcasts on key issues in conflict prevention and resolution: www.crisisgroup.org/. Recommended ☆

The *Stockholm International Peace Research Institute* (SIPRI) conducts research on conflict, arms control and security issues, and its website offers access to its databases and to a wealth of published resources such as briefs, fact sheets, policy papers, research reports and its yearbook with global security trends: www.sipri.org/

The Canadian *Human Security Report Project* (HSRP) is a research institute working on the trends, causes and consequences of conflict and organized violence; its website provides access to reports, briefs, security statistics and the *Human Security Gateway*, a database with thousands of related resources: www.hsrgroup.org/ and www.humansecuritygateway.com/, respectively.

The *International Institute for Strategic Studies* (IISS) researches international security and politico-military issues, and its website provides access to its publication series with assessment reports, research papers, journal articles and reviews, and to its Armed Conflict Database, available through paid subscription: www.iiss.org/

The South Africa-based *Institute for Security Studies* (ISS) conducts policy research on issues of human security on the continent; its website includes the latest news, links to relevant organizations and various publications from journal articles and briefings to research papers and conflict analysis reports: www.iss.co.za/default.php

Please see also resources under 'Justice and reconciliation'.

Development associations

The *European Association of Development Research and Training Institutions* (EADI) is a professional network for development studies in Europe, and its website offers information about the latest events and activities of its working groups as well as access to EADI's training database with training programmes and institutions and to the EADI portal with publications from its member institutions: www.eadi.org/

The *Development Studies Association* (DSA) connects and promotes the work of the development research community in the UK and Ireland, and its website provides access to its member and research programme directories, to its *Journal of International Development* and a few member resources: www.devstud.org.uk/

Aiming to become a useful source of reference, the *DevDir* website provides a directory of development (international, government, private, research, civil society and media) organizations, arranged by regions and countries: www.devdir.org/index.html

Development guides

As part of IDS Knowledge Services, *Eldis* is probably the best web portal, offering access to thousands of documents on development research, policy and practice, to country profiles with relevant links and to useful resource guides to the major development topics: www.eldis.org/. Recommended ☆

The Development Gateway website provides access to *Zunia*, an online knowledge-sharing network with the latest news, publications and best practices on the major development issues from various organizations: http://zunia.org/

SciDev.Net (the Science and Development Network) is a knowledge-sharing portal focusing on the use of science and technology for sustainable development; it offers hundreds of documents on relevant issues, regional and thematic (agriculture, climate change, health, science and technology) guides and links to related organizations: www.scidev.net/en/

The *OneWorld Group* is a portal of the OneWorld Network advocating for a fairer and greener world through the use of internet and mobile phone applications; its website offers guides to key development topics as well as country briefings on poverty, food security and climate change issues: www.oneworldgroup.org/

The *WWW Virtual Library*, the oldest web catalogue, offers a webpage with links to the major development portals, organizations and their resources: www2.etown.edu/vl/intldev.html

Disability

Source is an online information support centre managed by Handicap International which offers a variety of resources on health, disability and development organized in key subject areas and including manuals, reports, policy and working papers, and links to related websites and databases: www.asksource.info/

UN Enable is the website of the Secretariat for the Convention on the Rights of Persons with Disabilities (SCRPD), offering information on key issues in disability and related work by the UN system; it includes the Convention and other UN documents on disability, its newsletter with the latest developments and some resources on key themes such as disability and women, HIV and AIDS, emergencies, and sports: www.un.org/disabilities/

Handicap International is an independent organization working to improve the lives of disabled people in over 60 countries; its website presents its country programmes, toolkits and several policy papers on issues of health, rights and inclusive development along with good practices for assisting the disabled in emergencies and for mine risk education: www.handicap-international.org.uk/

Economic development

Made up of five institutions, the *World Bank Group* provides financial and technical assistance to developing countries on economic policy, trade, infrastructure, governance, agriculture, health and education. Its website offers plenty of resources, preferably accessed through the alphabetical topic list and including interesting policy research working papers, the annual World Development Report and evaluation and country documents; it also provides access to its project database and to datasets with tables and graphs such as the World Development Indicators (WDI) and the Africa Development Indicators, advertised as the most detailed dataset on Africa (http://data.worldbank.org/): www.worldbank.org/. Recommended ☆

The *OECD* has 34 member countries and promotes economic and social development with a focus on financial stability, effective governance, employment and green growth; its website includes various, thematically organized, resources. A good starting point is the website of OECD's Development Centre or the Topics as both include links to the OECD's specific development networks such as Aid Statistics, ENVIRONET, GOVNET, GENDERNET and POVNET. Alternatively, *OECD iLibrary* provides access to publications on key development challenges, such as journal articles, reports and working papers, to statistics and to the annual OECD Factbook, with major economic and social indicators: www.oecd.org/home/0,3675,en_2649_201185_1_1_1_1_1,00.html, www.oecd.org/topic/0,3699,en_2649_37413_1_1_1_1_37413,00.html and www.oecd-ilibrary.org/, respectively.

The *UN Industrial Development Organization* (UNIDO) works on industrial development through investment and technology promotion, trade capacity building, improved energy access and environmental sustainability; its website provides access to thematic working papers, reports and relevant legal resources as well as to industrial statistical databases and statistical country briefs: www.unido.org/

Please see also resources under *Finance*, and under *Trade and markets*.

Education

The *UN Educational, Scientific and Cultural Organization* (UNESCO) website includes legal documents, data and statistics, case studies, technical guides, global, regional and thematic reports on education, culture and sciences and links to its institutes, centres and country offices: www.unesco.org/. Recommended ☆

The *UN Girls' Education Initiative* (UNGEI) website includes recordings, country profiles and a wealth of resources published by UN, governmental and independent organizations on gender equality in education: www.ungei.org/

The *Forum for African Women Educationalists* (FAWE) is an African organization working to empower girls through gender-sensitive educational interventions, and its website provides information about its innovative programmes and best practices: www.fawe.org/

Emergencies and natural disasters

The *UN International Strategy for Disaster Reduction* (UNISDR) website includes fact sheets, policy and research papers, links to several related inter-agency initiatives for capacity development, risk management, gender and disaster and knowledge as well as to *PreventionWeb*, with many resources, including disaster data and statistics: www.unisdr.org/ and www.preventionweb.net/, respectively.

The *Asian Disaster Preparedness Center* (ADPC) website includes technical and working papers, country profiles and case studies, e-newsletters and articles on disaster risk management and reduction in the region: www.adpc.net/

The *Gender and Disaster Network* (GDN) website includes several resources published by various agencies on related topics, yet it is not well updated: www.gdnonline.org/

Employment

The *International Labour Organization* (ILO) website includes useful information organized by topics and regions, as well as programme documents, flagship reports and a working paper series; it also provides access to labour statistics and many related databases such as on international and national legislation, health and safety rules and social protection, the ILO thesaurus and Labordoc, ILO's database on global labour literature: www.ilo.org/

The *Anti-Slavery International* website includes fact sheets, case studies and reports on issues such as forced and bonded labour, slavery and trafficking: www.antislavery.org/english/

The ILO *International Programme on the Elimination of Child Labour* (IPEC) website provides a comprehensive overview of different forms of child labour, including trafficking, related legal documents, links to other key websites and training materials to combat child labour, fact sheets, case studies and policy and evaluation reports: www.ilo.org/ipec/lang--en/index.htm

The *Youth Employment Network* is a UN partnership aimed at improving youth employment opportunities in developing countries, and its website includes a few publications and links to partner agencies and to youth portals: http://www.ilo.org/public/english/employment/yen/

Environment

The *International Institute for Environment and Development* (IIED) conducts research on climate change, governance, settlements, natural resources and markets, and its website offers a wealth of related publications and links: www.iied.org/. Recommended ☆

The *UNEP* website contains reports, training manuals, databases, several e-books and multimedia resources on its six priority areas (climate change, disasters, ecosystem, governance, substances and resource efficiency) accessed through either each priority area or the UNEP Resource Kit, the agency's main resource repository: www.unep.org/

The website of the *International Union for Conservation of Nature* (IUCN), a global conservation network, offers access to its publications on biodiversity, climate change, sustainable energy, green economy and human wellbeing, and to its databases on threatened species, protected areas, law (ECOLEX) and ecosystem: www.iucn.org/

The *Stockholm Environment Institute* (SEI) conducts research on environment management, climate risk, governance and development alternatives, and its website includes reports, fact sheets, policy briefs, research papers and a few research tools: http://sei-international.org/

The Canadian-based *International Institute for Sustainable Development* (IISD) conducts policy research on issues of climate change, adaptation, trade, natural resources, technology, markets, environment and conflict, and its website provides access to its thematically organized resources: www.iisd.org/

Ethics

Codes of ethics for professional research associations offer a good reference point for ethical practice in social research. These include, for example, the *Social Research Association*: www.the-sra.org.uk/guidelines; the *Association of Social Anthropologists of the Commonwealth*: www.theasa.org/ethics.shtml; the *British Psychological Society*: www.bps.org.uk/the-society/code-of-conduct/code-of-conduct_home.cfm; and the *British Sociological Association*: www.britsoc.co.uk/about/equality/statement-of-ethical-practice.aspx

Europe

The website of *UNDP Europe and the Commonwealth of Independent States* (CIS) *Regional Office* offers information about its programmes and related publications such as country MDG progress reports and thematic studies: http://europeandcis.

undp.org/. It also offers access to a *Development and Transition* policy forum with articles on key issues, organized by theme and country: www.developmentandtransition.net/Home.89.0.html

The *European Bank for Reconstruction and Development* (EBRD) is the largest financial investor in the economic transformation of Central and Eastern European countries and the CIS, and its website includes country economic profiles, case studies and economic transition reports: www.ebrd.com/pages/homepage.shtml

Finance

The website of the *International Monetary Fund* (IMF) offers various publications on its country operations and global monetary matters, such as country reports and research and policy papers on key economic issues and financial prospects along with access to its databases on balance of payments, trade, government finance and international financial statistics: www.imf.org/external/index.htm

The *International Finance Corporation* (IFC) is a member of the World Bank Group, responsible for private sector investment in developing countries; its website provides access to issue briefs, project reports, policy papers and business manuals as well as to a joint *World Bank–IFC portal* with relevant resources such as an interactive map on the business environment in 183 countries, country business profiles, toolkits, policy briefs and access to several databases: www.ifc.org/ and http://rru.worldbank.org/, respectively.

The *Bretton Woods Project* is an ActionAid-hosted project challenging the two Bretton Woods Institutions, that is to say the World Bank and the IMF, and promoting alternative approaches for a fair and accountable global economic system; its website includes the Bimonthly Update, briefings and reports with critical analyses of key World Bank and IMF policies and projects on environment, rights, governance, poverty, finance and trade: www.brettonwoodsproject.org/index.shtml

Housed at the World Bank, the *Consultative Group to Assist the Poor* (CGAP) is a research and policy centre for financial services targeting the poor; its website includes information about its programmes, country profiles, thematic and donor briefs, reports and technical guides on key issues: www.cgap.org/p/site/c/home/. All its resources are also included and readily accessed in *CGAP's Microfinance Gateway*, a portal for the microfinance sector, which also includes links to other microfinance institutions: www.microfinancegateway.org/p/site/m/home/

The *Microfinance Information Exchange* (MIX) is a US-based organization supporting microfinance institutions (MFIs), and its website provides access to business information from donors and investors as well as to a database with information on the financial and social performance of over 1,900 MFIs worldwide, and to its Bulletin, articles and thematic and country reports: www.themix.org/

Food security and nutrition

The **International Food Policy Research Institute** (IFPRI) offers policy solutions to hunger and poverty; its website includes monographs, discussion papers, policy briefs, country reports and links to relevant journals and databases (such as the food security portal) on a wide range of topics from natural resource management and land tenure reforms to biosafety and trade policies: www.ifpri.org/. Recommended ☆

The *FAO* of the UN system works to fight hunger and improve human nutrition; its website includes a wealth of resources such as a knowledge forum providing access to the agency's best practices, expert networks and databases (including FAOLEX and FAOSTAT containing key legal documents and statistics, respectively) and an online library with flagship publications and working papers, as well as sections with country profiles, conference reports and information about its key topics and core activities: www.fao.org/

Using the rights-based approach to food security, FAO has established the *Right to Food Unit*, whose mission is to support the implementation of the human right to adequate food; its website includes a virtual library with resources covering five key areas (related laws, capacity, policy, monitoring and assessment) and ranging from conventions and country reports to training material and policy papers: www.fao.org/righttofood/index_en.htm

The *World Food Programme* (WFP) is a UN humanitarian agency fighting acute hunger in emergencies and chronic under-nutrition; its website provides information about its programmes, country food security analyses, fact sheets, annual reports and policy papers: www.wfp.org/

The *Global Alliance for Improved Nutrition* (GAIN) website provides information about the basic nutrition deficiencies and current approaches to tackling them, such as food fortification or salt iodization, the alliance's programmes based on public–private partnerships and their results, its annual reports and a few working papers: www.gainhealth.org/

Gender and women

Womenwatch is the main portal of all UN agencies containing information about the promotion of women's rights and gender equality, and relevant resources organized by topic, region and UN agency: www.un.org/womenwatch/. Recommended ☆

UN Women is the UN agency for gender equality and women's empowerment, with six distinctive focus areas: violence against women, peace and security, political representation, economic empowerment, gender-responsive budgeting and achievement of the related MDGs. Its website contains news, videos, links to relevant portals and useful resources organized by topic, region and document type, from legal documents and strategy papers to case studies, programme reports and working papers: www.unwomen.org/

BRIDGE is the gender-specific programme of IDS Knowledge Services, and its website offers a publication section consisting of bibliographies, briefings, reports and up-to-date overviews of existing knowledge and good practice on key gender issues; it also offers an online library (database) containing over 3,000 documents in English and several other languages organized by region and theme: www.bridge.ids.ac.uk/

The *International Center for Research on Women* (ICRW) is a US-based research institute working on issues of women's empowerment, gender equality and poverty alleviation in over 30 developing countries. Its website provides access to policy briefs, toolkits and programme and comparative reports on relevant issues ranging from reproductive health and nutrition to gender violence and property rights: www.icrw.org/

The Development Centre of the OECD is responsible for the organization's work on gender and development and has produced the *Gender, Institutions and Development Database* (GID-DB) which includes 60 indicators on gender discrimination in 160 countries (http://stats.oecd.org/Index.aspx?DatasetCode=GID2); the *Social Institutions and Gender Index* (SIGI), an innovative measure of gender equality in 102 non-OECD countries according to 12 social institution variables from the GID-DB (http://my.genderindex.org/); and *Wikigender,* an online project for the exchange of information on gender equality issues (www.wikigender.org/index.php/New_Home).

Please see also resources under *Violence against women and children.*

Governance and democratic reform

UNDP and its Democratic Governance Group support democratic governance principles and policies as essential to the achievement of MDGs, and *UNDP's Oslo Governance Centre* (OGC) has been created to manage governance assessment, review the agency's related work and provide training; its website provides access to publications and to the *Governance Assessment Portal* (GAP), a knowledge-sharing website with resources on the design and implementation of governance assessment, papers on specific governance areas, relevant indicators and databases of such initiatives: www.undp.org/governance/oslocentre.shtml and www.gaportal.org/, respectively.

Transparency International is a global coalition against corruption, and its website offers related indices and surveys, global and country reports, a working paper series and access to the *Anti-Corruption Research Network* (ACRN), a portal for the dissemination of research approaches and findings on key corruption issues: www.transparency.org/and http://corruptionresearchnetwork.org/, respectively.

The *International Institute for Democracy and Electoral Assistance* (IDEA) is an intergovernmental organization for sustainable democratic change, and its website offers access to relevant publications organized by theme and region, such as country reports, policy papers and newsletters, and to several databases: www.idea.int/

Government aid agencies

The website of the UK *Department for International Development* (DFID) provides project information by country and theme, aid statistics, operational plans and evaluation studies along with access to the Research for Development (R4D) portal, its online research repository with the latest research news, programmes and documents: www.dfid.gov.uk/

The website of the *US Agency for International Development* (USAID) offers access to its statistical databases with aid, economic and social indicators as well as to its Development Experience Clearinghouse (DEC), an online database of its technical and programme documents: www.usaid.gov

The website of the *German Agency for International Cooperation* (GIZ) provides information about its country programmes and related publications such as reports, research papers, case studies and manuals: www.giz.de/en/home.html

EuropeAid Development and Cooperation is the European Commission (EC) Directorate for European Union (EU) development policies and aid, and its website offers access to its information portal, with annual reports, thematic papers, manuals and several other publications as well as to an online knowledge platform (capacity4dev.eu) with resources for development practitioners: http://ec.europa.eu/europeaid/index_en.htm

Health and disease

The *World Health Organization* (WHO) website (www.who.int/en/) includes general and technical information about every health topic, very useful fact sheets, health and medicine regulations, country health profiles and various global, regional and thematic reports. It also provides access to several journals published by the organization, such as the monthly Bulletin focusing on developing countries; to major policy initiatives such as the Evidence Informed Policy Network (EVIPNet), which promotes the use of research evidence in health policy through partnerships in low- and middle-income countries; to the WHO *Global Health Observatory* (GHO), with over 50 datasets on key health topics, country statistics, thematic maps and annual global health statistics (http://apps.who.int/ghodata/), also available through the WHO *Statistical Information System* (WHOSIS) (www.who.int/whosis/whostat/en/index.html); and to the WHO *Global Health Library* (GHL) (www.who.int/ghl/en/). Recommended ☆

The *Pan American Health Organization* (PAHO, or OPS in Spanish) website contains the latest health news in the Americas, information about current projects, country reports, thematic studies and links to interactive disease maps, journals and health networks, along with regional data and statistics in English and Spanish: http://new.paho.org/

The US *National Library of Medicine* (NLM) is the world's largest medical library and its website provides access to its specialist databases, including PubMed and its 20 million biomedical literature citations: www.nlm.nih.gov/

Roll Back Malaria (RBM) is a global partnership for action against malaria, and its website provides country facts, links to related websites and online journals, latest news, a series of progress and impact papers and a toolbox with manuals and good practice guides: http://rbm.who.int

The *Global Alliance for Vaccines and Immunisation* (GAVI) is a public–private health partnership, and its website includes country information and a few policy and progress reports: www.gavialliance.org

HIV and AIDS

The *Joint UN Programme on HIV/AIDS* (UNAIDS) website provides epidemiological information, regional and country fact sheets, situation analyses and progress reports along with toolkits, policy briefs, global reports and links to related data portals, including the agency's own info database with visualization options: www.unaids.org/en/

The *Gender Equality and HIV/AIDS* website is a UN Women portal highlighting the gender dimensions of the disease, and providing published resources organized by type, region and subject, and links to related organizations: www.genderandaids.org/

The *AIDSPortal* aims to be a global information hub with links to related initiatives, publications on key issues, country resources, directories accessible to members and e-forums: www.aidsportal.org/web/guest/home

The website of the *International AIDS Vaccine Initiative* (IAVI) for safe and accessible access to all AIDS vaccines includes information about the current situation, country programmes, advocacy and research papers and policy briefs: www.iavi.org/Pages/home.aspx

Housing and urbanization

The website of the *UN Human Settlements Programme* (UN-HABITAT) offers information about its current country programmes, an e-library with reports, manuals, resolutions, declarations and best practices on climate change, land, disaster, social inclusion, sanitation and urban development and economy, a global urban indicators database and the *Urban Gateway*, a web platform for sharing urban management knowledge, with access to related resources and several networks, www.unhabitat.org and www.urbangateway.org/, respectively.

The website of the *Centre on Housing Rights and Evictions* (COHRE), an NGO promoting the right to housing, includes legal documents, fact sheets, regional and country reports and links to other international and grassroots organizations: www.cohre.org/

The website of the *Global Land Tool Network* (GLTN) for poverty alleviation through pro-poor land policies offers an e-library with resources on key land tools necessary for successful land reform, management and secure land rights: www.gltn.net/

The *Cities Alliance* is a coalition promoting local urban development strategies and slum upgrading for urban poverty reduction, and its website includes e-newsletters, regional and country reports and project documents: www.citiesalliance.org/ca/

Humanitarian issues

The website of *OCHA* contains daily situation reports and several policy and evaluation papers: www.unocha.org

The website of the *Humanitarian Practice Network* (HPN), a unique forum for the humanitarian community, offers network papers, good practice reviews, meeting reports and the Humanitarian Exchange Magazine, with articles on all aspects of humanitarian policy and practice: www.odihpn.org

The *International Committee of the Red Cross* provides humanitarian assistance to those affected by armed violence and conflict, and its website offers access to international humanitarian law (IHL), IHL national implementation and customary IHL databases and to publications on issues of IHL and humanitarian policy and practice: www.icrc.org/eng/index.jsp

The *Inter-Agency Standing Committee* (IASC) is the key inter-agency mechanism carrying out OCHA's coordination function, and its website includes guidelines, tools and several reports: www.humanitarianinfo.org/iasc/

The *Sphere Project* is an initiative to define and support basic humanitarian standards in disaster responses, and its website contains its key tool, the Sphere Handbook, in various languages, along with training materials and related reports: www.sphereproject.org

Human rights

The website of the UN *Office of the High Commissioner for Human Rights* (OHCHR) includes the Universal Declaration of Human Rights (UDHR) in 379 languages along with other key international legal instruments, fact sheets, training materials and the online reference services of the OHCHR Library: www.ohchr.org/EN/Pages/WelcomePage.aspx. It also includes the *Universal Human Rights Index*, a research tool offering access to country-specific human rights information: www.universalhumanrightsindex.org

The website of *Human Rights Watch* (HRW) offers the latest news, multimedia resources and excellent reports on all aspects of human rights worldwide from women's and sexual rights to labour and terrorism issues, organized by theme and country: www.hrw.org

Amnesty International campaigns against human rights abuses, and its website contains in its Library section the latest news, country information about the human rights situation and related reports: www.amnesty.org

The *UN Practitioner's Portal on Human Rights-Based Approach* (HRBA) *Programming* for the mainstreaming of human rights into development practice offers resources such as case studies, training materials and reports along with access to the HuriTALK Corner, the UN virtual network on human rights policy: http://hrbaportal.org

Information and communication technology

The *International Telecommunication Union* (ITU) is the UN agency for ICTs and the creation of the global information society, and its website provides access to several publications and statistics. The ITU also maintains *WSIS StockTaking*, a portal with information on all activities undertaken to implement the World Summit on the Information Society (WSIS); the portal provides access to a database of related initiatives and to the Global Repository with documents and presentations related to WSIS: www.itu.int/en/pages/default.aspx and http://groups.itu.int/stocktaking/HOME.aspx, respectively.

The *Global Knowledge Partnership* (GKP) is a network for the application of knowledge and technology in development issues, and its website provides access to information about such projects and relevant publications by various partners: www.globalknowledgepartnership.org/index.cfm

The *International Institute for Communication and Development* (IICD) uses ICTs to improve education, health, agriculture and governance in several African and Latin American countries, and its website provides information about its projects and related publications: www.iicd.org/

Justice and reconciliation

Conciliation Resources (CR) works on peace-building projects, and its website includes thematic policy briefs, the Accord publication series with reviews of conflict and peace processes and several videos: www.c-r.org/index.php

The website of the *African Centre for the Constructive Resolution of Disputes* (ACCORD) provides information about its programmes and access to useful resources such as journals, research papers and reports on conflict management and peace-making on the continent: www.accord.org.za/

The *UN Rule of Law Unit* coordinates relevant activities within the UN system, offers strategies and guidance and strengthens partnerships between all actors involved on issues of justice, security and reform; its website provides links to initiatives and training opportunities along with access to its document repository with related official UN documents and policy material, and to several other databases with resources on its main thematic areas: www.unrol.org/

The website of the *International Criminal Court* (ICC) provides access to information about its structure and operations, to Legal Tools, an online library of legal documents, and to official records, annual court reports and weekly updates: www. icc-cpi.int/Menus/ICC/

Please see also resources under *Conflict and security*.

Latin America

The UN *Economic Commission for Latin America and the Caribbean* (ECLAC, CEPAL in Spanish) website offers publications on economic, demographic and social development issues along with access to CEPALSTAT, with statistical information of all country members: www.eclac.org/

The website of the *Inter-American Development Bank* (IDB, BID in Spanish) offers access to its two organizations, INTAL for economic integration and INDES for professional training, as well as to country economic profiles, thematic newsletters, research reports and policy briefs on economic and social issues, and to several databases on trade, markets, governance, legislation and women's political participation: www.iadb.org/en/inter-american-development-bank,2837.html

The *Organization of American States* (OAS, OEA in Spanish) works on democracy, human rights, security and development issues, and relevant resources can be accessed through links to its key areas: www.oas.org

Migration

The website of the *International Organization for Migration* (IOM) provides access to the Migration Law Database, latest facts and figures, policy and project information, manuals, journals, the IOM research newsletter, country migration profiles, studies and the annual World Migration Report: www.iom.int/jahia/Jahia/lang/en/pid/1

The *UN Office on Drugs and Crime* (UNODC) works against human trafficking and migrant smuggling, and its website contains a few resources such as toolkits and manuals, issue papers, case studies and reports: www.unodc.org/unodc/en/human-trafficking/index.html?ref=menuside

The *UN Global Initiative to Fight Human Trafficking* (UN.GIFT) has an online knowledge hub offering programme information and a few handbooks and reports: www.ungift.org/knowledgehub/

The website of the *Centre on Migration, Policy and Society* (COMPAS) at the University of Oxford contains reports, working papers and briefings on issues of migration flows, labour migration, identity, integration and welfare provision: www.compas.ox.ac.uk; its *Migration Observatory* project focuses on migration in the UK: www.migrationobservatory.ox.ac.uk. COMPAS is part of the *MigrationOxford Initiative*, which also includes two other Oxford-based institutes, the International Migration Institute (IMI) and the Refugee Studies Centre (RSC), and provides online access to their research resources on the causes, effects and trends of global migration: www.migration.ox.ac.uk

Millennium Development Goals

The official *UN website for the MDG Indicators* offers official statistics and updated figures, progress reports, related links and information about statistical country capacity building for the production of development indicators: http://mdgs.un.org/unsd/mdg/

The *MDG Monitor* shows global and country progress towards the MDGs along with offering updated information and interactive maps visualizing existing data: www.mdgmonitor.org

Beyond 2015 is an international campaign for the creation of the post-2015 and MDGs development framework, and its website includes relevant news, articles and research papers: www.beyond2015.org/

The *UN* offers an additional *website for the MDG-related work of its agencies*, which also contains annual progress reports along with several regional and thematic ones, fact sheets, progress charts and links to each agency's related activities and statistical data: www.un.org/millenniumgoals/

Minorities and indigenous people

Minority Rights Group International campaigns for minorities and indigenous peoples, and its website contains a developing law section with key legal documents and related legal cases as well as programme and global reports, briefing papers and guides and the World Directory of Minorities and Indigenous Peoples: www.minorityrights.org

The website of the *UN Permanent Forum on Indigenous Issues* (UNPFII) contains several related resources, such as reviews, briefs, annual UN session reports, a quarterly newsletter and a recommendations database: www.un.org/esa/socdev/unpfii/index.html

Survival International works for tribal peoples' rights, and its website includes latest news, films and information about each tribe: www.survivalinternational.org

Monitoring and evaluation

The *Active Learning Network for Accountability and Performance in Humanitarian Action* (ALNAP) works to improve performance in humanitarian operations, and its website includes training materials, reviews and the Evaluative Reports Database (ERD), with over 1,000 documents: www.alnap.org

The *Humanitarian Accountability Partnership* (HAP) *International* aims to develop and uphold accountability principles to beneficiaries, and its website includes its key documents and policies, case studies and progress reports: www.hapinternational.org

The *One World Trust* is a think-tank working for more accountable global governance, and its website includes information and resources from its projects on the accountability of international, civil society and research organizations, and of global climate change and human security initiatives; it also provides access to a database of civil society self-regulatory initiatives and to a collection of accountability tools for policy researchers: www.oneworldtrust.org/

The *Independent Evaluation Office* (IEO) evaluates IMF policies and activities, and its website includes its two annual evaluation reports, issue papers and links to the evaluation offices of other international organizations: www.ieo-imf.org/

Capacity.org is a portal for knowledge sharing and support for development practitioners; it offers access to theoretical debates and approaches, practical applications, case studies and useful links on issues of building capacity, including planning, monitoring and evaluation: www.capacity.org/capacity/opencms/en/index.html

Population and reproductive issues

The *UN Population Fund* (UNFPA) works on population, reproductive health and gender equality, and its website offers information about its country programmes, links to statistical data, progress, thematic and global reports such as the annual State of World Population, case studies, issue and policy papers and several technical resources for practitioners: www.unfpa.org/public/

The *Population Council* works on reproductive health, HIV and AIDS and poverty, gender and youth issues, and its website offers excellent resources organized by topic and country, such as project reports, working papers and newsletters along with a data portal: www.popcouncil.org/

The website of the US-based *Population Reference Bureau* (PRB) contains country demographic profiles, data sheets, policy briefs and thematic webcasts along with links to its major project websites on gender, population dynamics and poverty with related resources:www.prb.org/

Ipas supports women's sexual and reproductive rights, and especially their right to safe abortion; its website offers resources largely on this topic, but also on sexual violence, youth and reproductive health issues: www.ipas.org/Index.aspx

Poverty and social protection

UNDP's *International Policy Centre for Inclusive Growth* (IPC-IG) works on issues of inclusive growth, social protection, equity and sustainable development, encouraging cooperation among developing countries, and its website provides resources such as national and evaluation reports, thematic research papers and policy briefs: www.ipc-undp.org/. Recommended ☆

The *Chronic Poverty Research Centre* (CPRC) has been established as an international partnership for researching persistent poverty, and its website provides access to excellent reports, working papers and research summaries along with a methodological toolbox: www.chronicpoverty.org/

The *World Bank* website includes a *Poverty* section with a few publications on its focus areas and poverty and inequality statistics: http://go.worldbank.org/ 33CTPS-VDC0; it also includes a separate Social Protection website with more documents on disability, labour markets, pensions, social funds and safety nets and transfers: http:// go.worldbank.org/FJ6LLR2LU0. However, more resources on various poverty-related issues can be accessed from its general Data and Research/Poverty Reduction webpage: http://go.worldbank.org/HHE354XGI0

Based at the University of Manchester, the *Brooks World Poverty Institute* (BWPI) conducts research on the causes and consequences of poverty worldwide and for policies to eradicate it; its website includes working papers, reports and global poverty-focused policy briefings: www.bwpi.manchester.ac.uk/index.php

The *Abdul Latif Jameel Poverty Action Lab* (J-PAL) is a Massachusetts Institute of Technology (MIT)-based research network using randomized evaluations (REs) to measure the effectiveness of poverty alleviation programmes and support the scaling-up of the most successful ones; its website provides access to its RE database and related research and policy publications: www.povertyactionlab.org/

Refugees and displacement

The website of the Office of the *UN High Commissioner for Refugees* (UNHCR) offers multiple relevant resources, from country profiles and operational plans to legal documents, research papers and evaluation reports, a statistical population database with visualization options provided by RefScout and *Refworld*, a daily updated portal with news, links and key documents: www.unhcr.org/cgi-bin/texis/ vtx/home and www.unhcr.org/cgi-bin/texis/vtx/refworld/rwmain, respectively.

The *Internal Displacement Monitoring Centre* (IDMC) of the Norwegian Refugee Council (NRC) monitors and analyses conflict-induced internal displacement all around the world, and its website offers access to its internally displaced person (IDP) database with country profiles, statistics, links and reports: www.internal-displacement.org/

The **Refugee Studies Centre** (RSC) conducts multidisciplinary research on the causes and consequences of forced migration, and its website provides access to research papers and policy briefings, to the Forced Migration Review (FMR) on key issues and to **Forced Migration Online** (FMO), a portal with a wealth of resources: www.rsc.ox.ac.uk/ and www.forcedmigration.org/, respectively.

The website of the **UN Relief and Works Agency** (UNRWA), the UN agency for Palestine refugees, provides programme information, statistics, reports and several studies: www.unrwa.org/

The **Women's Refugee Commission** website offers information and reports about its field and research work on refugee women, children and youth: www.womensrefugeecommission.org/

Research institutes

The **Center for Global Development** (CGD) researches the development policies of global powers and institutions, and offers practical ideas for global prosperity and security; its website offers good working papers, briefs, reports and multimedia resources on globalization, growth, migration, health and climate change: www.cgdev.org/

The Canadian **International Development Research Centre** (IDRC, CRDI in French) supports research on issues of agriculture, health, technology and social and economic policies in developing countries, and its website provides access to a project database, and to its Digital Library (IDL), with various resources such as e-books, manuals and research reports: www.idrc.ca/EN/Pages/default.aspx

Based at the University of Sussex, **IDS** is a leading research, training and communication centre with an extensive network of partners and a website offering a wealth of excellent resources on all key development research, policy and practice issues: www.ids.ac.uk/.

The **Overseas Development Institute** (ODI) is a leading British think-tank on development and humanitarian research, policy and practice, and its website offers excellent briefing and working papers, articles and reports, interesting blogposts and videos of its weekly events on key development issues: www.odi.org.uk

The **UN Research Institute for Social Development** (UNRISD) is the UN agency for applied research on social policies, democracy, governance, identities, markets and gender, and its website provides access to policy briefs, reports and research papers, organized by date, country and theme: www.unrisd.org/

Research methodology

Sage Research Methods Online (SRMO) is an online research methods tool offering project design support, quantitative and qualitative methodologies and assistance in writing-up along with links to research ethics, research organizations and free statistical software: http://srmo.sagepub.com/

The Economic and Social Research Council (ESRC) includes the **National Centre for Research Methods** (NCRM), a network of research and training in social sciences research methods; its website offers access to information about the latest training opportunities across the UK and its projects, and to its repository with resources on scientific research such as working papers, methodological reviews and other reports: www.ncrm.ac.uk/

Closely related to the NCRM is the ESRC *Researcher Development Initiative* (RDI) for the training and development of researchers in the social sciences; its website offers access to the latest training opportunities and online training resources for both qualitative and quantitative data based on RDI's projects: www.rdi.ac.uk/

The website of the American *Centers for Disease Control and Prevention* (CDC) offers Epi Info™, a collection of software tools used by public health professionals for data collection, statistical analyses and mapping: wwwn.cdc.gov/epiinfo/

The *Resource Centers for Participatory Learning and Action* (RCPLA) *Network* is an international alliance for the empowerment of disadvantaged communities through participation; its website facilitates the exchange of information about Participatory Learning and Action (PLA) approaches and offers several resources and best practices: www.rcpla.org/index.html

Sexuality and sexual rights

The *IDS Sexuality and Development Programme* offers partner links and information about its research projects and related publications: www.ids.ac.uk/go/sexualityanddevelopment

The website of *Sexuality Policy Watch* (SPW), a forum for sexual rights and related policy debates, provides access to relevant UN and other legal documents, working papers, reports and articles: www.sxpolitics.org/?cat=1

The website of the *Africa Regional Sexuality Resource Centre* (ARSRC) provides access to the latest news, its quarterly magazine and its e-library with resources on sexual health, education, gender and HIV and AIDS: www.arsrc.org

The Spanish and Portuguese websites of the *Latin America Center on Sexuality and Human Rights* (CLAM) provide access to articles, reviews and reports on sexuality, sexual rights and minorities issues in the region:www.clam.org.br/

Sport

The website of the *UN Office on Sport for Development and Peace* (UNOSDP) provides information about its initiatives and partners within the UN system, related UN resolutions and conventions and a few fact sheets and reports www.un.org/wcm/content/site/sport

The website of the *Sports and Development Platform* offers several resources, such as thematic bibliographies, case studies, manuals, an e-newsletter and related links: www.sportanddev.org

Statistics

Created by the UN Statistics Division (UNSD), the *UNdata* website offers thematic data from 33 databases along with country profiles with economic, social, environment and trade indicators, and links to national statistical services with relevant publications: http://data.un.org. Recommended ☆

Managed by UNICEF, *DevInfo* is a database system which contains the 48 standard MDG indicators along with several more, and monitors human development; its website offers access to global, regional and country data on human development themes such as child protection, child labour, immunization, maternal health, AIDS, migration and urbanization. It also allows for the generation of tables, graphs and maps of chosen indicators for which data are available: www.devinfo.org/

The website of the *OECD* provides access to its datasets for OECD and some non-member countries, including its well-known ODA data: http://stats.oecd.org/Index.aspx; other important indicators are also available to download as Excel tables: www.oecd.org/document/0,3746,en_2649_201185_46462759_1_1_1_1,00.html

The website of *UNDP's Human Development Report* (HDR) provides access to the data and the composite indices of the report along with country profiles with tables and graphs of the available human development indicators, a global map, comparison and country rankings with a visualization option, Human Development Index (HDI) trends and the option to select one's own data and create a personal index: http://hdr.undp.org/en/statistics/

StatPlanet is an interactive visualizing application for the creation of thematic maps and graphs using key demographic, health, education and other socioeconomic indicators of several international organizations: www.sacmeq.org/statplanet/; *StatPlanet World Bank* includes all indicators from its database and visualizes them through selected maps and graphs: www.statplanet.org/

Developed by H. Rosling and the Gapminder Foundation, *Gapminder* is a fascinating application converting datasets into moving graphics and thus enabling the visualization of the evolution of over 400 development indicators over time and of how countries have developed since 1800: www.gapminder.org/

The *Demographic and Health Surveys* (DHS) project collects, analyses and disseminates key national data on population, health, HIV, nutrition and gender through surveys conducted in over 80 countries with the aim of monitoring and improving relevant programmes: www.measuredhs.com/

Tourism

The *UN World Tourism Organization* (UNWTO) supports the development of responsible and sustainable tourism, and its website provides information about its initiatives, such as the Global Code of Ethics for Tourism, the protection of children in tourism and the Sustainable Tourism-Eliminating Poverty (ST-EP) programme, along with access to the *e-unwto database* with all its resources, thematically and regionally organized: http://unwto.org/en/ and www.e-unwto.org/home/main.mpx, respectively.

UNEP has a *Tourism and Environment Programme* for sustainable tourism development, and its website provides information about its initiatives and related publications: www.unep.fr/scp/tourism/

Trade and markets

The website of the *UN Conference on Trade and Development* (UNCTAD) for the integration of developing countries into the global economy provides programme information, policy briefs, thematic and regional reports and research papers along with access to UNCTADSTAT and its databases: www.unctad.org

The *World Trade Organization* (WTO) deals with the rules that structure the global multilateral trading system, and its website provides access to its document database with legal texts, General Agreement on Tariffs and Trades (GATT) documents, reports and policy reviews, and to its statistics database: www.wto.org

The *International Centre for Trade and Sustainable Development* (ICTSD) promotes trade policies that support sustainable development, and its website provides access to periodicals, policy briefs and research papers on the issues of agriculture, aid for trade, China, competitiveness, country trade rights, natural resources and intellectual property: http://ictsd.org/

The US-based *Institute for Agriculture and Trade Policy* (IATP) supports fair trade policies, sustainable resource management and food safety, and its online resources are organized in five resource centres, on trade, agriculture, health, forestry and climate: www.iatp.org

United Nations

The *UN* website (www.un.org/en/) provides information about its structure, main bodies, agencies (www.un.org/en/aboutun/structure/index.shtml) and the UN major thematic areas: peace and security, development, human rights, humanitarian affairs and international law. It also offers a wealth of resources ranging from multimedia such as webcasts and videos to general and mission maps, included in the *UN Cartographic Section* (www.un.org/Depts/Cartographic/english/htmain.htm), and official documents in the six official UN languages contained in the *Official Document System* (ODS), the database of UN documents (www.un.org/en/documents/ods/), and in the *UN Bibliographic Information System* (UNBISnet), the catalogue of UN documents, publications, speeches and voting records (http://unbisnet.un.org/). Many publications can be downloaded through the thematically organized publications section (https://unp.un.org/). A very useful link to access the libraries and publications of each one of the UN bodies and agencies is www.unsystem.org/en/libraRies/index.html; links to its major databases and statistics can be found at: www.un.org/en/databases/

UNDP works on poverty reduction, democratic governance, crisis prevention, environment, HIV and AIDS, women's empowerment and capacity development, and coordinates efforts for the achievement of the MDGs. Its website provides access to its flagship publication, the Global HDR, to the data used for the composite indices included and to country rankings according to their HDI and other indices; it also provides access to regional and national reports, MDG reports, fact papers, publications on the main themes of the agency and links to country offices websites with relevant resources: www.beta.undp.org/undp/en/home.html

UNDESA analyses global economic and social challenges, supports development and equality for all and monitors the implementation of relevant agreements and policies;

its website provides access to policy briefs, interesting working papers and reports on key economic, social and environmental issues: www.un.org/en/development/desa/index.html

Violence against women and children

UNiTE to End Violence against Women is the UN Secretary-General's campaign and framework for all relevant initiatives, and *Say NO-UNiTE* is the UN Women platform for the advancement of this campaign; its website provides some facts and figures, a few publications and access to the 2006 UN Secretary-General Study on Violence against Women: www.saynotoviolence.org/

Engagingmen.net is a network promoting the engagement of boys and men as a central strategy for gender equality, peace and justice, and its website provides information on regional networks and relevant initiatives along with several resources: www.engagingmen.net/

The *UN Secretary-General's database on violence against women* includes national and UN reports, country profiles with laws, national strategies and programmes and a few good practices: http://webapps01.un.org/vawdatabase/home.action

The *WHO* website provides several useful *resources on violence against women*, including its ground-breaking 2005 Multi-country Study on Women's Health and Domestic Violence against Women: www.who.int/reproductivehealth/publications/violence/en/index.html

The website of the 2006 *UN Secretary-General Study on Violence against Children* provides access to the study and a few related resources: www.unviolencestudy.org/

Water and sanitation

The *IRC International Water and Sanitation Centre* (IRC) website provides information and reports about water supply, sanitation programmes and major topics, links to key organizations of the sector and access to E-Source with the latest news and to the IRC WASH Library with open access to related journals: www.irc.nl/

The *International Water Management Institute* (IWMI) is a research centre working to improve the management of water resources for poor communities in developing countries; its website offers useful policy briefs, research reports and working papers, and access to the WaterData portal: www.iwmi.cgiar.org/index.aspx

UN-Water coordinates water and sanitation initiatives within the UN system, and its website contains information about its related programmes, reports, papers and policy briefs along with several links to water data and statistics: www.unwater.org/

WaterAid is an NGO working to provide water and sanitation to poor people, and its website offers synthesis and project reports, briefings and policy papers organized by theme and country: www.wateraid.org/

Administered by the World Bank, the *Water and Sanitation Program* (WSP) works with governments in 25 countries; its website offers interesting reports, case studies and comparative reviews of its programmes: www.wsp.org/wsp/

GLOSSARY

Abstract: Summary of a larger report, article or other document. Serves to quickly condense the main points of the material for the reader. Abstracts always appear before the introduction.

Action research: Research explicitly concerned with change. Action research tends to be defined as a participatory process aimed at the development of practical knowledge through participation in action and reflection, theory and practice, and in pursuit of practical solutions to issues of concern for individual persons and their communities.

Advisory group: A group of knowledgeable authorities (researchers, policy experts) and key stakeholders (representatives of funding organizations, partner agencies, community members/those being studied, etc.) formed to assist staff through the various stages of research while ensuring transparency.

Analysis: Breaking something down into its component parts. To do this, it is necessary to trace things back to their underlying sources, so analysis involves probing beneath the surface appearance of something to discover the component elements which have come together to produce it. Examination of data for trends, comparisons, relationships and themes.

Appraise: To examine something objectively and in detail; to evaluate; to make judgements.

Audit trail: Information provided to an audience, enabling them to understand how the research has been collected and analysed.

Averages: Midpoint of a set of values. There are three kinds of averages in mathematics: mean, median and mode. Collectively referred to as 'measures of central tendency'.

Axis, axes: Denotes the horizontal (x-axis) and the vertical (y-axis) of a line or bar graph. These are typically used to plot two variables in relation to each other.

Bar chart: Type of chart used to present basic information about frequencies, using bars along the x-axis with heights proportional to their representative values. Bar charts are used to graphically display discrete data and separate categories. (See Chapter 14.)

Baseline study: A collection of data about a population before a programme or project is set up. Data can then be compared with later evidence about the same characteristics in order to see what has changed.

Bias: Any influence which distorts or unduly influences the results of an investigation – perhaps as a result of the research method employed, sampling approaches or the researcher's presuppositions. Some kinds of bias may be inevitable. To avoid accusations of distortion, it is important to identify any factors you think may introduce bias.

Bivariate analysis: The study of the relationship between two variables simultaneously (e.g. income and gender).

Blog: A 'weblog' – more commonly just 'blog' – is a type of online journal posting content such as brief informal updates, short essays and comments, typically supplemented with external links. Blog posts are easy to write, and can be helpful tools for research promotion.

Body mapping: A participatory mapping method in which people draw images of how bodies work – used by researchers to find out people's names for parts and functions within the body, and to open up discussion of all kinds of health-related issues.

Bookmarks (also known as 'favourites'): When using the internet, bookmarks enable you to mark a web page you may want to return to.

Brief (research) (or terms of reference): A plan of action, describing the tasks to be carried out; includes aims and objectives; methods; outcomes. (See Chapter 3.)

Card index: Tool for referencing data, in which a card is allocated to each category, on which the researcher writes notes on material collected and cross-referencing to other relevant cards.

Case study: Research method focused around an in-depth investigation of a single issue, individual, group or event.

Category: A group that has similarities; a class (in the sense of classification) or set. Categories are generally mutually exclusive groupings – or are intended to be so.

Causal relationship: A relationship between two or more factors in which one factor directly explains a change in another.

Causation: The causal relationship between two or more variables. Remember the difference between causation and *correlation*: two variables correlated together do not alone imply causality.

CEL framework: The Overseas Development Institute (ODI) Research and Policy in Development (RAPID) programme Context Evidence Links (CEL) framework is a conceptual framework designed to help researchers and policy entrepreneurs understand the role evidence-based research plays in influencing policy.

Census: A government-sponsored, universal and obligatory survey of all individuals in a geographical area (also used to refer to non-government-sponsored population counts).

Charting: An analysis technique in which charts are created, using large sheets of paper, with categories and sub-categories arranged along the top of the page and cases (interviews, focus group transcripts, observations notes) down the side in a consistent order. This enables the researcher to see the whole 'story' for each case easily.

Citizens' juries: A mechanism of action research in which local people are selected to sit as a 'jury' and cross-question an expert on a particular topic. The jury then produces a short summary of their conclusions to an advisory panel of experts.

Classification: Aims to place together all instances of a phenomenon whose similarities, and differences from all other types of phenomenon, are such as to justify the classification for particular theoretical purposes.

Cluster sample: A method of sampling in the population is broken down into natural groups of cases called clusters. Samples of clusters are chosen at random and, within each sample, units are listed and then sampled randomly.

Coaching: On-the-job training, working individually to help someone to learn new skills through the tasks they carry out.

Codebook: A document containing all codes and meanings for a research project's data.

Coding: A method of transforming qualitative information into quantifiable information by categorization. Categorization is according to particular themes or patterns, and these categories can be numbered so complex information is simplified into manageable and meaningful groupings. Each possible answer is given a code, and then each person's answer is assigned the appropriate code. (See Section 13.4.)

Cohort: A group of persons possessing a common characteristic (e.g. born in the same year). (See also Longitudinal study.)

Communication strategy: A plan to aid in systematically thinking through the full communication cycle of a research project or programme. A communication strategy helps to set concrete communication goals for a research project, map how these goals are best to be achieved, consider the internal and external challenges and opportunities for maximizing overall impact and establish feedback mechanisms to learn from the experience.

Community consultation: Consultation, or user involvement, where community/ service users are actively engaged in giving feedback on decisions relating to a service. While this often uses research methods, it is a directly political process rather than traditional research.

Community member: Used here as a general term to refer to those the development worker/researcher relates to. They might be the people who live in a particular geographical area, or may form part of a different kind of community, such as disabled people or sex workers, for example. It is recognized that community links and support may be strong or weak.

Consent: See informed consent

Consultation: User involvement in the research process through the taking of advice from people and asking their opinions, rather than simply recording their experiences or collecting information.

Control group: A group matched with the group which will receive an intervention in all aspects except that it is not treated with the intervention whose effect is to be studied. A control group is an essential part of an experimental design, since comparison is needed to establish whether or not any change is due to the intervention. In the social world, looking at complex interventions, it is often difficult to identify suitable control groups, given the number of factors potentially affecting any particular outcome.

Convenience sampling: A method of sampling in which samples are drawn from whichever respondents happen to be conveniently available at the time of study. Difficult to defend.

Copyright library: A library which serves as a primary repository of published works.

Correlation: The association between two variables such that when one changes the other does also. A positive correlation means that one variable tends to increase together with another variable. Negative correlation means that one variable decreases as the other one increases. The strength of any correlation can be expressed statistically, and tests can establish whether or not any correlation is statistically significant. Correlation does not prove causation (see above). (See Chapter 13.)

Criterion (pl. criteria): Standard of judgement, test.

Critical friending: Workshop exercise in which colleagues constructively criticize a particular document, policy or argument, asking intentionally difficult questions to prompt discussion and refinement.

Cross-tabulation: A two-way table which uses the classes of a second variable to further subdivide each class of the first. Cross-tabulation is used to establish the occurrence and degree of relationship of connected variables. (See Section 13.8.)

Cut and paste technique: Analysis technique in which the researcher photocopies the whole of their dataset, then physically cuts it up with scissors and pastes part of it onto other sheets according to sorting categories.

Data: Used to describe all types of information gathered by researchers. 'Raw data' refer to information which has been collected but not processed or analysed.

Delphi technique: A structured communication technique which involves collecting views from experts in a field and generating discussion among them to interrogate these views.

Demography: The study of human populations, especially statistics of birth, fertility and death. Includes study of the structure of and changes in populations, for example by sex, age, ethnic origin, etc.

Depth interviews: See Unstructured interviews.

Design, research: See Research design.

Disaggregate: To break down into smaller units; from 'aggregate', to bring together into one mass.

Discipline: Refers to different systems of learning, realms of knowledge, for example sociology, anthropology, medicine.

Documentary sources: Texts and documents, including official government publications, academic scholarship, newspapers, census publications, media, etc. Documentary sources can be found in a range of formats, including paper and electronic.

Donors: Organizations which give funds for development work.

Double coding: The process in which a researcher enters their data twice, the second time with either a different researcher or a computer check to ensure the initial researcher is typing the exact same data typed previously.

Empirical: Comes from the Greek word for experience – empirical knowledge is knowledge derived from experience. Experience here means sensory experience – hearing, seeing, smelling, tasting or touching. However, sense data are also filtered, translated, shaped and transformed through mental processes. We understand things, even at the most basic level ('hot', 'loud', 'sweet') through words we have learnt for them, so these concepts also shape our experience.

Episode studies: An exercise useful for isolating a particular change in policy in order to help to identify the degree to which a research project contributed to said change. Episode studies revolve around the collaborative constructive of a narrative timeline reconstructing key policy decisions, events and documents leading up to the policy change with key policymakers and stakeholders.

Factor: One of the circumstances, facts or influences which produce a result. Some feature of the situation which must be taken into account when describing or attempting to alter it.

Favourites (internet): See Bookmarks.

Field: (As in 'fieldwork', 'field research') refers to any real-world setting where research takes place ('field' research as opposed to laboratory experiments); (in relation to databases) spaces reserved for specified data; columns of data in tables.

Focus groups: A facilitated group interview, where six to 12 people are brought together for a discussion. (See Section 11.3.)

Force field analysis: Strategic planning tool used for visualizing the various forces influencing a policy issue and understanding their relative strengths. In a small group, researchers draw a central column containing a specific policy objective. Next, all the forces driving this desired change forward are drawn and ranked down the left of the column, with forces holding back change down the right.

Formative (evaluation): Ongoing evaluation or monitoring with continuous feedback and use of information gathered so as to amend and improve or 'form' a service or piece of work. (As opposed to 'summative' evaluation, which looks at the whole picture at the end of a period of time.)

Frequency: The number of times a particular item of data occurs – for example, a specific answer to a question. In quantitative research, a frequency count might tell you simply how many people gave a particular response.

Gantt Chart: Planning tool which visually represents the duration of specific tasks and the order in which they must be completed.

Generalizability: The feature of research which enables statements to be made about a broader population than the one directly studied.

Generalizable: From 'generalization', the degree to which findings may be expected to apply beyond the specific situation in which they occurred. The case for applying such findings in more general situations. Making a statement about the whole population (or a larger population) on the basis of information about only part of that group.

Grey material: Unpublished documents produced by various organizations – governmental and non-governmental agencies.

Grid (questionnaire): Table or grid provided to record answers to two or more questions at the same time on a questionnaire.

Health gain: An objectively measurable improvement in the health status of the population (e.g. fewer babies die in the first year of life).

Hypothesis: A hunch or educated guess as to why something occurs. Statement of a predicted outcome which the research will either support or disprove. An initial prediction or statement of results which is tested through research. (See Section 3.3.)

Impact (research): The degree of change – in behaviour, knowledge, attitudes, practices, policies and programming – which a research project ultimately generates.

Incentive: Payment – monetary or otherwise – made to respondents as inducements to take part in research as a way to increase response rates.

Index: A list of references, regularly updated, which contains references to published works and information on a particular subject. Indexes are available in libraries, as well as electronic formats and online.

Indicator: Objective way of measuring (indicating) that progress is being achieved. These must relate to the aims and objectives of the project. Indicators are evidence that something has happened. They are not proof.

Informant: See Respondent.

Informed consent: refers to a person's agreement to allow information to be provided for research purposes. Agreement is based on full exposure of the facts the person needs to make the decision intelligently, including awareness of any risks involved, of uses and users of the data, and of alternatives to providing the data. See Section 9.2.3.

Instrument, research: See Research instrument.

Interval: The range of values in a set of observations.

Interviewer effect: The effect resulting from the influence of interviewers on the answers of respondents, arising from many sources, including behaviour, and characteristics beyond the interviewer's control.

IRB: Institutional research board. See Research ethics committees.

ISBN: International standard book number, a numeric identification scheme based around a nine-digit code for commercial publications.

Issue tree (also known as **'logic tree'**): A visual strategic tool which helps you to take your central research question and think about the sub-questions you will have to address in order to answer the high-level question, depicted graphically as branches.

IT: Information technology.

Iterative: Repeating, doing over again; can be seen as a trial-and-error procedure for solving problems, often represented as a cycle where a proposal is made, then tested, then adjusted, then tested again.

Iterative process: An approach to data analysis centred around cycles ('iterations') of analysis, conceptualization and re-categorization.

'Leading' question: Question asked which implies or encourages the answer the interviewer is searching for.

Line graph: Type of graph used for depicting development or progression in a sequence of data, most commonly used to show change over time.

List (questionnaire): A list of items is offered in a questionnaire, any of which may be selected by the respondent. For example, a question may ask about types of crop grown and the respondent may grow several types of crop which she can indicate using the list provided.

Literature review (study): The process of critically assessing and evaluating published and unpublished information materials which are relevant to your research.

Literature search: The process of locating the existing published (and perhaps unpublished) information materials which are relevant to your research.

Literature survey: Summarizes as accurately as possible the published information relevant to your research.

Longitudinal study: A piece of research that extends over a long period of time and collects data at different, regular, planned points in time. It builds in the assumption that the passage of time is important to understanding the phenomenon being studied. A 'motion picture' as opposed to a 'snapshot', taken at just one point in time.

Market research: The study of problems relating to the marketing of goods and services, including the study of customer characteristics and preferences.

Matched sample: A sample in which two subgroups similar in some way are compared. Units (which can range from a whole community or an individual) are purposefully matched by researchers so as to share as many relevant characteristics as possible.

Mean: A type of average calculated by adding up all the values in a dataset and dividing the total by the total number of values added.

Measurement bias: A measurement error caused by systematic bias occurring consciously or unconsciously in data collection and analysis of quantitative data. (See also Systematic bias.)

Measures of spread: Measurements which describe the way data are arranged around the midpoint.

Median: A type of average calculated by identifying the middle value of a set, when the values are arranged in order of size.

Methodology: (From the study of methods) correctly used to refer to an overall or underlying theory of research practice – the abstract logical basis of 'finding out' and 'knowing' itself (sometimes called philosophy of science). Includes theoretical rules, guidelines and principles. Also includes methods used, but if you mean methods or techniques, use the simpler term.

Mixed method approach/mixed method research: When researchers seek to use both qualitative and quantitative evidence to strengthen their arguments and 'triangulate' their findings.

Mobility maps: A mapping method designed to provide information about spatial mobility. Respondents are asked to draw a map of their routes of travel and routine over a certain time period, allowing the researcher to record, compare and analyse the mobility of different groups of people in a community. (See Section 12.4.)

Mode: A type of average identified by counting the number of times each value occurs. The value which occurs most often in a set is considered the mode.

Most Significant Change analysis: An exercise which draws on innovation histories recounting most significant change stories. These stories collected from key stakeholders are in turn vetted by several layers of review panels to select particularly useful examples for subsequent analysis and lesson learning.

Multivariate analysis: The study of the relationship between more than two variables simultaneously (e.g. income, age and gender).

Needs assessment: A method for determining unaddressed needs among individuals, organizations and communities which deviate from desired conditions, widely used by development workers in programming.

Non-probability (purposive) sampling: A sampling approach based around a set of intentional criteria selected by the researcher. Includes *quota sampling, snowball sampling* and *convenience sampling*, among others. (See Chapter 10.)

Non-response: Failure to obtain data from some of those in the sample because they do not respond or cannot be contacted. May cause bias in the achieved sample if non-respondents are different from respondents. (See Chapter 10.)

Normative (e.g. need): Establishing a norm or standard.

Omnibus survey: A research service consisting in a survey conducted periodically by a commercial market research supplier, serving a number of clients. Clients insert one or more question/s of their choosing into the survey, which is usually of a representative, national sample of consumers.

Ordinal data: Data where it is known that some items are more or less, bigger or smaller, than each other. For example, measurements of population size in several different cities are considered 'ordinal'.

Outputs (research): The final material produced by a research project – data, final reports, policy briefs, etc. In monitoring and evaluation, 'outputs' refer to the scale of the practical activities undertaken, such as number of people provided with a service.

Overheads: The costs one incurs simply by 'being there' during a project – rent, heat and light, phone rental and someone to answer the phone, someone to pay wages and keep track of finances, etc.

Panel studies: Surveys in which information is collected from the sample units two or more times. Here, 'panel' refers to a group of respondents who are surveyed periodically over time. Panel studies are useful for measuring change over time and causal processes.

Parsimonious: Data may be considered 'parsimonious' when they exclude any variable that is not strictly related to the observed phenomenon.

Participant observation: An observation strategy involving the researcher living closely alongside a community of researched people, typically over an extended period of time, in order to gain a better grounded, contexualized knowledge of the issues that affect them. A principle of participant observation is that the researcher herself becomes an active 'participant' in the daily life of the community, contributing to it in some tangible way instead of merely observing passively.

Participatory Learning and Action: A research approach in which the knowledge, opinions and perspectives of local communities are consulted for the planning and management of development programmes. Includes numerous participatory tools, techniques and methods.

Participatory mapping: A participatory research approach in which community members are asked to draw certain types of maps to graphically illustrate a range of concepts, issues and observations. These include *mobility maps, body mapping* and *transects*, among other tools and techniques.

Participatory Rural Appraisal: See Participatory Learning and Action.

Partner agencies: Organizations which cooperate in the planning and/or implementation of a piece of work. May include community-based organizations; local or national government bodies; non-governmental organizations; or international organizations.

Peer research: Involves people participating actively in research with others like themselves, for example young people interviewing other young people. (See Chapter 12.)

Phenomenology: A major school of philosophy based on the view that humans are active creators of their own rules. It underpins an important branch of social constructionist research, with the primary task of achieving a more essential understanding of the social and personal world. A study of life as it is experienced by self and others.

Photo research: Research which relies on respondents being given cameras and asked to provide photos and accompanying commentary of subjects that illustrate the issues under investigation. (See Chapter 12.)

Pie chart: Type of chart which presents data as segments of a whole pie, clearly showing the proportions of each category which contribute to the total. Individual segments are typically presented as percentages. (See Chapter 14.)

Pilot test: Pre-test; try-out before putting into general use.

Pinpoint sessions: A workshop exercise in which the facilitator helps participants to build on each other's ideas.

Plain English: A term for writing styles which deliberately avoid overly technical, jargon-filled language in favour of brevity, clarity, simplicity and accessibility for a particular target audience. This is by no means confined to English – research written in any language can follow the same principles.

Policy brief: A short report used as a development research communication tool for reaching policymakers, containing a summary of the key components of your research project and findings.

Population: The complete set of cases about which generalizations are to be made.

Positivism: A form of scientific methodology which believes there is a single true world 'out there', independent of the observer, and that, through detached observation, science can identify causes and laws regarding that world. It proceeds on an assumption that any unverifiable (or unfalsifiable) statements are meaningless. It assumes that the principles of natural science apply equally to investigative methods in the social sciences. (See Section 2.2.)

Post-modernism: Theories (in the arts as well as in social science) implicated in or accounting for change from modernity to post-modernity. Post-modernity is seen as involving such features as a world of 'flux, flow and fragmentation', without absolute values, an end of the dominance of an overarching belief in 'scientific' rationality and a unitary theory of progress.

Pre-coded: Questions are 'pre-coded' when the respondent is given a fixed set of alternative answers to choose from. See also Coding. (See Chapters 11 and 13.)

Press release: A short statement of a research project's key findings sent to journalists for the purposes of promotion.

Primary data: Data generated directly for the purposes of a study.

Probability: The likelihood that a particular event or events will occur. Can be expressed numerically as the ratio of the number of equally likely ways in which a particular event can occur to the total number of occurrences possible.

Probability sampling: A sampling approach designed to produce a sample, without consideration of particular characteristics, which can be considered representative of a population. Includes *simple random sampling, systematic sampling, stratified random sampling* and *cluster sampling,* among others.

Proposal, research: Detailed research plan proposed, usually to a funding body. Often used interchangeably with 'brief', 'terms of reference'.

Protocol: A complete plan for a piece of research, explaining procedures to be followed in detail. (See Section 3.4.)

Purposive (sample): Sample chosen on the basis of the judgement of the researcher in relation to the purpose of the study. The researcher tries to obtain as wide a representation as possible, taking account of likely sources of differences between individuals. (See Chapter 10.)

Qualitative: Describes the nature of answers (evidence) in terms of their verbal, written or other descriptive nature. Asks who, which, what, when, where and why – in contrast with 'quantitative' answers addressing how much or how many. Qualitative research approaches belong to a family of approaches concerned with collecting in-depth data about human social experiences and contexts. (See also Section 2.2.)

Quantitative: Data that are in numerical form – answering 'how many', 'to what extent' or 'how much' questions. Involves counting and other computation. Quantitative research is concerned with the collection of data in the form of various measures and indices, and its description and analysis by means of statistical methods.

Quantity (questionnaire): A type of response consisting of an exact or approximate number which gives the amount of some characteristics.

Questionnaire: A written list of questions, either given or posted to respondents. Information is gathered directly from people through a series of questions, many of which are likely to offer the respondent some possible ('pre-coded') replies to tick.

Quota sampling: A sampling approach which employs information about the target population to describe the types of units to be included in the sample. Individuals are then sought who fit these characteristics, for example by age, sex, housing type, location, etc.

Random error: Any aspect of the environment, the circumstances or anything else beyond the researcher's control which results in failure to capture the real value of a given variable.

Random (sample): A representative sample chosen from a population in such a way that every unit in that population is equally likely to be selected. The method of selection is based on chance but carried out in a systematic way. A type of probability sample. (See Chapter 10.)

Randomized controlled trial (RCT): A type of experimental study design considered most appropriate for medical research, testing new drugs or other interventions. 'Controlled' refers to the use of a matched control group which does not receive treatment. 'Randomized' refers to random allocation of patients to groups receiving different or no treatments.

Range: The simplest measure of spread. Calculated by subtracting the lowest value from the highest one. Affected strongly by extreme outliers.

Ranking and scoring methods: Research methods which rely on respondents placing something in order. 'Ranking' here relates to putting things in order; 'scoring' relates to the weight people give to different items.

Ranking questions: A type of question in which the respondent is asked to place something in rank order. For example, they might be asked to place qualities or characteristics in order of importance to them.

Rapid Rural Appraisal: See Participatory Learning and Action.

RAPID: The Overseas Development Institute (ODI) Research and Policy in Development programme, which works to understand the relationship between research, policy and practice and promote evidence-informed policymaking. RAPID uses insights from global research to provide practical expertise, to help to develop skills and competencies for policy influence.

Red teaming: A workshop role-playing exercise in which some research staff assume the roles of stakeholders likely to be opposed to an idea, in order to think through and anticipate potential challenges.

Reflexivity: Open reflection on the researcher's own point of view and how it influences their perceptions.

Reliability: The dependability of data collected, or of the test or measurement used to collect them. A reliable measure is one which gives the same results if the same individuals are measured on more than one occasion. Research instruments need to be consistent, so any variation in the results obtained through using the instrument owes entirely to variations in the thing being measured, not to the nature of the instrument itself. See also Validity. (See Section 13.8.)

Reliable: Data may be considered reliable when they are consistent or repeatable.

Research design: The method of planning research to gather the most appropriate information, in the correct way, and to analyse the results effectively. (See Chapters 3 and 7.)

Research ethics committees: Formal review committees established by universities, organizations, donors, etc., to ensure ethical standards are met by a research project. Also known as Institutional research boards.

Research instrument (or research tool): A technique used by the researcher to collect and record data. A global term used to describe the various data collection techniques used – for example interview schedules, observation checklists, questionnaires.

Respondent: Someone who 'responds', taking part in an interview, questionnaire or other research activity.

Response rate: The proportion of all sampled individuals who actually respond.

RSS: Really Simple Syndication, a format for the delivery of regularly changing web-based content. Users can subscribe to an RSS 'feed', which delivers to them a continually updating stream of content in a standardized format relevant to whatever specified issue or issues they request.

Sample: A selection of units chosen to represent the target population. Often also used loosely to refer to respondents within a study, even if no formal sampling process has occurred (i.e. people were self-selecting).

Sample size: The total number of units selected from the population.

Sampling frame: A complete list or map of all the units in the target population. The nature of the existing sampling frame is an important consideration in determining the sample design.

Sampling population: The complete set of cases about which generalizations are to be made.

Search engines: On the internet, these are tools to find relevant web pages. You enter your search terms, and the search engine searches its database and returns a list of results or 'hits'. Try several different ones. (See Sections 5.1 and 5.3.)

Secondary data: Data used for a study which were previously generated for other purposes or which pre-existed the study.

Self-completion questionnaire: A questionnaire which respondents fill in themselves.

Semi-structured interview: Interview method which relies largely on a predetermined framework of themes and specific questions, but which is flexible enough to allow space for new questions to be asked over the course of the interview.

Serials (as in libraries): Periodicals, journals.

Significance (statistical): Occurs when the probability of a given numerical difference or relationship occurring by chance alone is equal to, or less than, 0.05 ($p < 0.05$). The statistical significance of results increases as their probability decreases. The conventional cut-offs are: significant ($p < 0.05$); very significant ($p < 0.01$); highly significant ($p < 0.001$ or less). Note that a relationship can be statistically significant but have no practical significance – this depends on how meaningful it is in relation to the issue being studied.

Simple random sample: A sample designed so each combination of units in the population holds an equal chance (i.e. probability) of selection.

Snowball sampling: A form of sampling which begins with a few initial respondents, who provide the researcher with references to additional respondents of similar interest. A broader sample begins to grow like a 'snowball' as it accrues more and more references.

Social constructionism: A broad term used to emphasize the way in which reality, especially social institutions and social life generally, is socially produced rather than naturally given or determined. (See Section 2.2 and Chapter 7.)

Social media: A collective term for the range of internet-based applications that enable interactive communication between online communities.

Spreadsheet: Computer program which produces a matrix for managing numbers. (See Chapter 13.)

Spurious: A study is spurious when it fails to capture all the variables that might partially explain the phenomenon under observation.

Stakeholder: A person, group or institution with an interest in something, for example a project or programme. See Stakeholder analysis. (See Chapters 9 and 12.)

Stakeholder analysis: A process carried out as part of research and programme planning, in which actors with interests in a project or programme – people, groups, institutions, governments, etc. – are identified and analysed in terms of interests, needs, capabilities, opportunities and threats to determine strategies for engagement. It is useful to distinguish between primary stakeholders (those directly affected by an intervention or issue) and secondary stakeholders (who serve as intermediaries in the aid process or are less directly affected).

Standard deviation: A measurement of how the data you collect deviate from the *mean* (i.e. the value you expect to see). Lower standard deviations suggest the data do not differ from their anticipated values – higher standard deviations imply the opposite.

Statistical confidence: The statistical degree of confidence regarding a result – findings deemed statistically 'significant' are unlikely to have occurred by chance, whereas statistically 'insignificant' findings imply the opposite.

Statistical software package: Computer programs designed to aid in quantitative data analysis.

Steering group: See Advisory group.

Stratified random sample: A form of sampling in which an initial population is subdivided into mutually exclusive groups called *strata* based on one or more relevant criteria. Simple random samples are next drawn from these strata, and joined together to form a final, 'stratified' random sample.

Structured interview: Interview method in which a predetermined set of questions is asked of respondents in a specified order, without change across individual interviews. Commonly used in quantitative research and surveys.

Survey: A study that involves a relatively large number of respondents, generally chosen by some form of sampling and involving formal, usually fairly standardized, data collection procedures. Used to gather a broad range of information about a population.

SWOT Analysis: Useful method for strategic analysis, in which your project's 'strength, weaknesses, opportunities, threats' are systematically addressed and considered.

Synthesis: Combination of separate things or concepts to form a complex whole; process of recombining and making sense of what has been analysed.

Systematic bias: Any factor systematically affecting the measurement of a variable across a sample.

Systematic sample: A version of simple random sampling in which a random unit from the sampling frame is selected and then every nth unit from that unit onwards is selected.

Tally: Count or reckoning.

Terms of reference: See Brief (research).

Theory: A general statement about how something works. A theory is a proposition (or idea) about the relationship between things. Any abstract general account of an area of reality, usually involving the formulation of general concepts.

Tool, research: See Research instrument.

Transects: A participatory visual method comprising a diagram of main land use zones, helpful in research relating to natural resources and in learning quickly about a new place. Transect diagrams are made with the help of community members from a range of backgrounds, who each walk the researcher through their village, indicating important factors along the way.

Trends: Patterns within data.

Triangulation: Looking at things from different points of view. The employment of a number of different research techniques, in the belief that a variety of approaches gives the best chance of achieving validity. (See Section 7.3.)

Typology: A collection of types, a classification, a set of abstract categories derived from empirical evidence. For example, a typology of families might include the nuclear family, extended family, modified extended, etc.

Unstructured interview: Interview method in which questions asked are open ended and typically adapted to the particular subject or subjects being interviewed on a case-by-case basis.

Uptake (research): The degree to which research is read, cited and adopted for use among others – in short, the attention it receives when it is released.

Validity: Relates to the extent to which research data and the methods for obtaining them are deemed accurate (reflecting truth and reality; honest; and cover crucial matters). In terms of the methods used to obtain data, validity addresses the question 'Are we measuring suitable indicators of the concept and are we getting accurate results?' See also Reliability. (See Chapters 10 and 13.)

Variable: An element, feature or value which varies or undergoes change. *Independent variables* typically refer to the value that is manipulated or changed, whereas the *dependent variable* is the observed result of that manipulation.

Verbal questions: Questions for which the expected response is a word, a phrase or an extended comment. Gives respondents a chance to give their own views on the issue.

Verbatim: Word for word.

Weblog: see Blog.

 ## Further reading

Robinson, D. and Reed, Val. (eds) (1998) *The A to Z of Social Research Jargon*. London: Ashgate.

With thanks also to Denscombe (1998), Nichols (1991) and Wadsworth (1997), which contain useful definitions.

BIBLIOGRAPHY

Books and journal articles

Agresti, A. and Finlay, B. (2009) *Statistical Methods for the Social Sciences*. Upper Saddle River, NJ: Pearson Education, Inc.

Alasuutari, P., Bickman, L. and Brannen, J. (2008) *The Sage Handbook of Social Research Methods*. London: Sage.

Alderson, P. and Morrow, V. (2004) *Ethics, Social Research and Consulting with Children and Young People*. Barkingside: Barnardo's.

Alkire, S. (2010) 'Human development, definitions, critiques and related concepts', *Human Development Research Paper 1*. New York: UN Development Programme.

Alvesson, M. and Skoldberg, K. (2009) *Reflexive Methodology: New Vistas for Qualitative Research*. New Delhi, Thousand Oaks, CA, London: Sage.

Anderson, A. (2005a) 'An introduction to theory of change', *Evaluation Exchange/HFRP*, XI (2). Available online at: www.hfrp.org/evaluation/the-evaluation-exchange/issue-archive/evaluation-methodology/an-introduction-to-theory-of-change

Anderson, A., (2005b) *The Community Builder's Approach to Theory of Change: A Practical Guide to Theory and Development*. New York: The Aspen Institute Roundtable on Community Change. Available online at: www.aspeninstitute.org/sites/default/files/content/docs/roundtable%20on%20community% 20change/rcccommbuildersapproach.pdf

Anzul, M., Downing, M., Ely, M. and Vinz, R. (1997) *On Writing Qualitative Research: Living By Words*. London: Falmer Press.

Argyrous, G. (2005) *Statistics for Research*. Thousand Oaks, CA: Sage.

Arnstein, S. (1969) 'Eight rungs on the ladder of citizen participation', reprinted in Cahn, E. and Passett, B. (eds), (1971) *Citizen Participation: Effecting Community Change*. New York: Praeger Publishers.

Ashby, J.A. and Sperling, L. (1995) 'Institutionalizing participatory, client-driven research and technology development in agriculture', *Development and Change*, 26 (4): 753–70.

Babbie, E. (2009) *The Practice of Social Research*, 12th edn. Belmont, CA: Wadsworth.

Barbour, R. (2007) *Doing Focus Groups*. New Delhi, Thousand Oaks, CA, London: Sage.

Barnett, M. and Finnemore, M. (2004) *Rules for the World: International Organizations in Global Politics*. Ithaca, NY: Cornell University Press.

Bauer, M. and Gaskell, G. (eds) (2000) *Qualitative Researching with Text, Image and Sound*. New Delhi, Thousand Oaks, CA, London: Sage.

Bell, E. and Brambilla, P. (2001) *Gender and Participation: Supporting Resources Collection*. Brighton: Institute of Development Studies.

Belli, P., Anderson, J.R., Barnum, H.N., Dixon, J.A. and Tan, J.-P. (2000) *Economic Analysis of Investment Operations: Analytical Tools and Practical Applications*. Washington, DC: World Bank.

Bell, J. (2010) *Doing Your Research Project: A Guide for First-time Researchers in Education, Health and Social Science*, 5th edn. Maidenhead: Open University Press.

Bergh, G., Duvendack, M. and Walker, D. (2012) 'Adapted systematic reviews for social research in international development – concepts and lessons from practice', *Background Note*. London: Overseas Development Institute.

Berry, R. (2004) *The Research Project: How to Write It*, 5th edn. London: Routledge.

Bigwood, S. and Spore, M. (2003) *Presenting Numbers, Tables, and Charts*. Oxford: Oxford University Press.

Blaxter, L., Hughes, C. and Tight, M. (1996) *How to Research*. Buckingham: Open University Press (latest edition 2010).

Blaxter, L., Hughes, C. and Tight, M. (2010) *How to Research*, 3rd edn. Maidenhead: Open University Press.

Bloor, M., Frankland, J., Thomas, M. and Robson, K. (2001) *Focus Groups in Social Research*. New Delhi, Thousand Oaks, CA, London: Sage.

BOND (1999) 'Advocacy training guidance notes: monitoring and evaluating advocacy', *Guidance Note*. London: BOND.

Boyden, J. and Ennew, J. (eds) (1997) *Children in Focus – A Manual for Participatory Research with Children*. Stockholm: Save the Children Sweden.

Brabeck, M. and Brabeck, K. (2009) 'Feminist perspectives on research ethics ', in P. Alasuutari, L. Bickman and J. Brannen (eds), *The Handbook of Social Research Ethics*. London: Sage.

Bramberg, M. (2000) *Integrating Quantitative and Qualitative Research in Development Projects*. Washington, DC: International Bank for Reconstruction and Development/World Bank.

Brannen, J. (2005) 'Mixing methods: the entry of qualitative and quantitative approaches into the research process', *International Journal of Social Research Methodology*, 8 (3): 173–84.

Buchanan-Smith, M. (2005) 'How the sphere project came into being: a case study of policy making in the humanitarian-aid sector and the relative influence of research', in J. Court, I. Hovland and J. Young (eds), *Bridging Research and Policy in Development: Evidence and the Change Process*. Rugby: ITDG.

Bulmer, M. (1982) *The Uses of Social Research: Social Investigation in Public Policy-making*. London: George Allen and Unwin.

Bulmer, M. (1998) 'The problem of exporting social survey research', *The American Behavioral Scientist*, 42 (2): 153–67.

Campbell, J. (2002) 'A critical appraisal of participatory methods in development research', *International Journal of Social Research Methodology: Theory and Practice*, 5 (18): 19–30.

Carden, F. (2009) *Knowledge to Policy: Making the Most out of Development Research*. New Delhi, Thousand Oaks, CA, London: Sage.

Chambers, R. (1992) 'Rural appraisal: rapid, relaxed and participatory', *Discussion Paper 311*. Brighton: Institute of Development Studies.

Chambers, R. (1996) 'Participatory rural appraisal and the reversal of power', *Cambridge Anthropology*, 19 (1): 5–23.

Chambers, R. (2002) *Participatory Workshops: A Sourcebook of 21 Sets of Ideas and Activities*. Oxford: Earthscan.

Christensen, P. and James, A. (2008) *Research with Children: Perspectives and Practices*, 2nd edn. London: Jessica Kingsley.

Cohen, A. (2004) *Custom and Politics in Urban Africa: A Study of Hausa Migrants in Yoruba Towns*. London: Routledge Classic Ethnographies.

Collier, P., Radwan, S. and Wangwe, S. with Wagner, A. (1986) *Labour and Poverty in Rural Tanzania*. Oxford: Oxford University Press and International Labour Organization.

Conley-Tyler, M. (2005) 'A fundamental choice: internal or external Evaluation?' *Evaluation Journal of Australasia*, 4 (1–2): 3–11.

Cooke, B. and Kothari, U. (eds) (2001) *Participation: The New Tyranny?* London: Zed Books.

Cornwall, A. (1992) 'Body mapping in health RRA/PRA', *RRA Notes*, 16, Special Issue on Applications for Health, London, International Institute for Environment and Development, pp. 69–76.

Costello, A. and Zumla, A. (2000) 'Moving to research partnerships in developing countries', *British Medical Journal*, 321: 827–9.

Court, J., Hovland, I. and Young, J. (2005) *Bridging Research and Policy in Development: Evidence and the Change Process.* Rugby: ITDG.

Craig, G. (1998) *Women's Views Count: Building Responsive Maternity Services.* London: College of Health.

Creswell, J.W. (2009) *Research Design: Qualitative, Quantitative and Mixed Method Approaches.* New Delhi, Thousand Oaks, CA, London: Sage.

Cuninghame, C., Griffin, J. and Laws, S. (1996) *Water Tight: The Impact of Water Metering on Low-income Families.* London: Save the Children.

Davies, H., Nutley, S. and Walter, I. (2005) 'Assessing the impact of social science research: conceptual, methodological and practical issues', *Background Paper for Economic and Social Research Council Symposium on Assessing Non-academic Impact of Research.* London: Overseas Development Institute.

Deaton, A. (1997) *The Analysis of Household Surveys.* Washington, DC: World Bank.

Della Porta, D. and Keating, M. (2008) *Approaches and Methodologies in the Social Sciences: A Pluralist Perspective.* Cambridge: Cambridge University Press.

Denscombe, M. (2010) *The Good Research Guide for Small-scale Social Research Projects,* 4th edn. Buckingham and Philadelphia, PA: Open University Press.

Department for International Development (DFID) (1998) 'DDT impact assessment project, Zimbabwe'. Evaluation Summary EV621. London: DFID.

Department for International Development (DFID) (2006) *Maximising the Impact of Development Research: How Can Funders Encourage More Effective Research Communication?* London: DFID.

Desai, V. and Potter, R. (2006) *Doing Development Research.* New Delhi, Thousand Oaks, CA, London: Sage.

Earl, S., Carden, F. and Smutylo, T. (2001) *Outcome Mapping: Building Learning and Reflection into Development Programs.* Ottawa: IDRC.

Economic and Social Research Council (ESRC) (2010) *ESRC Framework for Research Ethics.* Swindon: ESRC.

Edwards, M. and Hulme, D. (1995) *Non-governmental Organisations: Performance and Accountability.* London: Earthscan.

Eldridge, C. (1993) 'A participatory learning and action study on the 1992 drought in Malawi, Zambia and Zimbabwe'. Unpublished report.

Elliott, C. (1999) *Locating the Energy for Change: An Introduction to Appreciative Inquiry.* Winnipeg: International Institute for Sustainable Development.

Escobar, A. and Roberts, B. (1998) 'Surveys as instruments of modernization: the case of Mexico', *The American Behavioral Scientist,* 2 (2): 237–51.

Fairhead, J. and Leach, M. (1996) 'Rethinking the forest–savannah mosaic: colonial science and its relics in West Africa', in M. Leach and R. Mearns (eds), *The Lie of the Land: Challenging Received Wisdom on the African Environment.* Oxford: Heinemann and the International African Institute, with James Currey Ltd.

Finch, J. (1986) *Research and Policy. The Uses of Qualitative Methods in Social and Educational Research.* London: Falmer.

Flick, U. (2009) *An Introduction to Qualitative Research,* 4th edn. New Delhi, Thousand Oaks, CA, London: Sage.

Gainsbury, S. and Brown, C. (2006) 'How is research communicated professionally?' in V. Desai, V. and R. Potter (eds), *Doing Development Research.* New Delhi, Thousand Oaks, CA, London: Sage.

Gattenhof, S. and Radvan, M. (2009) 'In the mouth of the imagination: positioning children as co-researchers and co-artists to create a professional children's theatre production', *Journal of Applied Theatre and Performance,* 14 (2): 221–4.

Gaventa, J. and Atwood, H. (1998) 'Synthesizing PRA and case study Materials: a participatory process for developing outlines, concepts and synthesis reports', in participation group (eds), *Participatory Poverty Assessments Topic Pack*. Brighton: Institute of Development Studies.

Gilbert, N. (2008) *Researching Social Life*, 3rd edn. New Delhi, Thousand Oaks, CA, London: Sage.

Girvan, N. (2007) 'Power imbalances and development knowledge'. Theme Paper for Southern Perspectives on Reform of the International Development Architecture project. 887th Wilton Park Conference in Sussex, England,19 May.

Glaser, B. and Strauss, A. (1967) *The Discovery of Grounded Theory: Strategies for Qualitative Research*. New York: Aldine.

Goetz, A.-M. and Jenkins, R. (2002) 'Voice, accountability and human development: the emergence of a new agenda', *Technical Report*. New York: UN Development Programme.

Golafshani, N. (2003) 'Understanding reliability and validity in qualitative research', *Qualitative Report*, 8 (4): 597–607.

Gosling, L., with Edwards, M. (2003) *Toolkits: A Practical Guide to Planning, Monitoring, Evaluation and Impact Assessment*. London: Save the Children.

Greene, S., Ahluwalia, A., Watson, J., Tucker, R., Rourke, S.B., Koornstra, J., Sobota, M.Monette, L. and Byers, S.(2009) 'Between skepticism and empowerment: the experiences of peer research assistants in HIV/AIDS, housing and homelessness community-based research', *International Journal of Social Research Methodology*, 12 (4): 361–73.

Guhathakurta, M. (2008) 'Theatre in participatory action research: experiences from Bangladesh', in P. Reason and H. Bradbury (eds), *The Sage Handbook of Action Research, Participative Inquiry and Practice*. New Delhi, Thousand Oaks, CA, London: Sage.

Gustavsen, B. (2003) 'New forms of knowledge production and the role of action research', *Action Research*, 1 (2): 153–64.

Hagen-Zanker, J., McCord, A. and Holmes, R. (2012) 'Making systematic reviews work for international development research', *Discussion Paper*. London: Overseas Development Institute.

Hakim, C. (2000) *Research Design: Successful Designs for Social Economics Research*. London: Routledge.

Hall, D. and Hall, I. (1996) *Practical Social Research: Project Work in the Community*. Basingstoke: Macmillan.

Hare, K. and Reynolds, L. (2005) *The Trainer's Toolkit: Bringing Brain-friendly Learning to Life*. Bancyfelin: Crown House Publishing.

Harper, C. (1997) 'Do the facts matter: NGOs, research and international advocacy', in M. Edwards and J. Gaventa (eds), *Global Citizen Action*. Boulder, CO: Lynne Rienner.

Harper, D. (2002) 'Talking about pictures: a case for photo elicitation', *Visual Studies*, 17 (1): 14–26.

Harris, E. (2004) 'Building scientific capacity in developing countries', *EMBO Reports*, 5 (1): 7–11.

Hart, R. (1992) 'Children's participation: from tokenism to citizenship', *Essay 4*. Florence: Innocenti Research Centre, UN Children's Fund.

Hawtin, M. and Percy-Smith, J. (2007) *Community Profiling: A Practical Guide*. Oxford: Oxford University Press.

HelpAge International (1999) 'The contribution of older people to development: the research process', *Research Updates 1–4*. London: HelpAge International.

Hennink, M.M. (2007) *International Focus Group Research: A Handbook for the Health and Social Sciences*. Cambridge: Cambridge University Press.

Hertel, S., Singer, M. and van Cott, D. (2009) 'Field research in developing countries: hitting the road running', *PS: Political Science and Politics*, 42 (2): 305–9.

Highmore Sims, N. (2006) *How to Run a Great Workshop: The Complete Guide to Designing and Running Brilliant Workshops and Meetings*. Harlow: Prentice Hall.

Hill, M., Davis, J., Prout, A. and Tisdall, K. (2004) 'Moving the participation forward', *Children and Society*, 18 (2): 77–96.

Hillman, M., Adams, J. and Whitelegg, J. (1990) *One False Move: A Study of Children's Independent Mobility*. London: Policy Studies Institute.

Holland, J., with Blackburn, J. (1998) *Whose Voice? Participatory Research and Policy Change*. London: Intermediate Technology Publications.

Holland, J. and Munro, M. (1997) 'Profiling the purposive: some thoughts on site selection in PPAs', *Participatory Poverty Assessments (PPA): PPA Topic Pack*. Brighton: IDS.

Huff, D. (1973) *How to Lie with Statistics*. Harmondsworth: Pelican.

Hughes, R. (1999) 'Why do people agree to participate in social research? The case of drug injectors', *International Journal of Social Research Methodology*, 1 (4): 315–24.

Impey, A. (2005) 'Culture, conservation and community reconstruction: explorations in advocacy ethnomusicology in the Dukuduku Forests, Northern KwaZulu Natal', in J. Post (ed.), *Ethnomusicology: A Contemporary Reader*. New York: Routledge.

Jacobsen, Y. (2000) *Our Right to Learn: A Pack for People with Learning Difficulties and Staff Who Work With Them Based on the Charter for Learning*. Leicester: National Organization for Adult Learning.

James, A. and Prout, A. (eds) (1990) *Constructing and Reconstructing Childhood*. London: Falmer.

James, A., Jenks, C. and Prout, A. (1998) *Theorising Childhood*. Cambridge: Polity.

Johansson, L. (1994) 'Interactive media technology and "instant video" in rural development', *Forests, Trees and People Newsletter*. Uppsala: Swedish University of Agricultural Sciences.

Johnson, H. and Mayoux, L. (1998) 'Investigation as empowerment: using participatory methods', in A. Thomas, J. Chataway and M. Wuyts (eds), *Finding out Fast: Investigative Skills for Policy Development*. London: Sage, pp. 147–72.

Jones, H., Shaxson, L. and Walker, D. (2012) *Knowledge, Policy and Power in International Development: A Practical Guide*. Bristol: Policy Press.

Jones, N. and Sumner, A. (2011) *Child Poverty, Evidence and Policy: Mainstreaming Children in International Development*. Bristol: Policy Press.

Jones, N., Bailey, M. and Lyytikäinen, M. (2007) *Research Capacity Strengthening in Africa: Trends, Gaps and Opportunities*. London: Overseas Development Institute.

Jones, N., Jones, H. and Datta, A., with Evidence-based Policy in Development Network partners (2009) *Knowledge, Policy and Power: Six Dimensions of the Knowledge-Policy Interface*. London: Overseas Development Institute.

Jowett, M. and O'Toole, G. (2006) 'Focusing researchers' minds: contrasting experiences of using focus groups in feminist qualitative research', *Qualitative Research*, 6 (4): 453–72.

Kass, N. (2007) 'The structure and function of research ethics committees in Africa', *PLoS Med*, 4 (3): 595–6.

Khan, S. (1997) *A Street Children's Research*. Dhaka: Save the Children UK and Chinnamul Shishu Kishore Sangstha.

Kelly, L., Regan, L. and Burton, S. (1995) 'Defending the indefensible? Quantitative methods and feminist research', in J. Holland and M. Blair, with S. Sheldon (eds), *Debates and Issues in Feminist Research and Pedagogy*. Clevedon: Multilingual Matters/Open University Press.

King, G., Keohane, R. and Verba, S. (1994) *Designing Social Inquiry: Scientific Inference in Qualitative Research*. Princeton, NJ: Princeton University Press.

Kirby, P. (1999) *Involving Young Researchers: How to Enable Young People to Design and Conduct Research*. York: Joseph Rowntree Foundation.

Krueger, R. and Casey, M. (2000) *Focus Groups: A Practical Guide for Applied Research*, 3rd edn. New Delhi, Thousand Oaks, CA, London: Sage.

Laws, S. (1998) *Hear Me! Consulting with Young People on Mental Health Services*. London: Mental Health Foundation.

Laws, S., Armitt, D., Metzendorf, W., Percival, P. and Reisel, J. (1999) *Time to Listen: Young People's Experiences of Mental Health Services*. London: College of Health, National Lottery Charities Board, Mental Health Foundation, BYPASS and Save the Children.

Leedy, P. (1997) *Practical Research: Planning and Design*, 6th edn. Englewood Cliffs, NJ: Prentice Hall.

Leksmono, C., Young, J., Hooton, N., Muriuki, H. and Romney, D. (2006) 'Informal traders lock horns with the formal milk industry: the role of research in pro-poor dairy policy shift in Kenya', *Working Paper 266*. London: Overseas Development Institute.

Levitas, R. and Guy, W. (1996) *Interpreting Official Statistics*. London: Routledge.

Lewis, J. (2010) *Project Planning, Scheduling and Control*, 5th edn. New York: McGraw Hill.

Lewis, M. and Kirby, P. (2001) *Consulting Children and Young People with Disabilities in Hammersmith and Fulham*. London: Save the Children.

Liamputtong, P. (2006) *Researching the Vulnerable: A Guide to Sensitive Research Methods*. New Delhi, Thousand Oaks, CA, London: Sage.

McCartney, I. (2000) *Children in Our Midst: Voices of Farmworkers' Children*. Harare: Weaver Press and Save the Children.

McCrum, S. and Hughes, L. (1998) *Interviewing Children: A Guide for Journalists and Others*. London: Save the Children.

Mabry, L. (2008) 'Governmental regulation in social science', in L. Bickman and J. Brannen (eds), *The Sage Handbook of Social Research Methods*. London: Sage.

Mack, N., Woodsong, C., MacQueen, K., Guest, G. and Namey, E. (2005) *Qualitative Research Methods: A Data Collector's Field Guide*. Research Triangle Park, NC: Family Health International.

Maguire, P. (1987) *Doing Participatory Research: A Feminist Approach*. Amherst, MA: UMass Center for International Education.

Marouani, M. and Ayuk, E. (2007) *Policy Paradox in Africa: Strengthening Links between Economic Research and Policymaking*. Trenton, NJ: Africa World Press and International Development Research Centre.

Matheson, J. (2007) 'The voice transcription technique: use of voice recognition software to transcribe digital interview data in qualitative research', *The Qualitative Report*, 12 (4): 547–60.

May, T. (2003) *Social Research: Issues, Methods and Process*, 3rd edn. Buckingham: Open University Press.

Mayer, S. (1998) 'Critical issues in using data', in A. Thomas, J. Chataway and M. Wuyts (eds), *Finding Out Fast*. Buckingham and London: Open University Press and Sage.

Mertens, D. and Ginsberg, P. (eds) (2009) *Handbook of Social Research Ethics*. New Delhi, Thousand Oaks, CA, London: Sage.

Mikkelsen, B. (2005) *Methods for Development Work and Research: A New Guide for Practitioners*, 2nd edn. New Delhi, Thousand Oaks, CA, London: Sage.

Mollison, S. (2000) 'Pratham: a challenge to social development?' Unpublished paper.

Moore, N. (2006) *How to Do Research: The Practical Guide to Designing and Managing Research Projects*, 3rd edn. London: Facet.

Mordaunt, J. and O'Sullivan, T. (2010) *Resources from Organisations, Winning Resources and Support*, 2nd edn. Buckingham: Open University Press.

Morrow, V. (1999) 'If you were a teacher, it would be harder to talk to you: reflections on qualitative research with children in school', *International Journal of Social Research Methodology*, 1 (4): 297–313.

Morse, S. (2006) 'Writing an effective research report or dissertation', in V. Desai and R. Potter *Doing Development Research*. New Delhi, Thousand Oaks, CA, London: Sage.

Moser, C.A. and Kalton, G. (1971) *Survey Methods in Social Investigation*, 2nd edn. London: Heinemann.

Mosse, D. (1994) 'Authority, gender and knowledge: theoretical reflections on the practice of participatory rural appraisal', *Development and Change*, 25 (3): 497–526.

Mukherjee, N. (2002) *Participatory Learning and Action – With 100 Field Methods*. New Delhi: Concept Publishing Company.

Newell, A.F. (2011) *Design and the Digital Divide: Insights from 40 Years' Research into Computer Support for Older and Disabled People*. London: Morgan and Claypool.

Nichols, P. (1991) 'Social survey methods: a field guide for development workers', *Development Guidelines* 6. Oxford: Oxfam.

Norton, A. (1998) 'Some reflections on the PPA process and lessons learned', in J. Holland with J. Blackburn (eds), *Whose Voice? Participatory Research and Policy Change*. London: Intermediate Technology Publications.

Nutley, S., Walter, I. and Davies, H. (2007) *Using Evidence: How Research Can Inform Public Services*. Bristol: The Policy Press.

Nuyens, Y. (2005) *No Development without Research – A Challenge for Research Capacity Development*. Geneva: Global Forum for Health Research.

O'Keeffe, C. (2004) 'Object and subject: the challenges of peer research in community justice', *British Journal of Community Justice*, 3(1). Available online at: www.cjp.org.uk/publications/bjcj/volume-3-issue-1/]

O'Laughlin, B. (1998) 'Interpreting institutional discourses', in A. Thomas, J. Chataway and M. Wuyts (eds), *Finding Out Fast*. Buckingham and London: Open University Press and Sage.

Oakley, A. and Roberts, H. (eds) (1996) *Evaluating Social Interventions*. Basildon: Barnardo's.

Oppenheim, A.N. (1992) *Questionnaire Design, Interviewing and Attitude Measurement*, 2nd edn. London: Pinter.

Owen, D. (1998) 'The Mozambique PPA: lessons learned from the process', in J. Holland with J. Blackburn (eds), *Whose Voice? Participatory Research and Policy Change*. London: Intermediate Technology Publications.

Oyelaran-Oyeyinka, B. (2005) 'Partnerships for building science and technology capacity in Africa'. Paper for the Africa–Canada–UK Exploration: Building Science and Technology Capacity with African Partners, London, 30 January–1 February.

Parker, M., Allen, T. and Hastings, J. (2008) 'Resisting control of neglected tropical diseases: dilemmas in the mass treatment of schistosomiasis and soil-transmitted helminths in north-west Uganda', *J Biosoc Sci*, 40 (2):161–81.

Patton, M. (2001) *Qualitative Research and Evaluation Methods*, 3rd edn. New Delhi, Thousand Oaks, CA, London: Sage.

Peters, K., Laws, S. and Dorbor, E. (2003) *When Children Affected by War Go Home: Lessons Learned from Liberia*. London: Save the Children.

Pettinger, R., Nelson, B. and Economy, P. (2007) *Managing For Dummies*, 2nd edn. Chichester: John Wiley and Sons.

Pinnock, H with Vijayakumar, G. (2009) *Language and Education: The Missing Link: How the Language Used in Schools Threatens the Achievement of Education for All*. London: CfBT Education Trust and Save the Children.

Pratt, B. and Loizos, P. (1992) 'Choosing research methods: data collection for development workers'. *Development Guidelines* 7. Oxford: Oxfam.

Pridmore, P. and Bendelow, G. (1995) 'Images of health: exploring beliefs of children using the "draw-and-write" technique', *Health Education Journal*, 54 (4): 473–88.

Prime Minister's Strategy Unit (2004) *The Strategy Survival Guide*. London: Prime Minister's Strategy Unit, Her Majesty's Government.

Princen, T. and Finger, M. (1994) *Environmental NGOs in World Politics: Linking the Local and the Global*. London and New York: Routledge.

Pye-Smith, C. (1999) 'Truth games', *New Scientist*, 161: 16–18.

Qvortrup, J. (1994) 'Childhood and modern society: a paradoxical relationship?' in J. Brannen and M. O'Brien (eds), *Childhood and Parenthood: Proceedings of ISA Committee for Family Research Conference on Children and Families*. London: Institute of Education, University of London.

Rahnema, M. (1992) *Participation. The Development Dictionary.* London: Zed Books.

Reason, P. (1998) 'Three approaches to participative enquiry', in N.K. Denzin and Y.S. Lincoln (eds), *Strategies of Qualitative Enquiry.* Thousand Oaks, CA: Sage.

Reason, P. and Bradbury, H. (2008) *The Sage Handbook of Action Research, Participative Inquiry and Practice.* New Delhi, Thousand Oaks, CA, London: Sage.

Ridley, D. (2008) *The Literature Review: A Step-by-step Guide for Students.* New Delhi, Thousand Oaks, CA, London: Sage.

Ritchie, J. and Spencer, L. (1994) 'Qualitative data analysis for applied policy research', in A. Bryman and R. Burgess (eds), *Analyzing Qualitative Data.* London: Routledge.

Robb, C. (2002) *Can the Poor Influence Policy? Participatory Poverty Assessments in the Developing World,* 2nd edn. Washington, DC: International Monetary Fund and World Bank.

Robinson, D. and Reed, V. (eds) (1998) *The A to Z of Social Research Jargon.* London: Ashgate.

Robson, C. (2002) *Real World Research: A Resource for Social Scientists and Practitioner-Researchers,* 2nd edn. Oxford: Blackwell.

Roper, L. (2002) 'Achieving successful academic-practitioner research collaborations', *Development in Practice,* 12 (3–4): 338–45.

Rumsey, S. (2008) *How to Find Information: A Guide for Researchers,* 2nd edn. Maidenhead: Open University Press.

Saukko, P. (2003) *Doing Research in Cultural Studies: An Introduction to Classical and New Methodological Approaches.* New Delhi, Thousand Oaks, CA, London: Sage.

Save the Children (1993) *Participatory Needs Assessment – Thanh Chuong District, Vietnam.* Hanoi: Save the Children.

Save the Children (1997a) *Stitching Footballs: Voices of Children in Sialkot, Pakistan.* Islamabad: Save the Children.

Save the Children (1997b) 'PLA case study 1: Ghana', *Gender and HIV/AIDS Guidelines.* London: Save the Children.

Schöpfel, J. and Farace, D.J. (2010) 'Grey literature', in M.J. Bates and M.K. Maack (eds), *Encyclopedia of Library and Information Sciences,* 3rd edn. New York: CRC Press.

Shadish, W., Cook, T. and Campbell, D. (2002) *Experimental and Quasi-Experimental Designs for Generalized Causal Inference.* Boston, MA: Houghton Mifflin.

Shaw, C., Brady, L. and Davey, C. (2011) *Guidelines for Research with Children and Young People.* London: National Children's Bureau.

Singleton R. and Straits, B. (1999) *Approaches to Social Research,* 3rd edn. Oxford: Oxford University Press.

Slocum, N. (2003) *Participatory Methods Toolkit: A Practitioner's Manual.* Bruges: UNU Institute on Comparative Integration.

Spivak, G.C. (1988) 'Can the subaltern speak?', in C. Nelson and L. Grossberg (eds), *Marxism and the Interpretation of Culture.* Chicago, IL: University of Illinois Press.

Stachowiak, S. (2007) *Pathways for Change: Six Theories About How Policy Change Happens.* Seattle: ORS.

Start, D. and Hovland, I. (2004) *Tools for Policy Impact: A Handbook for Researchers.* London: Overseas Development Institute.

Stubbs, S. (1999) 'Engaging with difference: soul-searching for a methodology in disability and development research', in E. Stone (ed.), *Disability and Development: Learning from Action and Research on Disability in the Majority World.* Leeds: The Disability Press.

Sutcliffe, S. and Court, J. (2006) *A Toolkit for Progressive Policymakers in Developing Countries.* London: Overseas Development Institute.

Tarling, R. (2006) *Managing Social Research: A Practical Guide.* London: Routledge.

Tashakkori, A. and Teddlie, C. (2003) *Handbook of Mixed Methods in Social and Behavioral Research.* Thousand Oaks, CA: Sage.

Tesfu, M. and Magrath, P. (2007) 'Water and sanitation access for people with motor disabilities'. *Research Report.* Addis Ababa: WaterAid Ethiopia.

Theis, J. and Grady, H.M. (1991) *Participatory Rapid Appraisal for Community Development.* London: International Institute for Environment and Development and Save the Children Federation.

Thomas, A. and Mohan, G. (2007) *Research Skills for Policy and Development: How to Find Out Fast.* New Delhi, Thousand Oaks, CA, London: Sage.

Tofteng, D. and Husted, M. (2011) 'Theatre and action research: how drama can empower action research processes in the field of unemployment', *Action Research*, 9 (1): 27–41.

Tolich, M. and Fitzgerald, M. (2006) 'If ethics committees were designed for ethnography', *Journal of Empirical Research on Human Research Ethics*, 1(2), 71–8.

Treseder, P. (1997) *Empowering Children and Young People: Promoting Involvement in Decision-making.* London: Save the Children.

Trochim, W. and Donnelly, J. (2008) *The Research Methods Knowledge Base,* 3rd edn. Mason, OH: Cengage Learning.

Utting, P. (2006) *Reclaiming Development Agendas: Power and International Policy Making.* Gordonsville: Palgrave Macmillan.

United Nations Development Programme (UNDP) (2002) *Handbook on Monitoring and Evaluating for Results.* New York: UNDP.

University of Chicago Press (2010) *The Chicago Manual of Style,* 16th edn. Chicago, IL: University of Chicago Press.

Velho, L. (2004) 'Research capacity building for development: from old to new assumptions', *Science Technology and Society*, 9 (2): 171–207.

Wadsworth, Y. (1997) *Do It Yourself Social Research*, 2nd edn. St Leonards: Allen and Unwin.

Wang, C., Cash, J. and Powers, L. (2000) 'Who knows the streets as well as the homeless? Promoting personal and community action through Photovoice', *Health Promotion Practice*, 1 (1): 81–9.

Ward, L. (1997) *Seen and Heard: Involving Disabled Children and Young People in Research and Development Projects.* York: Joseph Rowntree Foundation.

Weisberg, H., Krosnick, J.A. and Bowen, B. (1996) *Introduction to Survey Research, Polling, and Data Analysis.* New Delhi, Thousand Oaks, CA, London: Sage.

Weiss, C.H. and Bucuvalas, M.J. (1977) 'The challenge of social research to decision making', in C.H. Weiss (ed.), *Using Social Research in Public Policy Making.* Lexington, MA: Lexington Books, pp. 213–33.

West, A. (1995) *You're on Your Own: Young People's Research on Leaving Care.* London: Save the Children.

White, S. (1996) 'Depoliticising development: the uses and abuses of participation', *Development in Practice*, 6 (1): 142–55.

Worrall, S. (2000) *Young People as Researchers: A Learning Resource Pack.* London: Save the Children.

Young, E. and Quinn, L. (2002) 'Writing effective public policy papers: a guide to policy advisers in Central and Eastern Europe'. Budapest: Local Government and Public Reform Initiative. http://lgi.osi.hu/publications_datasheet.php?id=112.

Young, L. and Barrett, H. (2000) 'Adapting visual methods: action research with Kampala street children', *Area*, 33 (2): 141–52.

Youngman, M. B. (1986) *Analysing Quesitionaires.* Nottingham: University of Nottingham School of Education.

Online publications/resources

Association of Social Anthropologists of the Commonwealth 'Ethical guidelines for good practice', revised 1999. Available online at: www.theasa.org/ethics.shtml

British Sociological Association. www.bps.org.uk/the-society/code-of-conduct/code-of-conduct_home.cfm

Blagescu, M. and Young, J. (2006) 'Capacity development for policy advocacy: current thinking and approaches among agencies supporting civil society organisations', *Working Paper* 260. London: Overseas Development Institute. Available online at: www.odi.org.uk/resources/download/136.pdf

Chenail, R.J. (1995) 'Presenting qualitative data', *The Qualitative Report*, 2 (3). Available online at: www.nova.edu/ssss/QR/QR2-3/presenting.html

Evidence for Policy and Practice Information and Co-ordinating (EPPI) Centre (2009) What is a Systematic Review? Available online at: http://eppi.ioe.ac.uk/cms/Default.aspx?tabid=67

Gilbert, N. (ed.) (1996) 'Social research update'. Guildford: Department of Sociology, University of Surrey. Available online at: http://sru.soc.surrey.ac.uk/index.html

Girvan, N. (2007) 'Power imbalances and development knowledge'. Theme Paper. Montreal: The North-South Institute. Available online at: www.oecd.org/dataoecd/57/21/39447872.pdf

Guijt, I. and Woodhill, J. (2002) *Managing for Impact in Rural Development: A Guide for Project M&E*. Rome: International Fund for Agricultural Development. Available online at: www.ifad.org/evaluation/guide/index.htm

Higgins, J. and Green, S. (2011) *Cochrane Handbook for Systematic Reviews of Interventions*. Version 5.1.0. Available online at: www.cochrane-handbook.org/The Cochrane Collaboration.

High, C. (2010) 'What is participatory video?' Available online at: www.ncrm.ac.uk/TandE/video/RMF2010/pages/29_ParticipateVid.php

Hovland, I. (2007) 'Making a difference: M&E of policy research', *Working Paper* 281. Available online at: www.odi.org.uk/resources/download/1751.pdf London: Overseas Development Institute.

International Institute for Environment and Development. 'Citizens' juries on the governance of food and agricultural research'. Available online at: www.excludedvoices.org/democratising-agricultural-research-food-sovereignty-west-africa

Jones, H. (2011) 'A guide to monitoring and evaluating policy influence', *Background Note*. London: Overseas Development Institute. Available online at: www.odi.org.uk/resources/download/5252.pdf

Jones, N. and Walsh, C. (2008) 'Policy briefs as a communication tool for development research', *Background Note*. London: Overseas Development Institute. Available online at: www.odi.org.uk/resources/download/425.pdf

Jones, N., Moore, K. and Villar-Marquez, E., with Broadbent, E. (2008) *Painful Lessons: The Politics of Preventing Sexual Violence and Bullying at School*. Woking and London: Plan International and Overseas Development Institute, Available online at: http://plan-international.org/learnwithoutfear/files/painful-lessons-english

Joseph Rowntree Foundation (2006) 'Strategic plan 2008–2011: search, demonstrate, influence'. York: Joseph Rowntree Foundation. Available online at: www.jrf.org.uk/sites/files/jrf/JRF-Strategic-Plan-2008-2011.pdf

Kirby, P. (2004) *A Guide to Actively Involving Young People in Research: For Researchers, Research Commissioners, and Managers*. Eastleigh: Involve. Available online at: www.conres.co.uk/pdfs/Involving_Young_People_in_Research_151104_FINAL.pdf

Laws, S. and Mann, G. (2004) 'So you want to involve children in research?', *Supporting Children's Meaningful and Ethical Participation in Work around Violence against Children series for the UN Study*. Stockholm: Save the Children Sweden. Full text available in print and online at SC Sweden. Available online at: http://shop.rb.se/Product/Product.aspx?ItemId=2965386. Also available in French http://shop.rb.se/Product/Product.aspx?ItemId=2967076&SectionId=2017325&MenuId=74347

Organizational Research Services. *Publications and Resources*. Available online at: www.organizationalresearch.com/publications_and_resources.htm#pfc6tahpch

Plan International (2010) 'Prevention pays: the economic benefits of ending violence in School', *Learn Without Fear*. Woking: Plan International. Available online at: http://plan-international.org/learnwithoutfear/prevention-pays-the-economic-benefits-of-ending-violence-in-schools-1

Smutylo, T. (2005) 'Outcome mapping: a method for tracking behavioural changes in development programs', *Institutional Learning and Change Brief* 7. Ottawa: IDRC.

Spaapen, J., Dijstelbloem, H. and Wamelink, F. (2007) *Evaluating Research in Context: A Method for Comprehensive Assessment*, 2nd edn. The Hague: COS. Available online at: www.nwo.nl/files.nsf/pages/NWOA_73VH8D_Eng/$file/eric_book_internet.pdf

Social Research Association 'Ethical Guidelines', published annually in its Directory of Members. www.the-sra.org.uk/guidelines.htm

Start, D. and Hovland, I. (2007) *Tools for Policy Impact: A Handbook for Researchers*. London: Overseas Development Institute.

Trochim, W. and Donnelly, J. (2008). *The Research Methods Knowledge Base*, 3rd edn. Cincinnati, OH: Atomic Dog Publishing. Available online at: www.socialresearchmethods.net/kb/

Ulrich's International Periodical Directory: *A Classified Guide to Current Periodicals, Foreign and Domestic*. New York: Bowker, annual. Available online at: www.ulrichsweb.com.

Wilcox, D. *A Guide to Effective Participation*. Available online at: www.partnerships.org.uk/guide/

World Bank (2004) *Monitoring and Evaluation: Tools Methods, and Approaches*. Washington, DC: World Bank. Available online at: www.worldbank.org/oed/ecd/me_tools_and_approaches.html

World Health Organization (2005) *Multi-country Study on Women's Health and Domestic Violence against Women*. Geneva: WHO. Available online at: www.who.int/gender/violence/who_multicountry_study/en

Websites

Capacity.Org. www.capacity.org/capacity/opencms/en/index.html

Comic Relief. *Vision and Principles for UK Grant-making*. www.comicrelief.com/apply-for-a-grant/vision-principles-uk-grant-making

Cornell University Participation Action Research Network. http://cornellparnetwork.blogspot.com/2011/02/cornell-participatory-action-research.html

Department for International Development (DFID). *Writing a Good Application – Part 2 of 3*. http://www.esrc.ac.uk/funding-and-guidance/guidance/applicants/application2.aspx

Department for International Development (DFID). *Research for Development*. www.dfid.gov.uk/r4d

ELDIS. www.eldis.org/participation/index.htm

Economic and Social Research Council (ESRC). *The Research Ethics Guidebook*. www.ethicsguidebook.ac.uk

Economic and Social Research Council (ESRC). *Interactive Media: Blogs. Part of the ESRC Impact Toolkit*. http://stage.esrc.ac.uk/funding-and-guidance/tools-and-resources/impact-toolkit/tools/interactive-media/index.aspx

Economic and Social Research Council (ESRC). *Developing a Website for Research Promotion. Part of the ESRC Impact Toolkit*. http://stage.esrc.ac.uk/funding-and-guidance/tools-and-resources/impact-toolkit/tools/interactive-media/index.aspx

Economic and Social Research Council (ESRC). *Guide to Publicizing Your Event*. www.esrc.ac.uk/_images/Guide_to_publicising_your_event_tcm8-5093.pdf

Economic and Social Research Council (ESRC). *Funding and Guidance: Writing a Good Proposal*. www.esrc.ac.uk/funding-and-guidance/guidance/applicants/application2.aspx

European Commission (EC). (2008) *Open Access – Opportunities and Challenges: A Handbook*. www.eldis.org/go/topics/dossiers/open-access-for-development&id=40011&type=Document

European Commission (EC). *Statistics Database*. http://epp.eurostat.ec.europa.eu/portal/page/portal/eurostat/home

European Union (EU). *A to Z Index*. http://europa.eu/documentation/index_en.htm

GDNet. *Disseminating Research Online*. Toolkit. www.gdnet.org/middle.php?oid=373

GDNet. *Disseminating Research Online*. http://cloud2.gdnet.org/cms.php?id=disseminating_research_online

Global Development Network (GDN). *Toolkit on Disseminating Research Online*. http://researcher.gdnet.org/cms.php?id=worries_about_online_dissemination

Global Partnership Forum. www.partnerships.org.uk/guide/index.htm

International Development Research Centre (IDRC). *Toolkit for Researchers*. http://publicwebsite.idrc.ca/EN/Resources/Tools_and_Training/Pages/Toolkit-for-researchers. aspx

International ISBN Agencies. *National ISBN Agencies*. www.isbn-international.org/agency

Life Drama.net. www.lifedrama.net

Merriam-Webster Online Dictionary. www.merriam-webster.com/dictionary/consult

Organisation for Economic Co-operation and Development (OECD). *Statistics Portal*. www.oecd.org/statsportal/0,2639,en_2825_293564_1_1_1_1_1,00.html

Overseas Development Institute (ODI). *RAPID Policy Impact Online Toolkit*. www.odi.org.uk/rapid/tools/toolkits/policy_impact/Tools.html

Overseas Development Institute (ODI). *Evidence-based Policymaking*. www.odi.org.uk/Rapid/Projects/PPA0117

Participatory Planning, Monitoring and Evaluation Online Resource Portal. http://portals.wi.wur.nl/ppme/index.php

Photovoice. www.Photovoice.org

Plan International. *Learn Without Fear Campaign*. http://plan-international.org/learnwithoutfear

Research Information Network. *Social Media: A Guide for Researchers*. www.rin.ac.uk/our-work/communicating-and-disseminating-research/social-media-guide-researchers

Restore. *The Managing Research Projects Toolkit*. www.restore.ac.uk/mrp/services/ldc/mrp/resources/resproskills

The Economist. *The Economist Style Guide*. www.economist.com/research/styleguide

The Wellesley Institute. *Peer Research in Action*. www.wellesleyinstitute.com/uncategorized/peer-research-in-action

The Open University. *The Development Management Project*. Available at www3.open.ac.uk/study/postgraduate/course/TU874.htm

UK Data Archive. www.data-archive.ac.uk/home

University of California Berkeley. *Finding Information on the Internet: A Tutorial*. www.lib.berkeley.edu/TeachingLib/Guides/Internet/FindInfo.html

World Bank. Data Portal: data.worldbank.org

World Bank. *Participation and Civil Engagement*. www.worldbank.org/participation

INDEX

CPSIA information can be obtained
at www.ICGtesting.com
Printed in the USA
BVHW090524040721
611013BV00002B/4

9 781446 252376